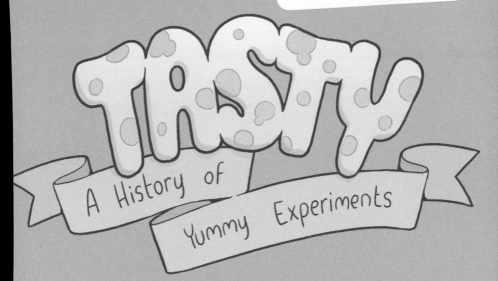

TASTY

A History of

Yummy Experiments

Also by Victoria Grace Elliott

*Yummy: A History of Desserts*

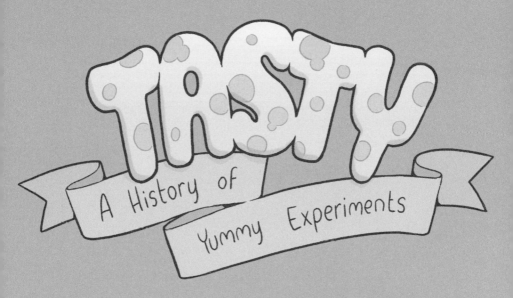

# TASTY

## A History of Yummy Experiments

Victoria Grace Elliott

RH
GRAPHIC

NEW YORK

*Tasty: A History of Yummy Experiments* was illustrated, colored, and lettered digitally. All recipes were made and enjoyed by the author.

All rights reserved. Published in the United States by RH Graphic, an imprint of Random House Children's Books, a division of Penguin Random House LLC, New York.

RH Graphic with the book design is a trademark of Penguin Random House LLC.

Visit us on the web! RHKidsGraphic.com • @RHKidsGraphic

Educators and librarians, for a variety of teaching tools, visit us at RHTeachersLibrarians.com

Library of Congress Cataloging-in-Publication Data is available upon request.
ISBN 978-0-593-42531-2 (trade paperback) — ISBN 978-0-593-42532-9 (hardcover)
ISBN 978-0-593-42534-3 (ebook)

Designed by Patrick Crotty

MANUFACTURED IN ITALY
10 9 8 7 6 5 4 3 2 1
First Edition

A comic on every bookshelf.

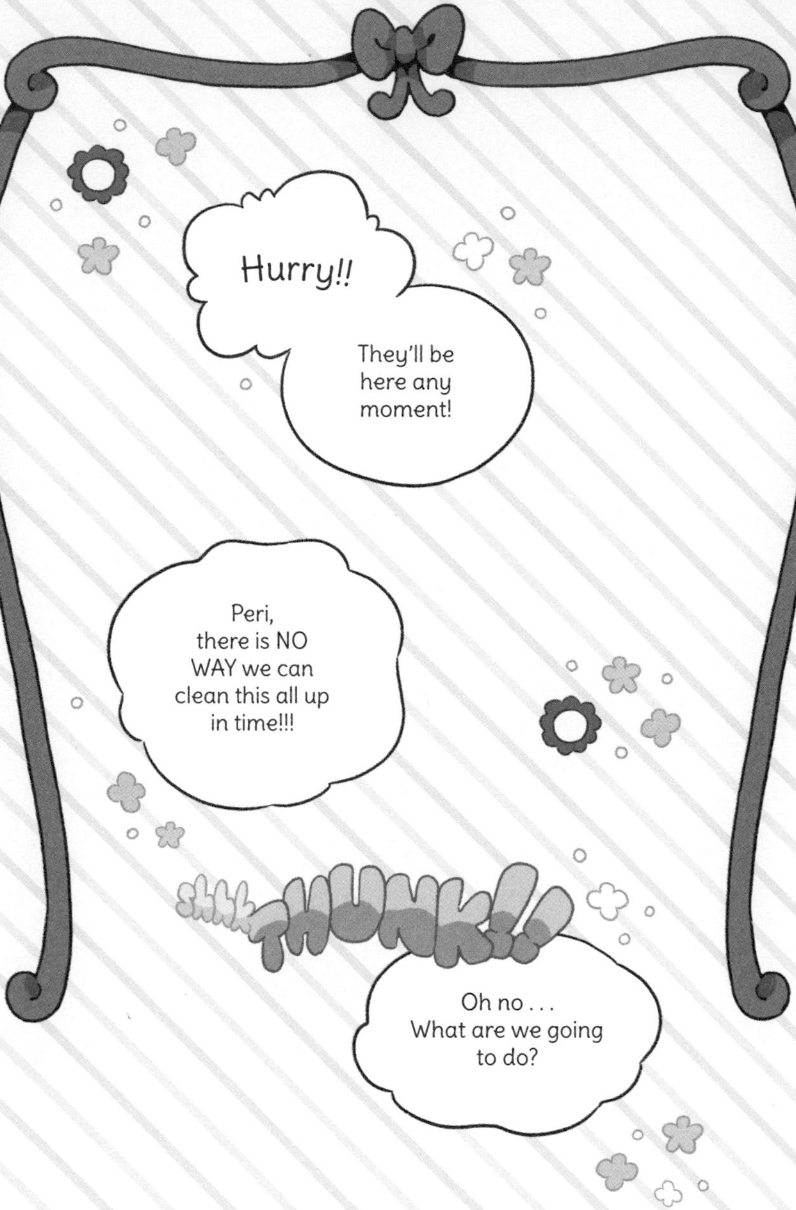
Hurry!!
They'll be here any moment!
Peri, there is NO WAY we can clean this all up in time!!!
shhk THUNK!!
Oh no . . . What are we going to do?

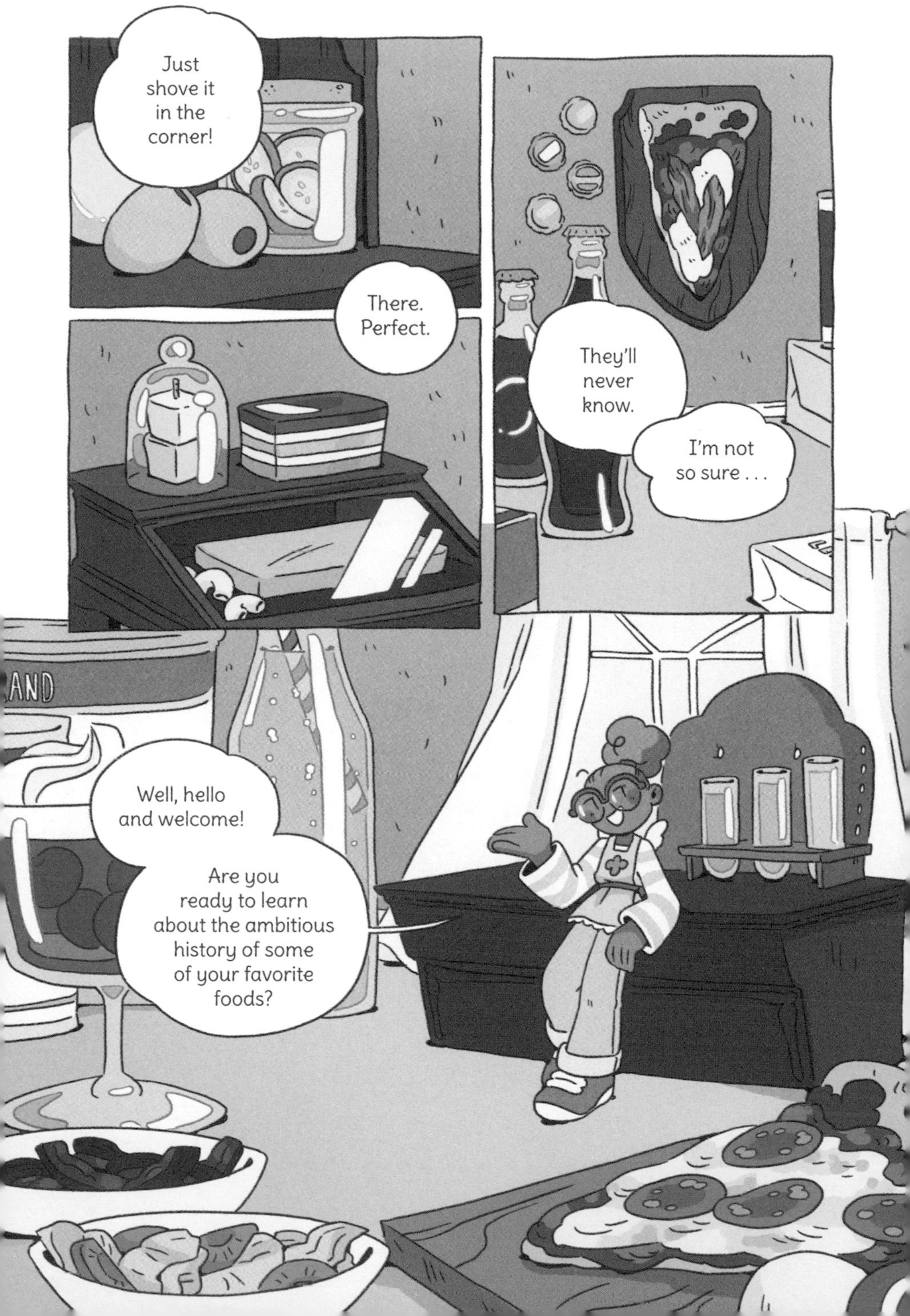
Just shove it in the corner!
There. Perfect.
They'll never know.
I'm not so sure . . .
Well, hello and welcome!
Are you ready to learn about the ambitious history of some of your favorite foods?

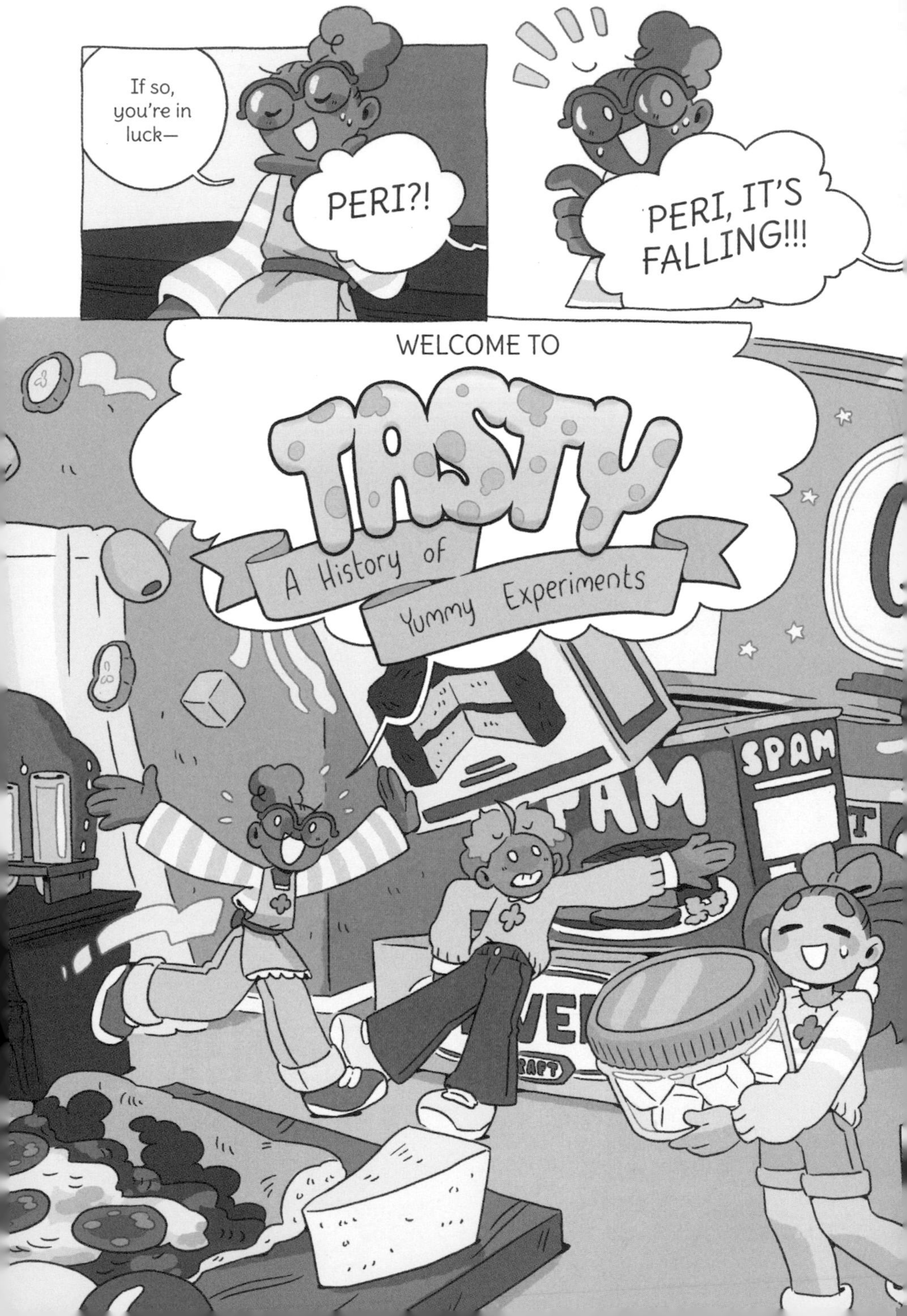
If so, you're in luck—
PERI?!
PERI, IT'S FALLING!!!
WELCOME TO
TASTY
A History of Yummy Experiments
SPAM
SPAM
VE
RAFT

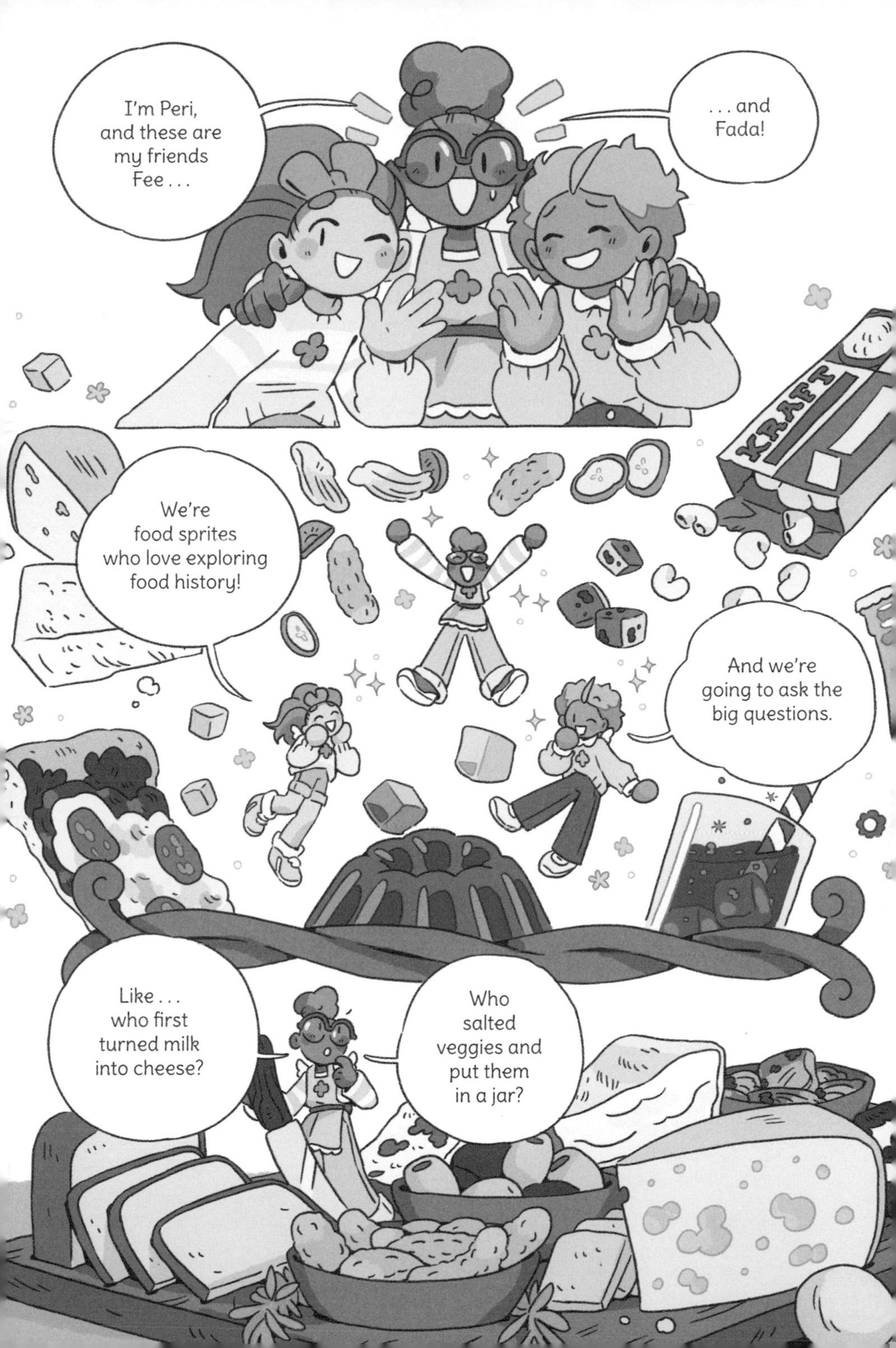
I'm Peri, and these are my friends Fee . . .
. . . and Fada!
We're food sprites who love exploring food history!
And we're going to ask the big questions.
Like . . . who first turned milk into cheese?
Who salted veggies and put them in a jar?
KRAFT

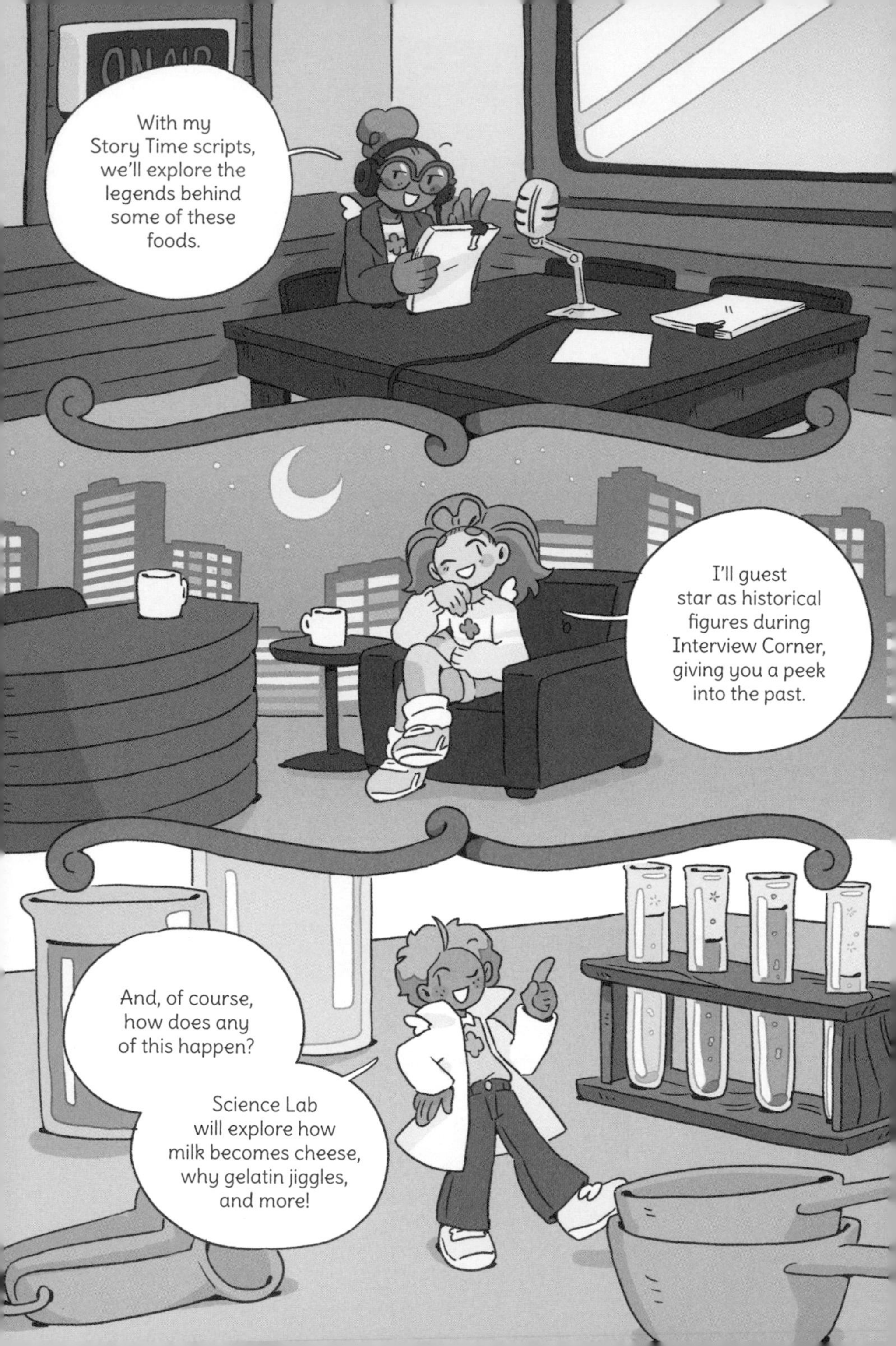
ON AIR
With my Story Time scripts, we'll explore the legends behind some of these foods.
I'll guest star as historical figures during Interview Corner, giving you a peek into the past.
And, of course, how does any of this happen?
Science Lab will explore how milk becomes cheese, why gelatin jiggles, and more!

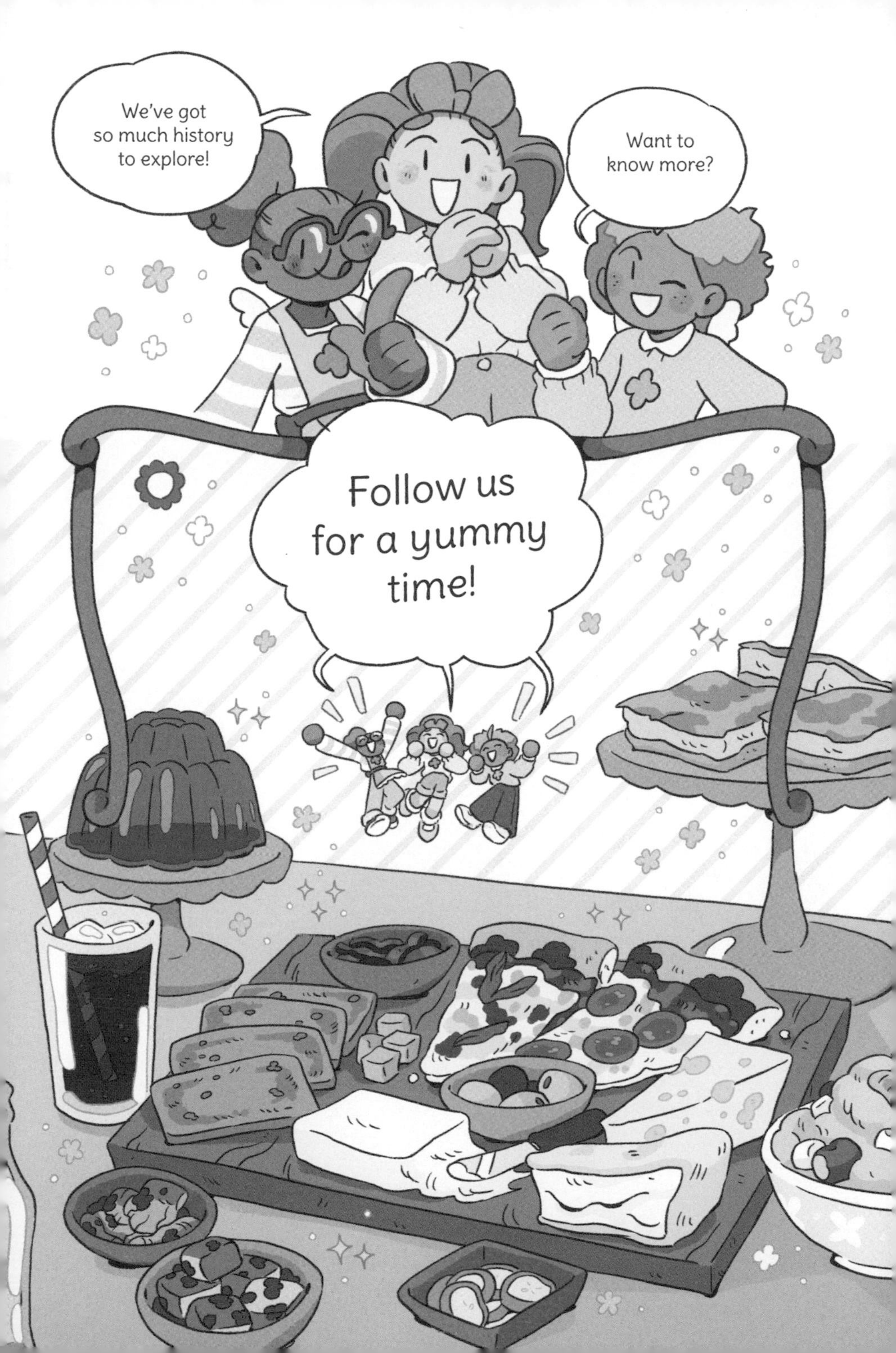
We've got so much history to explore!
Want to know more?
Follow us for a yummy time!

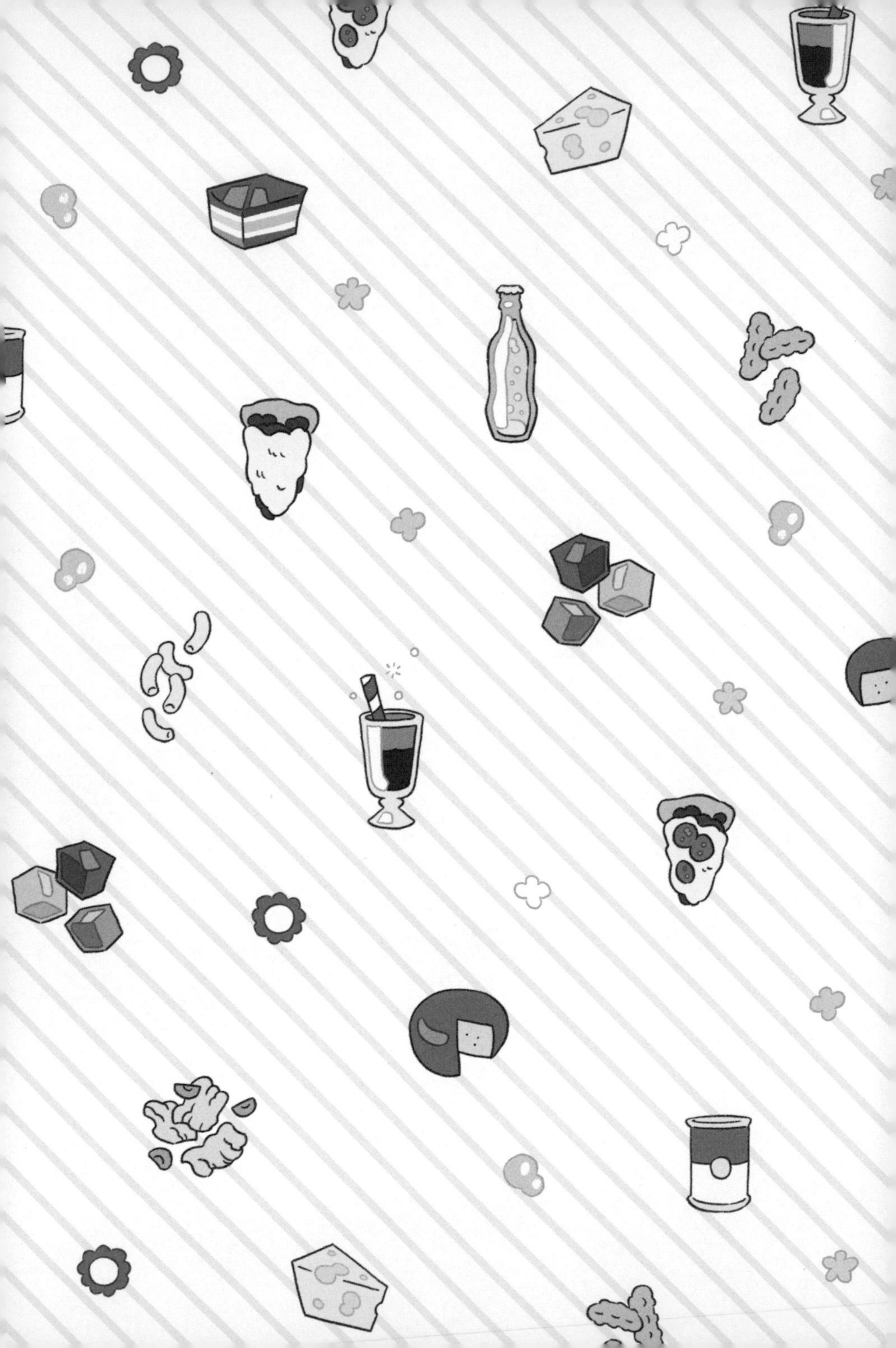

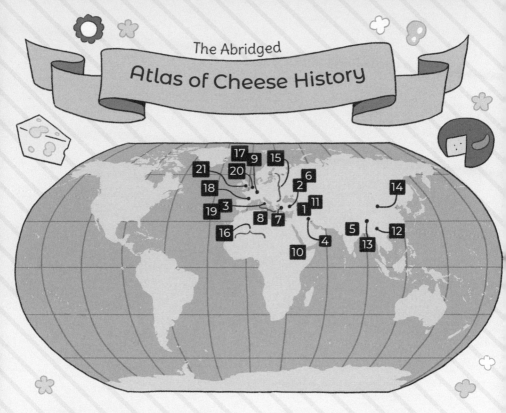

# The Abridged
# Atlas of Cheese History

1  Fertile Crescent

2  Turkish Çökelek

3  Italian Ricotta

4  Sumerian Goddess Inanna

5  Indian Paneer

6  Hittite Empire Hard Cheeses

7  Homer's *The Odyssey*

8  Mediterranean Pecorino and Caprino

9  Celtic Vatusican Creamy Cheese

10  Ethiopian Ayib

11  Middle Eastern/African Areesh

12  Yunnan Chinese Rubing

13  Tibetan Hard Cheese

14  Mongolian Byaslag

15  Holy Roman Brie

16  West African Wagashi

17  Swiss Gruyère and Swiss

18  French Roquefort

19  Italian Parmesan and Mozzarella

20  Holland Spice Cheese, Edam, and Gouda

21  British Cheddar

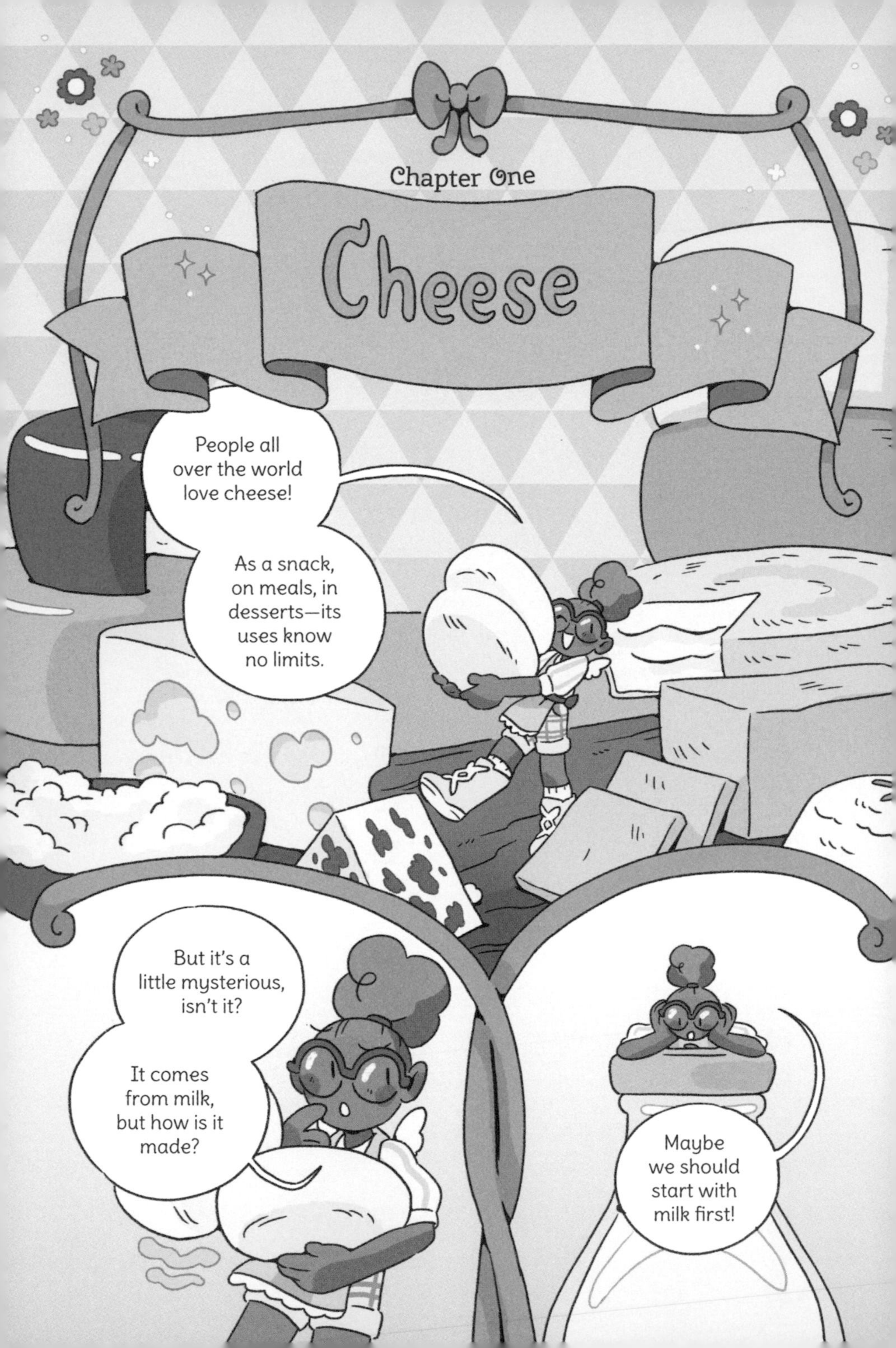
Chapter One
Cheese
People all over the world love cheese!
As a snack, on meals, in desserts—its uses know no limits.
But it's a little mysterious, isn't it?
It comes from milk, but how is it made?
Maybe we should start with milk first!

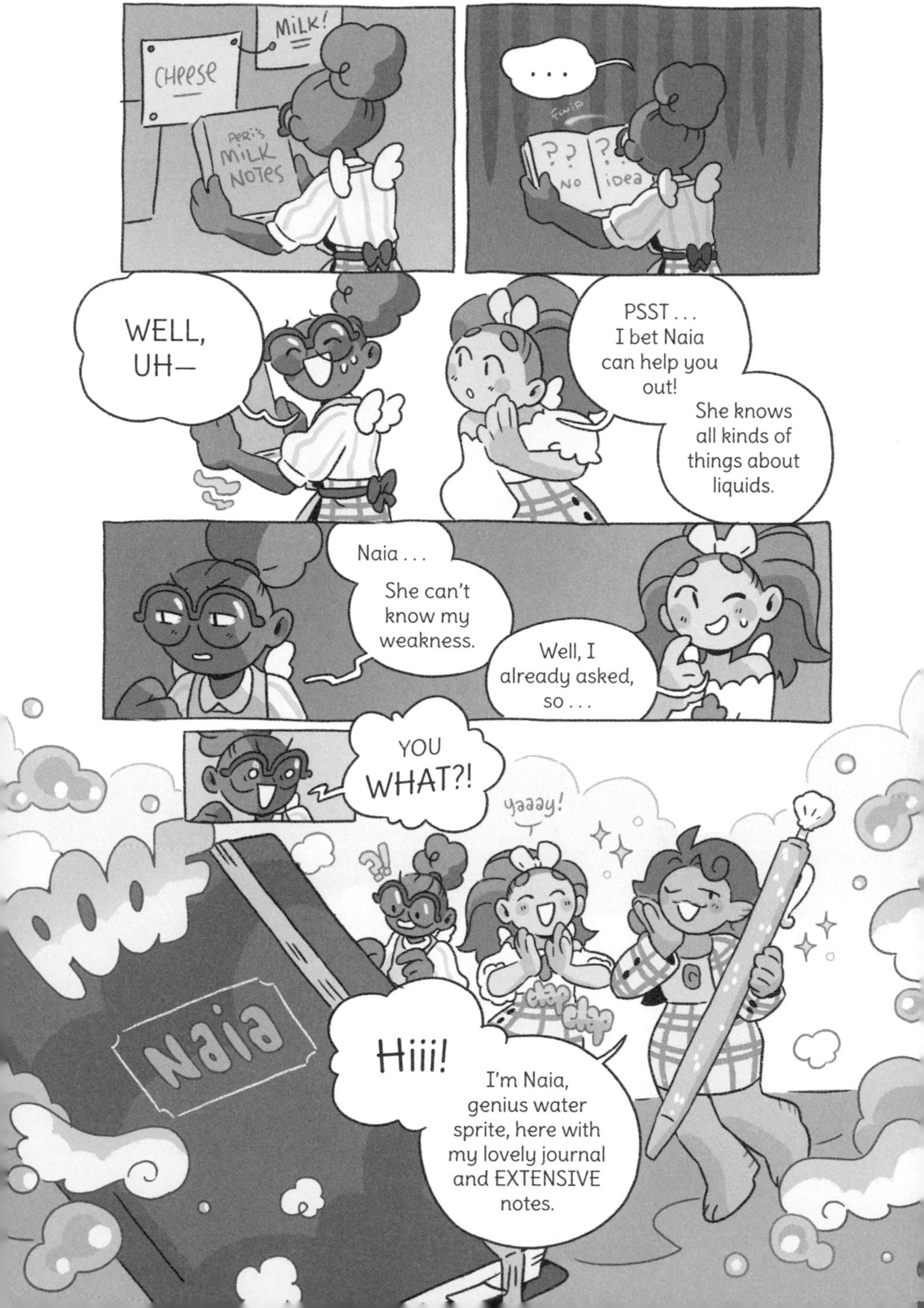
MILK!
CHEESE
PERI'S MILK NOTES
. . .
FWIP
?? NO
? IDEA
WELL, UH—
PSST . . . I bet Naia can help you out!
She knows all kinds of things about liquids.
Naia . . .
She can't know my weakness.
Well, I already asked, so . . .
YOU WHAT?!
yaaay!
?!
POOF
Naia
clap clap
Hiii!
I'm Naia, genius water sprite, here with my lovely journal and EXTENSIVE notes.

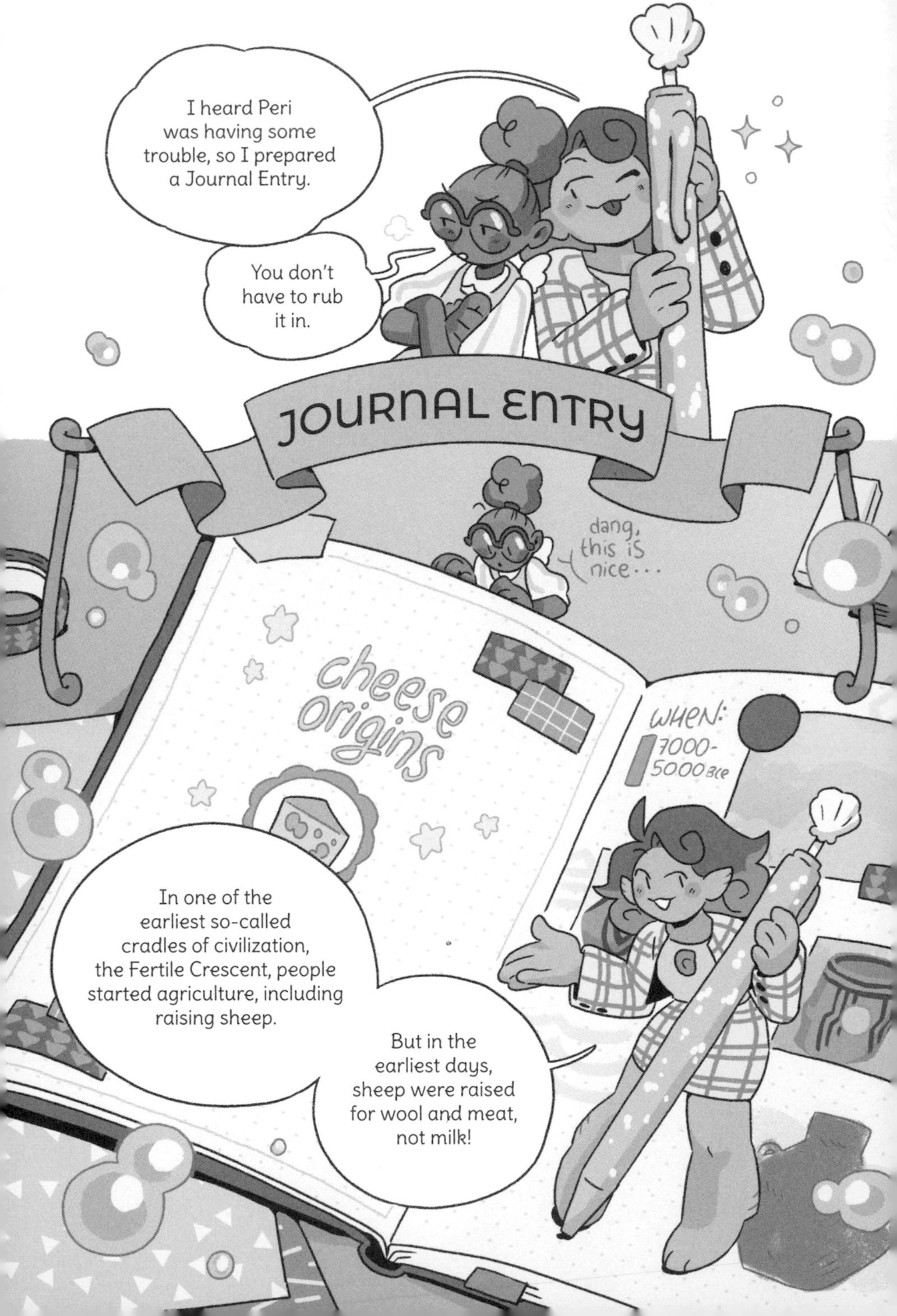
I heard Peri was having some trouble, so I prepared a Journal Entry.
You don't have to rub it in.
JOURNAL ENTRY
dang, this is nice...
cheese origins
WHEN: 7000-5000 BCE
In one of the earliest so-called cradles of civilization, the Fertile Crescent, people started agriculture, including raising sheep.
But in the earliest days, sheep were raised for wool and meat, not milk!

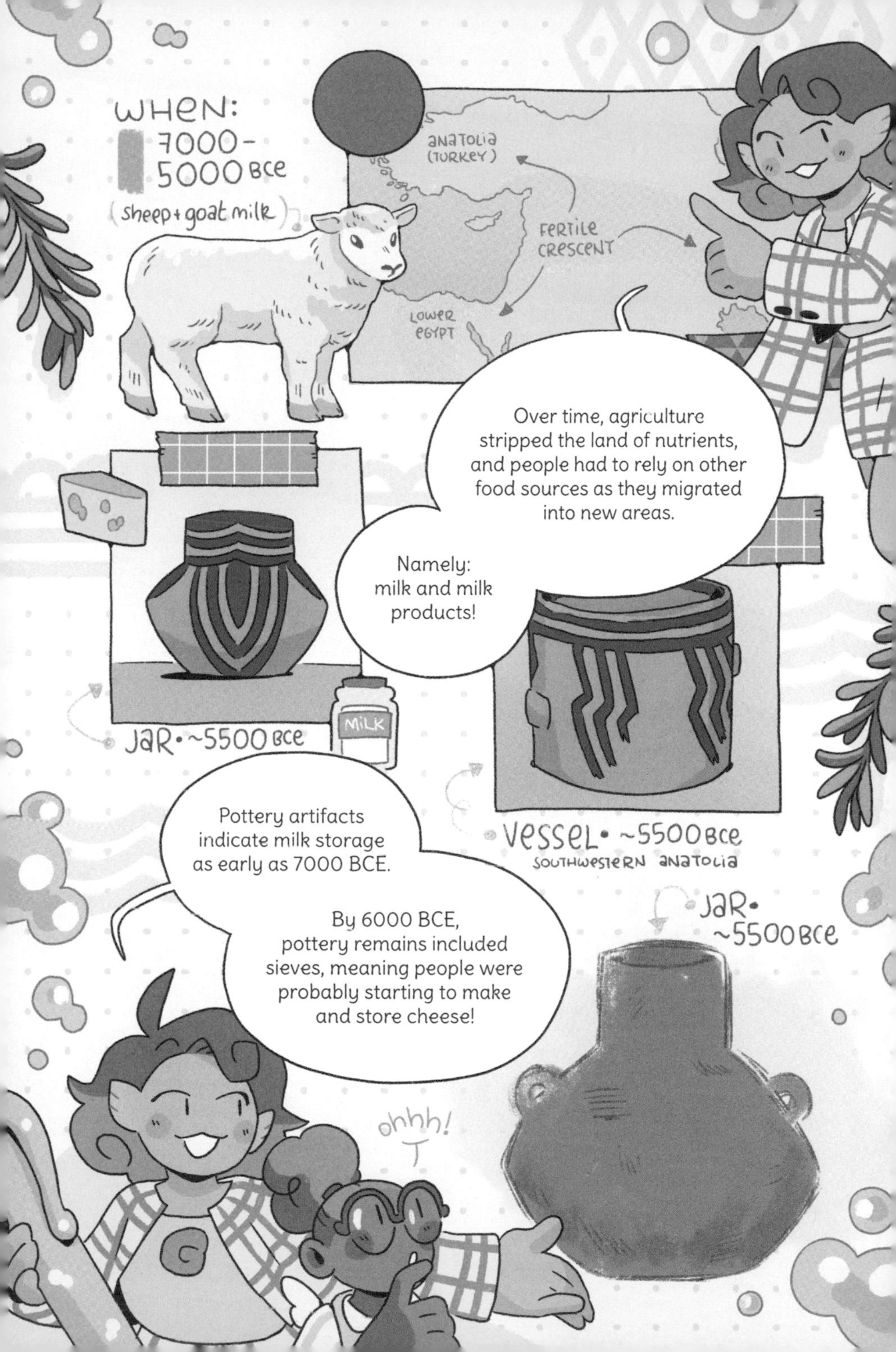
WHEN:
7000-
5000 BCE
(sheep + goat milk)
ANATOLIA
(TURKEY)
FERTILE
CRESCENT
LOWER
EGYPT
Over time, agriculture stripped the land of nutrients, and people had to rely on other food sources as they migrated into new areas.
Namely: milk and milk products!
JAR • ~5500 BCE
MILK
VESSEL • ~5500 BCE
SOUTHWESTERN ANATOLIA
Pottery artifacts indicate milk storage as early as 7000 BCE.
By 6000 BCE, pottery remains included sieves, meaning people were probably starting to make and store cheese!
JAR •
~5500 BCE
ohhh!

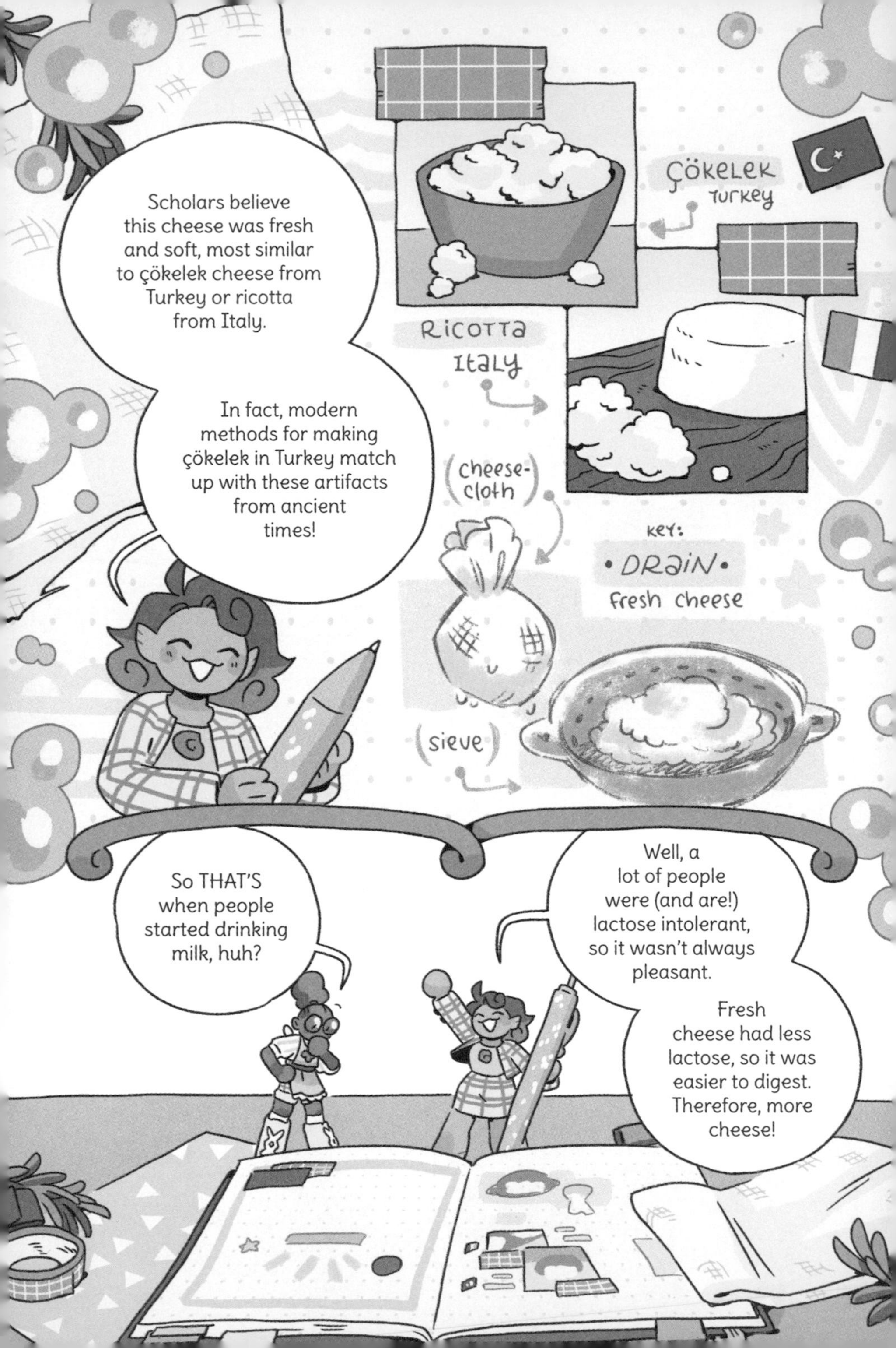
Scholars believe this cheese was fresh and soft, most similar to çökelek cheese from Turkey or ricotta from Italy.
In fact, modern methods for making çökelek in Turkey match up with these artifacts from ancient times!
Çökelek
Turkey
Ricotta
Italy
cheese-cloth
Key:
• DRAIN •
fresh cheese
sieve
So THAT'S when people started drinking milk, huh?
Well, a lot of people were (and are!) lactose intolerant, so it wasn't always pleasant.
Fresh cheese had less lactose, so it was easier to digest. Therefore, more cheese!

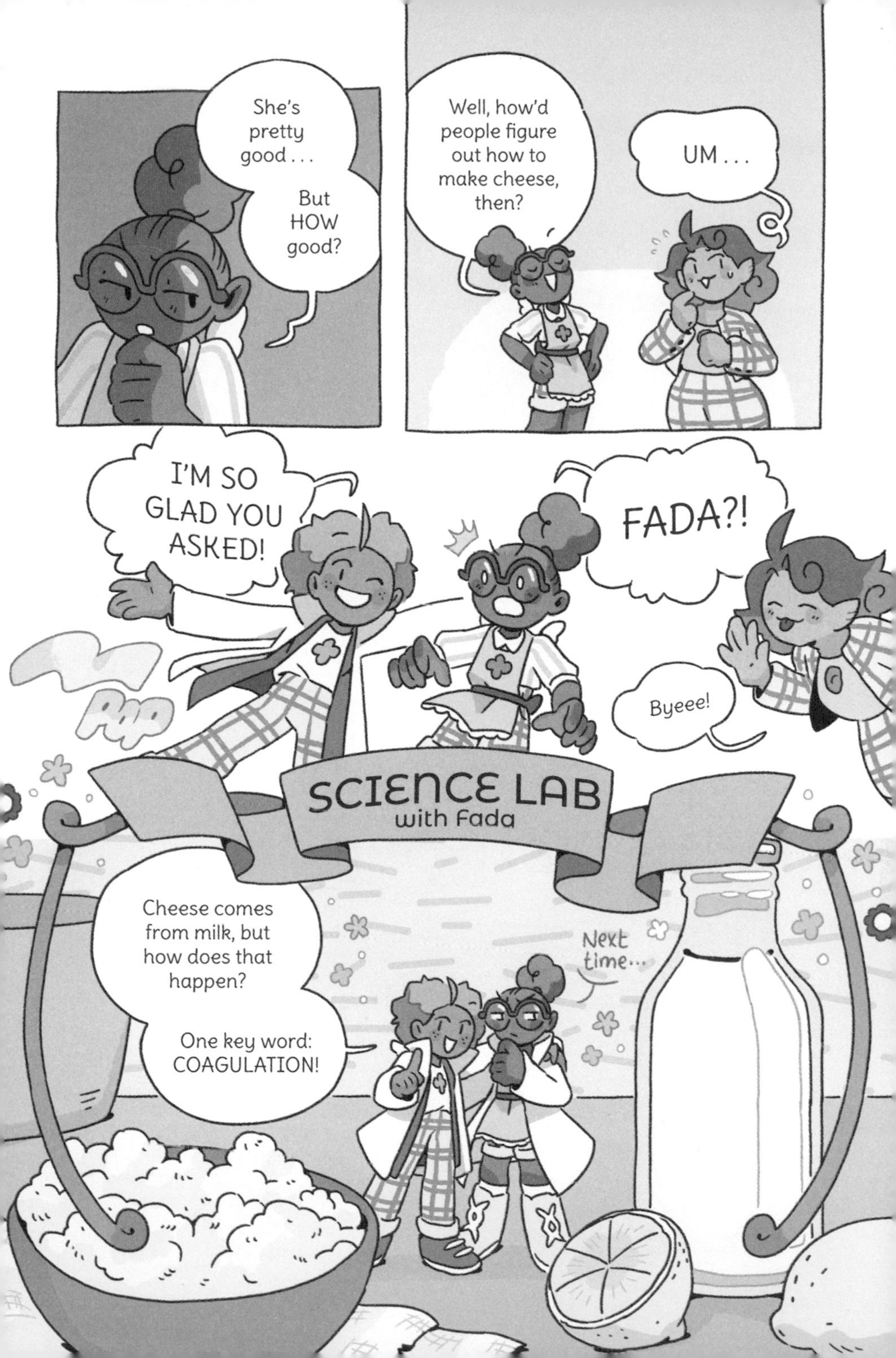

She's pretty good . . .
But HOW good?
Well, how'd people figure out how to make cheese, then?
UM . . .
I'M SO GLAD YOU ASKED!
FADA?!
POP
Byeee!
SCIENCE LAB
with Fada
Cheese comes from milk, but how does that happen?
One key word: COAGULATION!
Next time...

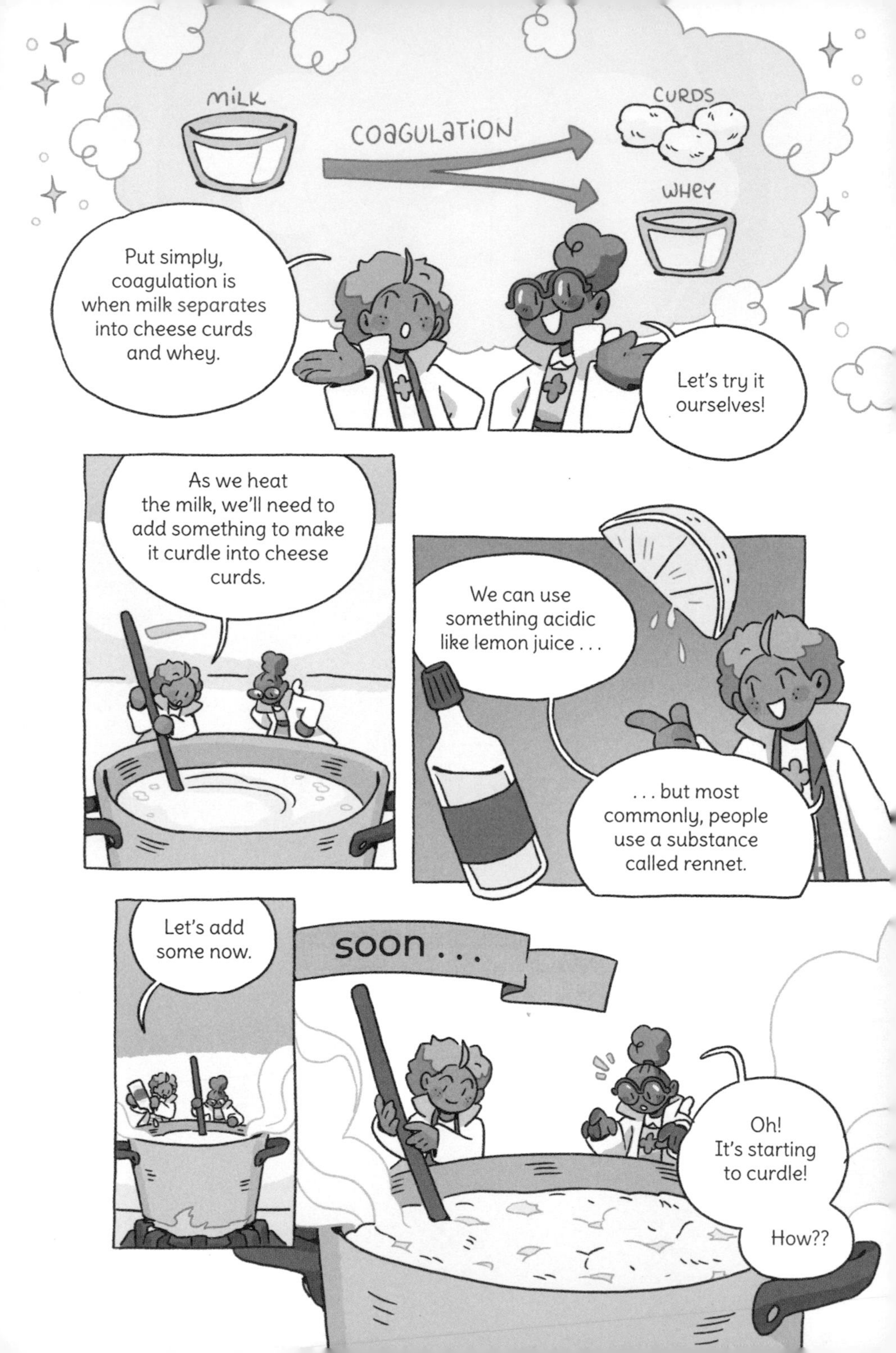
MILK
COAGULATION
CURDS
WHEY
Put simply, coagulation is when milk separates into cheese curds and whey.
Let's try it ourselves!
As we heat the milk, we'll need to add something to make it curdle into cheese curds.
We can use something acidic like lemon juice . . .
. . . but most commonly, people use a substance called rennet.
Let's add some now.
soon . . .
Oh! It's starting to curdle!
How??

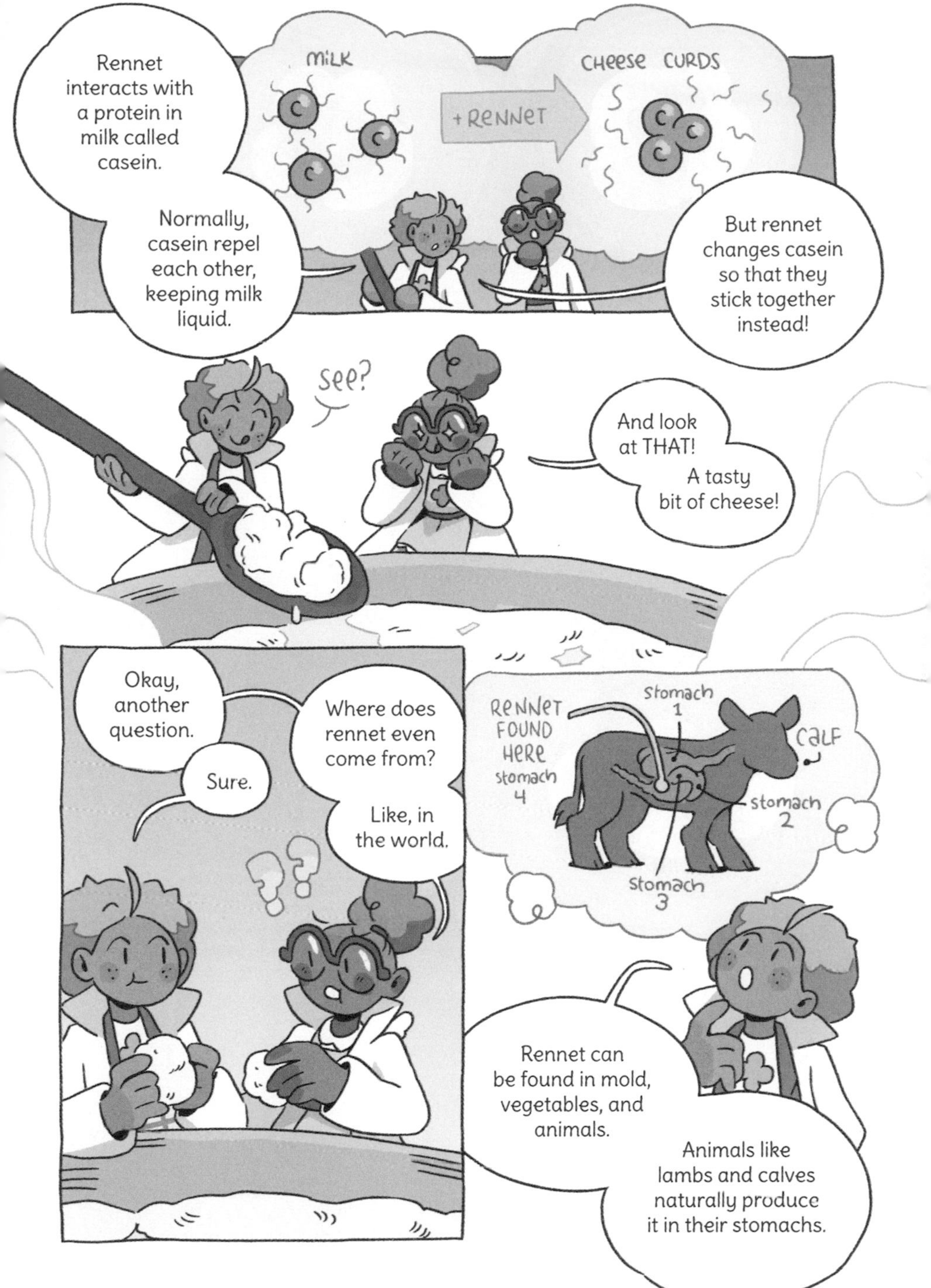
Rennet interacts with a protein in milk called casein.
MILK
+RENNET
CHEESE CURDS
Normally, casein repel each other, keeping milk liquid.
But rennet changes casein so that they stick together instead!
See?
And look at THAT!
A tasty bit of cheese!
Okay, another question.
Sure.
Where does rennet even come from?
Like, in the world.
RENNET FOUND HERE stomach 4
stomach 1
CALF
stomach 2
stomach 3
Rennet can be found in mold, vegetables, and animals.
Animals like lambs and calves naturally produce it in their stomachs.

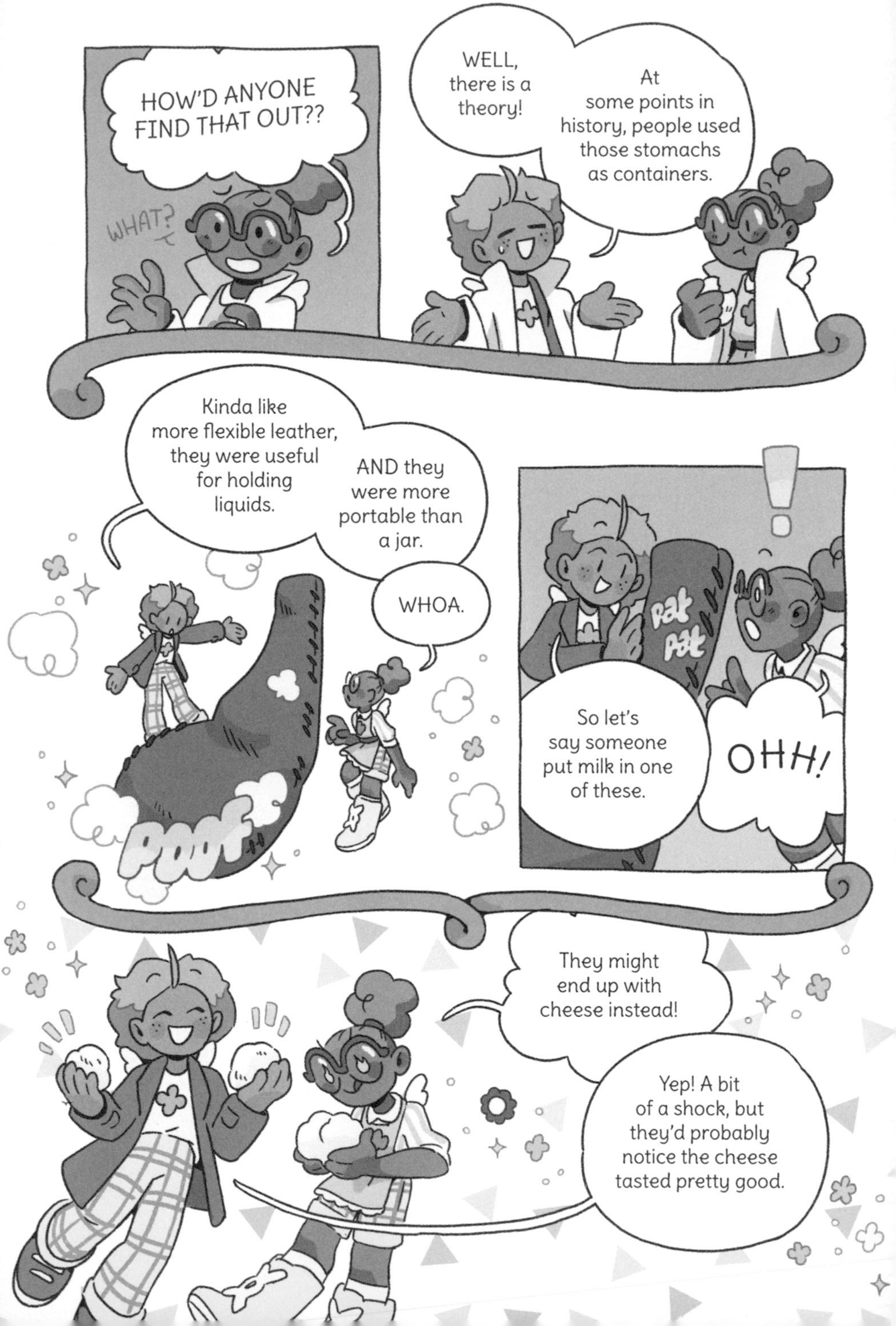
HOW'D ANYONE FIND THAT OUT??
WHAT?
WELL, there is a theory!
At some points in history, people used those stomachs as containers.
Kinda like more flexible leather, they were useful for holding liquids.
AND they were more portable than a jar.
WHOA.
POOF
PAT PAT
So let's say someone put milk in one of these.
OHH!
They might end up with cheese instead!
Yep! A bit of a shock, but they'd probably notice the cheese tasted pretty good.

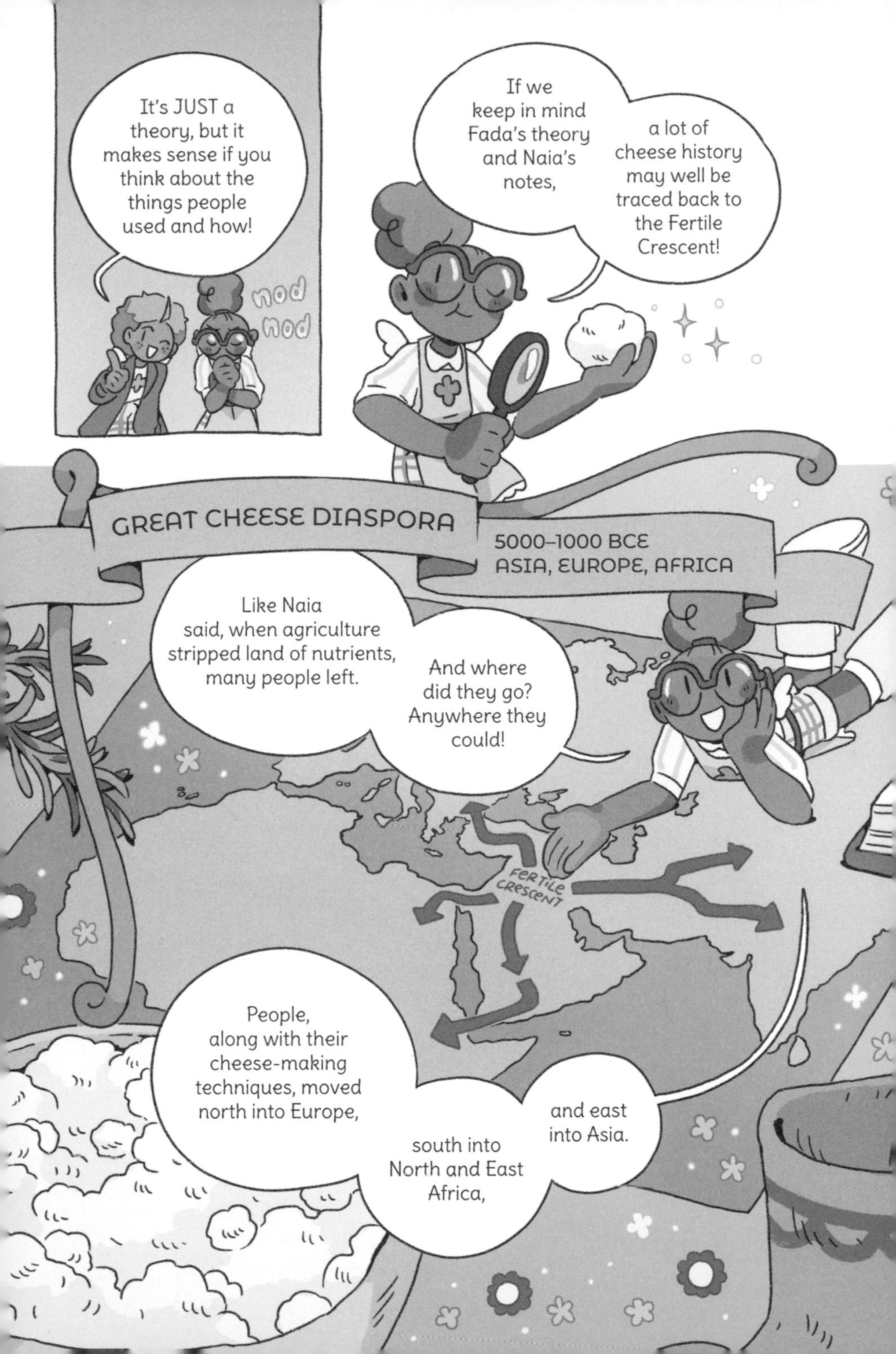
It's JUST a theory, but it makes sense if you think about the things people used and how!
nod nod
If we keep in mind Fada's theory and Naia's notes,
a lot of cheese history may well be traced back to the Fertile Crescent!
GREAT CHEESE DIASPORA
5000–1000 BCE
ASIA, EUROPE, AFRICA
Like Naia said, when agriculture stripped land of nutrients, many people left.
And where did they go? Anywhere they could!
FERTILE CRESCENT
People, along with their cheese-making techniques, moved north into Europe,
south into North and East Africa,
and east into Asia.

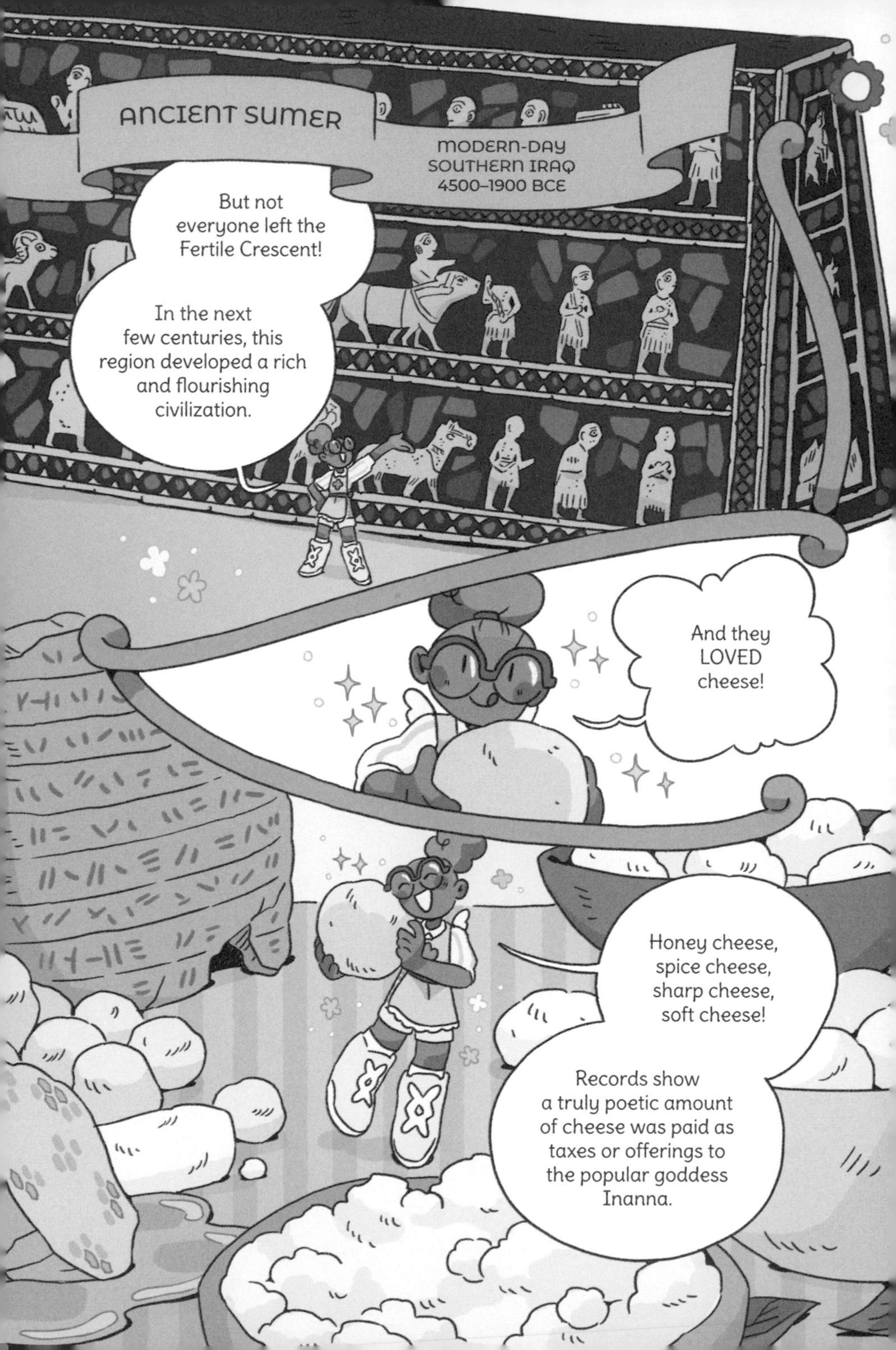
ANCIENT SUMER
MODERN-DAY SOUTHERN IRAQ 4500–1900 BCE
But not everyone left the Fertile Crescent!
In the next few centuries, this region developed a rich and flourishing civilization.
And they LOVED cheese!
Honey cheese, spice cheese, sharp cheese, soft cheese!
Records show a truly poetic amount of cheese was paid as taxes or offerings to the popular goddess Inanna.

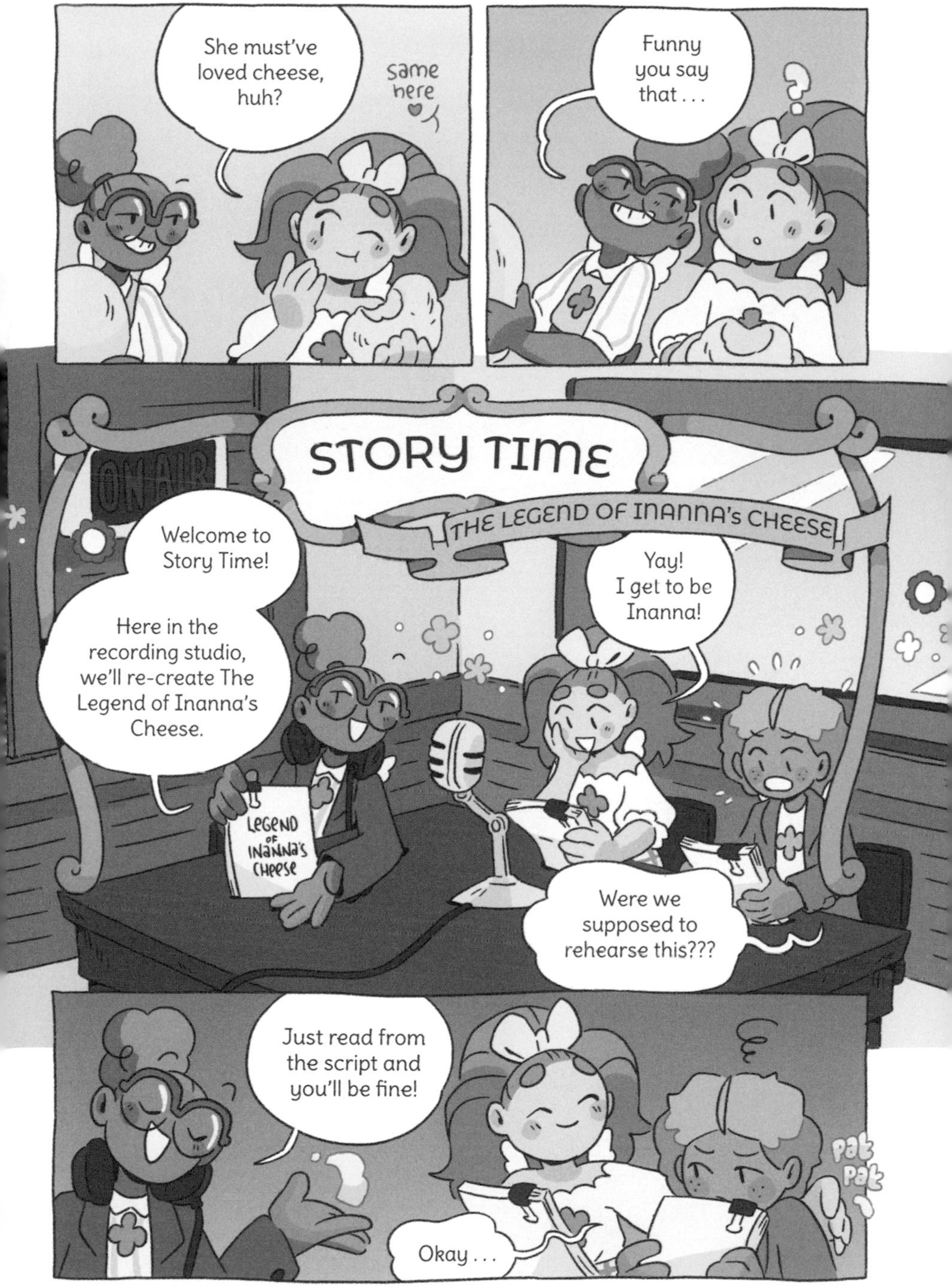
She must've loved cheese, huh?
same here
Funny you say that . . .
STORY TIME
THE LEGEND OF INANNA's CHEESE
ON AIR
Welcome to Story Time!
Here in the recording studio, we'll re-create The Legend of Inanna's Cheese.
Yay! I get to be Inanna!
LEGEND of INANNA's CHEESE
Were we supposed to rehearse this???
Just read from the script and you'll be fine!
PAT PAT
Okay . . .

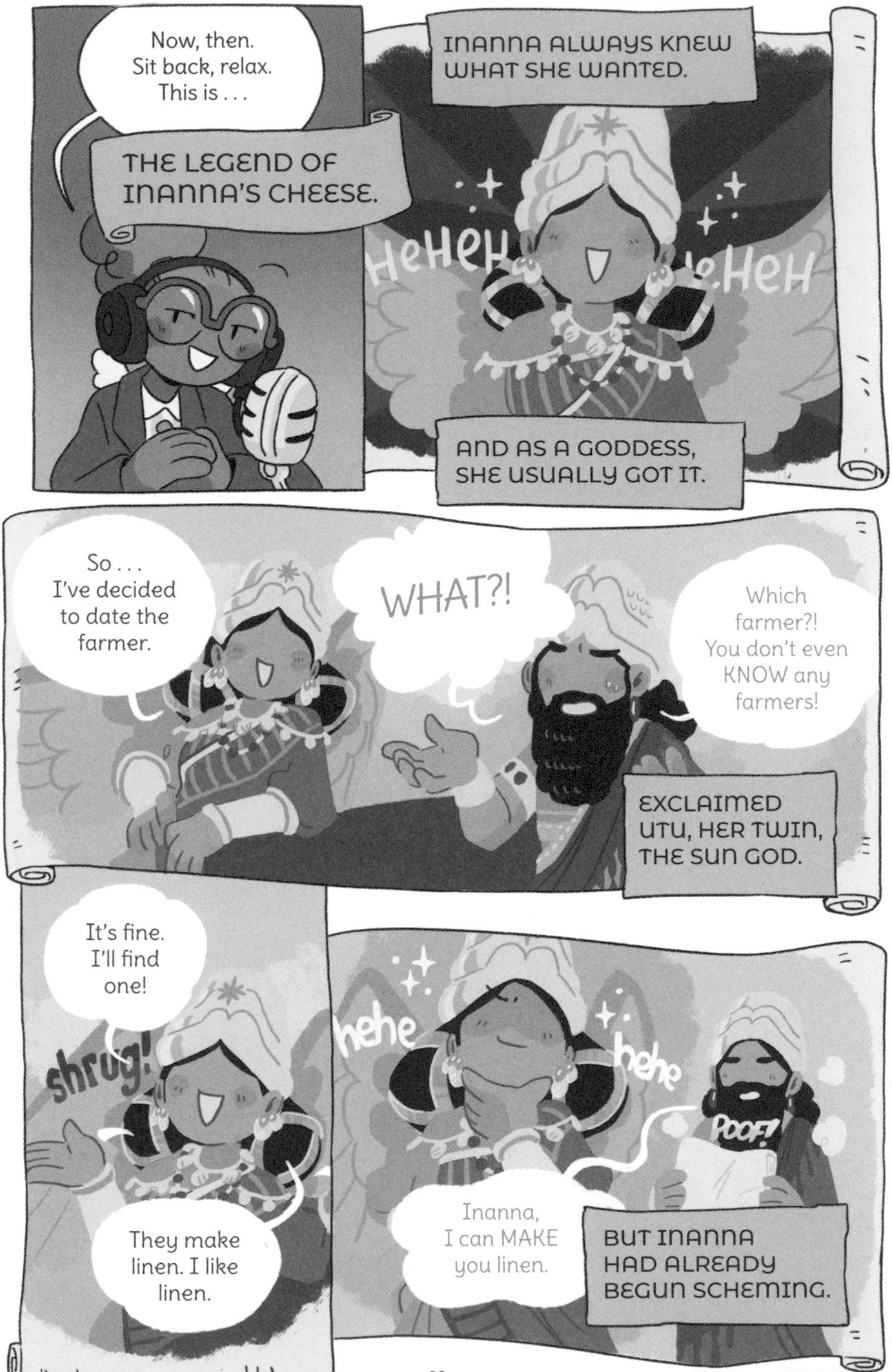
Now, then. Sit back, relax. This is . . .
THE LEGEND OF INANNA'S CHEESE.
INANNA ALWAYS KNEW WHAT SHE WANTED.
HEHEH
HEHEH
AND AS A GODDESS, SHE USUALLY GOT IT.
So . . . I've decided to date the farmer.
WHAT?!
Which farmer?! You don't even KNOW any farmers!
EXCLAIMED UTU, HER TWIN, THE SUN GOD.
It's fine. I'll find one!
shrug!
They make linen. I like linen.
hehe
hehe
POOF!
Inanna, I can MAKE you linen.
BUT INANNA HAD ALREADY BEGUN SCHEMING.

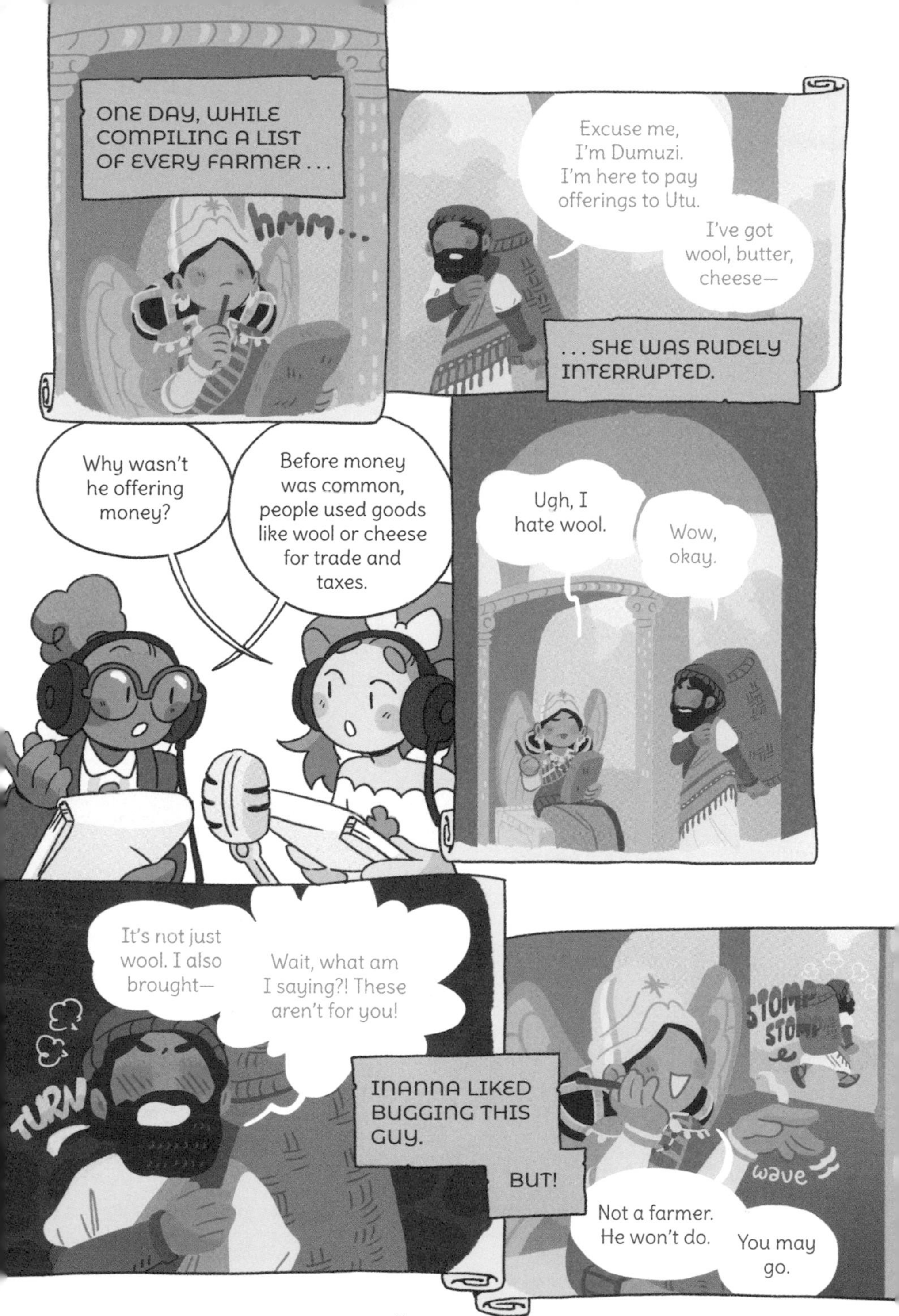
ONE DAY, WHILE COMPILING A LIST OF EVERY FARMER . . .
hmm...
Excuse me, I'm Dumuzi. I'm here to pay offerings to Utu.
I've got wool, butter, cheese—
. . . SHE WAS RUDELY INTERRUPTED.
Why wasn't he offering money?
Before money was common, people used goods like wool or cheese for trade and taxes.
Ugh, I hate wool.
Wow, okay.
It's not just wool. I also brought—
Wait, what am I saying?! These aren't for you!
TURN
INANNA LIKED BUGGING THIS GUY.
BUT!
STOMP
STOMP
wave
Not a farmer. He won't do.
You may go.

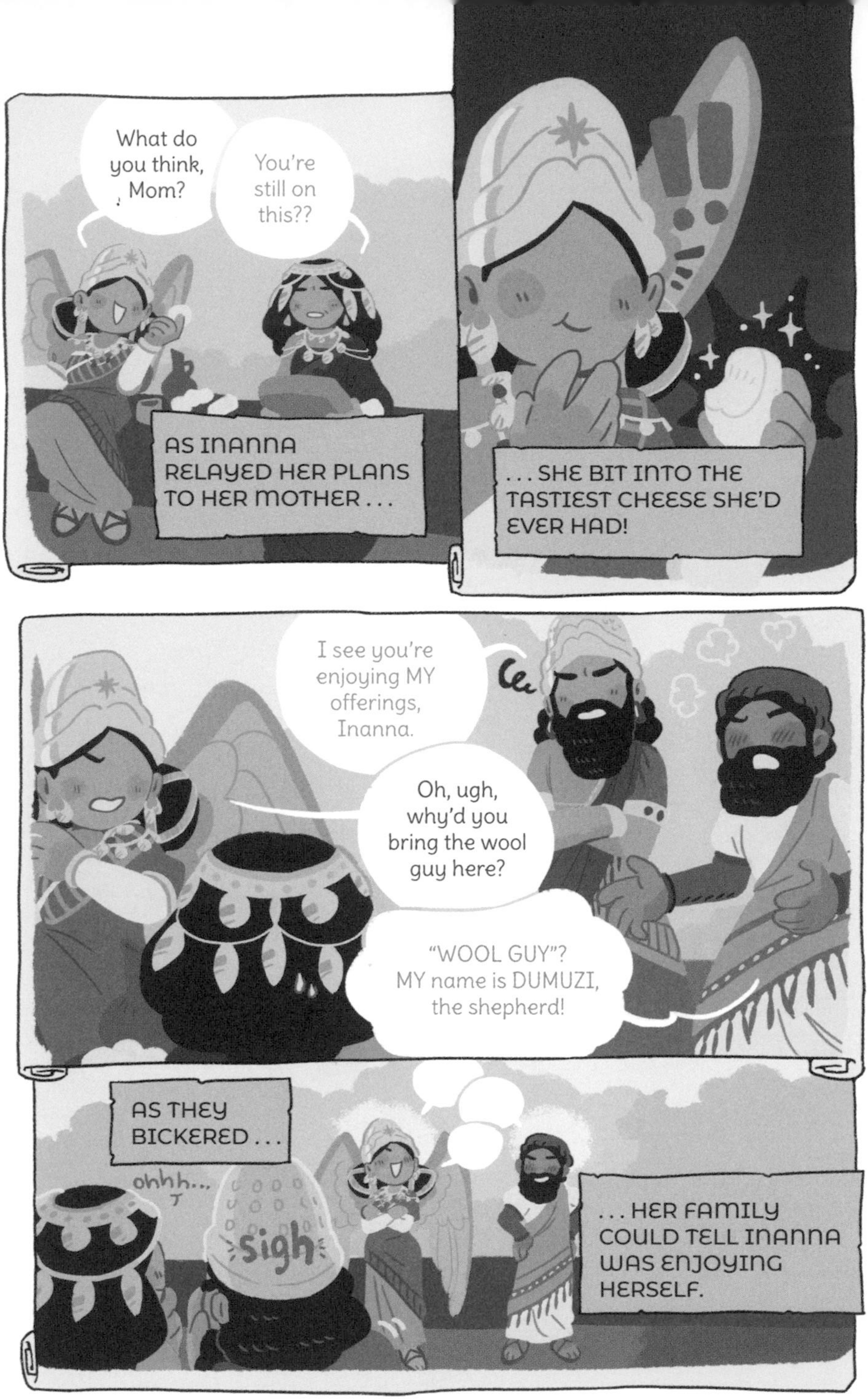
What do you think, Mom?
You're still on this??
AS INANNA RELAYED HER PLANS TO HER MOTHER . . .
. . . SHE BIT INTO THE TASTIEST CHEESE SHE'D EVER HAD!
I see you're enjoying MY offerings, Inanna.
Oh, ugh, why'd you bring the wool guy here?
"WOOL GUY"? MY name is DUMUZI, the shepherd!
AS THEY BICKERED . . .
ohhh...
sigh
. . . HER FAMILY COULD TELL INANNA WAS ENJOYING HERSELF.

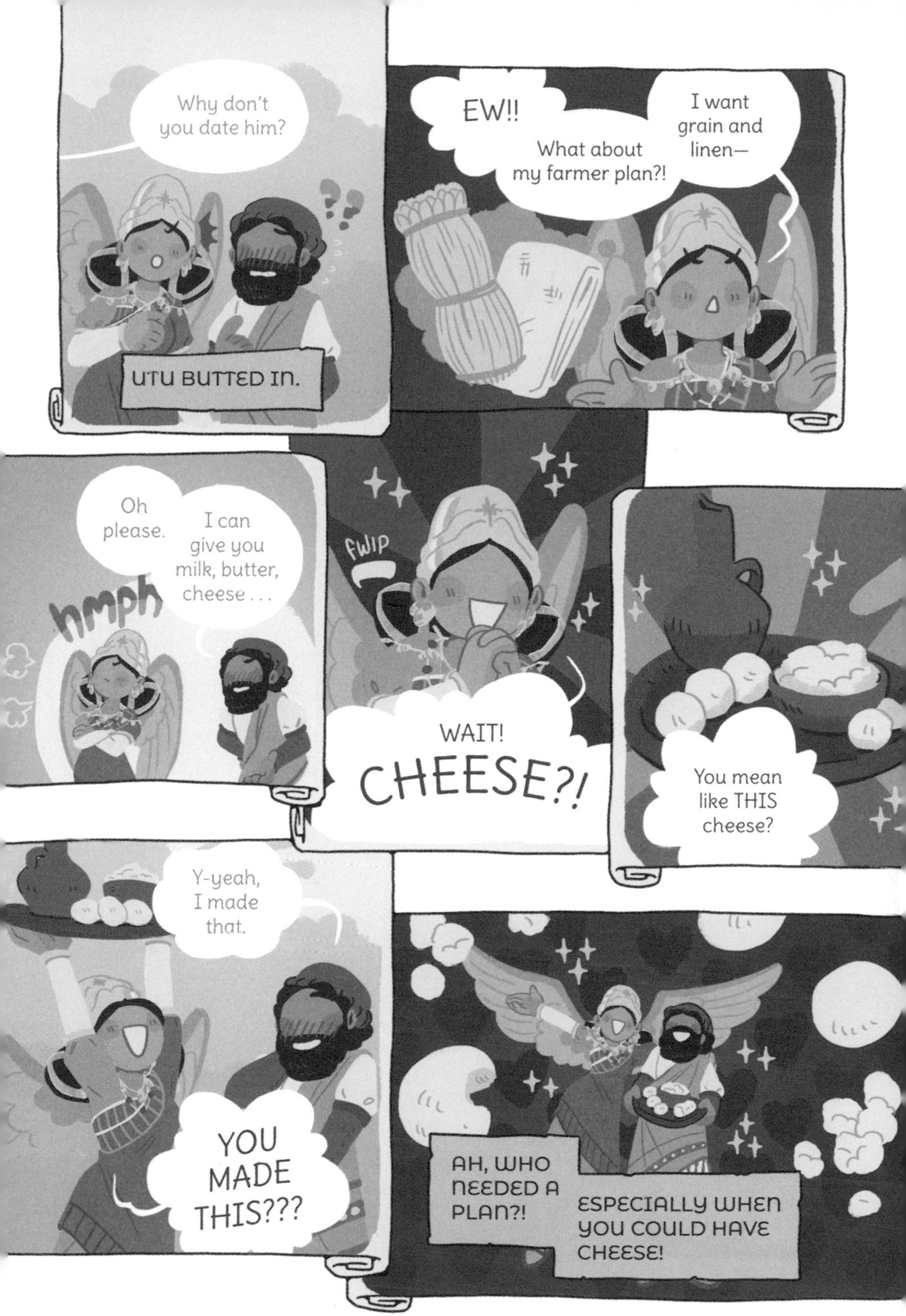
Why don't you date him?
UTU BUTTED IN.
EW!!
What about my farmer plan?!
I want grain and linen—
Oh please.
I can give you milk, butter, cheese . . .
hmph
FWIP
WAIT! CHEESE?!
You mean like THIS cheese?
Y-yeah, I made that.
YOU MADE THIS???
AH, WHO NEEDED A PLAN?!
ESPECIALLY WHEN YOU COULD HAVE CHEESE!

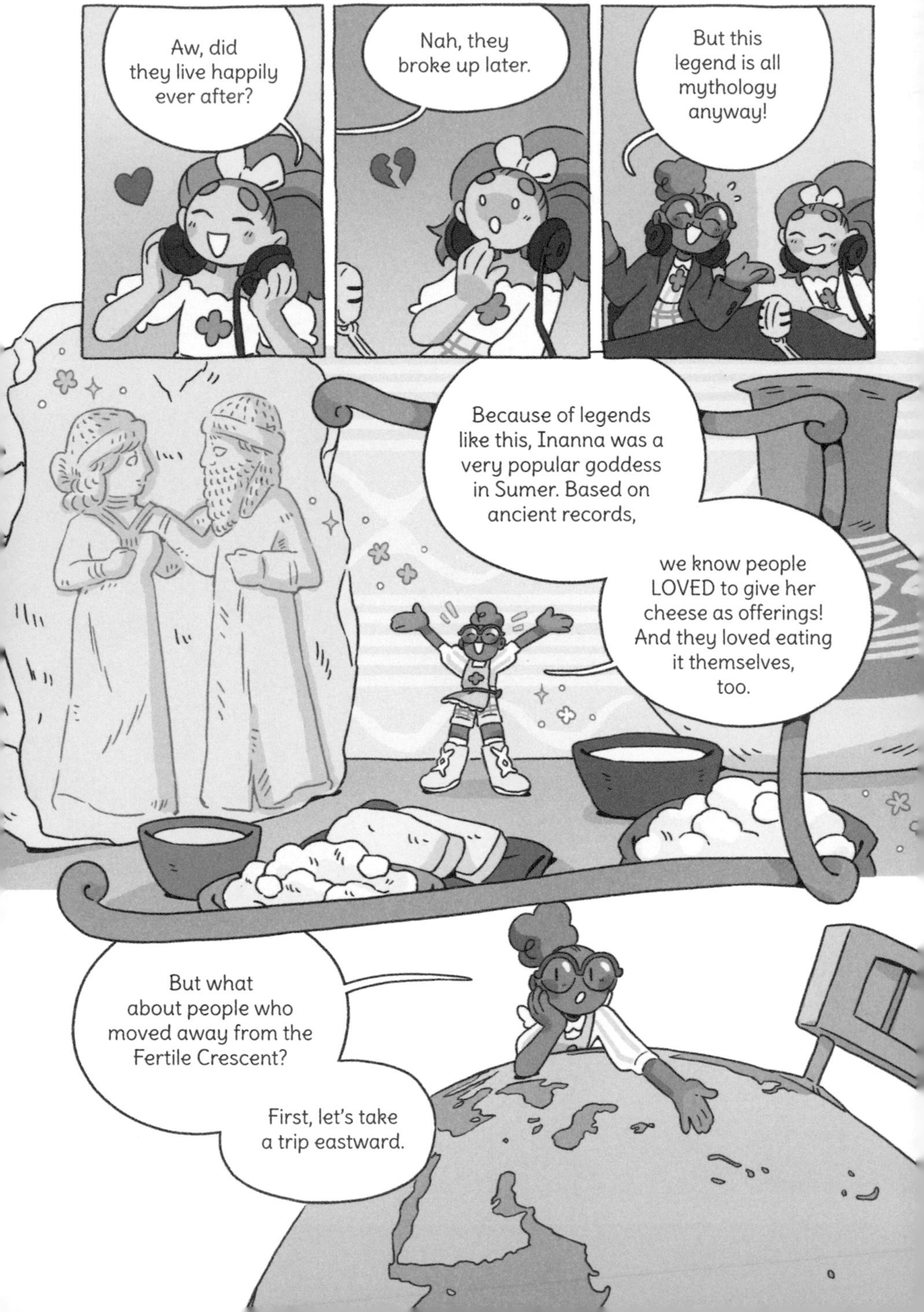
Aw, did they live happily ever after?
Nah, they broke up later.
But this legend is all mythology anyway!
Because of legends like this, Inanna was a very popular goddess in Sumer. Based on ancient records,
we know people LOVED to give her cheese as offerings! And they loved eating it themselves, too.
But what about people who moved away from the Fertile Crescent?
First, let's take a trip eastward.

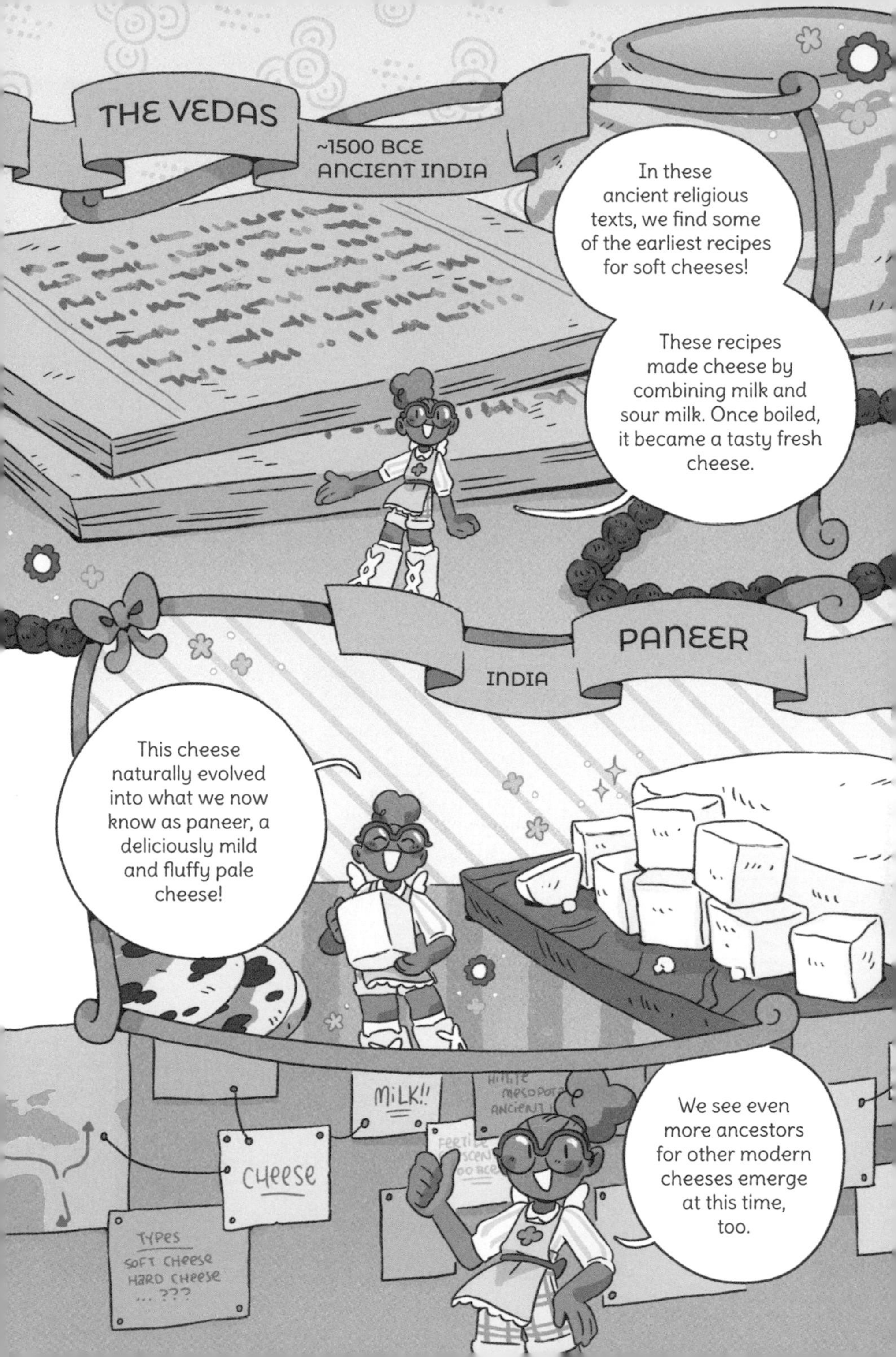
THE VEDAS
~1500 BCE
ANCIENT INDIA
In these ancient religious texts, we find some of the earliest recipes for soft cheeses!
These recipes made cheese by combining milk and sour milk. Once boiled, it became a tasty fresh cheese.
PANEER
INDIA
This cheese naturally evolved into what we now know as paneer, a deliciously mild and fluffy pale cheese!
MiLK!!
CHeese
TYPES
SOFT CHEESE
HARD CHEESE
... ???
We see even more ancestors for other modern cheeses emerge at this time, too.

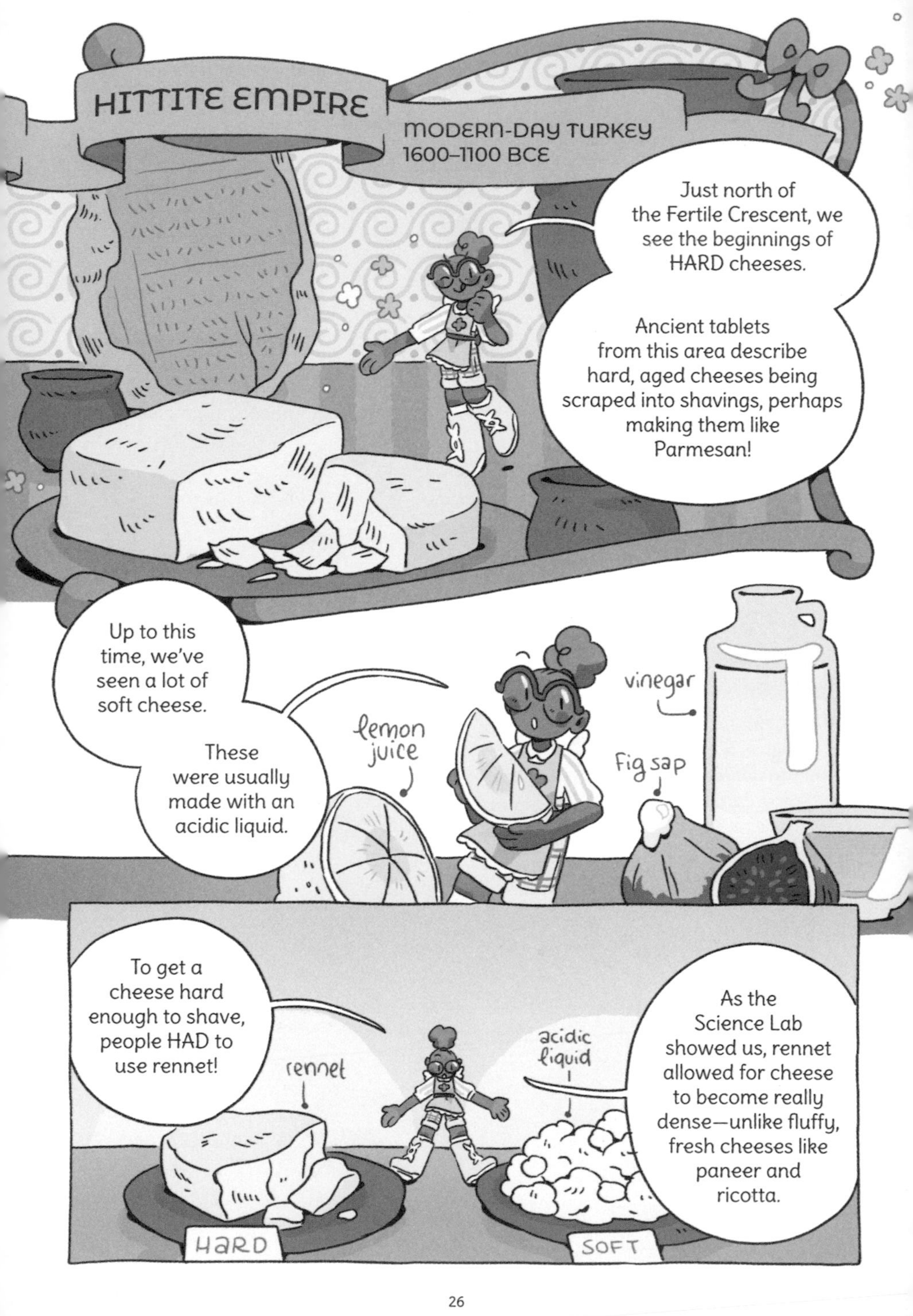
HITTITE EMPIRE
MODERN-DAY TURKEY
1600–1100 BCE
Just north of the Fertile Crescent, we see the beginnings of HARD cheeses.
Ancient tablets from this area describe hard, aged cheeses being scraped into shavings, perhaps making them like Parmesan!
Up to this time, we've seen a lot of soft cheese.
These were usually made with an acidic liquid.
lemon juice
vinegar
fig sap
To get a cheese hard enough to shave, people HAD to use rennet!
rennet
acidic liquid
As the Science Lab showed us, rennet allowed for cheese to become really dense—unlike fluffy, fresh cheeses like paneer and ricotta.
HARD
SOFT

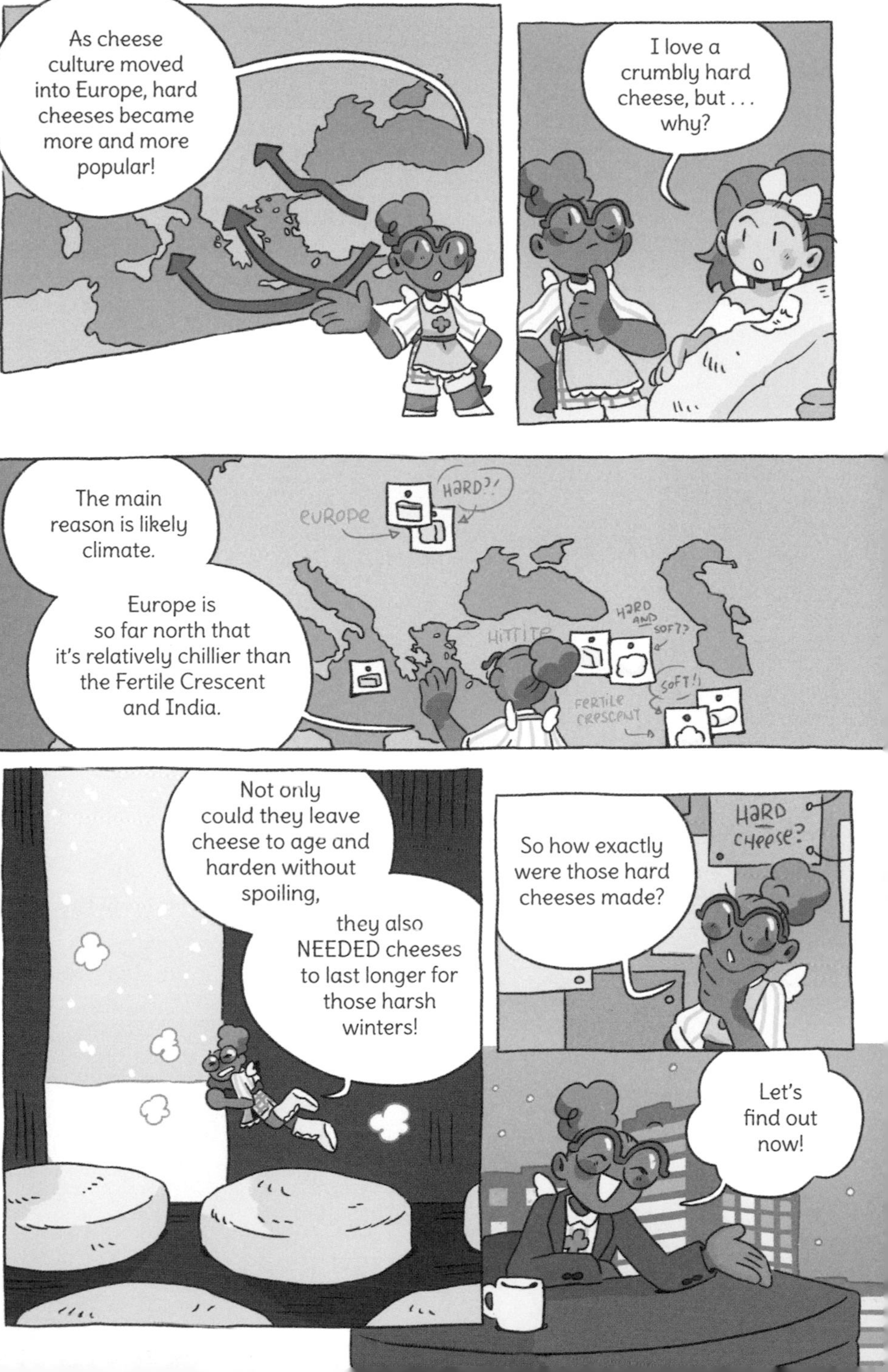

As cheese culture moved into Europe, hard cheeses became more and more popular!
I love a crumbly hard cheese, but . . . why?
The main reason is likely climate.
Europe is so far north that it's relatively chillier than the Fertile Crescent and India.
HARD?!
EUROPE
HARD AND SOFT?
HITTITE
SOFT!
FERTILE CRESCENT
Not only could they leave cheese to age and harden without spoiling,
they also NEEDED cheeses to last longer for those harsh winters!
So how exactly were those hard cheeses made?
HARD CHEESE?
Let's find out now!

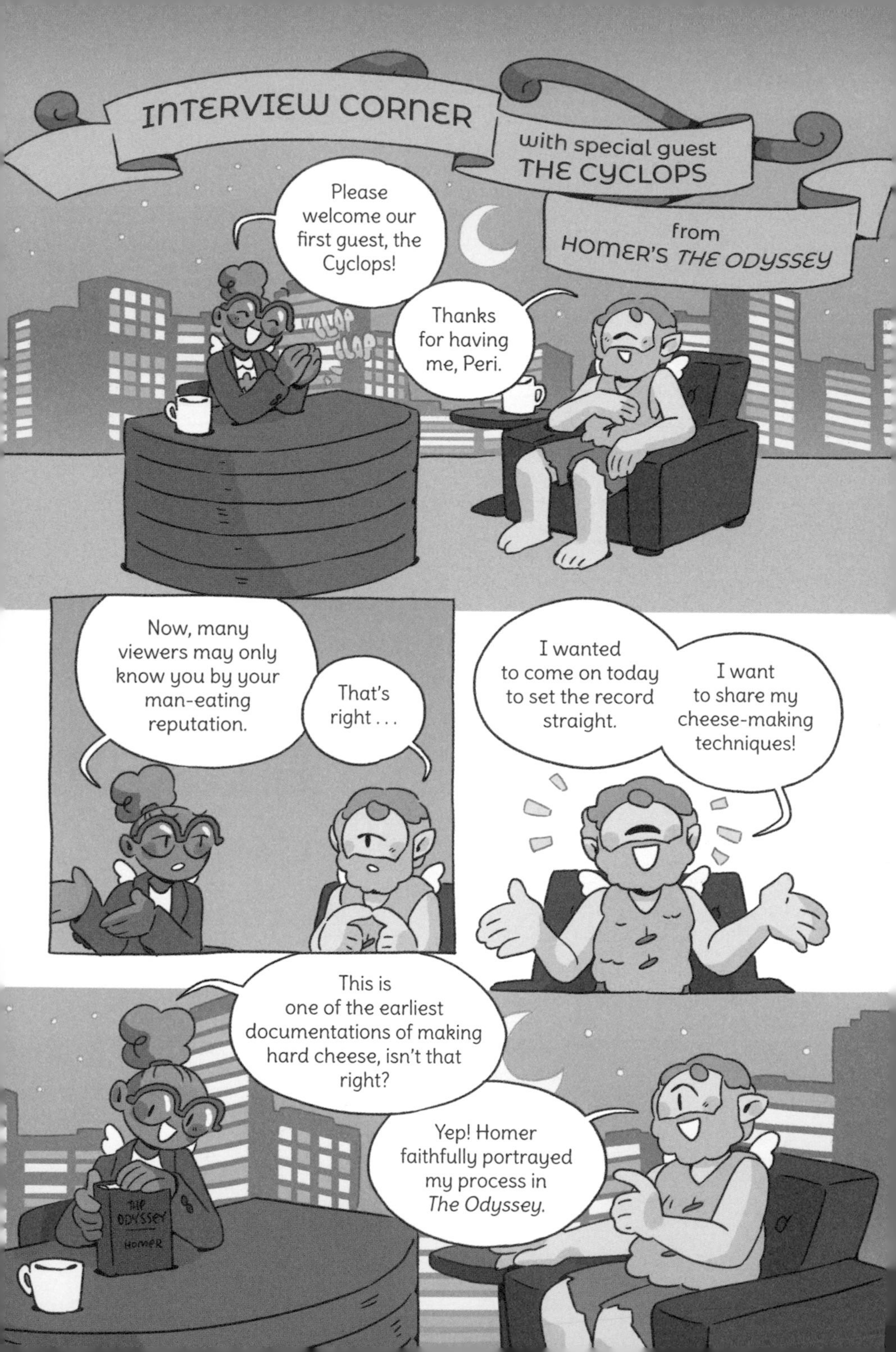
INTERVIEW CORNER
with special guest THE CYCLOPS
from HOMER'S *THE ODYSSEY*
Please welcome our first guest, the Cyclops!
CLAP CLAP
Thanks for having me, Peri.
Now, many viewers may only know you by your man-eating reputation.
That's right . . .
I wanted to come on today to set the record straight.
I want to share my cheese-making techniques!
This is one of the earliest documentations of making hard cheese, isn't that right?
THE ODYSSEY HOMER
Yep! Homer faithfully portrayed my process in *The Odyssey*.

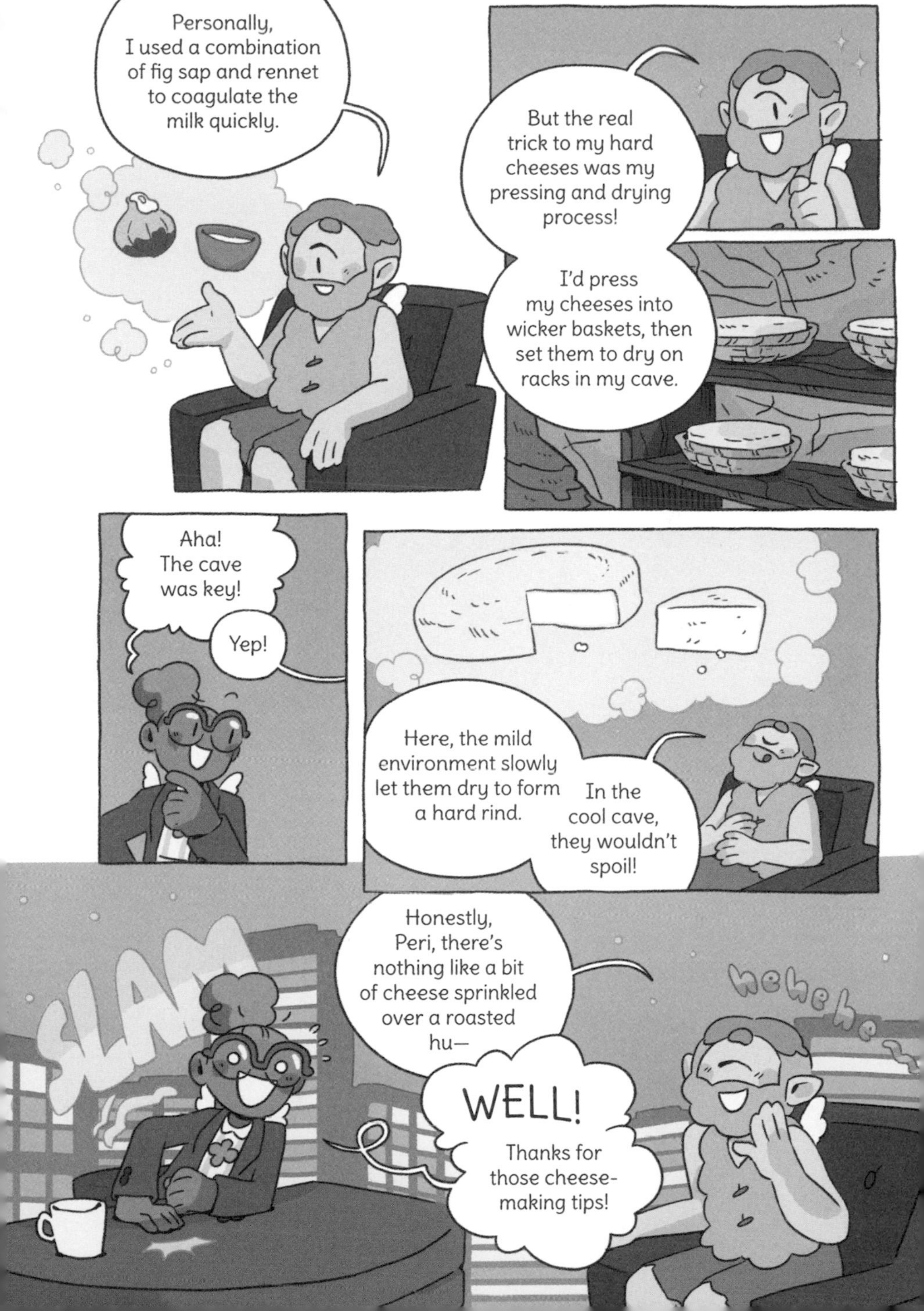
Personally, I used a combination of fig sap and rennet to coagulate the milk quickly.
But the real trick to my hard cheeses was my pressing and drying process!
I'd press my cheeses into wicker baskets, then set them to dry on racks in my cave.
Aha! The cave was key!
Yep!
Here, the mild environment slowly let them dry to form a hard rind.
In the cool cave, they wouldn't spoil!
Honestly, Peri, there's nothing like a bit of cheese sprinkled over a roasted hu—
SLAM
WELL!
Thanks for those cheese-making tips!
hehehe

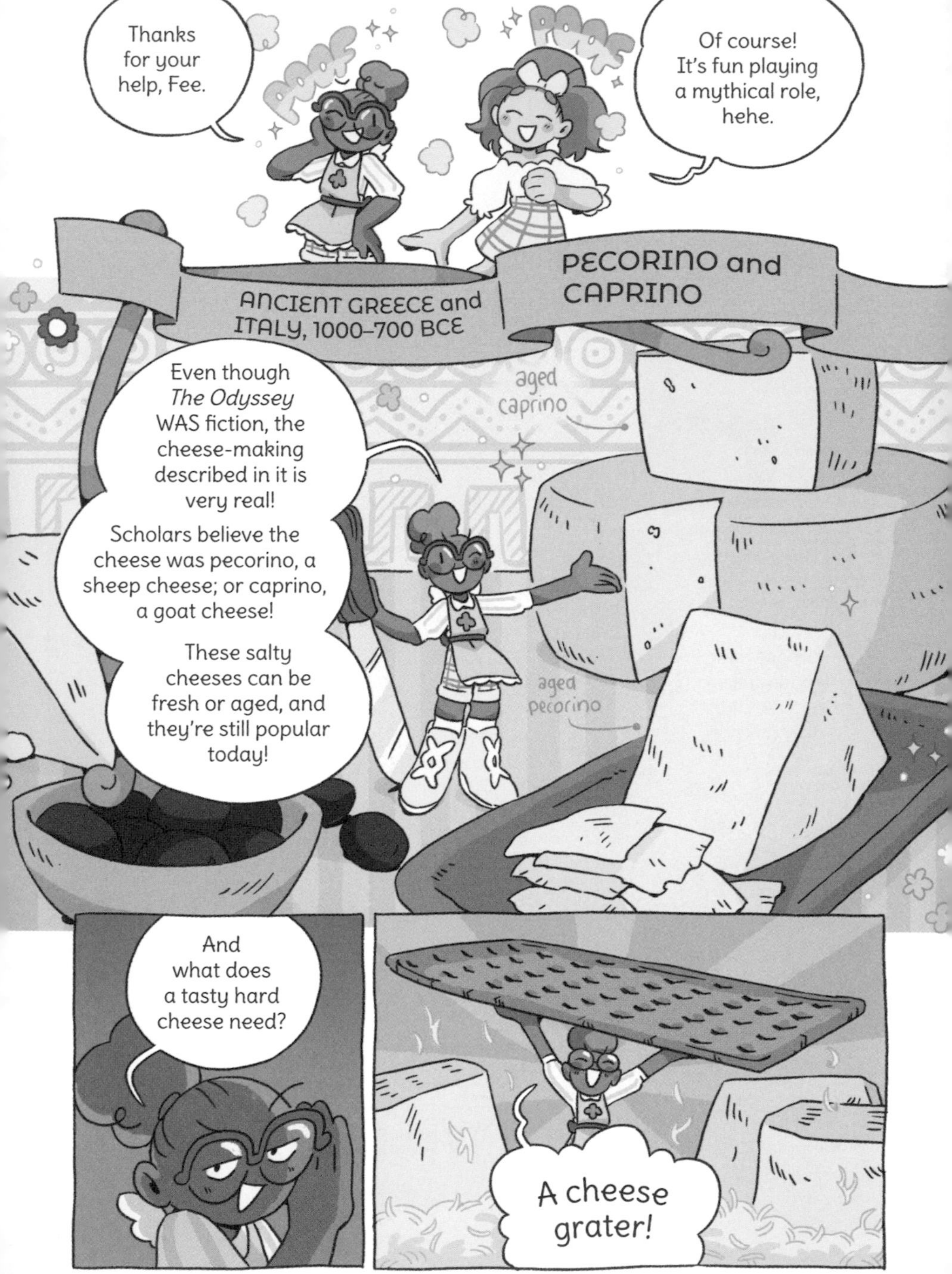
Thanks for your help, Fee.
POOF
POOF
Of course! It's fun playing a mythical role, hehe.
ANCIENT GREECE and ITALY, 1000–700 BCE
PECORINO and CAPRINO
Even though *The Odyssey* WAS fiction, the cheese-making described in it is very real!
Scholars believe the cheese was pecorino, a sheep cheese; or caprino, a goat cheese!
These salty cheeses can be fresh or aged, and they're still popular today!
aged caprino
aged pecorino
And what does a tasty hard cheese need?
A cheese grater!

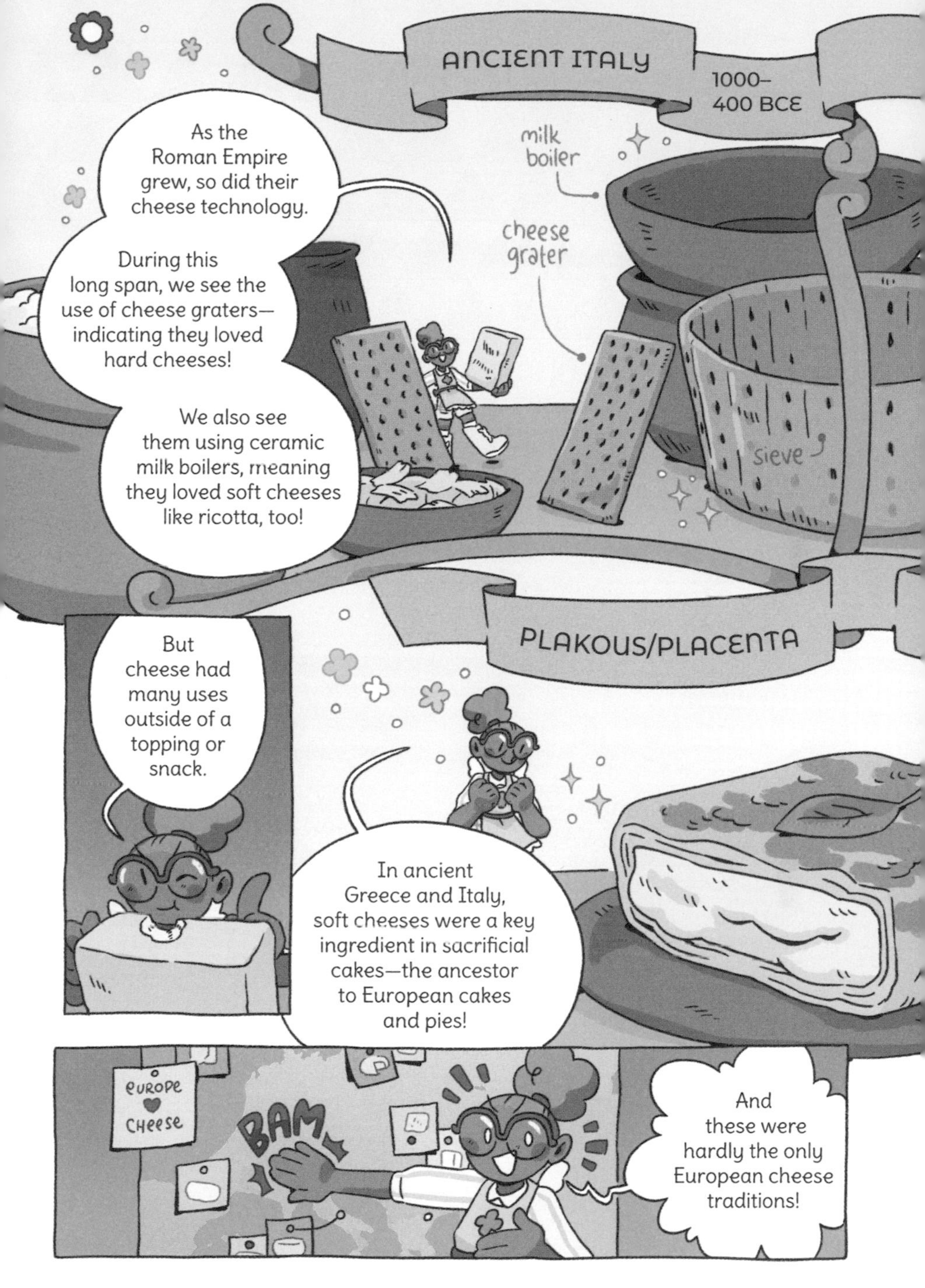
ANCIENT ITALY
1000–400 BCE
As the Roman Empire grew, so did their cheese technology.
During this long span, we see the use of cheese graters—indicating they loved hard cheeses!
We also see them using ceramic milk boilers, meaning they loved soft cheeses like ricotta, too!
milk boiler
cheese grater
sieve
But cheese had many uses outside of a topping or snack.
PLAKOUS/PLACENTA
In ancient Greece and Italy, soft cheeses were a key ingredient in sacrificial cakes—the ancestor to European cakes and pies!
EUROPE ♥ CHEESE
BAM
And these were hardly the only European cheese traditions!

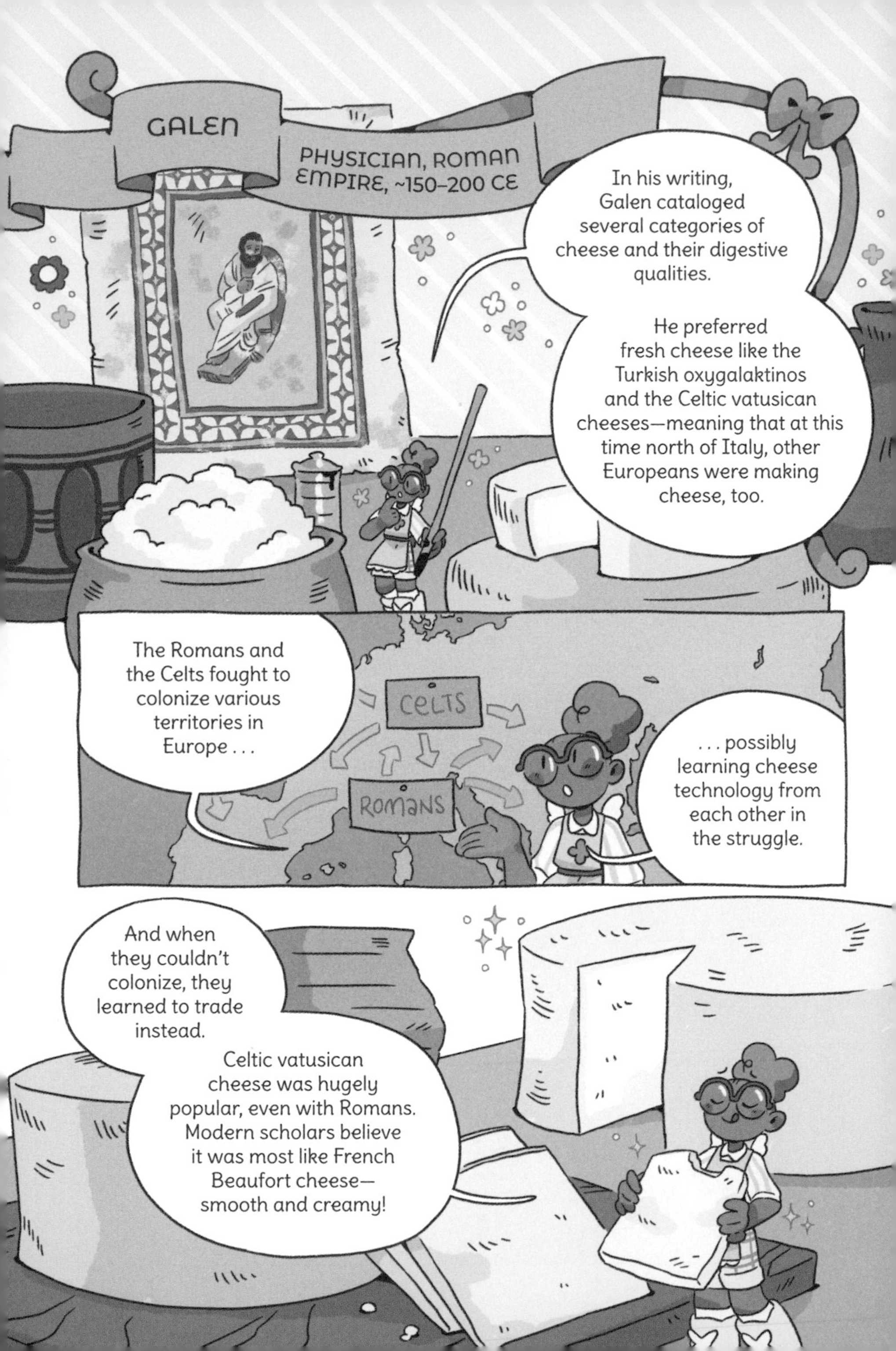
GALEN
PHYSICIAN, ROMAN EMPIRE, ~150–200 CE
In his writing, Galen cataloged several categories of cheese and their digestive qualities.
He preferred fresh cheese like the Turkish oxygalaktinos and the Celtic vatusican cheeses—meaning that at this time north of Italy, other Europeans were making cheese, too.
The Romans and the Celts fought to colonize various territories in Europe . . .
CELTS
ROMANS
. . . possibly learning cheese technology from each other in the struggle.
And when they couldn't colonize, they learned to trade instead.
Celtic vatusican cheese was hugely popular, even with Romans. Modern scholars believe it was most like French Beaufort cheese—smooth and creamy!

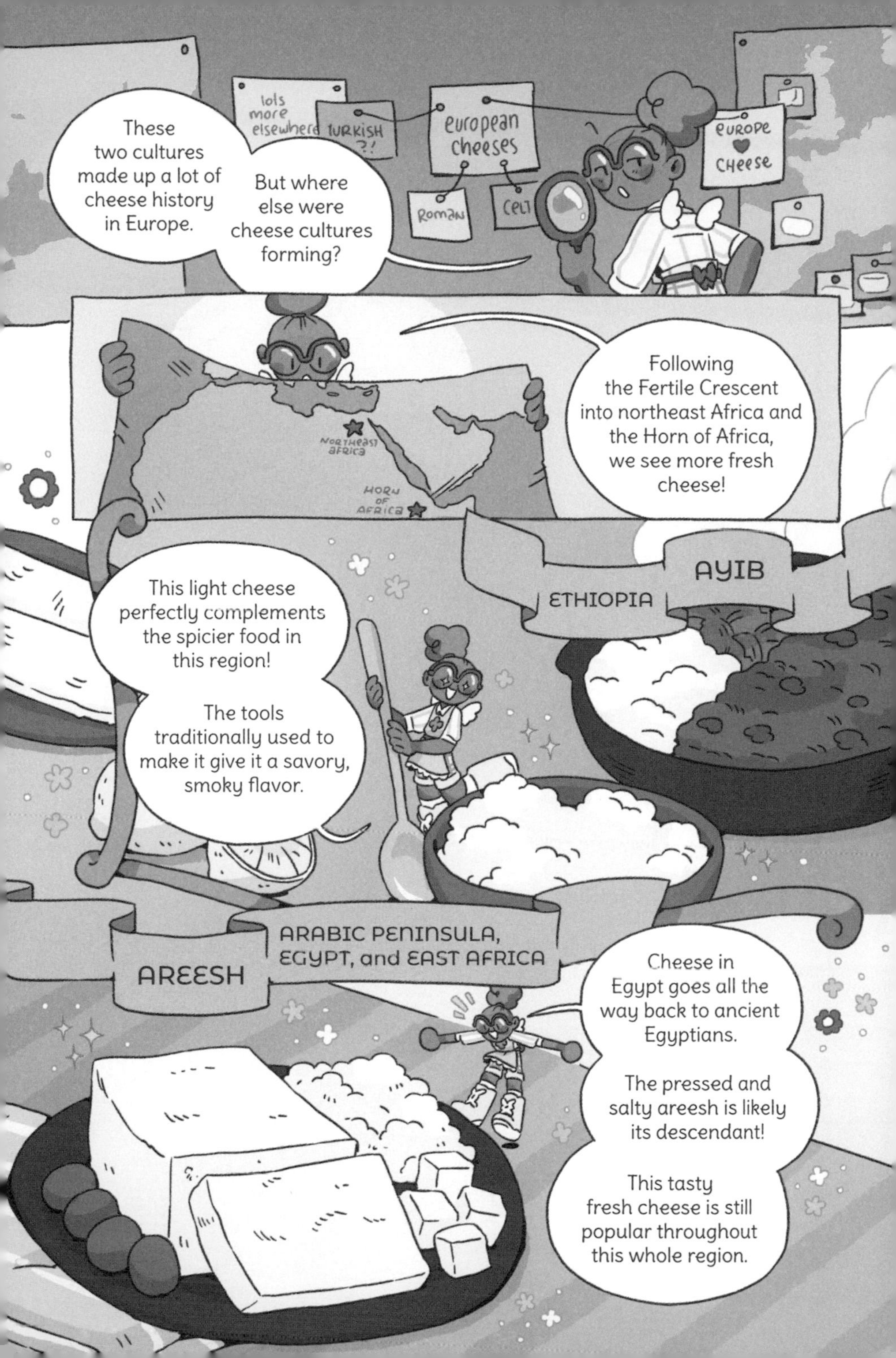
lots more elsewhere
TURKISH ?!
european cheeses
Roman
Celt
Europe ♥ Cheese
These two cultures made up a lot of cheese history in Europe.
But where else were cheese cultures forming?
NORTHEAST AFRICA
HORN OF AFRICA
Following the Fertile Crescent into northeast Africa and the Horn of Africa, we see more fresh cheese!
AYIB
ETHIOPIA
This light cheese perfectly complements the spicier food in this region!
The tools traditionally used to make it give it a savory, smoky flavor.
AREESH
ARABIC PENINSULA, EGYPT, and EAST AFRICA
Cheese in Egypt goes all the way back to ancient Egyptians.
The pressed and salty areesh is likely its descendant!
This tasty fresh cheese is still popular throughout this whole region.

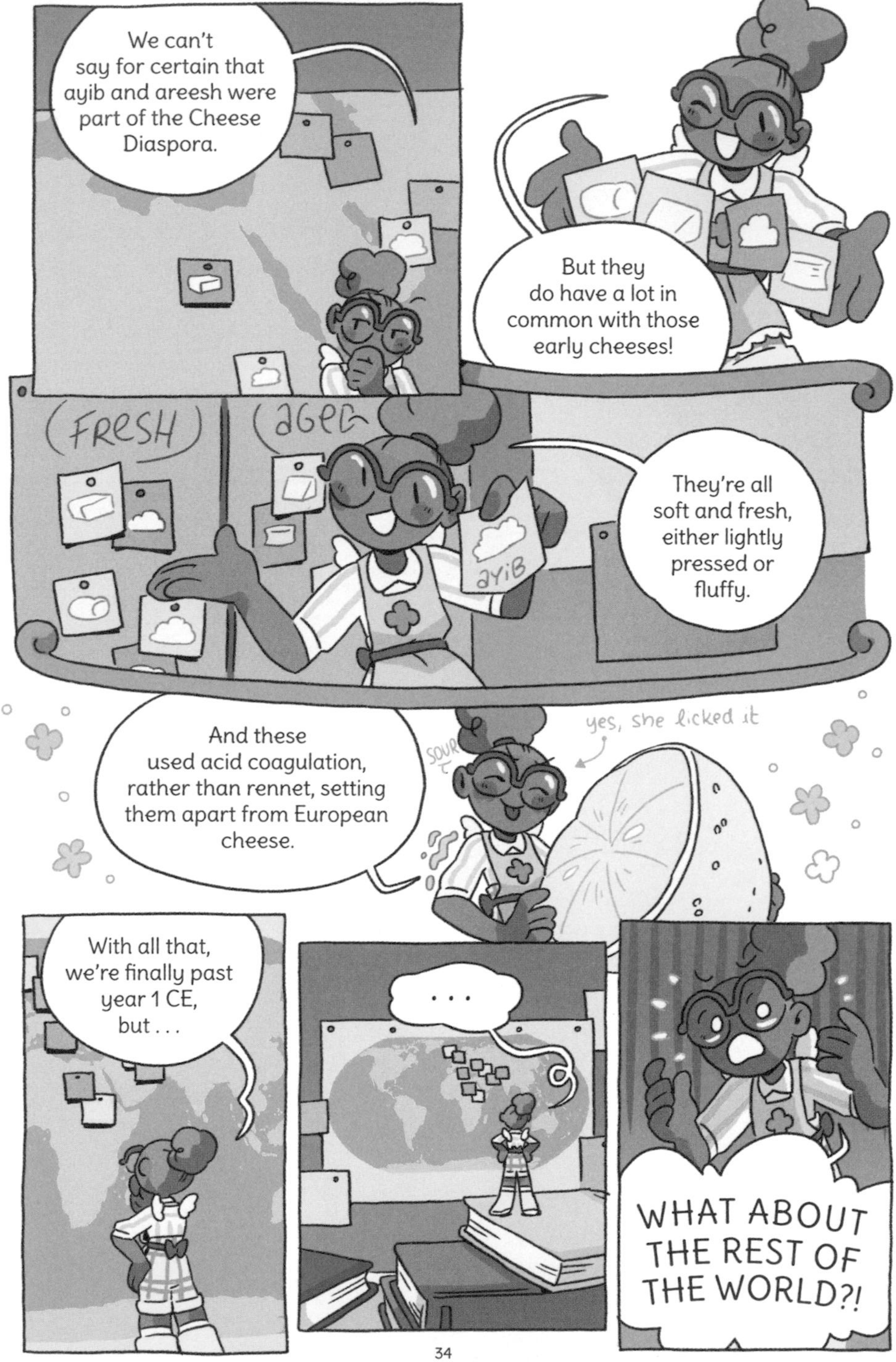
We can't say for certain that ayib and areesh were part of the Cheese Diaspora.
But they do have a lot in common with those early cheeses!
(FRESH)
(aged)
ayib
They're all soft and fresh, either lightly pressed or fluffy.
And these used acid coagulation, rather than rennet, setting them apart from European cheese.
SOUR
yes, she licked it
With all that, we're finally past year 1 CE, but . . .
. . .
WHAT ABOUT THE REST OF THE WORLD?!

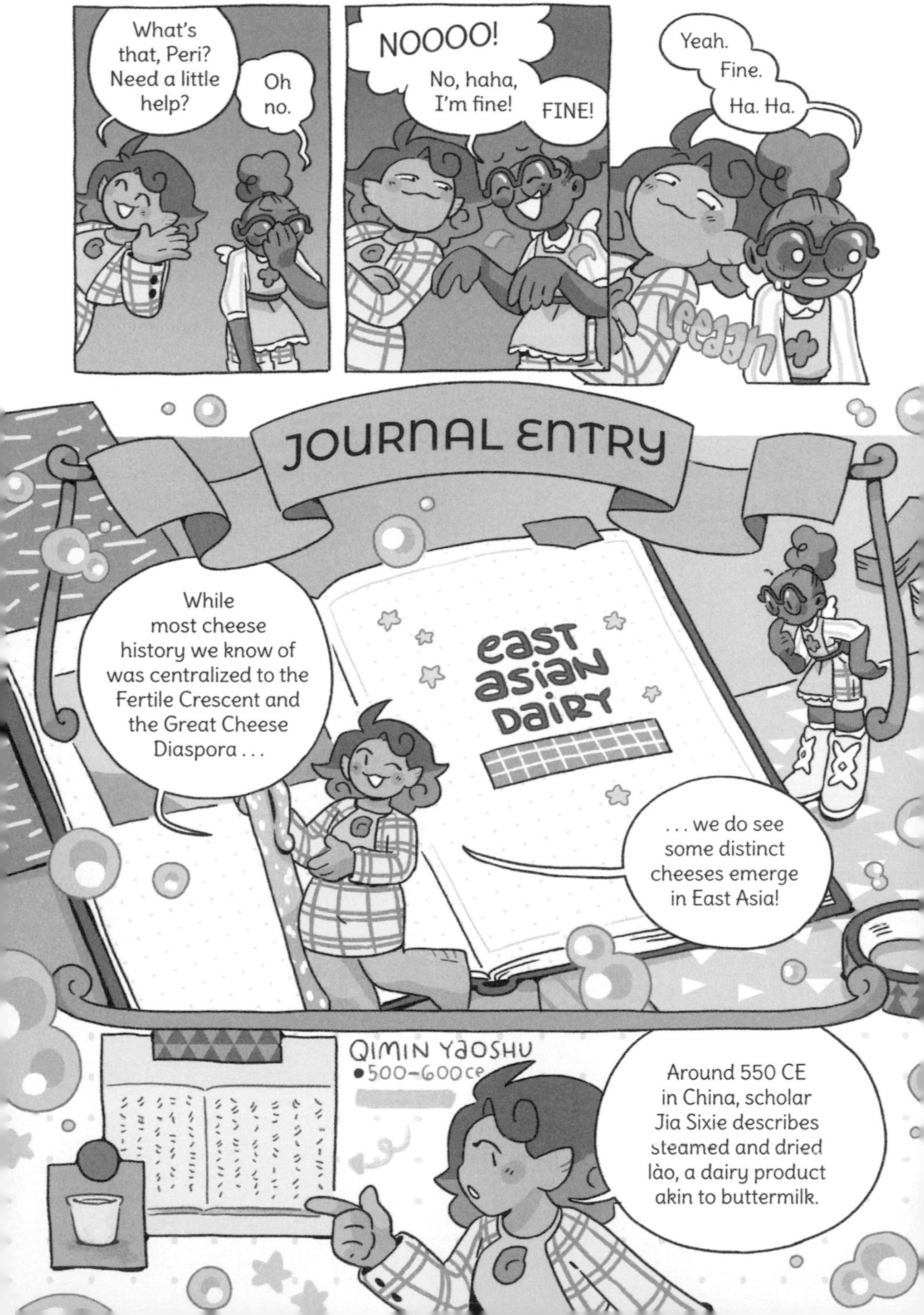
What's that, Peri? Need a little help?
Oh no.
NOOOO!
No, haha, I'm fine!
FINE!
Yeah.
Fine.
Ha. Ha.
LEEAAN
JOURNAL ENTRY
While most cheese history we know of was centralized to the Fertile Crescent and the Great Cheese Diaspora . . .
EAST ASIAN DAIRY
. . . we do see some distinct cheeses emerge in East Asia!
QIMIN YAOSHU
500–600CE
Around 550 CE in China, scholar Jia Sixie describes steamed and dried lào, a dairy product akin to buttermilk.

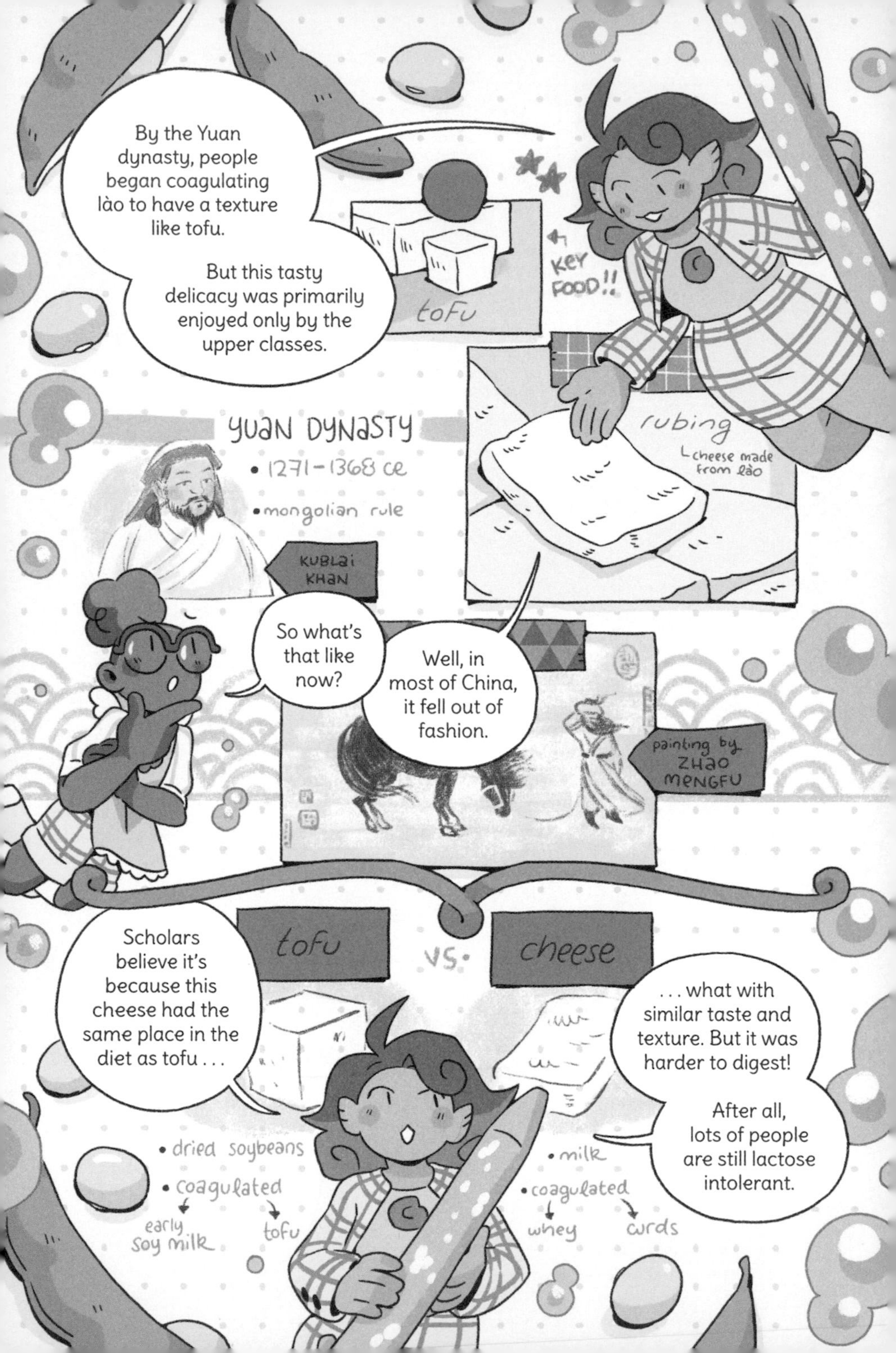
By the Yuan dynasty, people began coagulating lào to have a texture like tofu.
But this tasty delicacy was primarily enjoyed only by the upper classes.
tofu
KEY FOOD!!
YUAN DYNASTY
• 1271–1368 CE
• mongolian rule
KUBLAI KHAN
rubing
cheese made from lào
So what's that like now?
Well, in most of China, it fell out of fashion.
painting by ZHAO MENGFU
tofu
vs.
cheese
Scholars believe it's because this cheese had the same place in the diet as tofu . . .
. . . what with similar taste and texture. But it was harder to digest!
After all, lots of people are still lactose intolerant.
• dried soybeans
• coagulated
early soy milk
tofu
• milk
• coagulated
whey
curds

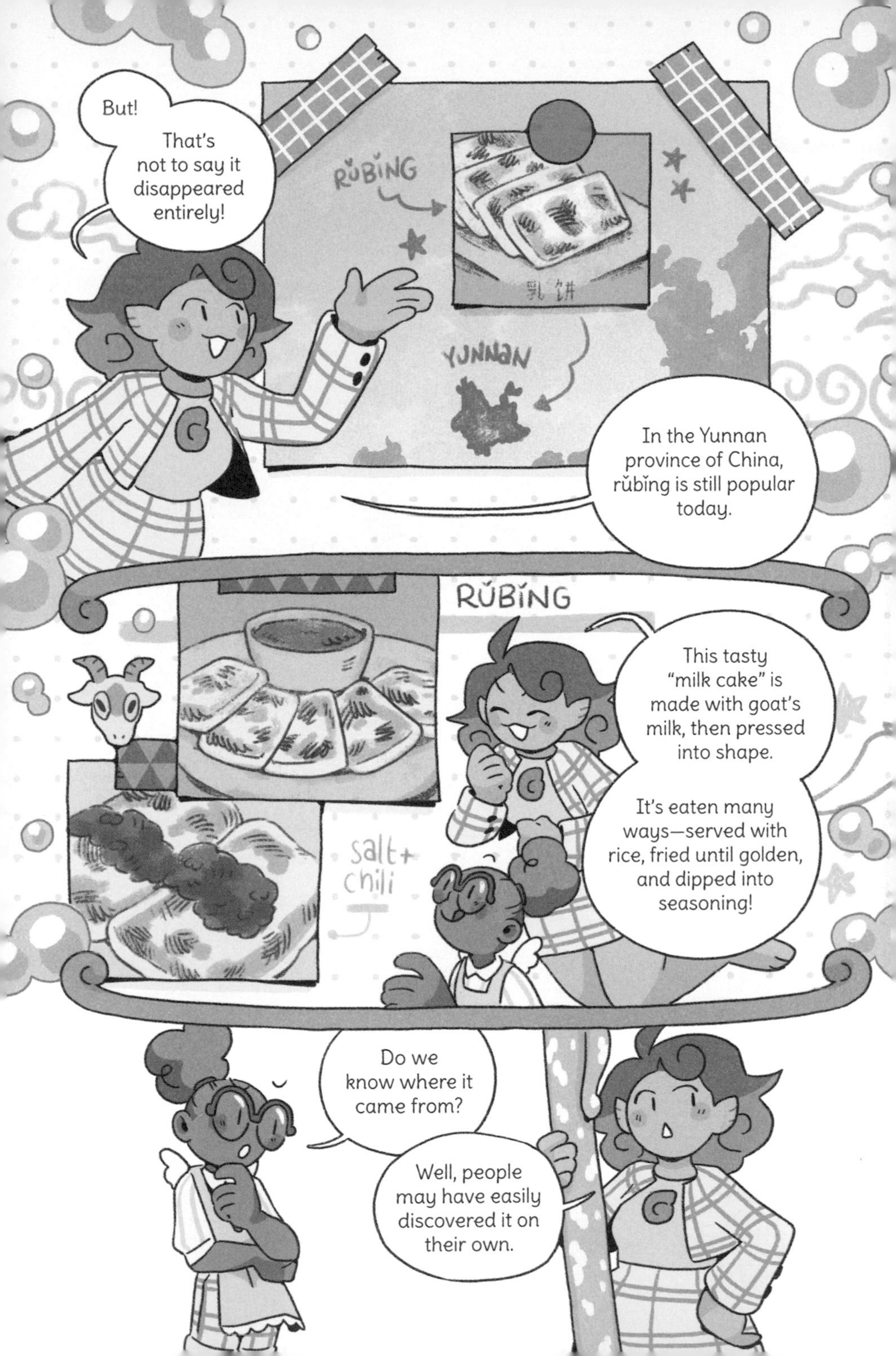
But!
That's not to say it disappeared entirely!
RŬBĬNG
乳饼
YUNNAN
In the Yunnan province of China, rŭbĭng is still popular today.
RŬBĬNG
This tasty "milk cake" is made with goat's milk, then pressed into shape.
It's eaten many ways—served with rice, fried until golden, and dipped into seasoning!
salt + chili
Do we know where it came from?
Well, people may have easily discovered it on their own.

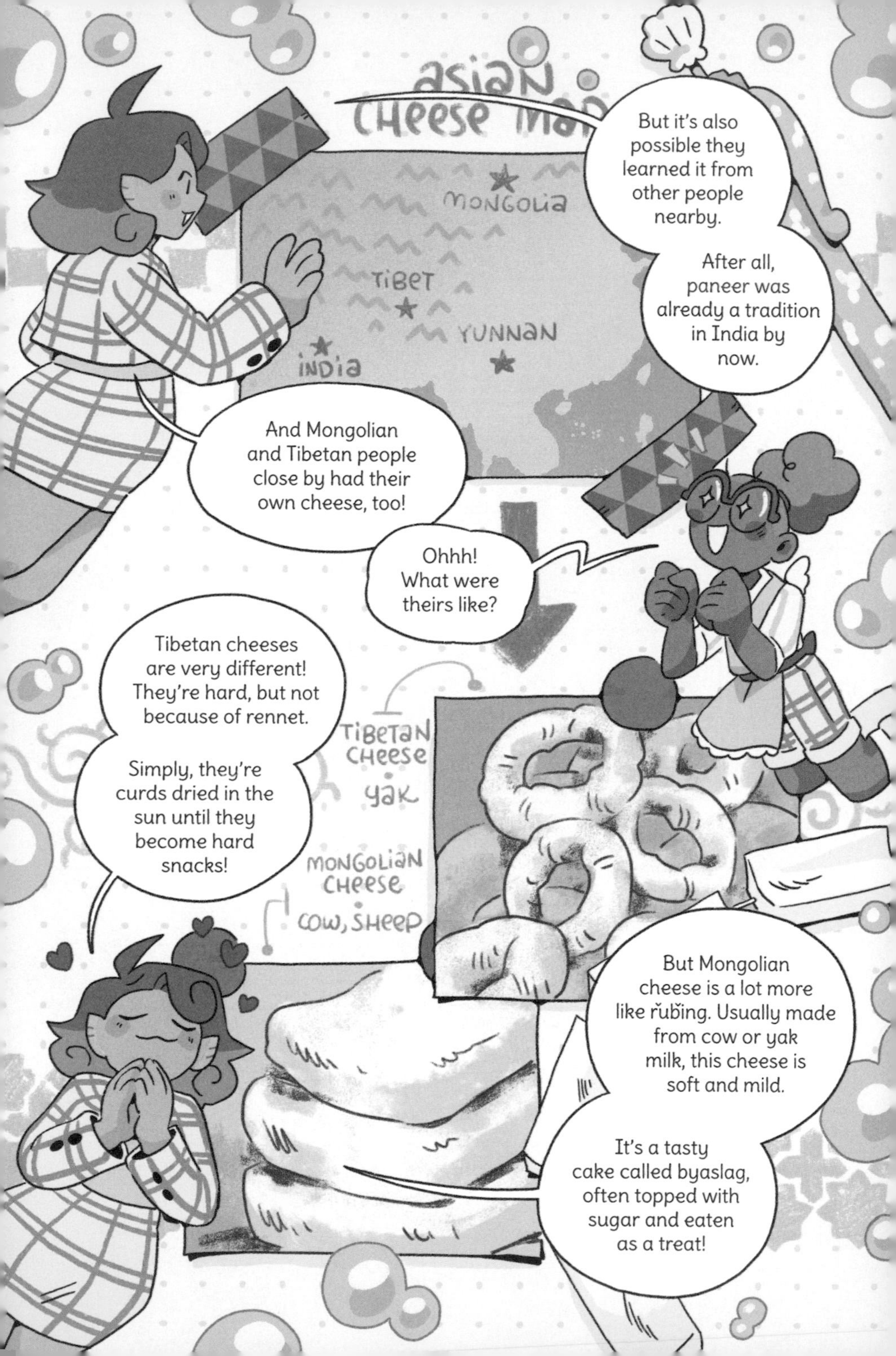
asian cheese map
MONGOLIA
TIBET
YUNNAN
INDIA
But it's also possible they learned it from other people nearby.
After all, paneer was already a tradition in India by now.
And Mongolian and Tibetan people close by had their own cheese, too!
Ohhh! What were theirs like?
Tibetan cheeses are very different! They're hard, but not because of rennet.
Simply, they're curds dried in the sun until they become hard snacks!
TIBETAN CHEESE
YAK
MONGOLIAN CHEESE
COW, SHEEP
But Mongolian cheese is a lot more like rǔbǐng. Usually made from cow or yak milk, this cheese is soft and mild.
It's a tasty cake called byaslag, often topped with sugar and eaten as a treat!

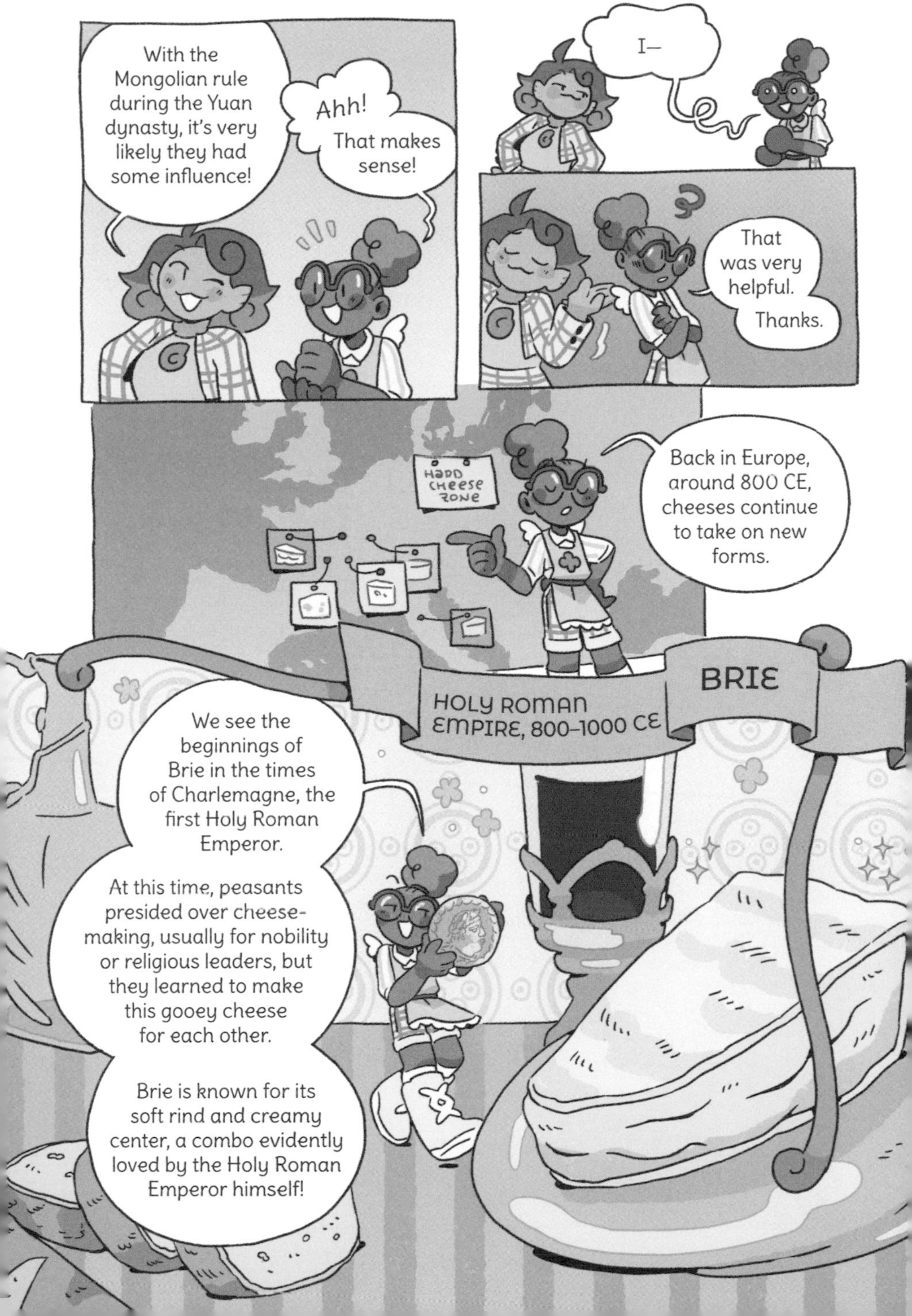

With the Mongolian rule during the Yuan dynasty, it's very likely they had some influence!
Ahh!
That makes sense!
I—
That was very helpful.
Thanks.
HARD CHEESE ZONE
Back in Europe, around 800 CE, cheeses continue to take on new forms.
HOLY ROMAN EMPIRE, 800–1000 CE
BRIE
We see the beginnings of Brie in the times of Charlemagne, the first Holy Roman Emperor.
At this time, peasants presided over cheese-making, usually for nobility or religious leaders, but they learned to make this gooey cheese for each other.
Brie is known for its soft rind and creamy center, a combo evidently loved by the Holy Roman Emperor himself!

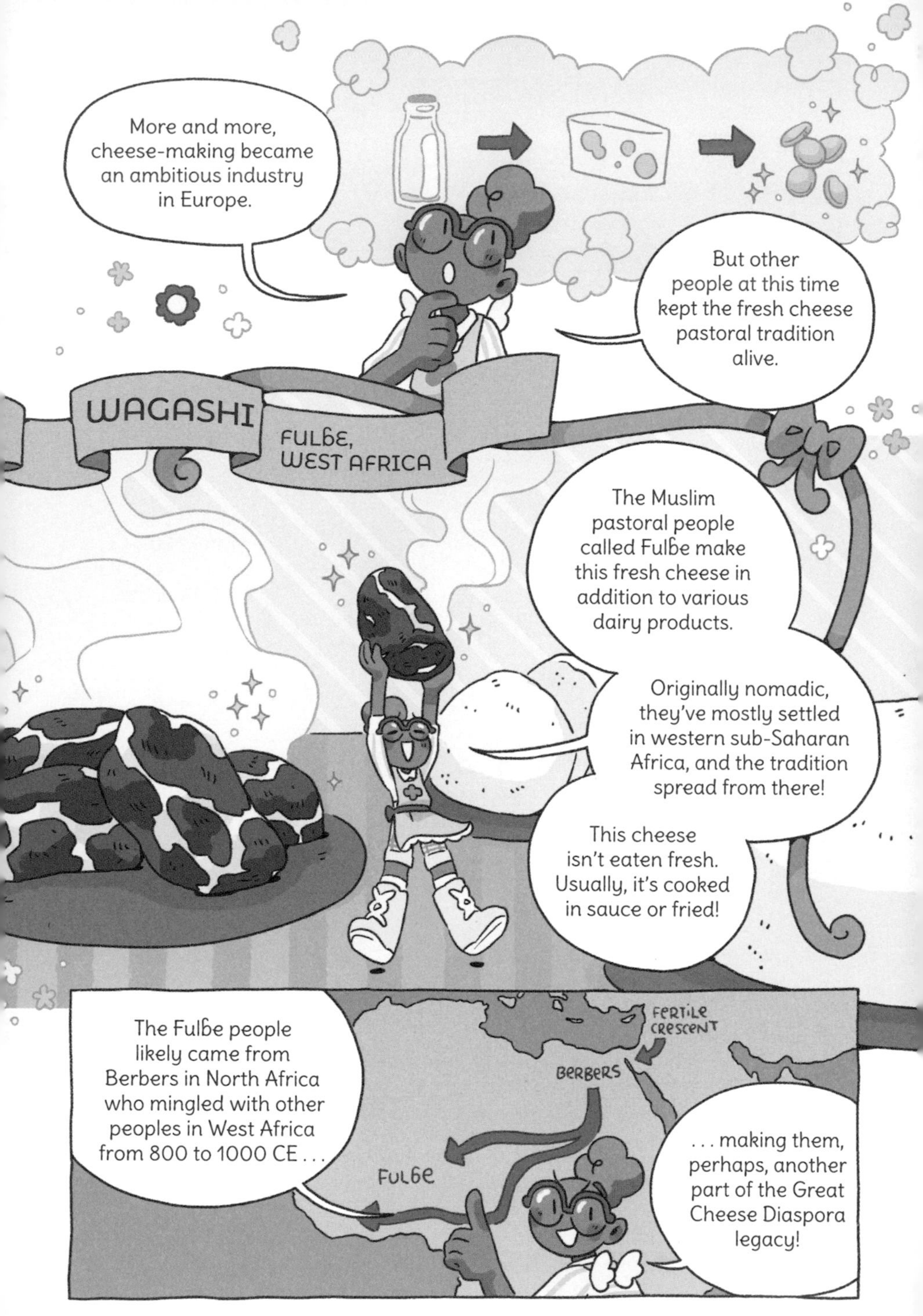

More and more, cheese-making became an ambitious industry in Europe.
But other people at this time kept the fresh cheese pastoral tradition alive.
WAGASHI
FULBE, WEST AFRICA
The Muslim pastoral people called Fulbe make this fresh cheese in addition to various dairy products.
Originally nomadic, they've mostly settled in western sub-Saharan Africa, and the tradition spread from there!
This cheese isn't eaten fresh. Usually, it's cooked in sauce or fried!
The Fulbe people likely came from Berbers in North Africa who mingled with other peoples in West Africa from 800 to 1000 CE . . .
FERTILE CRESCENT
BERBERS
FULBE
. . . making them, perhaps, another part of the Great Cheese Diaspora legacy!

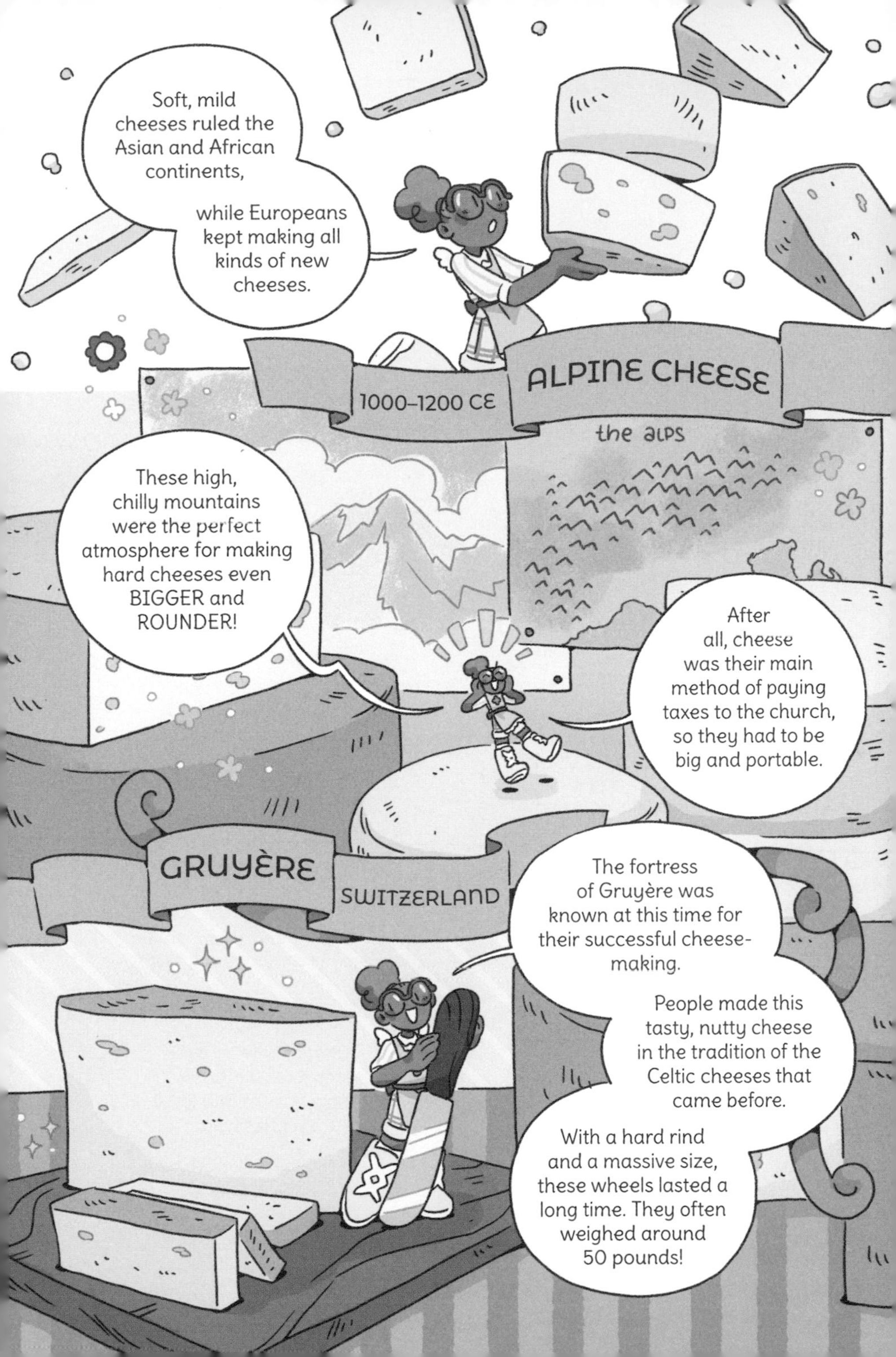

Soft, mild cheeses ruled the Asian and African continents,
while Europeans kept making all kinds of new cheeses.
ALPINE CHEESE
1000–1200 CE
the alps
These high, chilly mountains were the perfect atmosphere for making hard cheeses even BIGGER and ROUNDER!
After all, cheese was their main method of paying taxes to the church, so they had to be big and portable.
GRUYÈRE
SWITZERLAND
The fortress of Gruyère was known at this time for their successful cheese-making.
People made this tasty, nutty cheese in the tradition of the Celtic cheeses that came before.
With a hard rind and a massive size, these wheels lasted a long time. They often weighed around 50 pounds!

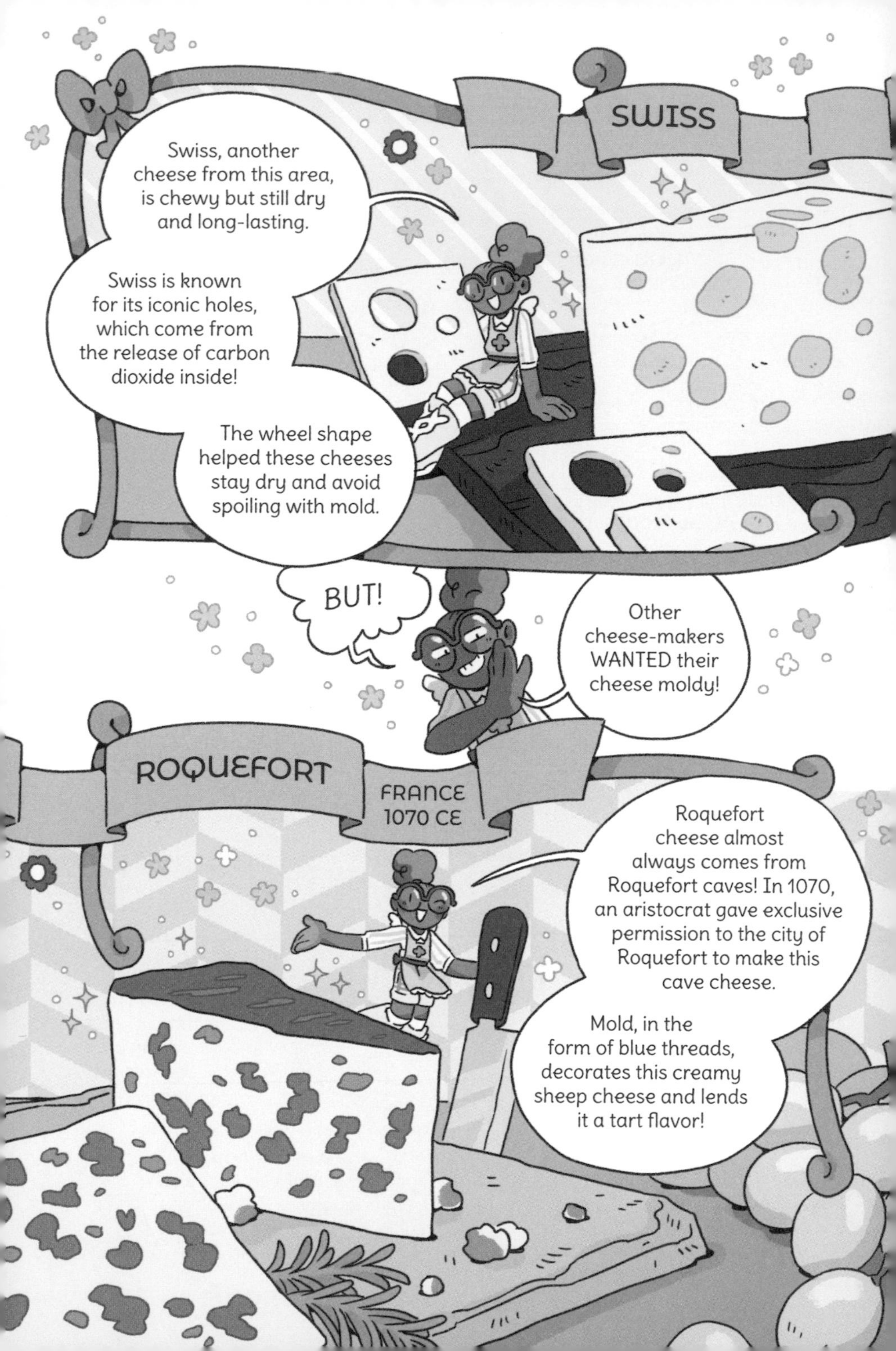
SWISS
Swiss, another cheese from this area, is chewy but still dry and long-lasting.
Swiss is known for its iconic holes, which come from the release of carbon dioxide inside!
The wheel shape helped these cheeses stay dry and avoid spoiling with mold.
BUT!
Other cheese-makers WANTED their cheese moldy!
ROQUEFORT
FRANCE 1070 CE
Roquefort cheese almost always comes from Roquefort caves! In 1070, an aristocrat gave exclusive permission to the city of Roquefort to make this cave cheese.
Mold, in the form of blue threads, decorates this creamy sheep cheese and lends it a tart flavor!

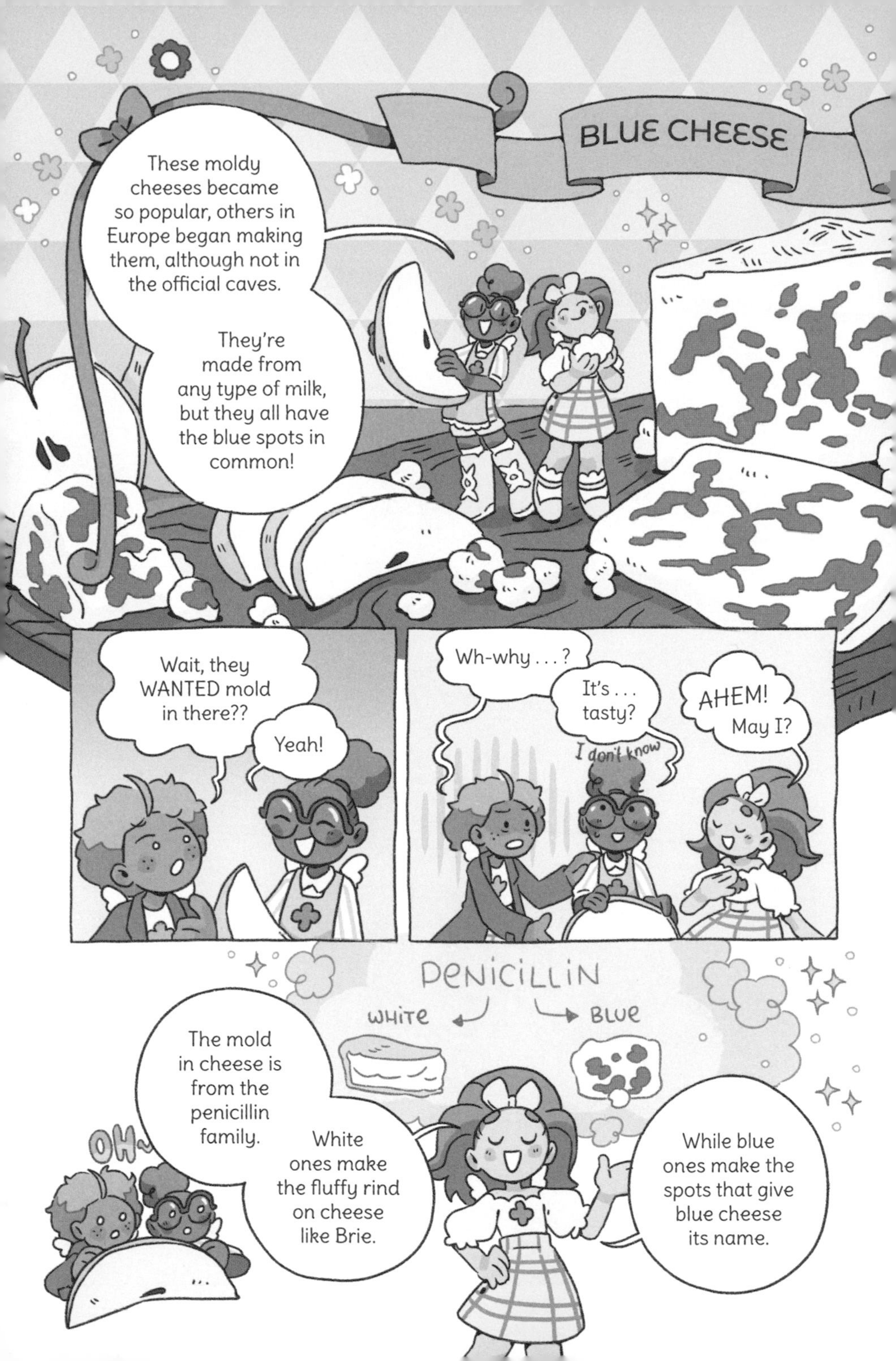

BLUE CHEESE
These moldy cheeses became so popular, others in Europe began making them, although not in the official caves.
They're made from any type of milk, but they all have the blue spots in common!
Wait, they WANTED mold in there??
Yeah!
Wh-why . . . ?
It's . . . tasty?
I don't know
AHEM!
May I?
PENICILLIN
WHITE
BLUE
The mold in cheese is from the penicillin family.
White ones make the fluffy rind on cheese like Brie.
While blue ones make the spots that give blue cheese its name.
OH~

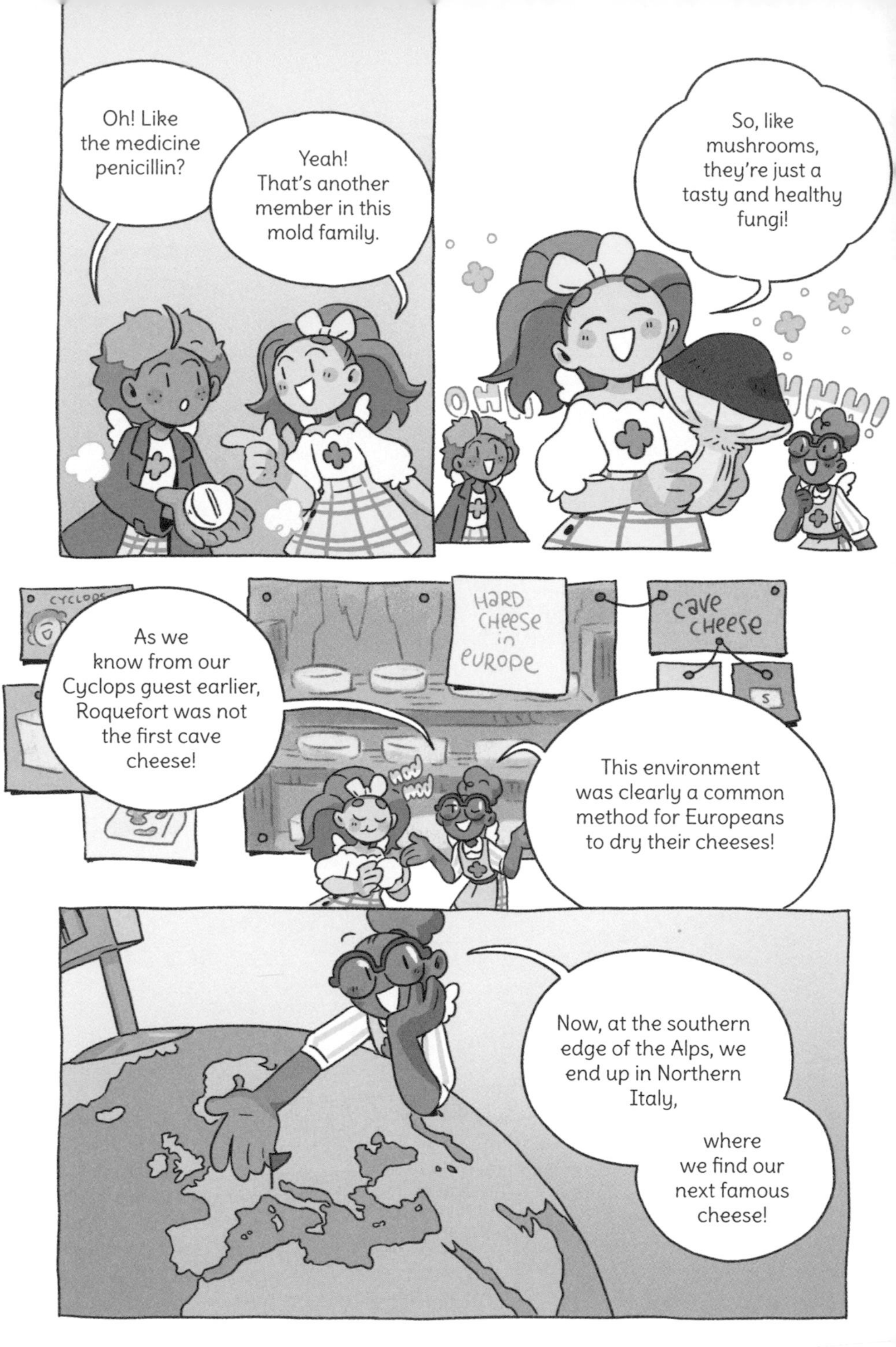
Oh! Like the medicine penicillin?
Yeah! That's another member in this mold family.
So, like mushrooms, they're just a tasty and healthy fungi!
HARD CHEESE in EUROPE
cave cheese
As we know from our Cyclops guest earlier, Roquefort was not the first cave cheese!
nod nod
This environment was clearly a common method for Europeans to dry their cheeses!
Now, at the southern edge of the Alps, we end up in Northern Italy,
where we find our next famous cheese!

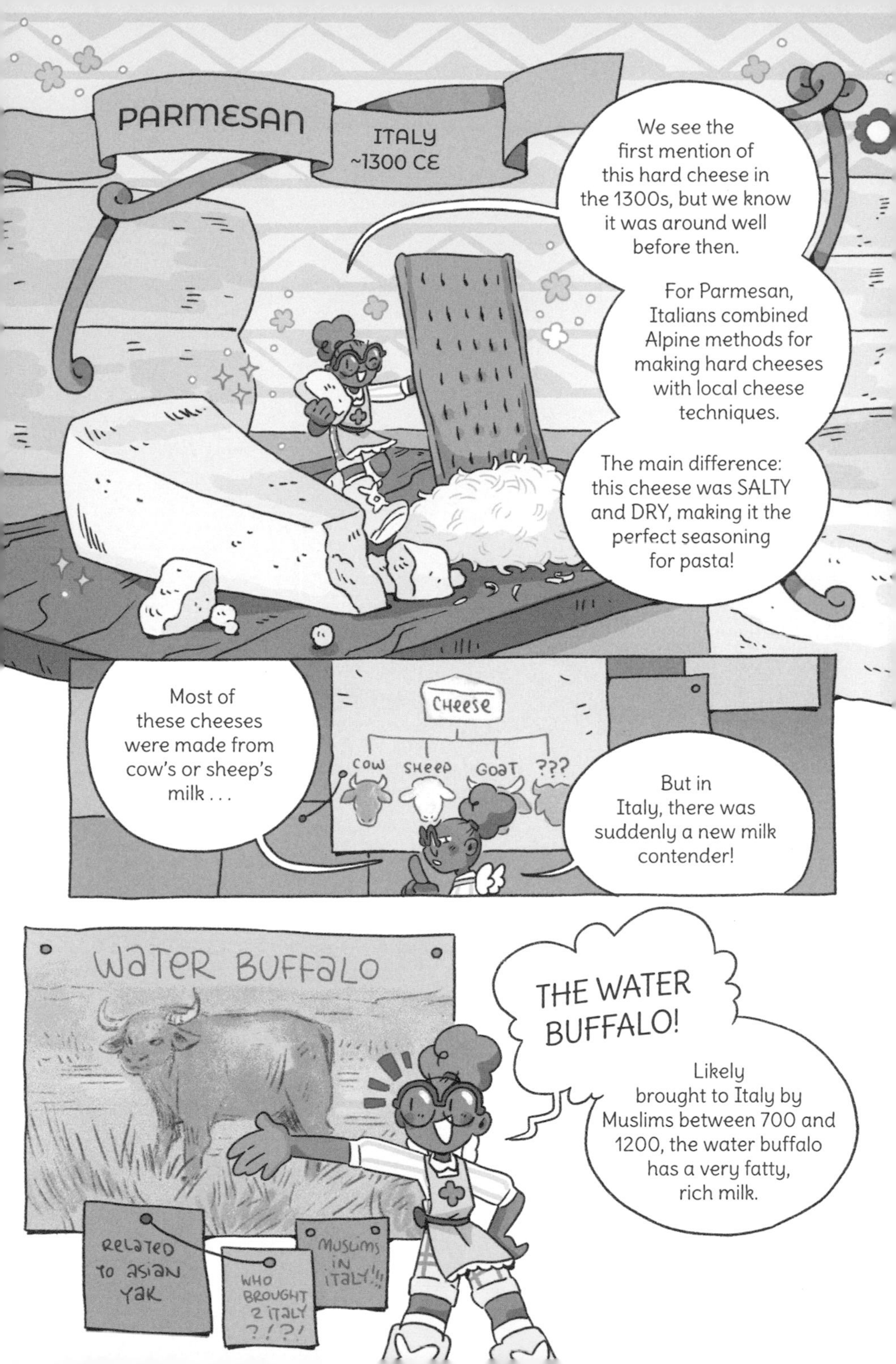

PARMESAN
ITALY
~1300 CE
We see the first mention of this hard cheese in the 1300s, but we know it was around well before then.
For Parmesan, Italians combined Alpine methods for making hard cheeses with local cheese techniques.
The main difference: this cheese was SALTY and DRY, making it the perfect seasoning for pasta!
Most of these cheeses were made from cow's or sheep's milk . . .
CHeese
COW
SHEEP
GOAT
???
But in Italy, there was suddenly a new milk contender!
WATER BUFFALO
THE WATER BUFFALO!
Likely brought to Italy by Muslims between 700 and 1200, the water buffalo has a very fatty, rich milk.
RELATED TO ASIAN YAK
WHO BROUGHT 2 ITALY ?!?!
MUSLIMS IN ITALY!!!

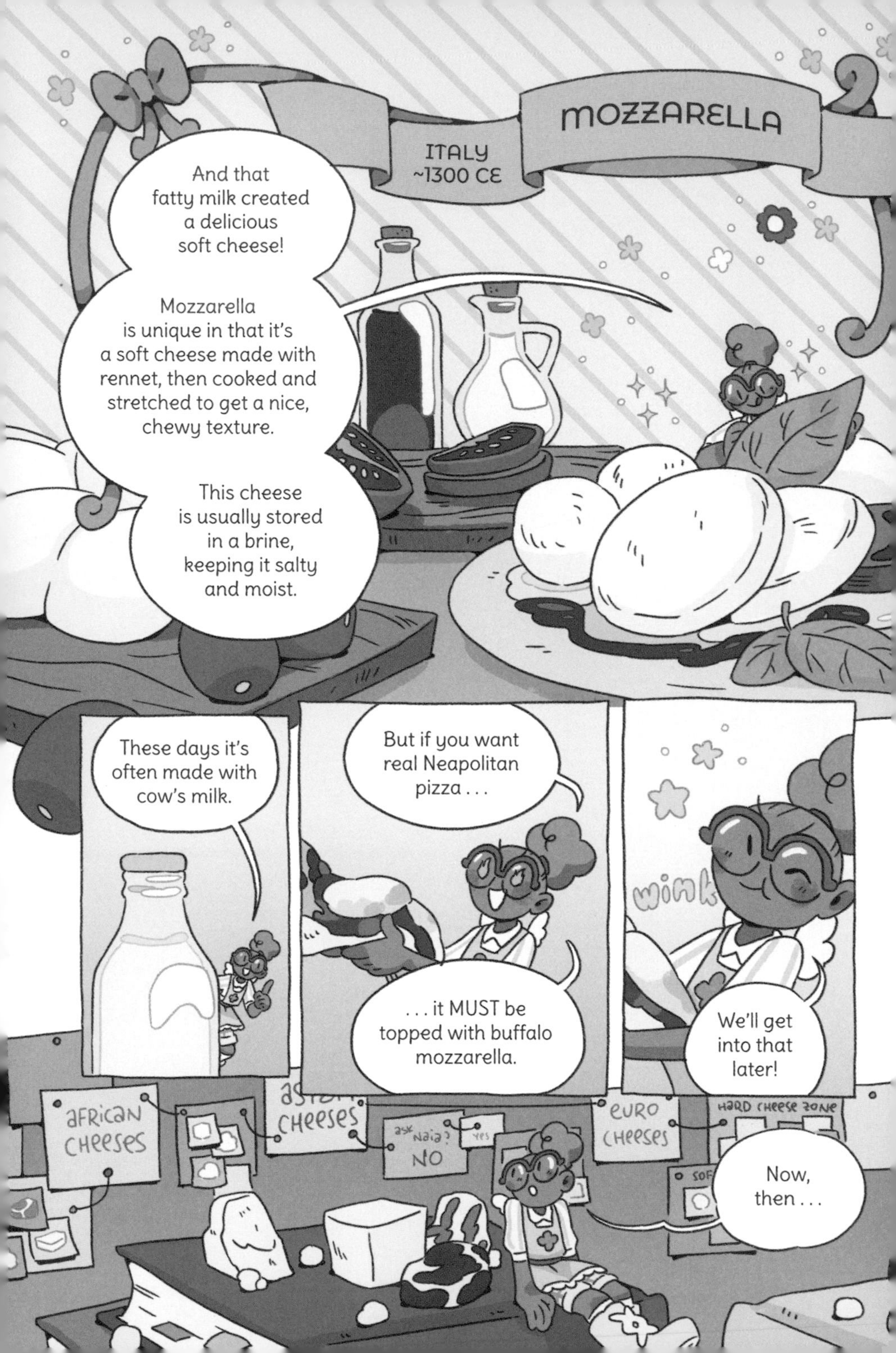
MOZZARELLA
ITALY
~1300 CE
And that fatty milk created a delicious soft cheese!
Mozzarella is unique in that it's a soft cheese made with rennet, then cooked and stretched to get a nice, chewy texture.
This cheese is usually stored in a brine, keeping it salty and moist.
These days it's often made with cow's milk.
But if you want real Neapolitan pizza . . .
. . . it MUST be topped with buffalo mozzarella.
wink
We'll get into that later!
african cheeses
ask Naia?
yes
NO
euro cheeses
HARD CHEESE ZONE
Now, then . . .

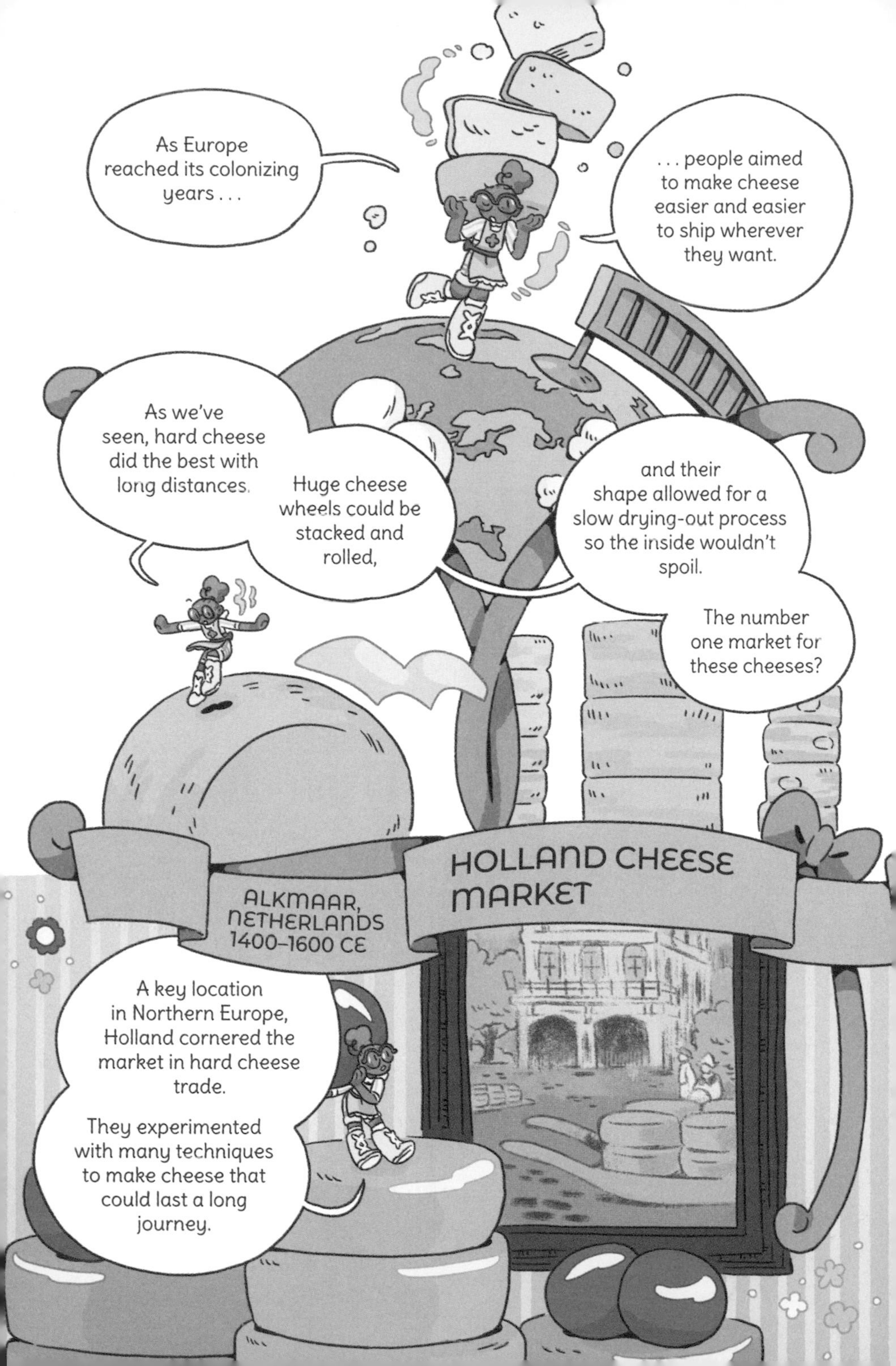
As Europe reached its colonizing years . . .
. . . people aimed to make cheese easier and easier to ship wherever they want.
As we've seen, hard cheese did the best with long distances.
Huge cheese wheels could be stacked and rolled,
and their shape allowed for a slow drying-out process so the inside wouldn't spoil.
The number one market for these cheeses?
ALKMAAR, NETHERLANDS 1400–1600 CE
HOLLAND CHEESE MARKET
A key location in Northern Europe, Holland cornered the market in hard cheese trade.
They experimented with many techniques to make cheese that could last a long journey.

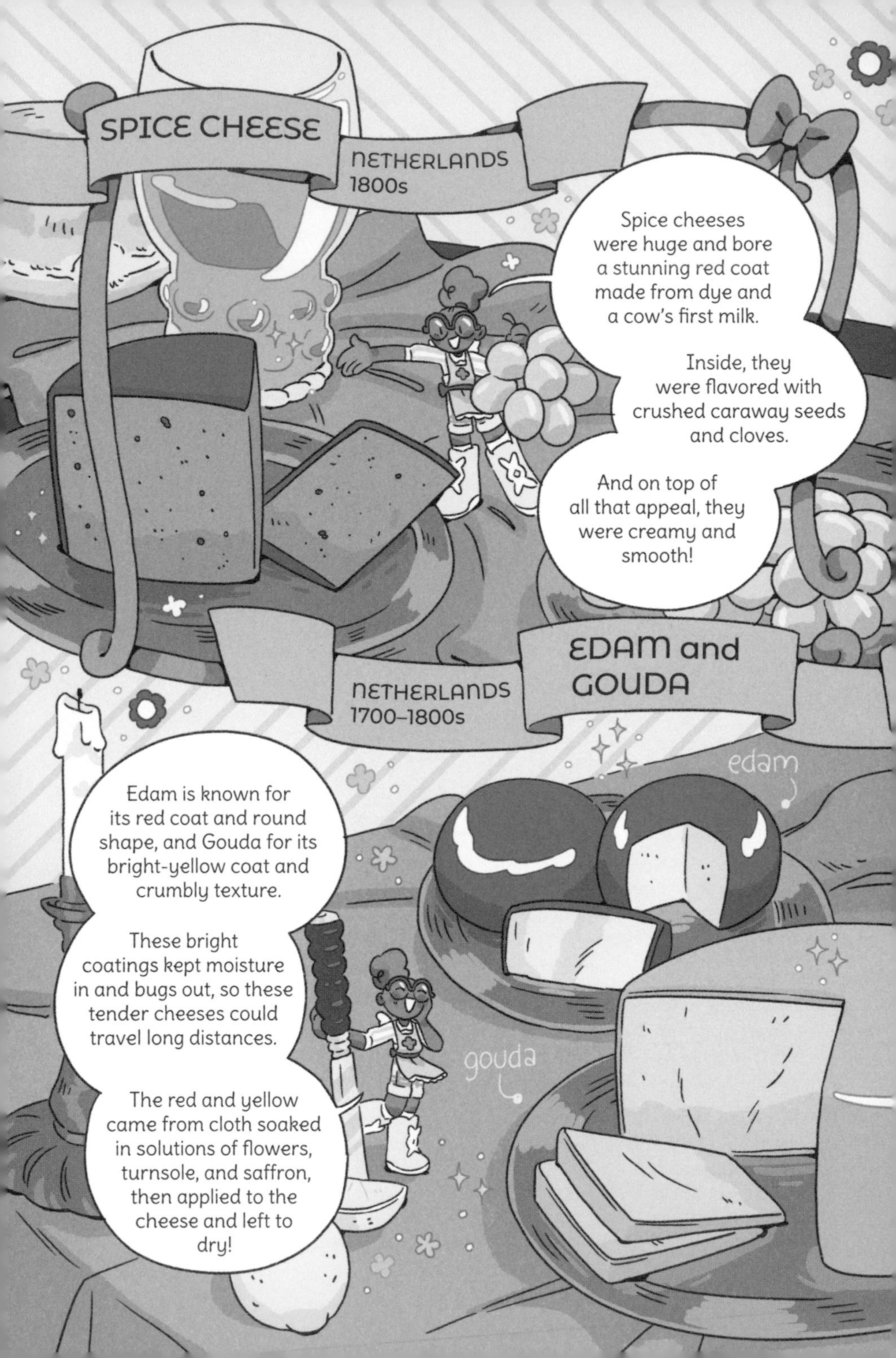

SPICE CHEESE
NETHERLANDS 1800s
Spice cheeses were huge and bore a stunning red coat made from dye and a cow's first milk.
Inside, they were flavored with crushed caraway seeds and cloves.
And on top of all that appeal, they were creamy and smooth!
EDAM and GOUDA
NETHERLANDS 1700–1800s
Edam is known for its red coat and round shape, and Gouda for its bright-yellow coat and crumbly texture.
These bright coatings kept moisture in and bugs out, so these tender cheeses could travel long distances.
The red and yellow came from cloth soaked in solutions of flowers, turnsole, and saffron, then applied to the cheese and left to dry!
edam
gouda

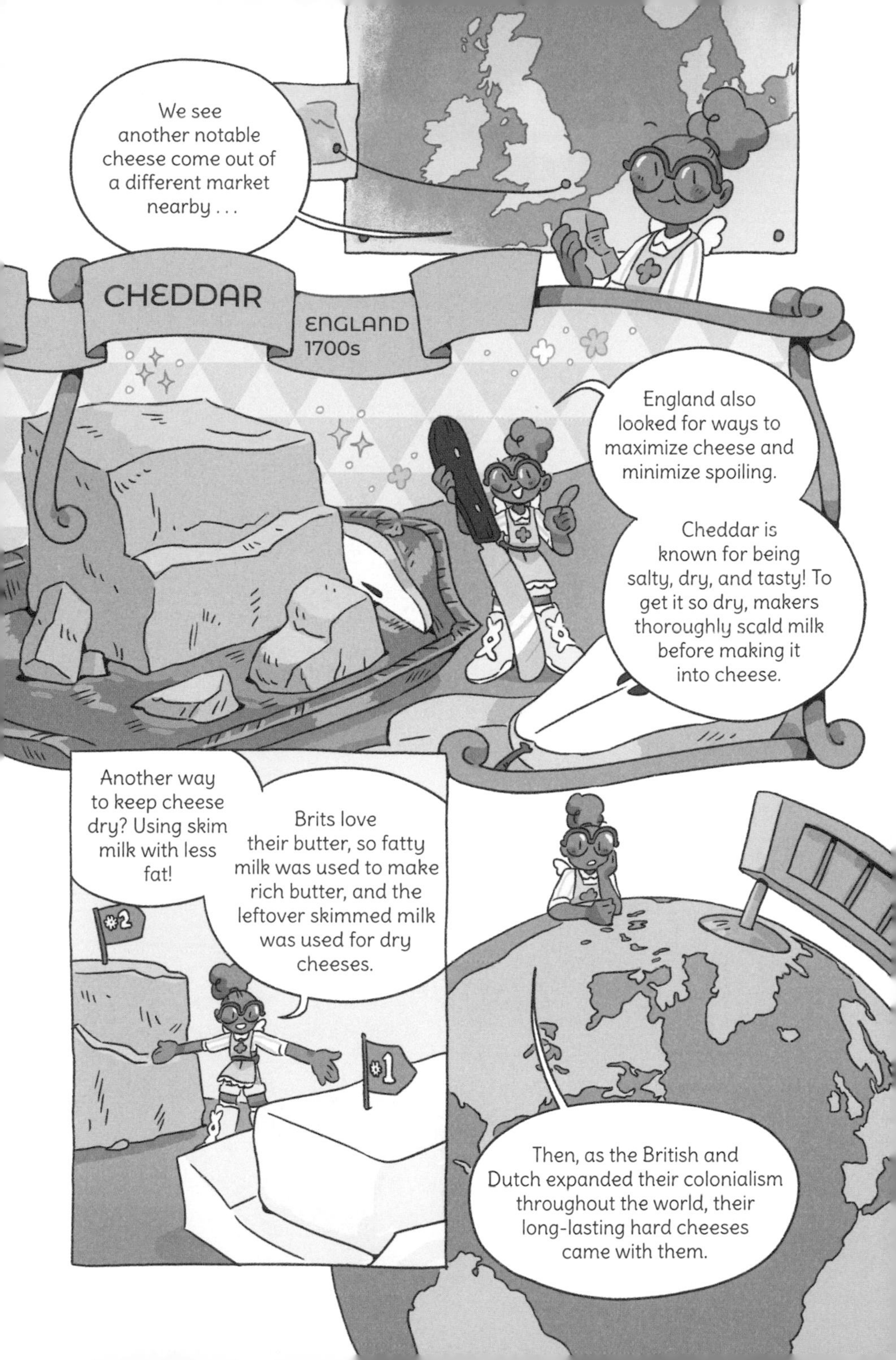
We see another notable cheese come out of a different market nearby . . .
CHEDDAR
ENGLAND 1700s
England also looked for ways to maximize cheese and minimize spoiling.
Cheddar is known for being salty, dry, and tasty! To get it so dry, makers thoroughly scald milk before making it into cheese.
Another way to keep cheese dry? Using skim milk with less fat!
Brits love their butter, so fatty milk was used to make rich butter, and the leftover skimmed milk was used for dry cheeses.
#2
#1
Then, as the British and Dutch expanded their colonialism throughout the world, their long-lasting hard cheeses came with them.

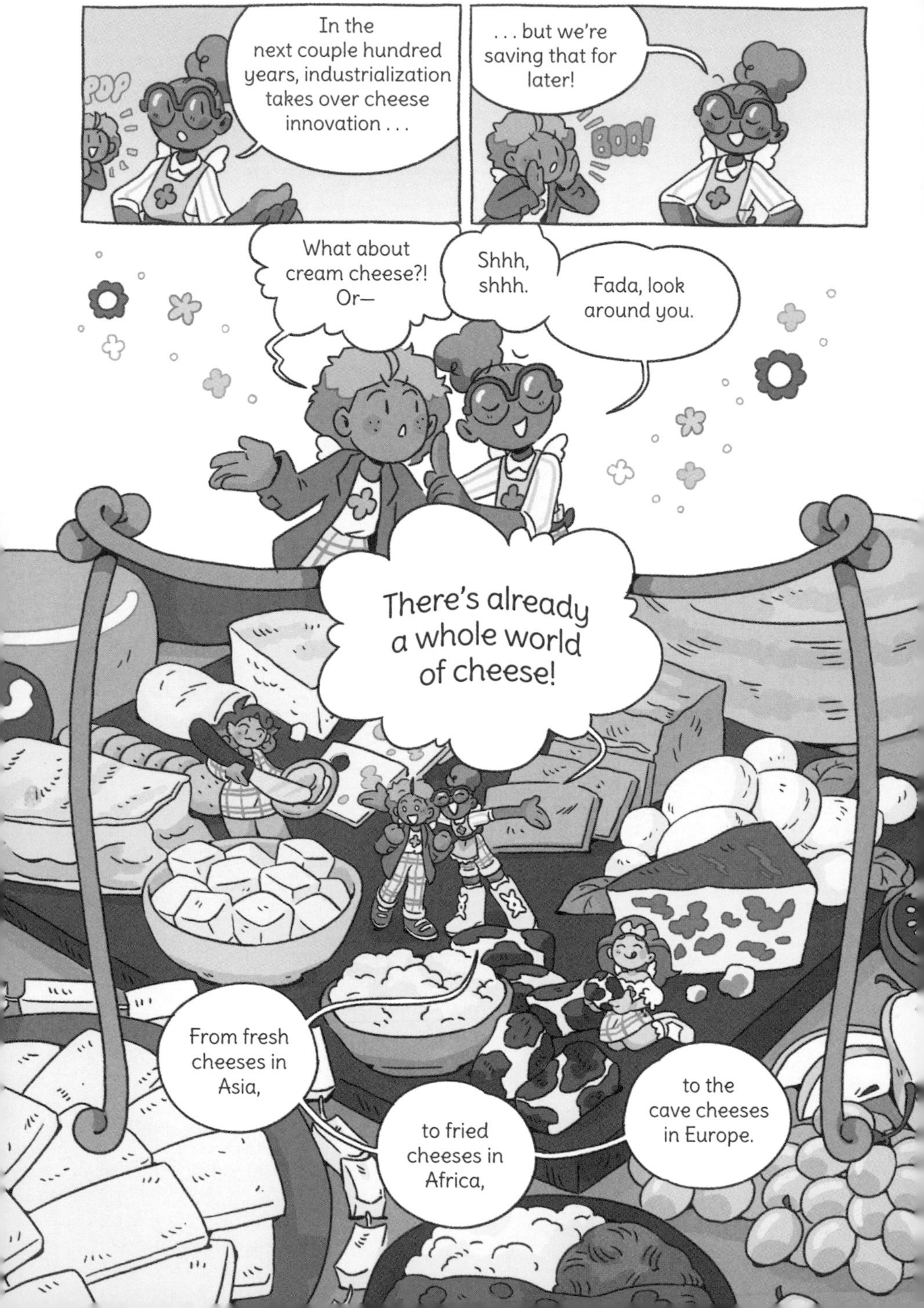
POP
In the next couple hundred years, industrialization takes over cheese innovation . . .
. . . but we're saving that for later!
BOO!
What about cream cheese?! Or—
Shhh, shhh.
Fada, look around you.
There's already a whole world of cheese!
From fresh cheeses in Asia,
to fried cheeses in Africa,
to the cave cheeses in Europe.

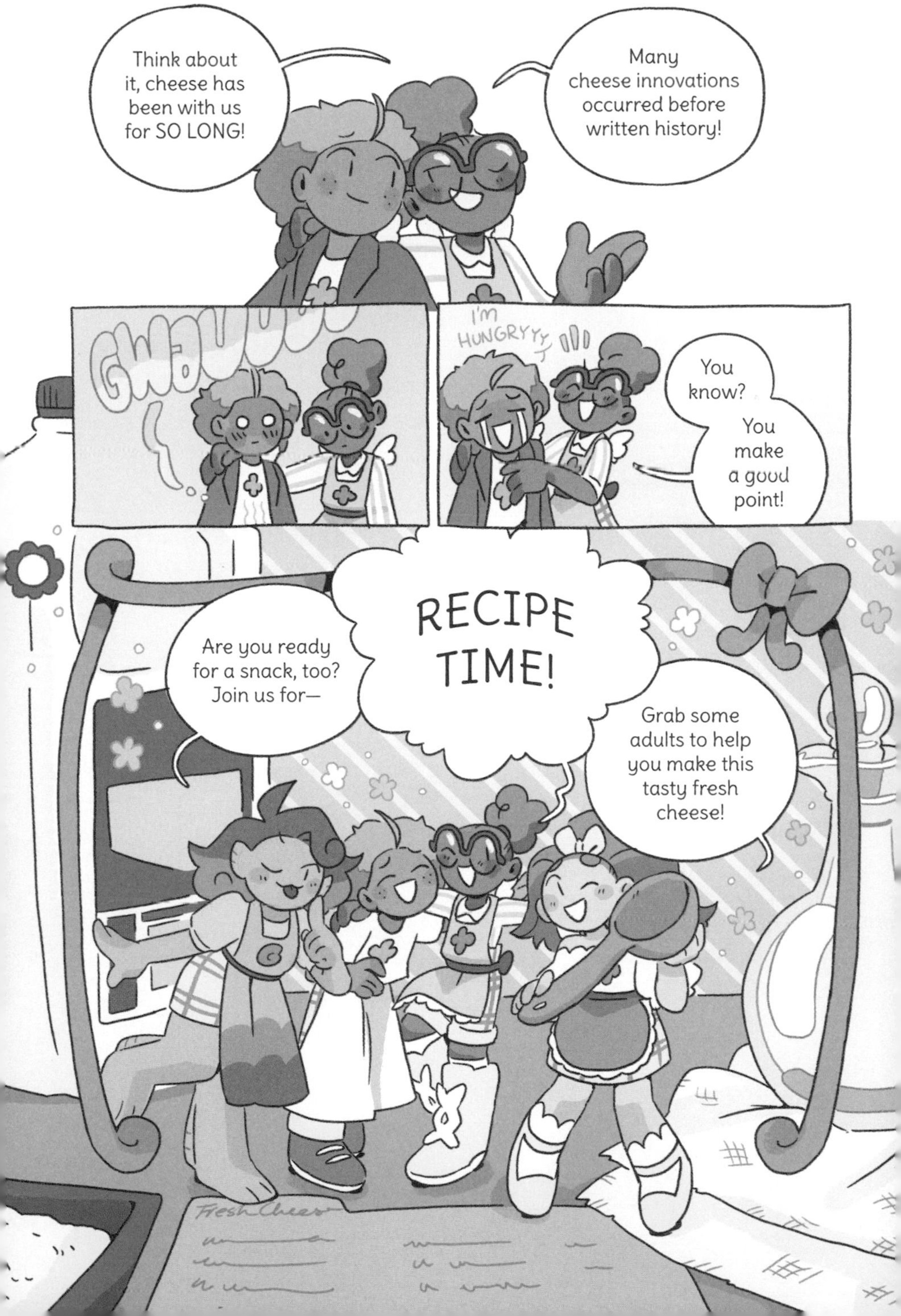
Think about it, cheese has been with us for SO LONG!
Many cheese innovations occurred before written history!
GWAUUU
I'M HUNGRYYY
You know?
You make a good point!
RECIPE TIME!
Are you ready for a snack, too? Join us for—
Grab some adults to help you make this tasty fresh cheese!
Fresh Chees

# FRESH CHEESE

YOU WILL NEED:

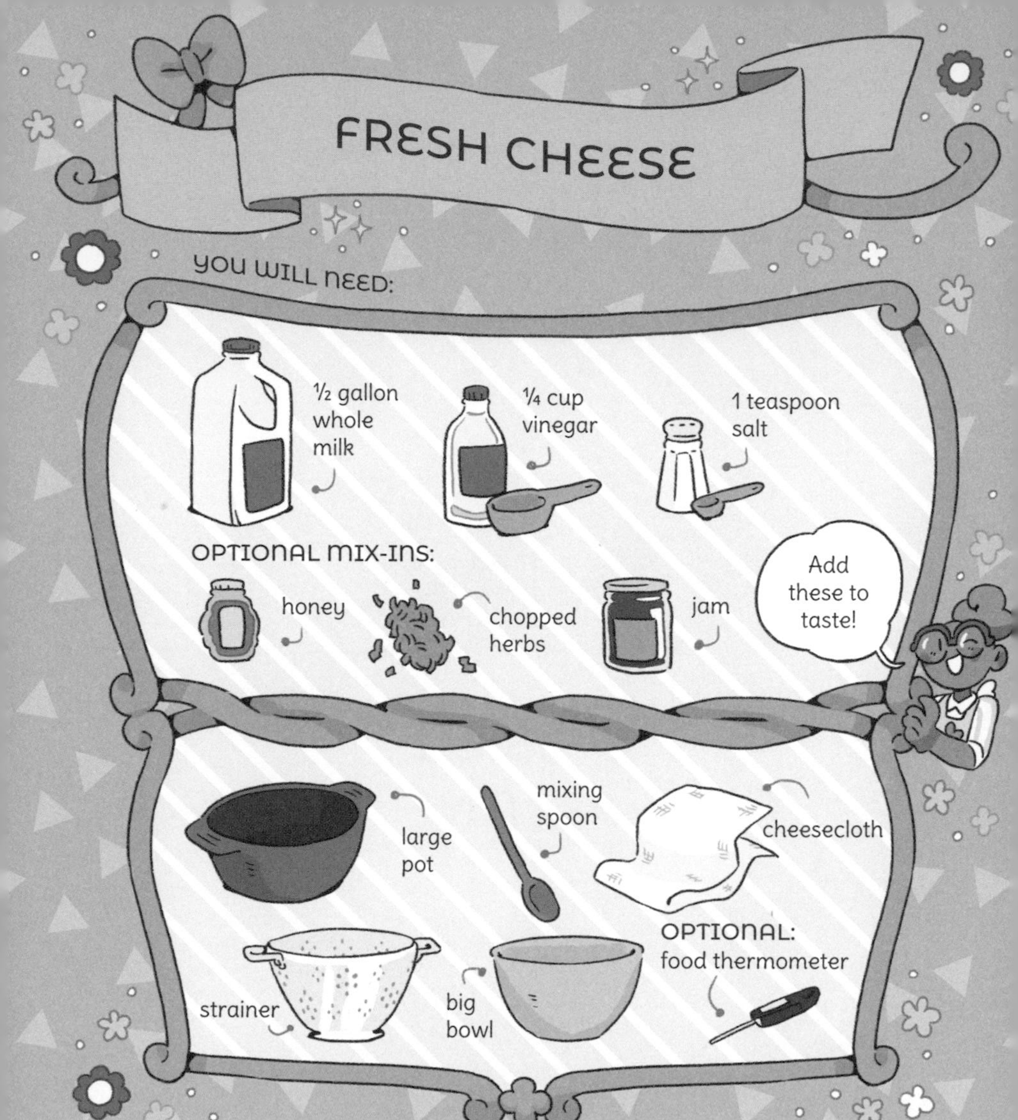

½ gallon whole milk
¼ cup vinegar
1 teaspoon salt
OPTIONAL MIX-INS:
honey
chopped herbs
jam
Add these to taste!
large pot
mixing spoon
cheesecloth
OPTIONAL:
food thermometer
strainer
big bowl


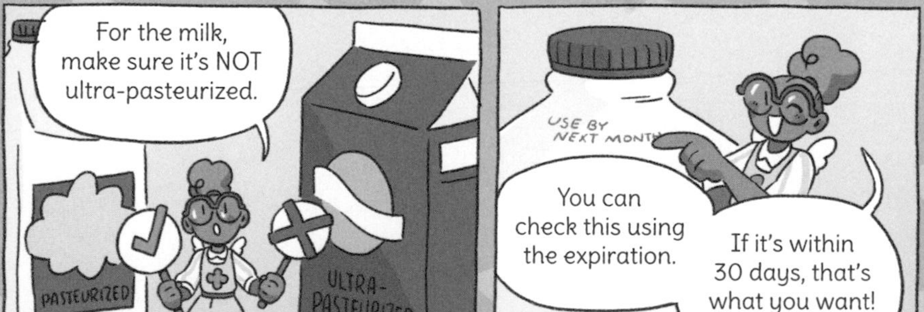

For the milk, make sure it's NOT ultra-pasteurized.
PASTEURIZED
ULTRA-PASTEURIZED
USE BY NEXT MONTH
You can check this using the expiration.
If it's within 30 days, that's what you want!

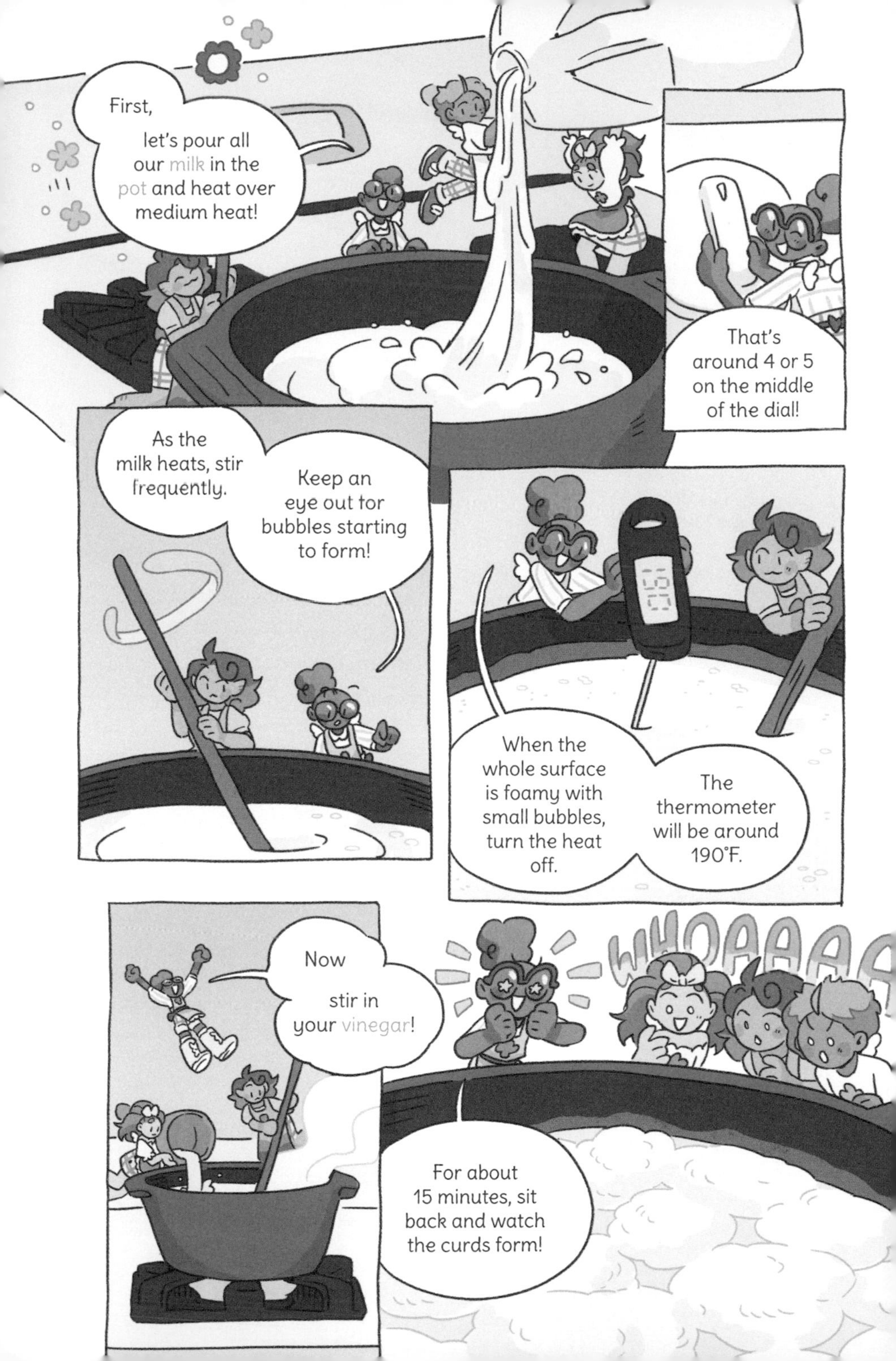

First,
let's pour all our milk in the pot and heat over medium heat!
That's around 4 or 5 on the middle of the dial!
As the milk heats, stir frequently.
Keep an eye out for bubbles starting to form!
When the whole surface is foamy with small bubbles, turn the heat off.
The thermometer will be around 190°F.
Now
stir in your vinegar!
WHOAAAA
For about 15 minutes, sit back and watch the curds form!

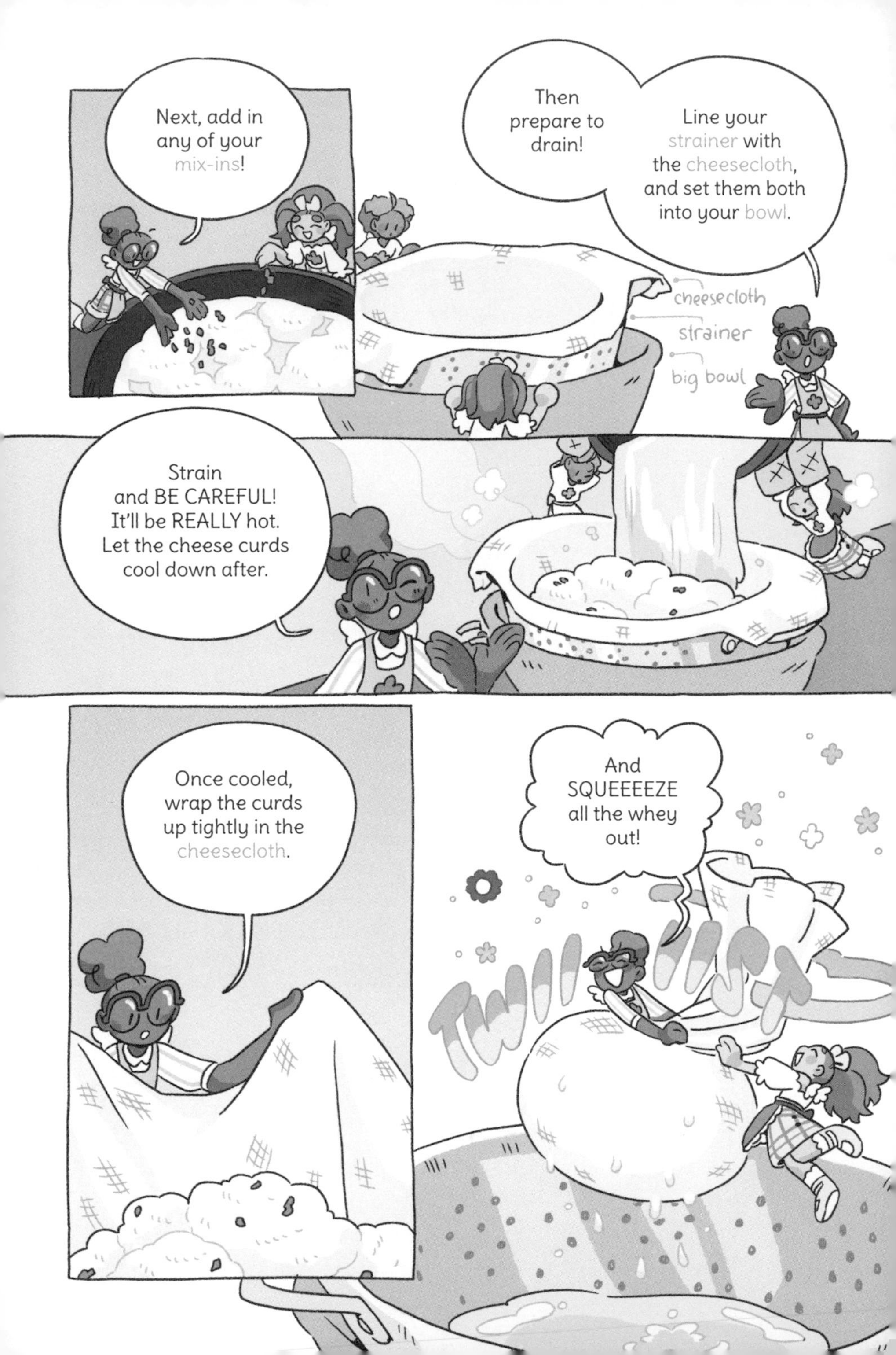
Next, add in any of your mix-ins!
Then prepare to drain!
Line your strainer with the cheesecloth, and set them both into your bowl.
cheesecloth
strainer
big bowl
Strain and BE CAREFUL! It'll be REALLY hot. Let the cheese curds cool down after.
Once cooled, wrap the curds up tightly in the cheesecloth.
And SQUEEEEZE all the whey out!

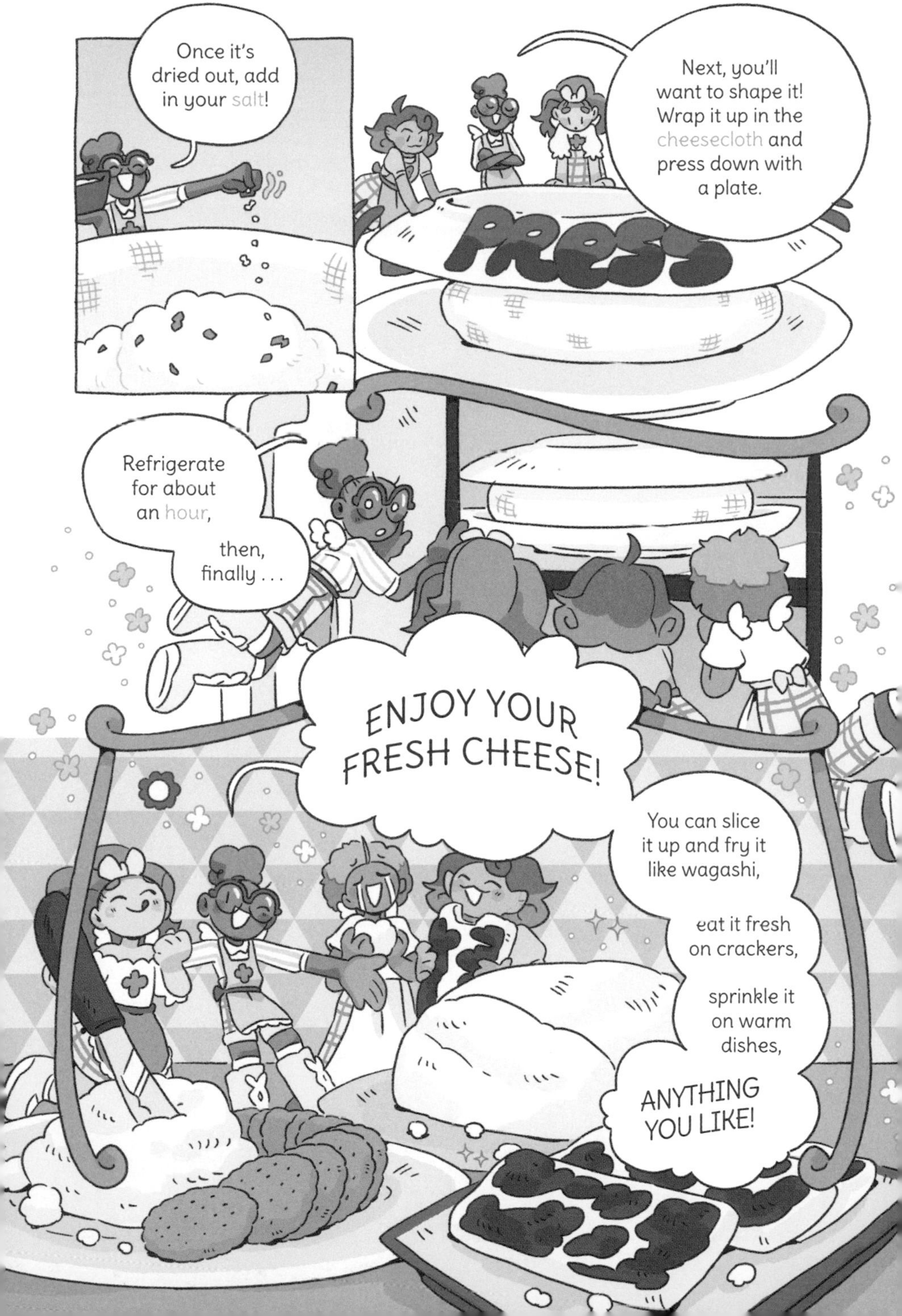
Once it's dried out, add in your salt!
Next, you'll want to shape it! Wrap it up in the cheesecloth and press down with a plate.
PRESS
Refrigerate for about an hour,
then, finally . . .
ENJOY YOUR FRESH CHEESE!
You can slice it up and fry it like wagashi,
eat it fresh on crackers,
sprinkle it on warm dishes,
ANYTHING YOU LIKE!

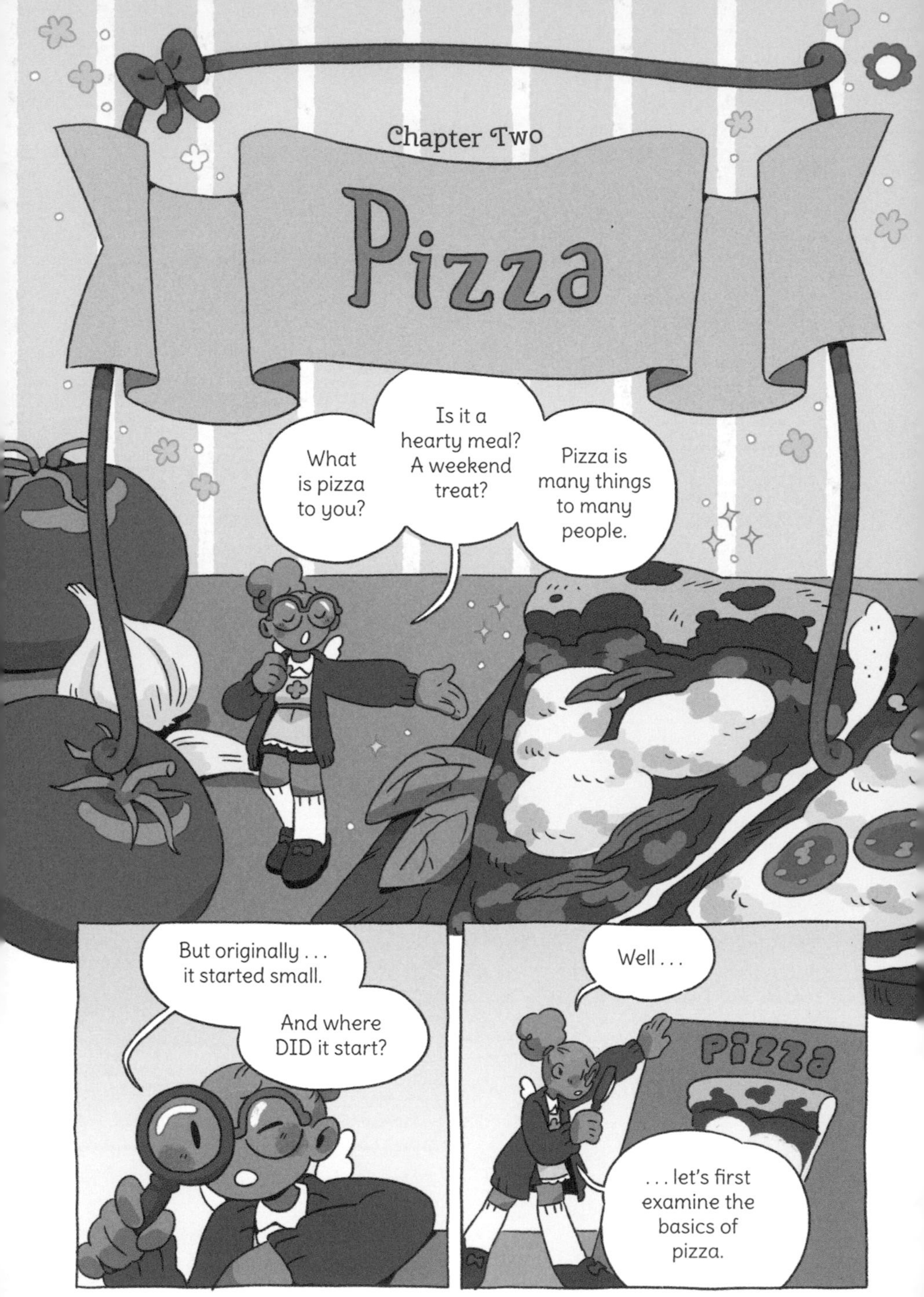
Chapter Two
Pizza
What is pizza to you?
Is it a hearty meal? A weekend treat?
Pizza is many things to many people.
But originally . . . it started small.
And where DID it start?
Well . . .
PIZZA
. . . let's first examine the basics of pizza.

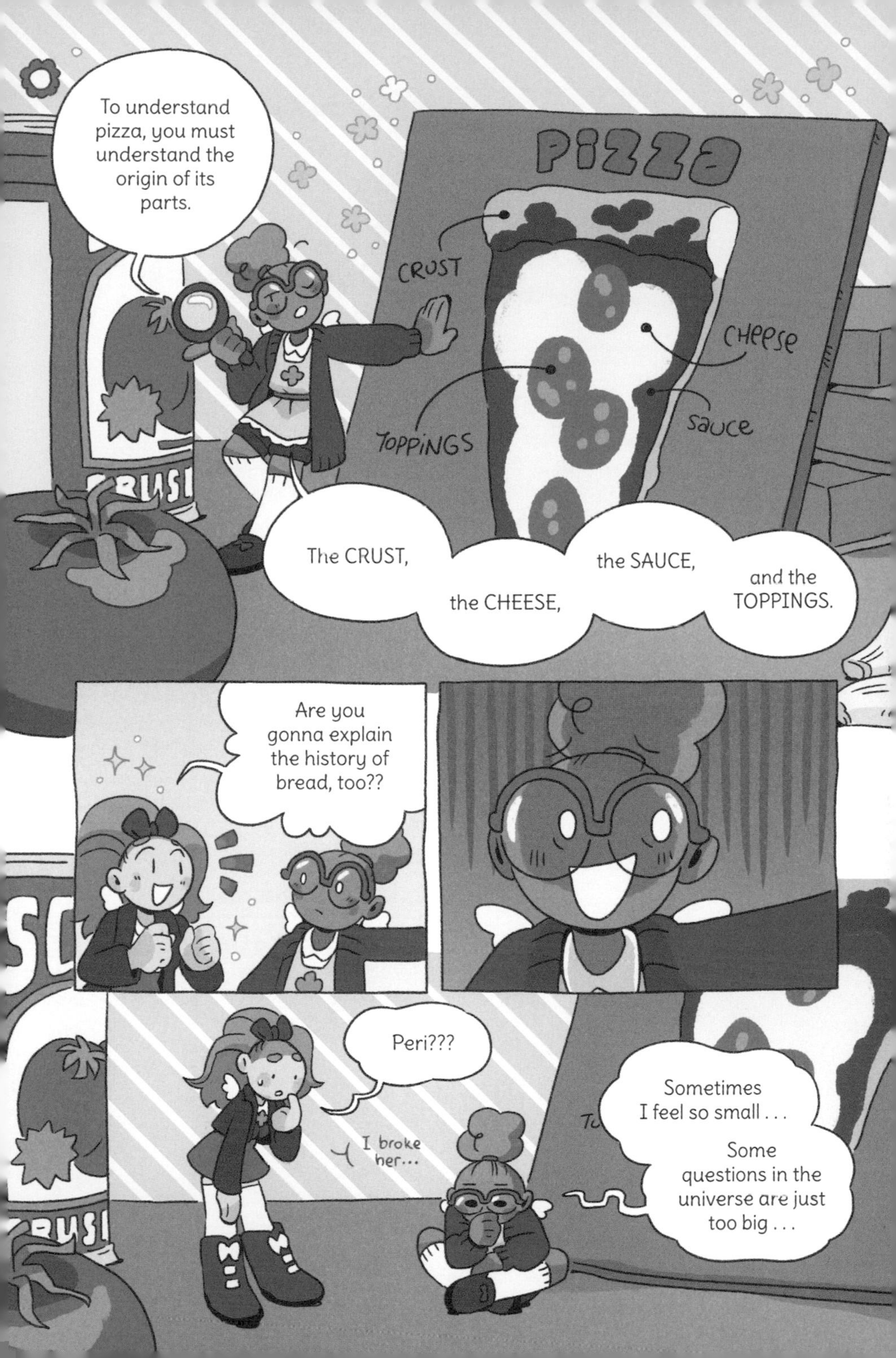

To understand pizza, you must understand the origin of its parts.
PIZZA
CRUST
CHEESE
TOPPINGS
SAUCE
The CRUST,
the CHEESE,
the SAUCE,
and the TOPPINGS.
Are you gonna explain the history of bread, too??
Peri???
I broke her...
Sometimes I feel so small . . .
Some questions in the universe are just too big . . .

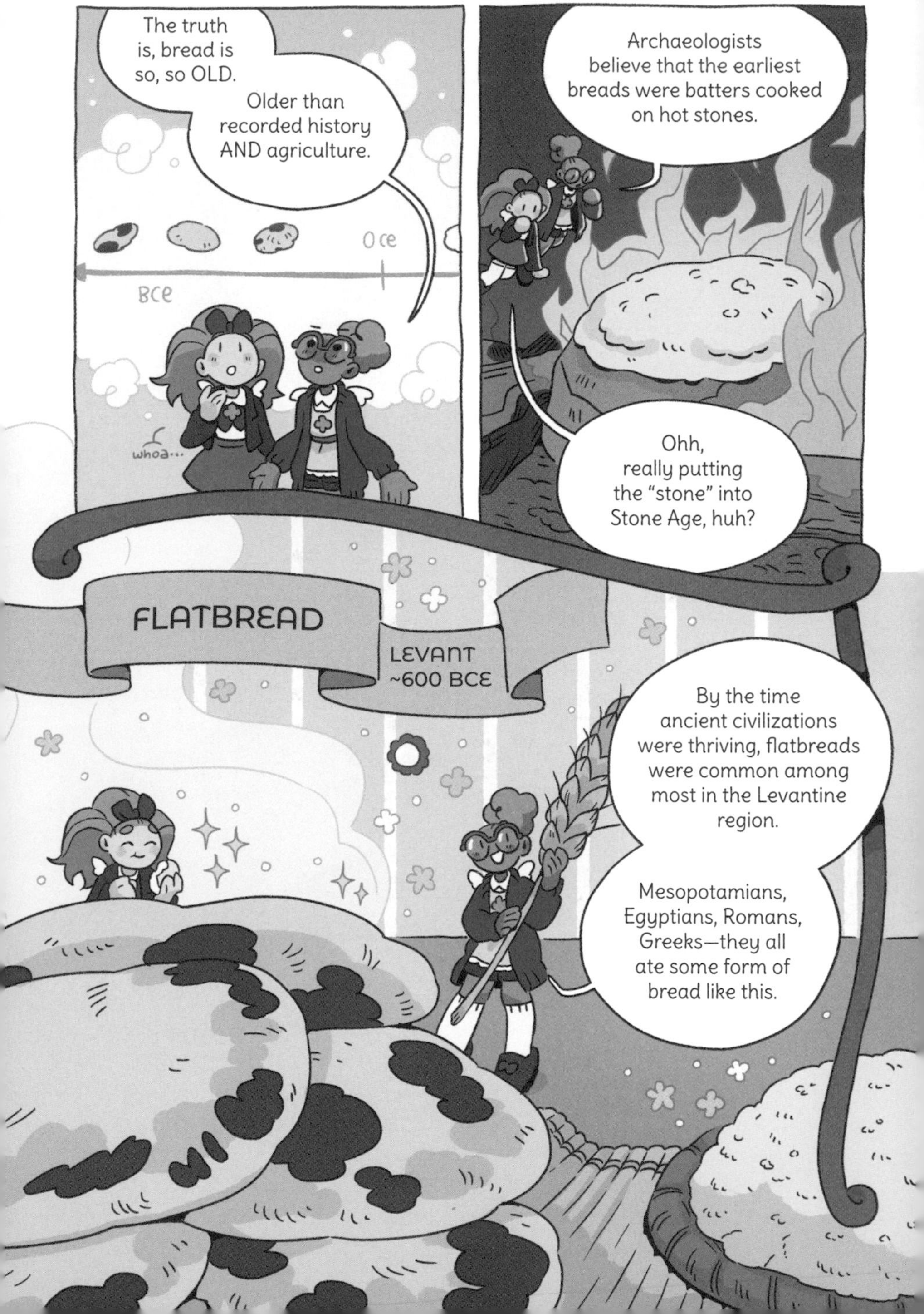

The truth is, bread is so, so OLD.
Older than recorded history AND agriculture.
0 ce
BCE
whoa...
Archaeologists believe that the earliest breads were batters cooked on hot stones.
Ohh, really putting the "stone" into Stone Age, huh?
FLATBREAD
LEVANT ~600 BCE
By the time ancient civilizations were thriving, flatbreads were common among most in the Levantine region.
Mesopotamians, Egyptians, Romans, Greeks—they all ate some form of bread like this.

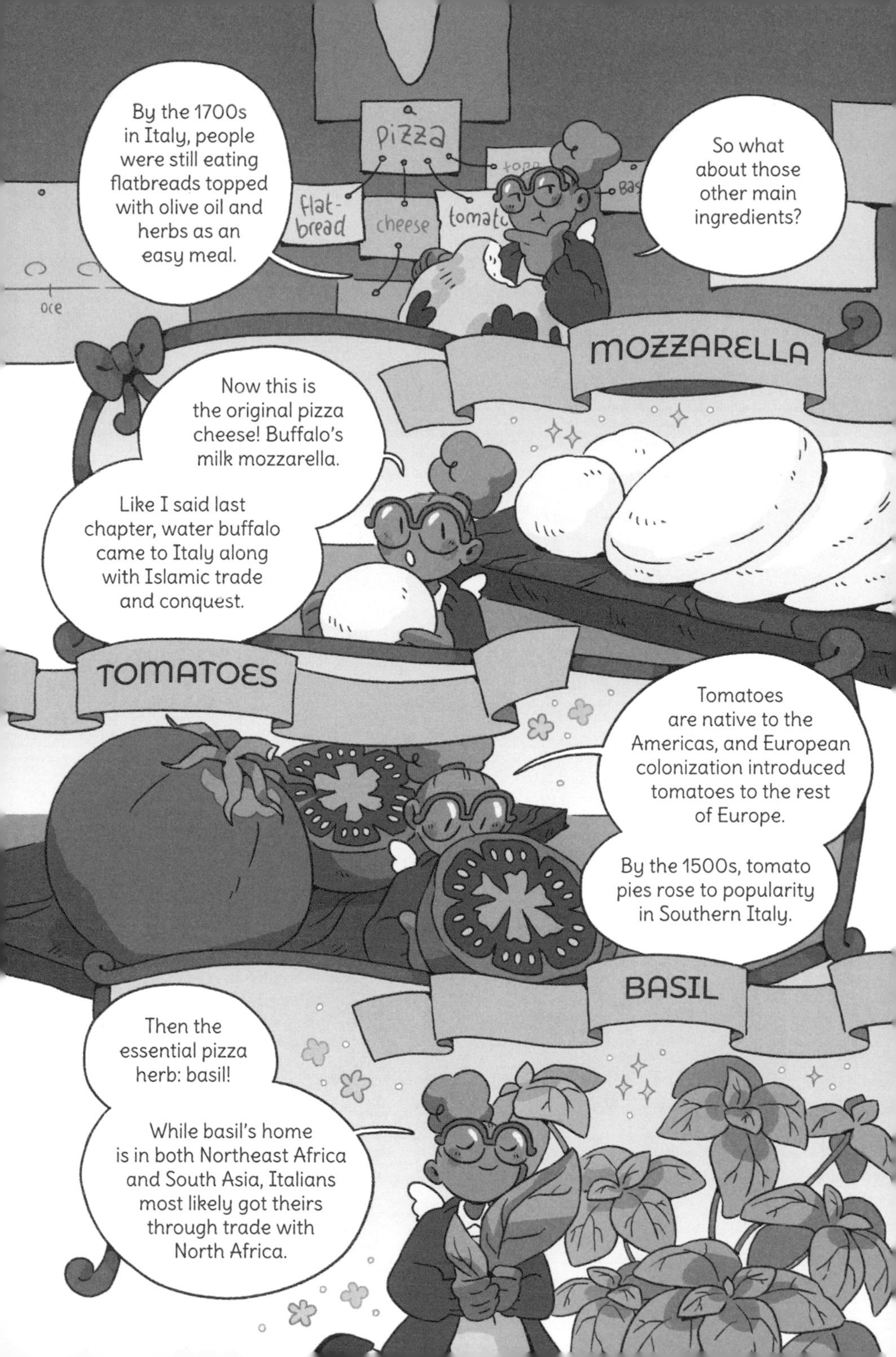
By the 1700s in Italy, people were still eating flatbreads topped with olive oil and herbs as an easy meal.
pizza
flat-bread
cheese
tomato
So what about those other main ingredients?
MOZZARELLA
Now this is the original pizza cheese! Buffalo's milk mozzarella.
Like I said last chapter, water buffalo came to Italy along with Islamic trade and conquest.
TOMATOES
Tomatoes are native to the Americas, and European colonization introduced tomatoes to the rest of Europe.
By the 1500s, tomato pies rose to popularity in Southern Italy.
BASIL
Then the essential pizza herb: basil!
While basil's home is in both Northeast Africa and South Asia, Italians most likely got theirs through trade with North Africa.

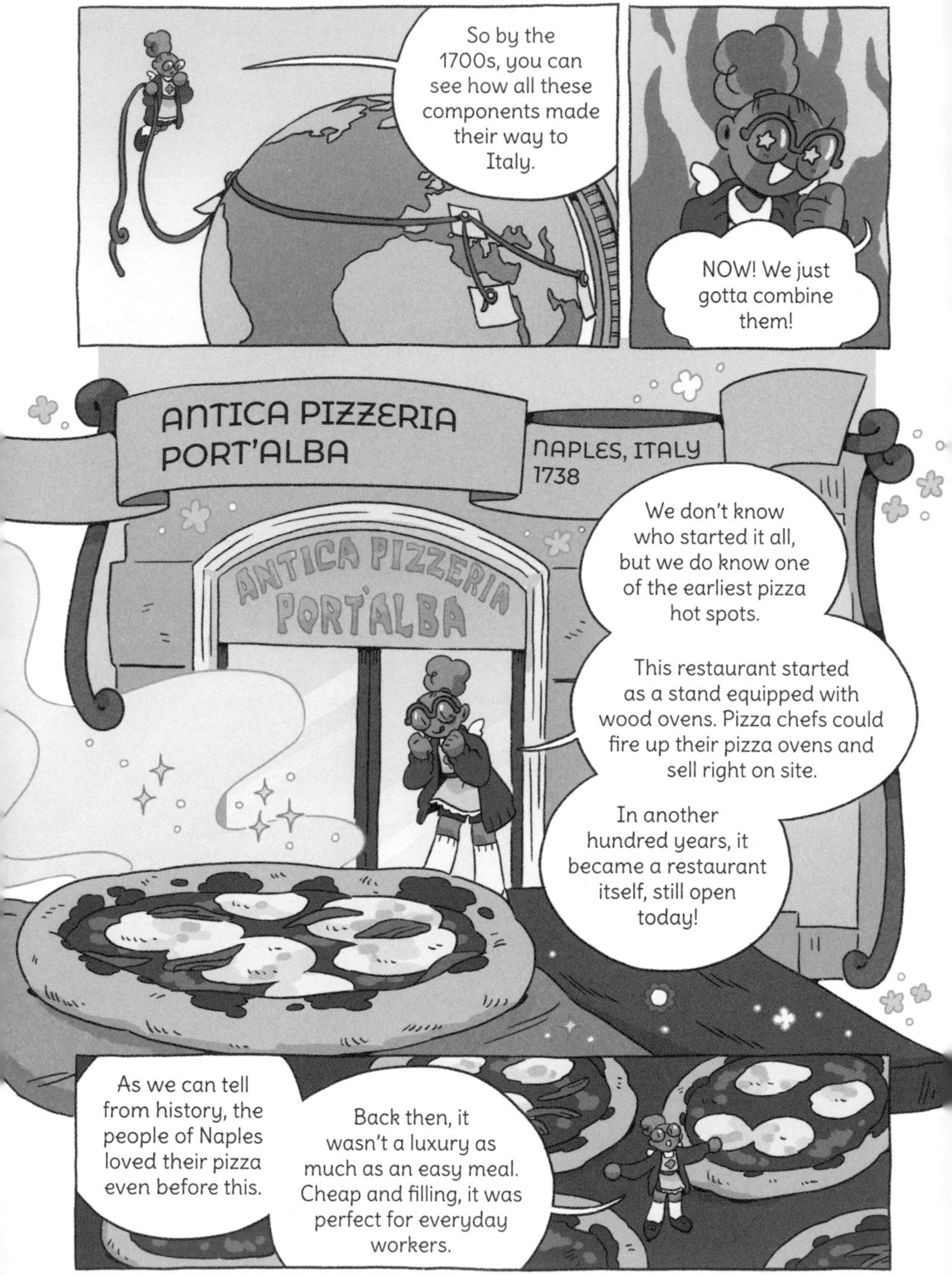
So by the 1700s, you can see how all these components made their way to Italy.
NOW! We just gotta combine them!
ANTICA PIZZERIA PORT'ALBA
NAPLES, ITALY 1738
ANTICA PIZZERIA PORT'ALBA
We don't know who started it all, but we do know one of the earliest pizza hot spots.
This restaurant started as a stand equipped with wood ovens. Pizza chefs could fire up their pizza ovens and sell right on site.
In another hundred years, it became a restaurant itself, still open today!
As we can tell from history, the people of Naples loved their pizza even before this.
Back then, it wasn't a luxury as much as an easy meal. Cheap and filling, it was perfect for everyday workers.

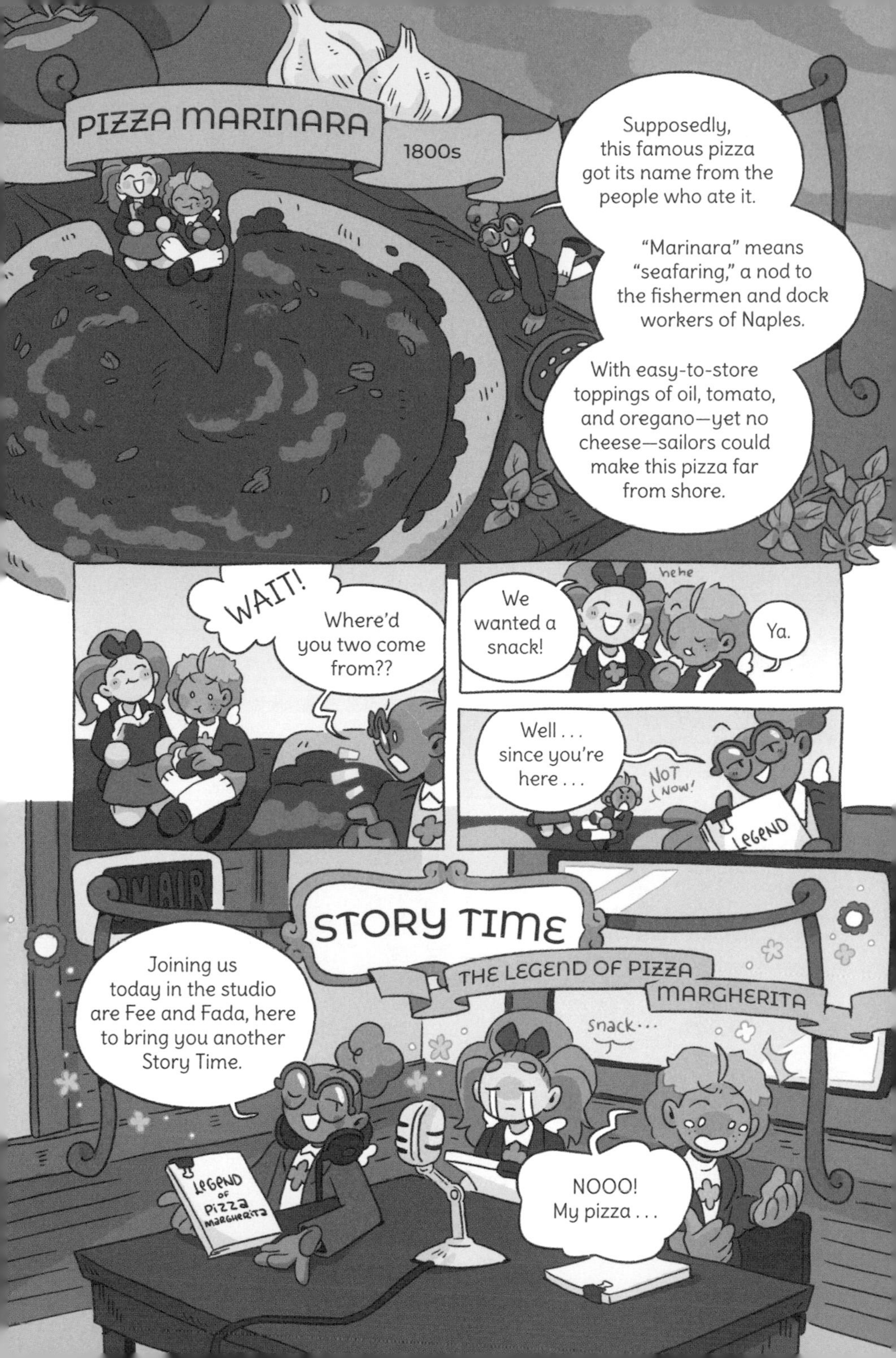
PIZZA MARINARA
1800s
Supposedly, this famous pizza got its name from the people who ate it.
"Marinara" means "seafaring," a nod to the fishermen and dock workers of Naples.
With easy-to-store toppings of oil, tomato, and oregano—yet no cheese—sailors could make this pizza far from shore.
WAIT!
Where'd you two come from??
We wanted a snack!
hehe
Ya.
Well . . . since you're here . . .
NOT NOW!
LEGEND
STORY TIME
THE LEGEND OF PIZZA MARGHERITA
Joining us today in the studio are Fee and Fada, here to bring you another Story Time.
snack . . .
LEGEND OF PIZZA MARGHERITA
NOOO! My pizza . . .

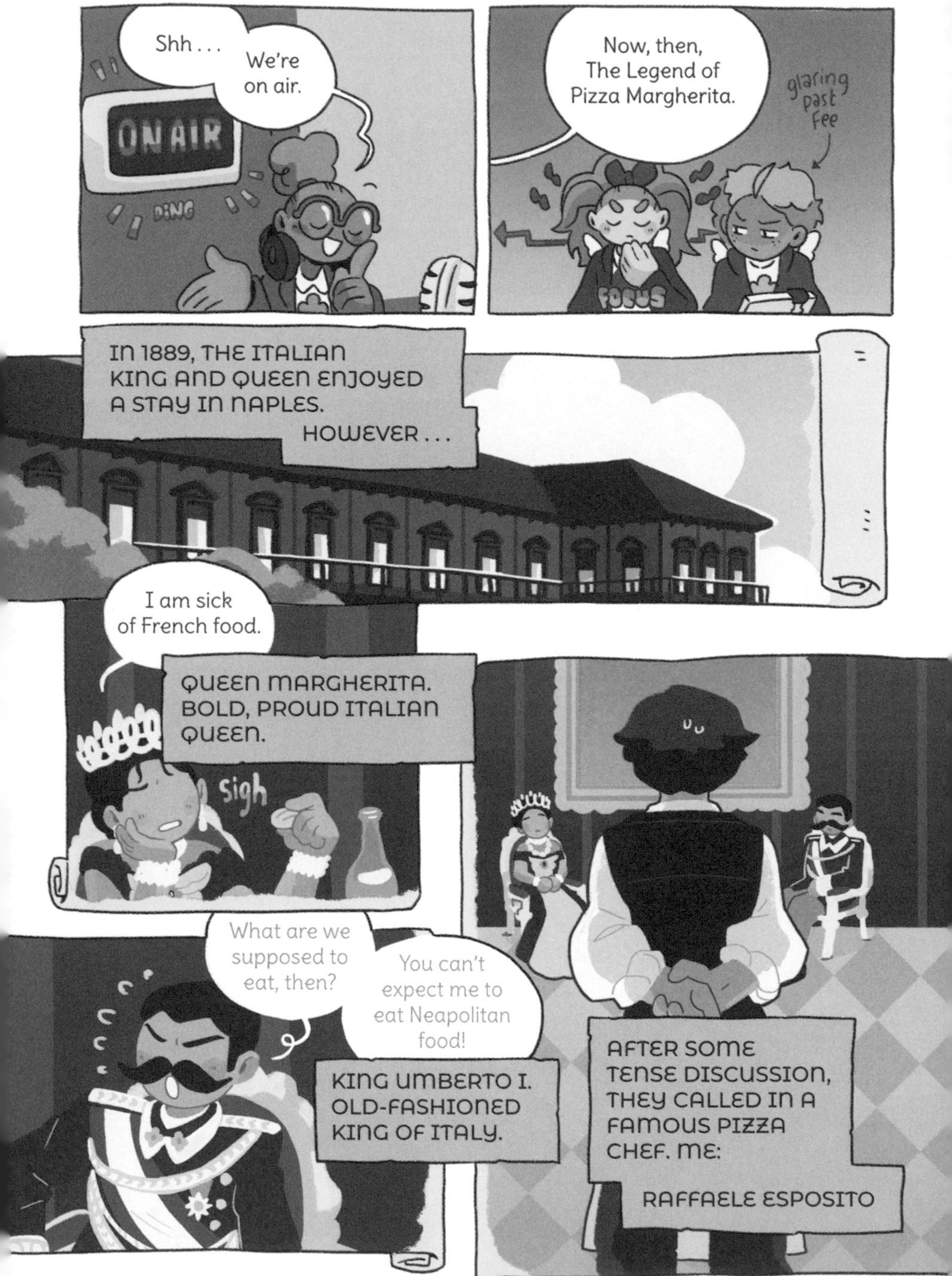

Shh . . .
We're on air.
ON AIR
DING
Now, then, The Legend of Pizza Margherita.
glaring past Fee
FOCUS
IN 1889, THE ITALIAN KING AND QUEEN ENJOYED A STAY IN NAPLES.
HOWEVER . . .
I am sick of French food.
QUEEN MARGHERITA. BOLD, PROUD ITALIAN QUEEN.
sigh
What are we supposed to eat, then?
You can't expect me to eat Neapolitan food!
KING UMBERTO I. OLD-FASHIONED KING OF ITALY.
AFTER SOME TENSE DISCUSSION, THEY CALLED IN A FAMOUS PIZZA CHEF. ME:
RAFFAELE ESPOSITO

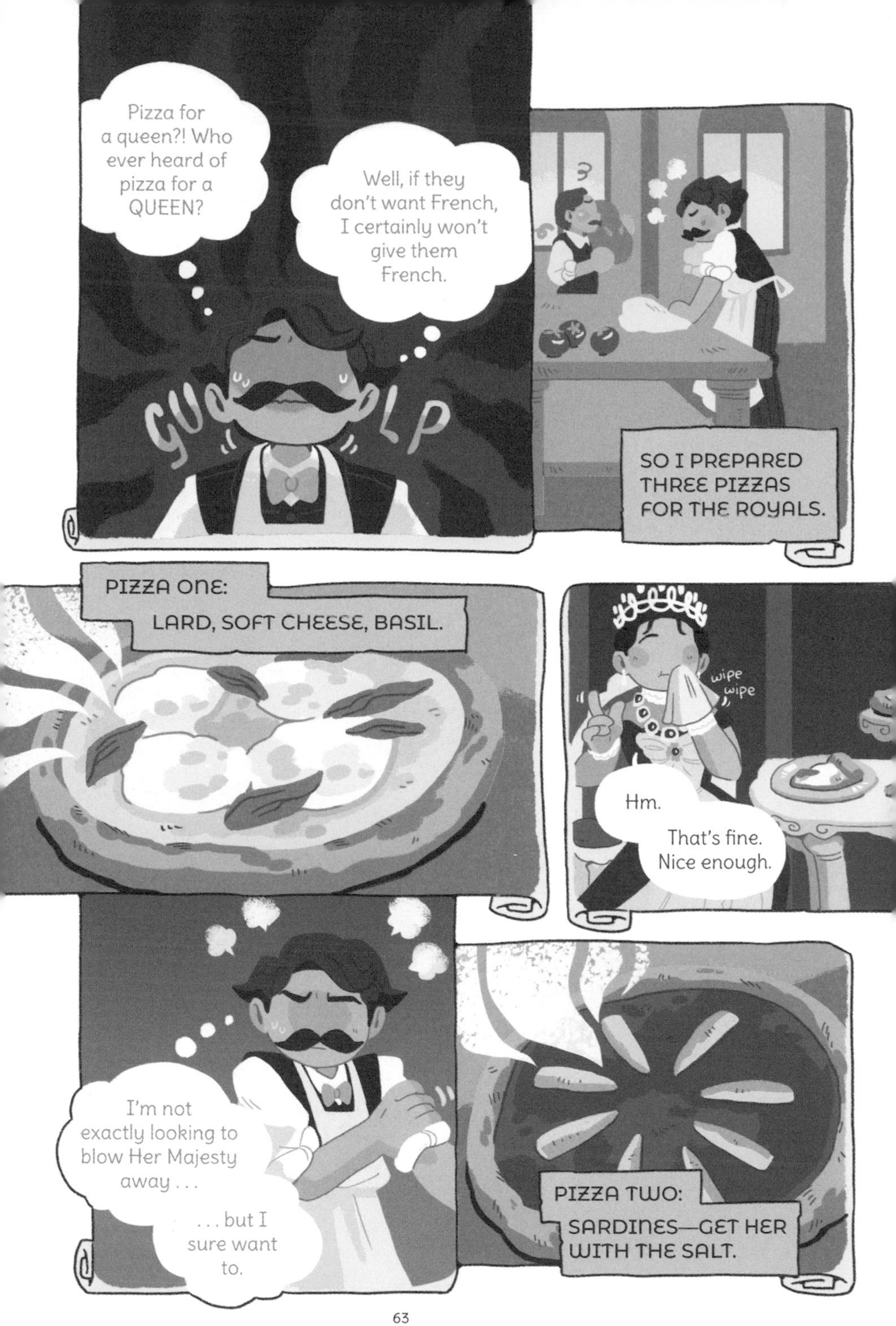
Pizza for a queen?! Who ever heard of pizza for a QUEEN?
Well, if they don't want French, I certainly won't give them French.
GULP
SO I PREPARED THREE PIZZAS FOR THE ROYALS.
PIZZA ONE:
LARD, SOFT CHEESE, BASIL.
wipe wipe
Hm.
That's fine. Nice enough.
I'm not exactly looking to blow Her Majesty away . . .
. . . but I sure want to.
PIZZA TWO:
SARDINES—GET HER WITH THE SALT.

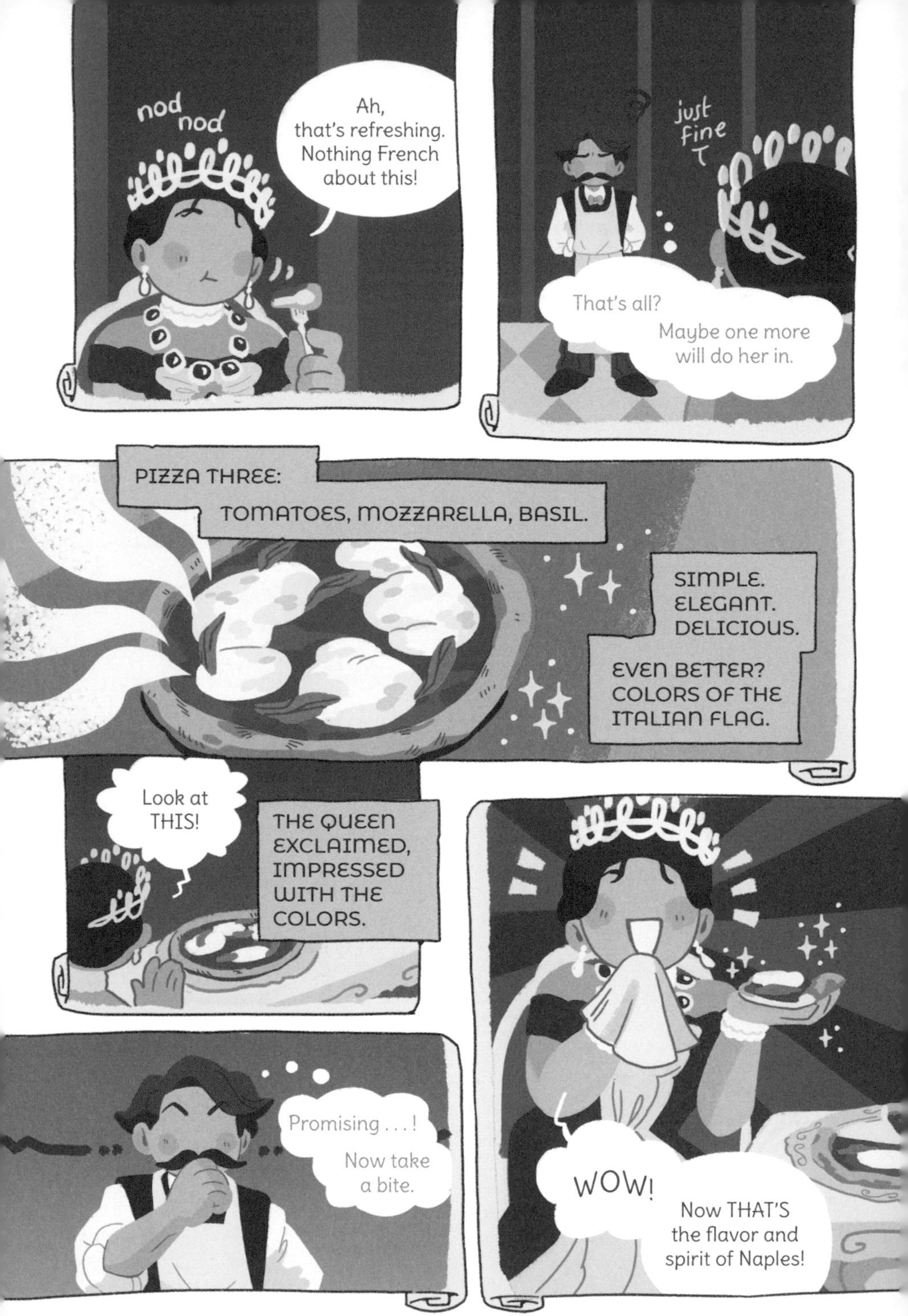
nod nod
Ah, that's refreshing. Nothing French about this!
just fine
That's all? Maybe one more will do her in.
PIZZA THREE:
TOMATOES, MOZZARELLA, BASIL.
SIMPLE. ELEGANT. DELICIOUS.
EVEN BETTER? COLORS OF THE ITALIAN FLAG.
Look at THIS!
THE QUEEN EXCLAIMED, IMPRESSED WITH THE COLORS.
WOW!
Now THAT'S the flavor and spirit of Naples!
Promising . . . !
Now take a bite.

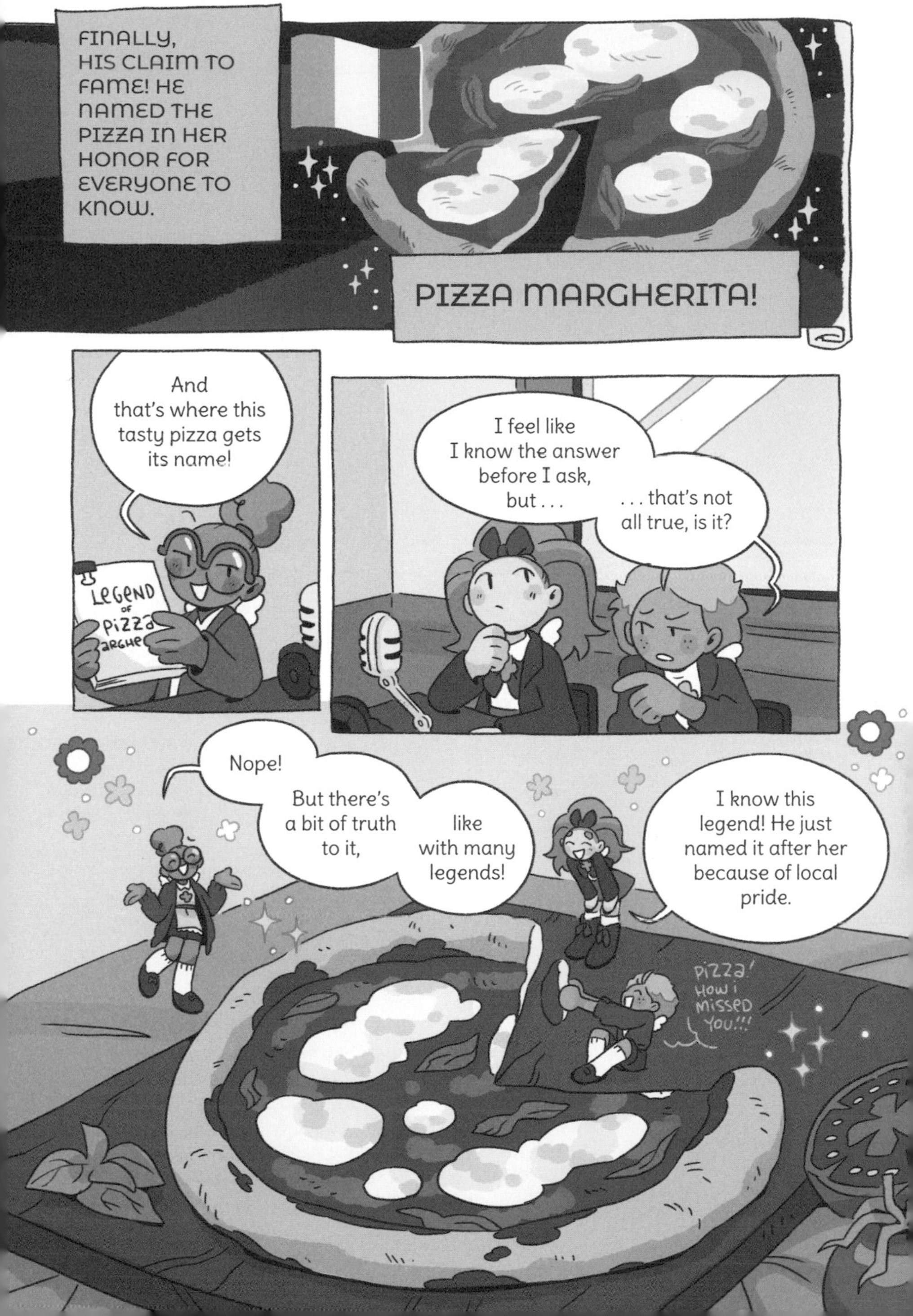

FINALLY, HIS CLAIM TO FAME! HE NAMED THE PIZZA IN HER HONOR FOR EVERYONE TO KNOW.
PIZZA MARGHERITA!
And that's where this tasty pizza gets its name!
LEGEND OF PIZZA
I feel like I know the answer before I ask, but . . .
. . . that's not all true, is it?
Nope!
But there's a bit of truth to it,
like with many legends!
I know this legend! He just named it after her because of local pride.
PIZZA! HOW I MISSED YOU!!!

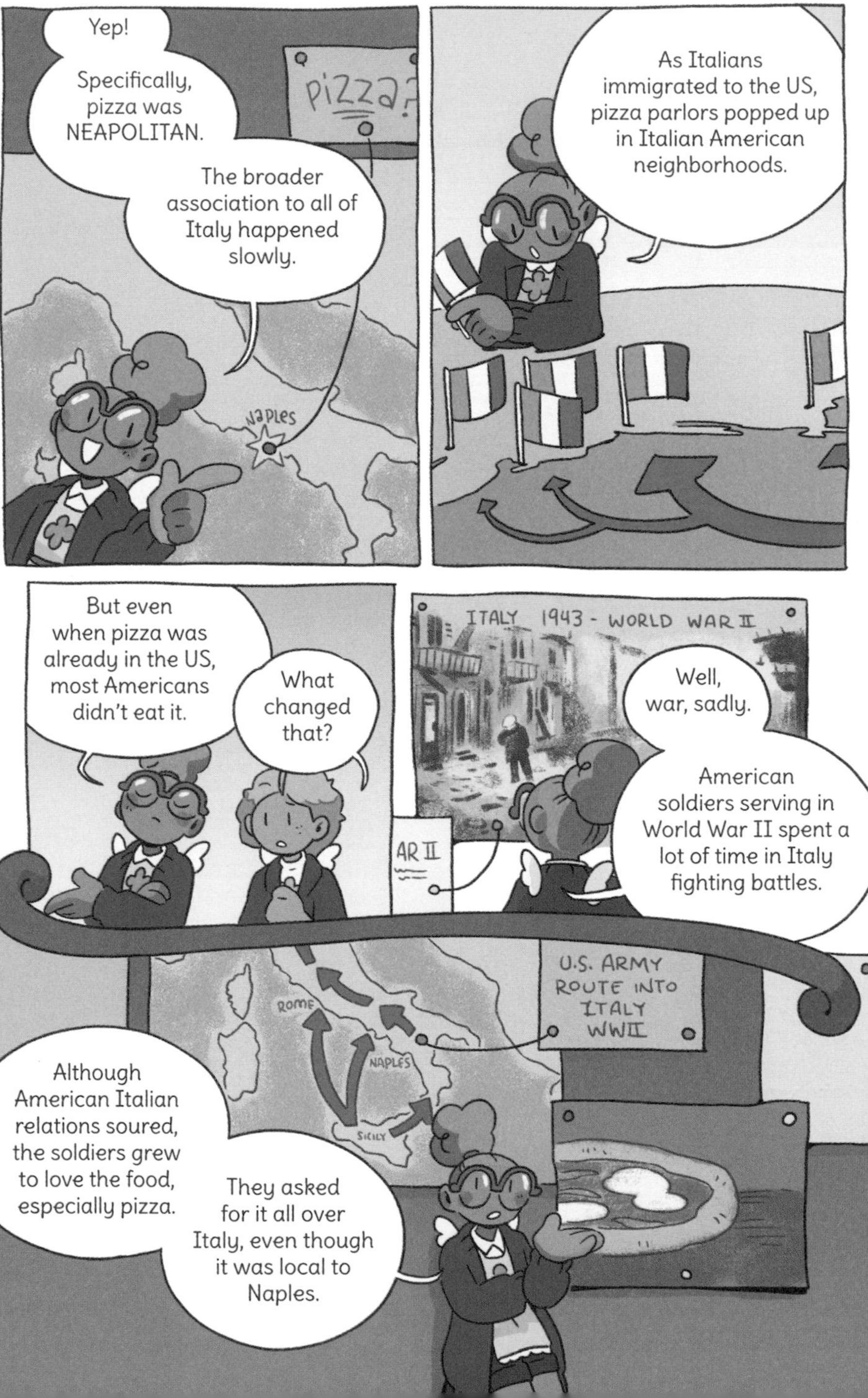
Yep!
Specifically, pizza was NEAPOLITAN.
PIZZA?
The broader association to all of Italy happened slowly.
NAPLES
As Italians immigrated to the US, pizza parlors popped up in Italian American neighborhoods.
But even when pizza was already in the US, most Americans didn't eat it.
What changed that?
ITALY 1943 - WORLD WAR II
Well, war, sadly.
American soldiers serving in World War II spent a lot of time in Italy fighting battles.
AR II
U.S. ARMY ROUTE INTO ITALY WWII
ROME
NAPLES
SICILY
Although American Italian relations soured, the soldiers grew to love the food, especially pizza.
They asked for it all over Italy, even though it was local to Naples.

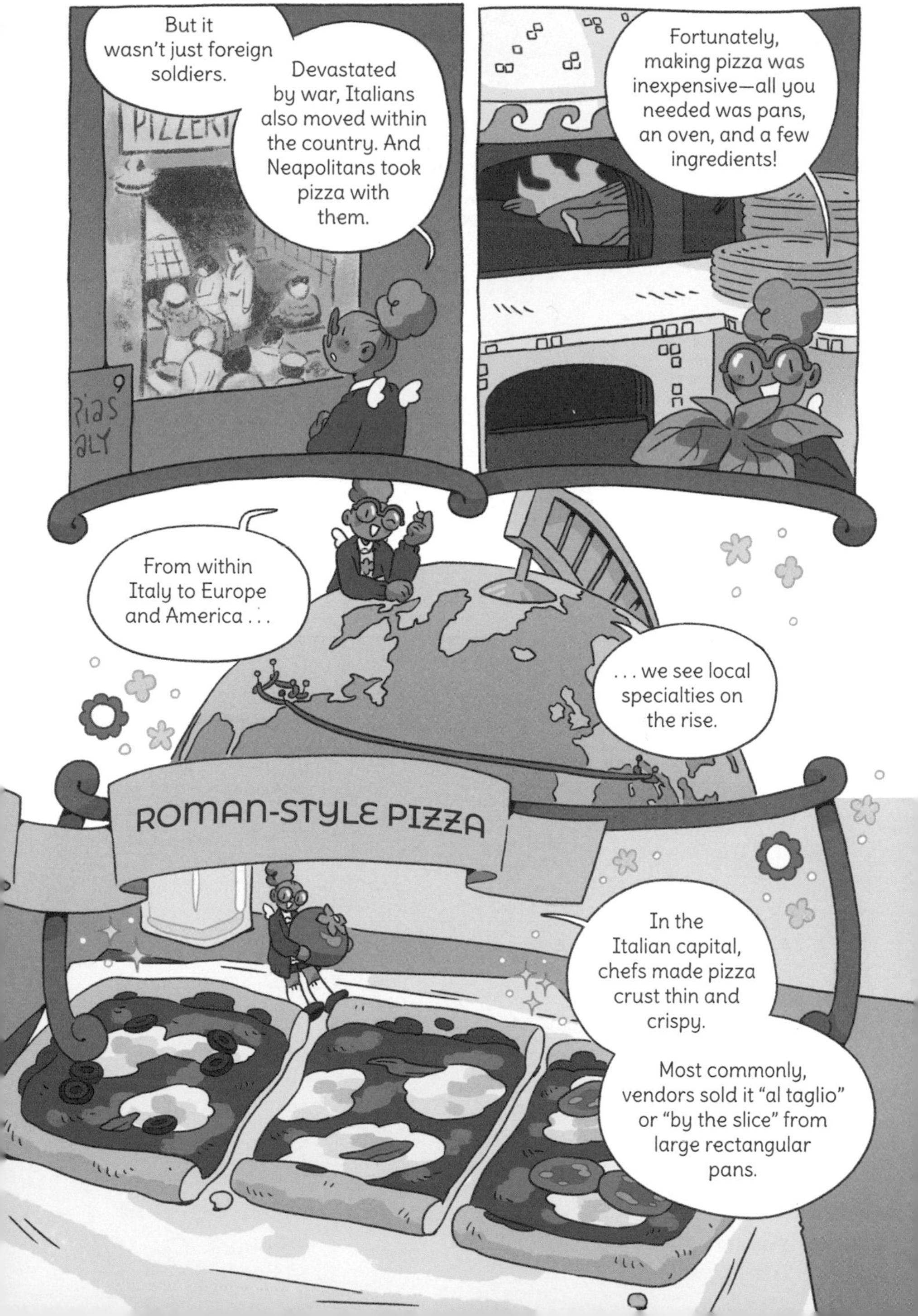
But it wasn't just foreign soldiers.
Devastated by war, Italians also moved within the country. And Neapolitans took pizza with them.
PIZZERI
Fortunately, making pizza was inexpensive—all you needed was pans, an oven, and a few ingredients!
From within Italy to Europe and America . . .
. . . we see local specialties on the rise.
ROMAN-STYLE PIZZA
In the Italian capital, chefs made pizza crust thin and crispy.
Most commonly, vendors sold it "al taglio" or "by the slice" from large rectangular pans.

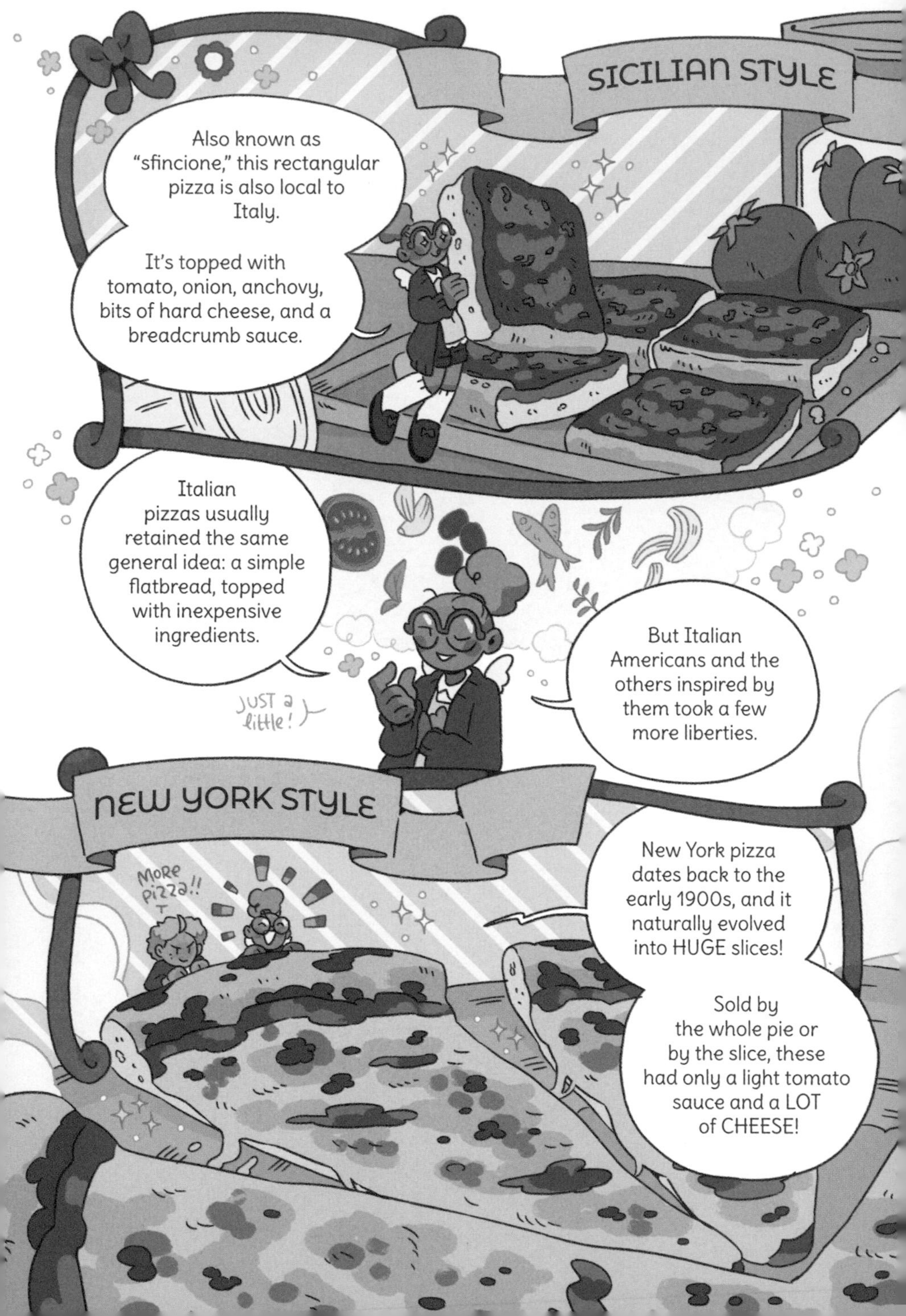
SICILIAN STYLE
Also known as "sfincione," this rectangular pizza is also local to Italy.
It's topped with tomato, onion, anchovy, bits of hard cheese, and a breadcrumb sauce.
Italian pizzas usually retained the same general idea: a simple flatbread, topped with inexpensive ingredients.
JUST a little!
But Italian Americans and the others inspired by them took a few more liberties.
NEW YORK STYLE
MORE pizza!!
New York pizza dates back to the early 1900s, and it naturally evolved into HUGE slices!
Sold by the whole pie or by the slice, these had only a light tomato sauce and a LOT of CHEESE!

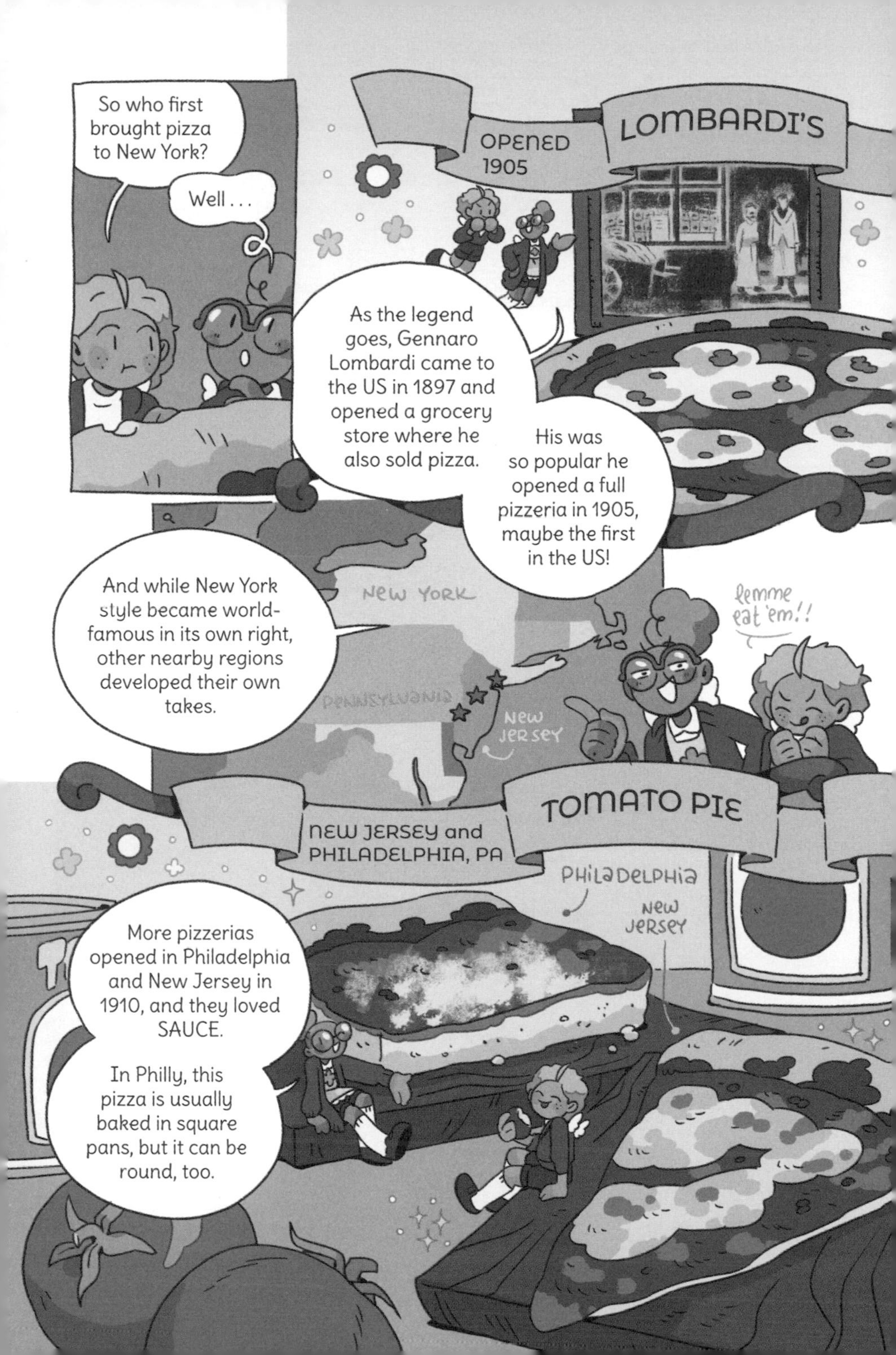

So who first brought pizza to New York?
Well . . .
LOMBARDI'S
OPENED 1905
As the legend goes, Gennaro Lombardi came to the US in 1897 and opened a grocery store where he also sold pizza.
His was so popular he opened a full pizzeria in 1905, maybe the first in the US!
NEW YORK
PENNSYLVANIA
NEW JERSEY
And while New York style became world-famous in its own right, other nearby regions developed their own takes.
lemme eat 'em!!
TOMATO PIE
NEW JERSEY and PHILADELPHIA, PA
PHILADELPHIA
NEW JERSEY
More pizzerias opened in Philadelphia and New Jersey in 1910, and they loved SAUCE.
In Philly, this pizza is usually baked in square pans, but it can be round, too.

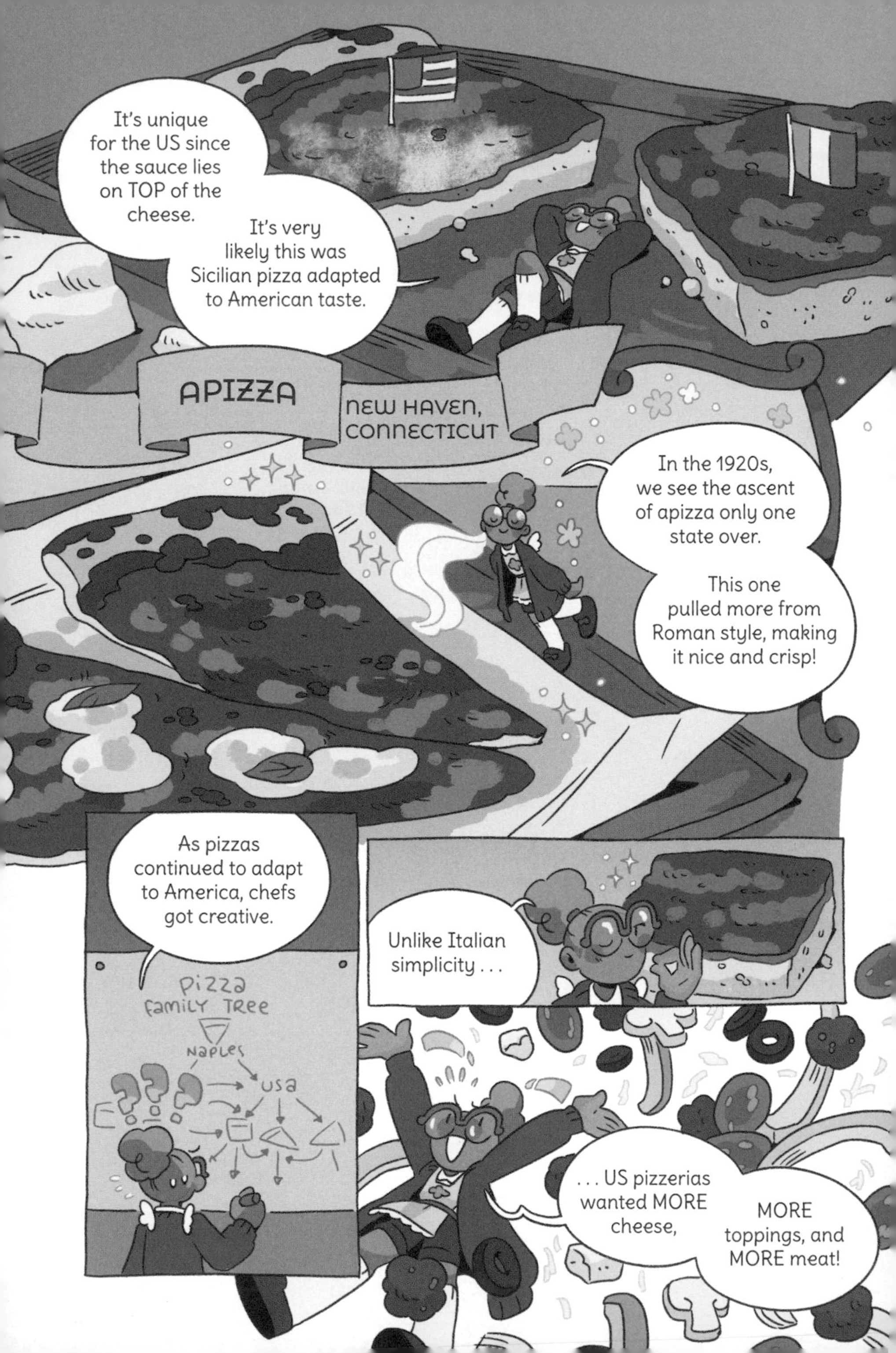

It's unique for the US since the sauce lies on TOP of the cheese.
It's very likely this was Sicilian pizza adapted to American taste.
APIZZA
NEW HAVEN, CONNECTICUT
In the 1920s, we see the ascent of apizza only one state over.
This one pulled more from Roman style, making it nice and crisp!
As pizzas continued to adapt to America, chefs got creative.
pizza family tree
Naples
usa
Unlike Italian simplicity . . .
. . . US pizzerias wanted MORE cheese,
MORE toppings, and MORE meat!

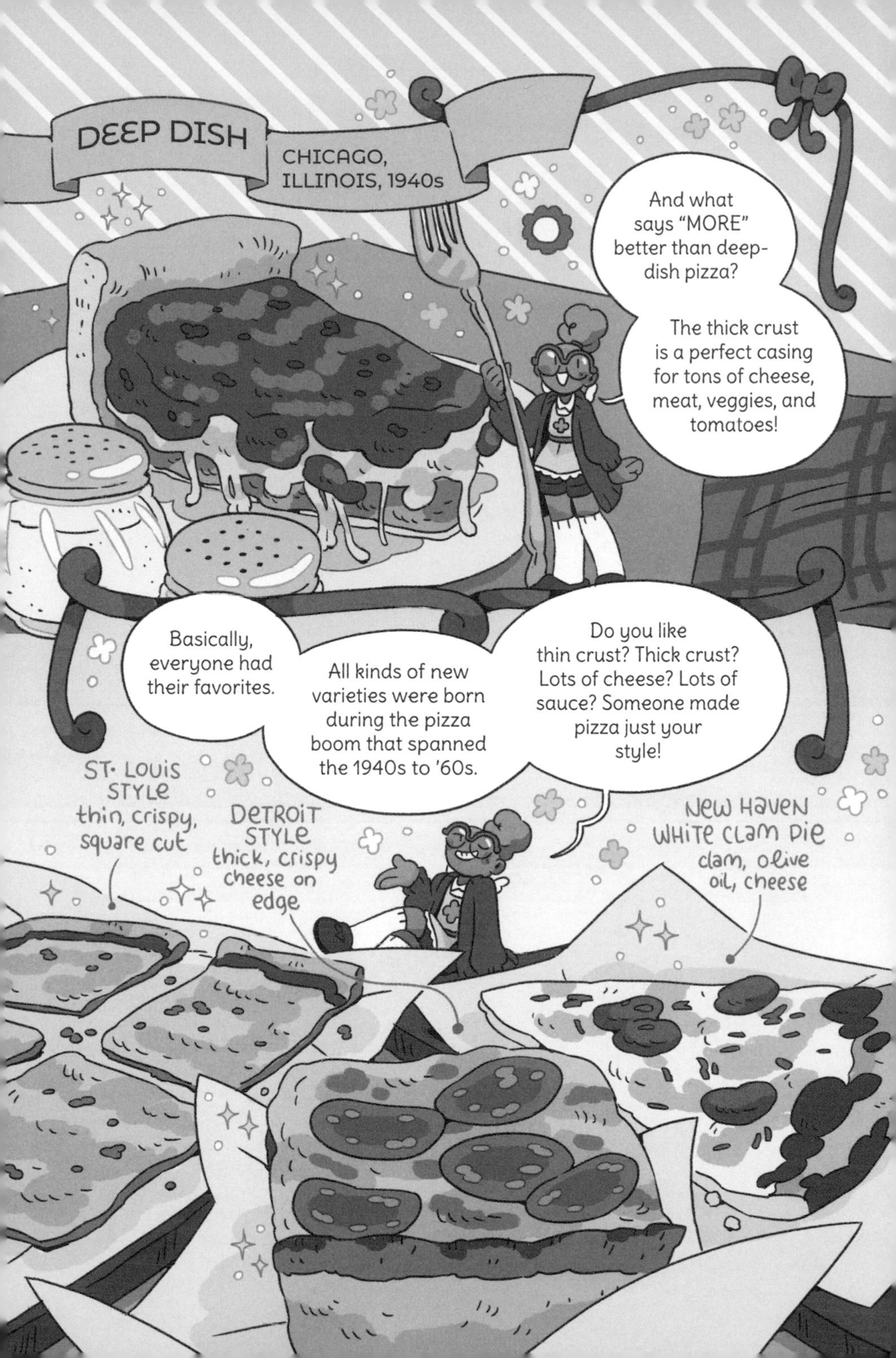
DEEP DISH
CHICAGO, ILLINOIS, 1940s
And what says "MORE" better than deep-dish pizza?
The thick crust is a perfect casing for tons of cheese, meat, veggies, and tomatoes!
Basically, everyone had their favorites.
All kinds of new varieties were born during the pizza boom that spanned the 1940s to '60s.
Do you like thin crust? Thick crust? Lots of cheese? Lots of sauce? Someone made pizza just your style!
ST. LOUIS STYLE
thin, crispy, square cut
DETROIT STYLE
thick, crispy cheese on edge
NEW HAVEN WHITE CLAM PIE
clam, olive oil, cheese

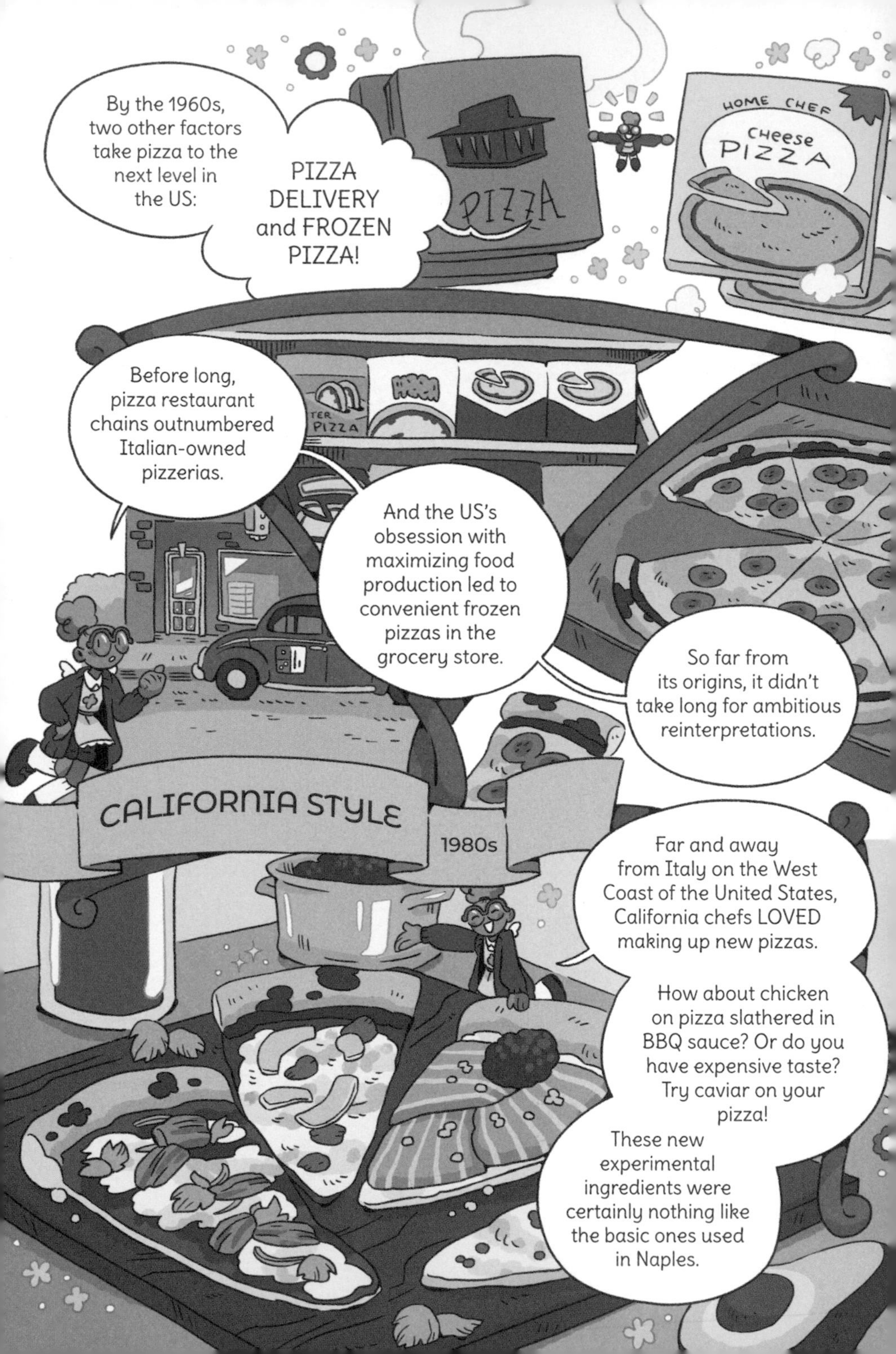
By the 1960s, two other factors take pizza to the next level in the US:
PIZZA DELIVERY and FROZEN PIZZA!
PIZZA
HOME CHEF
Cheese PIZZA
Before long, pizza restaurant chains outnumbered Italian-owned pizzerias.
And the US's obsession with maximizing food production led to convenient frozen pizzas in the grocery store.
So far from its origins, it didn't take long for ambitious reinterpretations.
CALIFORNIA STYLE
1980s
Far and away from Italy on the West Coast of the United States, California chefs LOVED making up new pizzas.
How about chicken on pizza slathered in BBQ sauce? Or do you have expensive taste? Try caviar on your pizza!
These new experimental ingredients were certainly nothing like the basic ones used in Naples.

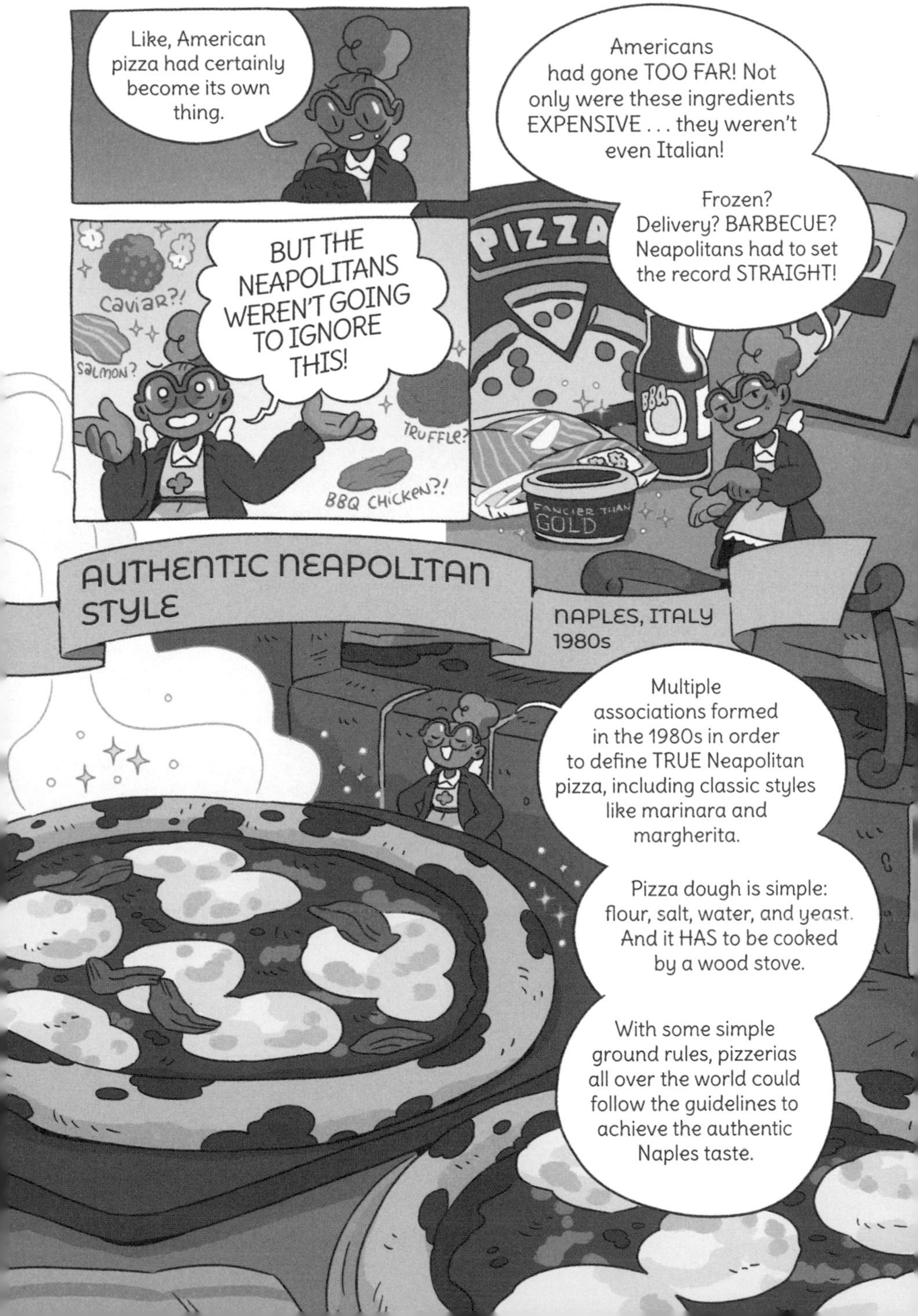

Like, American pizza had certainly become its own thing.
Americans had gone TOO FAR! Not only were these ingredients EXPENSIVE . . . they weren't even Italian!
BUT THE NEAPOLITANS WEREN'T GOING TO IGNORE THIS!
CAVIAR?!
SALMON?
TRUFFLE?
BBQ CHICKEN?!
PIZZA
BBQ
FANCIER THAN GOLD
Frozen? Delivery? BARBECUE? Neapolitans had to set the record STRAIGHT!
AUTHENTIC NEAPOLITAN STYLE
NAPLES, ITALY 1980s
Multiple associations formed in the 1980s in order to define TRUE Neapolitan pizza, including classic styles like marinara and margherita.
Pizza dough is simple: flour, salt, water, and yeast. And it HAS to be cooked by a wood stove.
With some simple ground rules, pizzerias all over the world could follow the guidelines to achieve the authentic Naples taste.

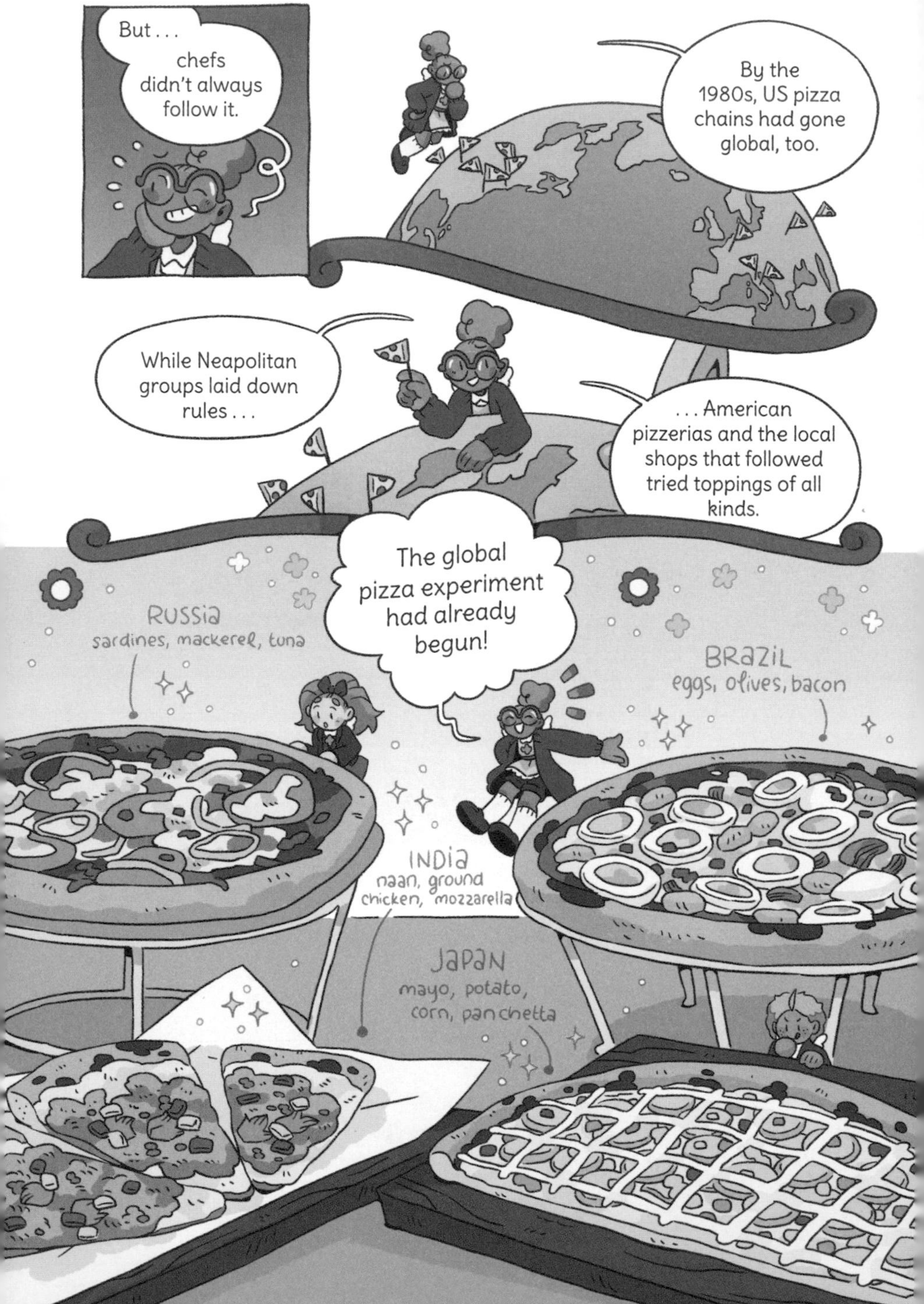
But . . .
chefs didn't always follow it.
By the 1980s, US pizza chains had gone global, too.
While Neapolitan groups laid down rules . . .
. . . American pizzerias and the local shops that followed tried toppings of all kinds.
The global pizza experiment had already begun!
RUSSIA
sardines, mackerel, tuna
BRAZIL
eggs, olives, bacon
INDIA
naan, ground chicken, mozzarella
JAPAN
mayo, potato, corn, panchetta

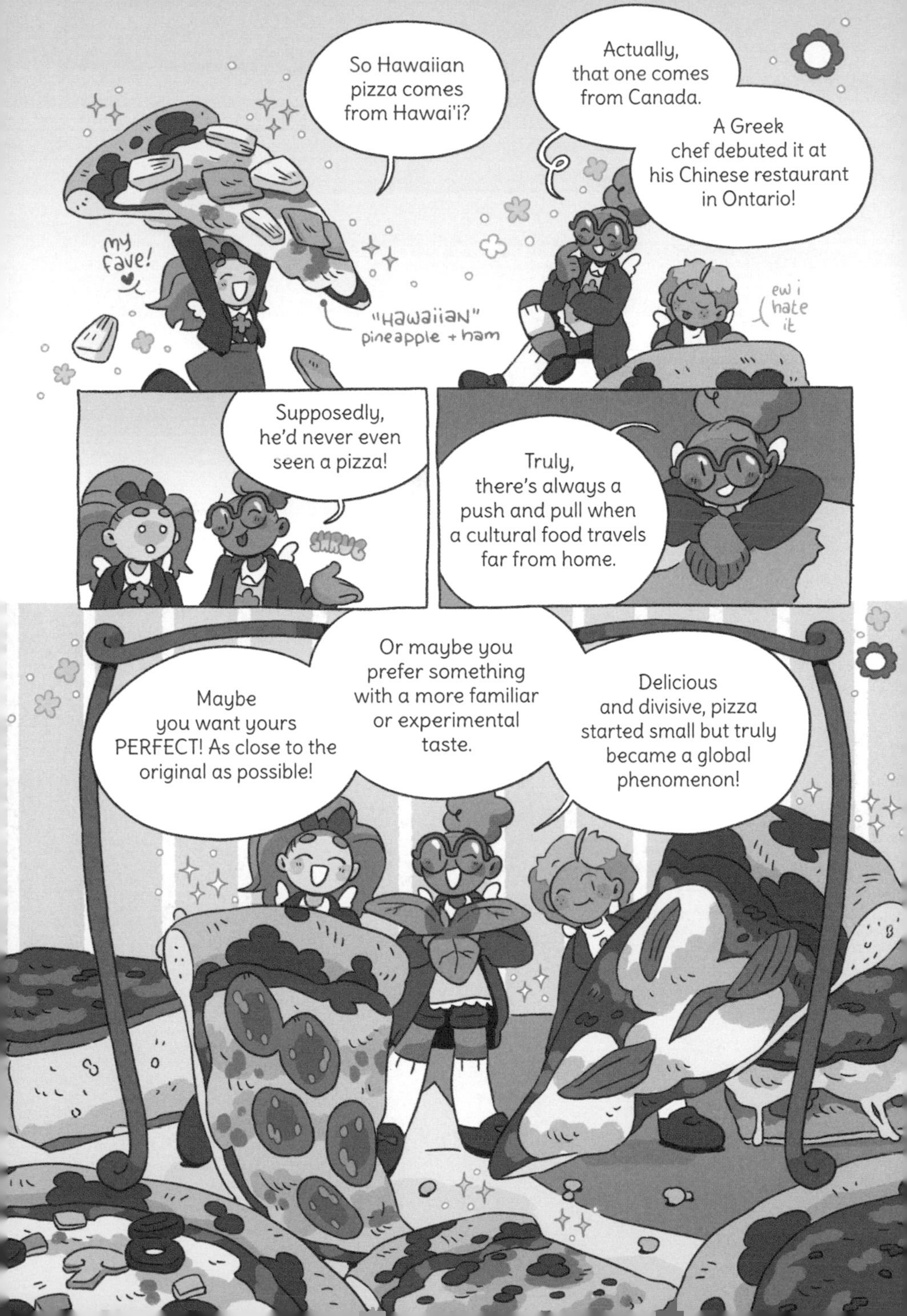
So Hawaiian pizza comes from Hawai'i?
Actually, that one comes from Canada.
A Greek chef debuted it at his Chinese restaurant in Ontario!
my fave!
"HAWAIIAN" pineapple + ham
ew i hate it
Supposedly, he'd never even seen a pizza!
SHRUG
Truly, there's always a push and pull when a cultural food travels far from home.
Maybe you want yours PERFECT! As close to the original as possible!
Or maybe you prefer something with a more familiar or experimental taste.
Delicious and divisive, pizza started small but truly became a global phenomenon!

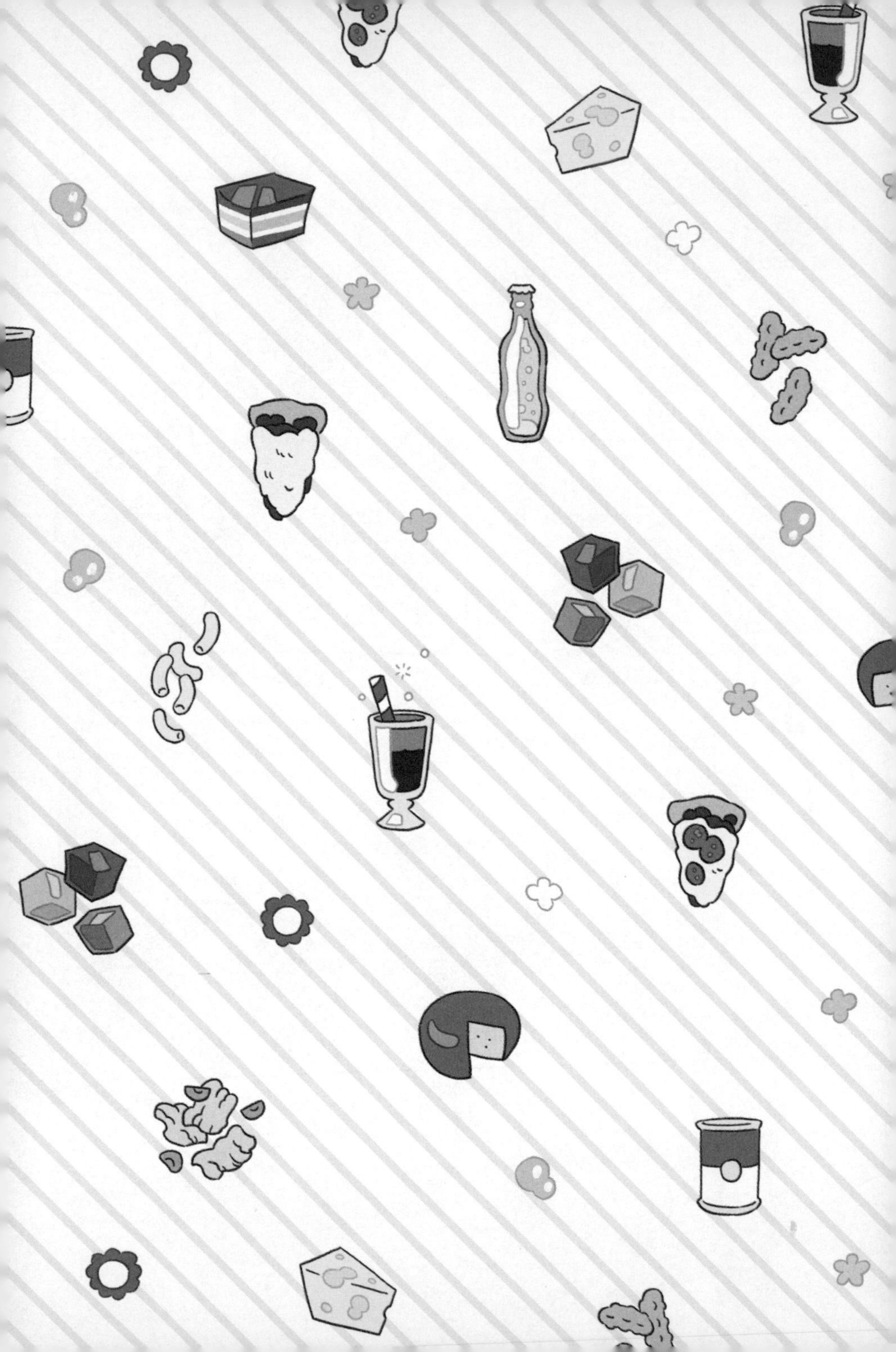

# The Abridged
# Atlas of Pickle History

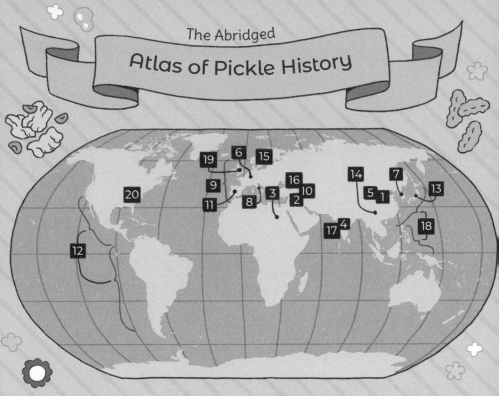

1. Confucius's *Book of Odes*
2. Mesopotamian Siqqu
3. Egyptian Pickled Geese
4. Indian Ayurvedic Pickles
5. Chinese Pickled Cabbage
6. European Sauerkraut
7. Korean Kimchi
8. Roman Pickled Olives
9. Jewish Diaspora Mishnah Pickles
10. Persian/Arabic Sikbaj
11. Iberian Pickled Eggplant
12. American Ceviche, Salsas, Escabeche Vegetales, and Pico de Gallo
13. Japanese Umeboshi, Tsukemono, and Nukazuke
14. Yunnan Chinese Zha
15. European Pickled Herring
16. Middle Eastern Torshi
17. South Asian Achar and Chutney
18. Southeast and East Asian Soy Sauce, Miso Paste, and Fish Sauce
19. British Chutney
20. American Ketchup

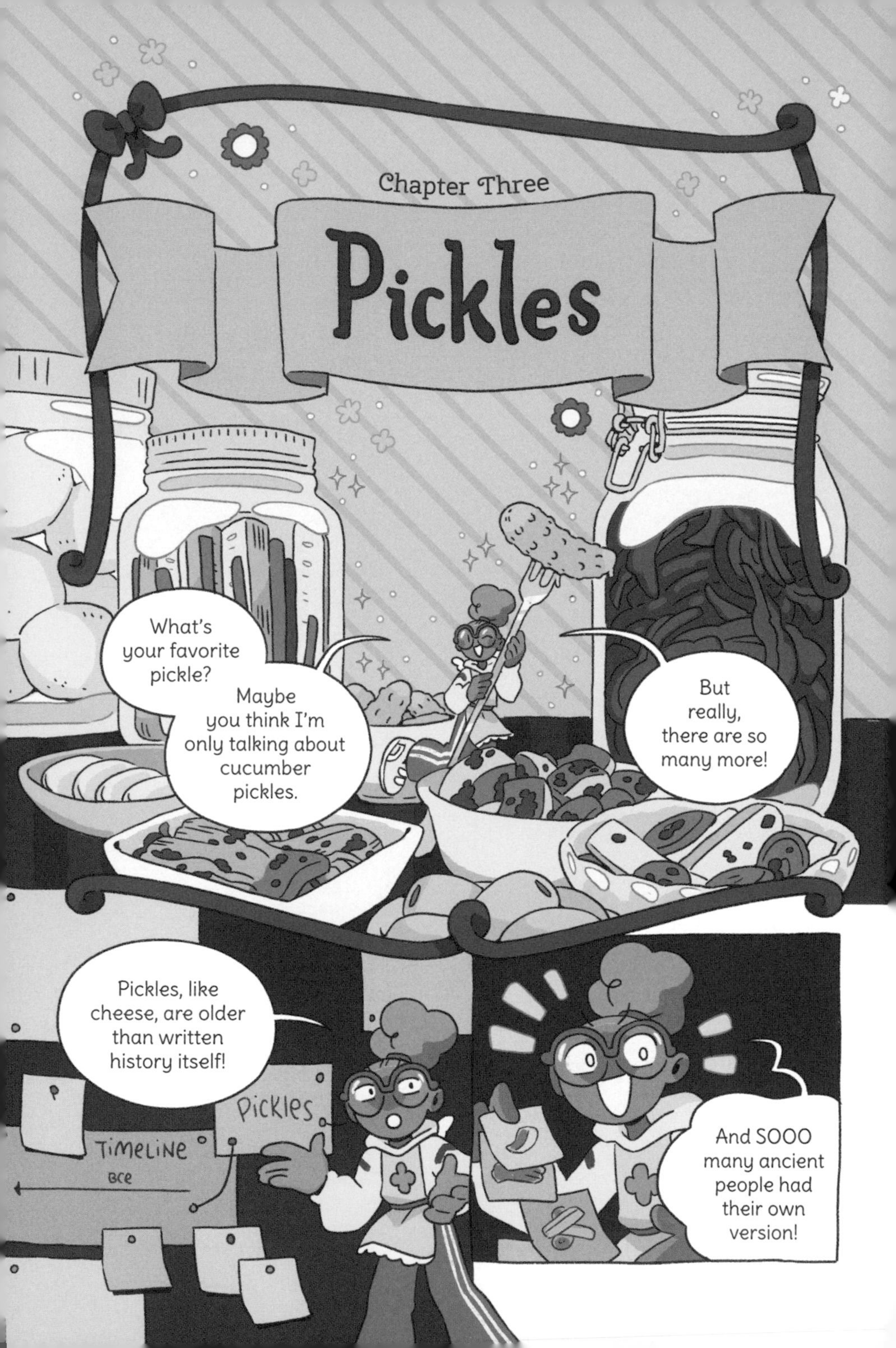
Chapter Three
Pickles
What's your favorite pickle?
Maybe you think I'm only talking about cucumber pickles.
But really, there are so many more!
Pickles, like cheese, are older than written history itself!
Pickles
Timeline
BCE
And SOOO many ancient people had their own version!

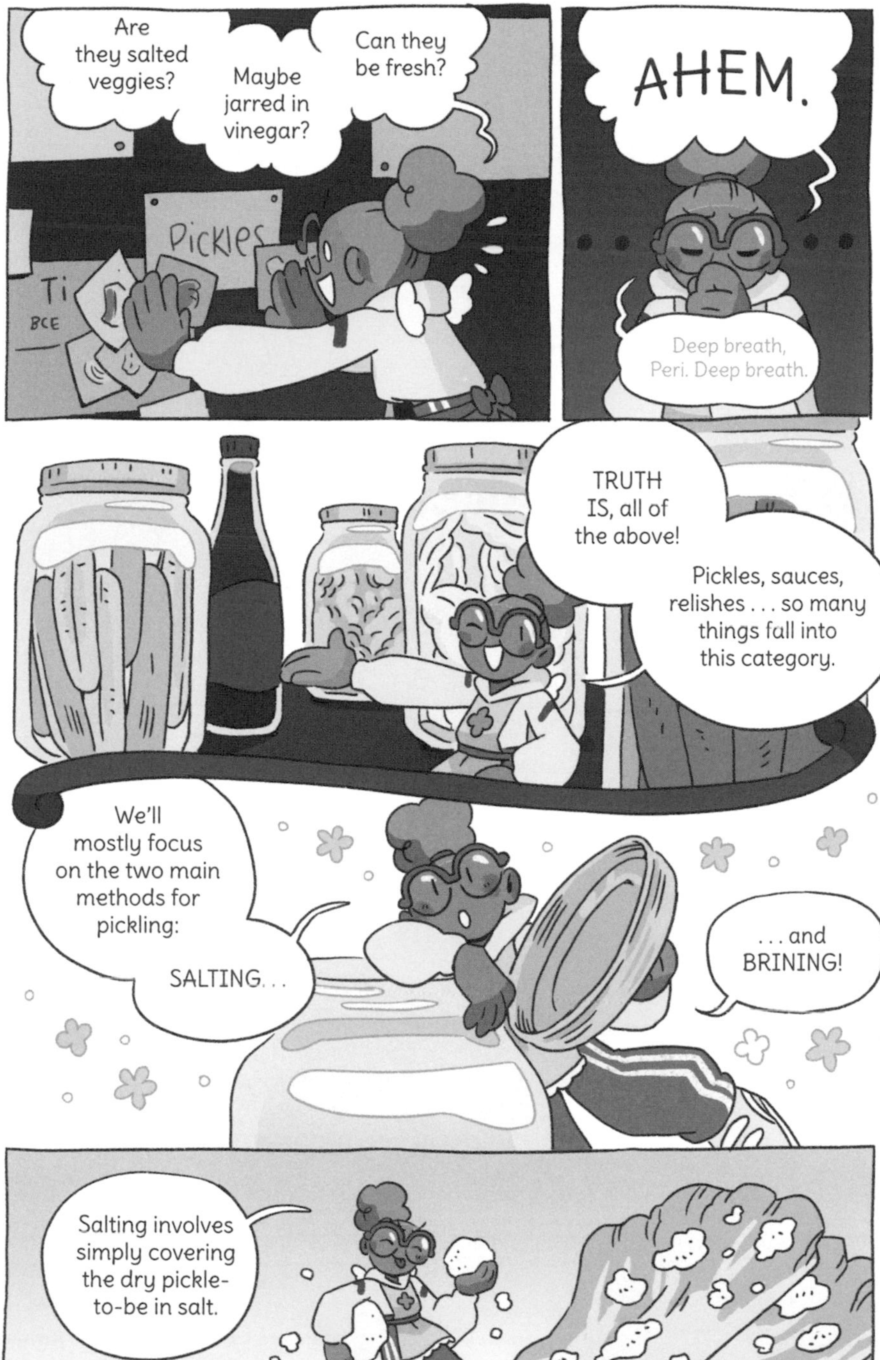
Are they salted veggies?
Maybe jarred in vinegar?
Can they be fresh?
Pickles
Ti
BCE
AHEM.
Deep breath, Peri. Deep breath.
TRUTH IS, all of the above!
Pickles, sauces, relishes . . . so many things fall into this category.
We'll mostly focus on the two main methods for pickling:
SALTING. . .
. . . and BRINING!
Salting involves simply covering the dry pickle-to-be in salt.

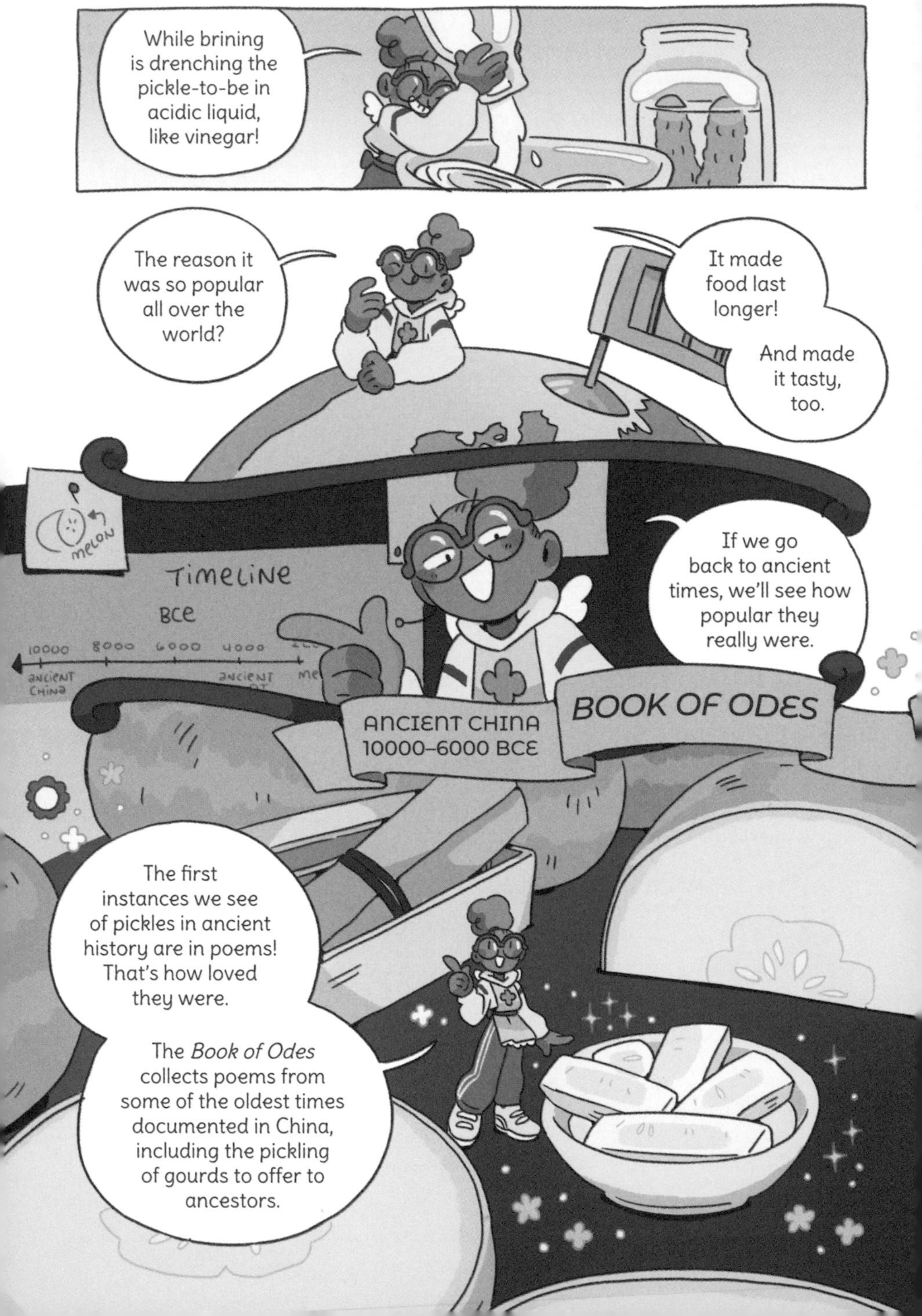
While brining is drenching the pickle-to-be in acidic liquid, like vinegar!
The reason it was so popular all over the world?
It made food last longer!
And made it tasty, too.
melon
TimeLine
BCE
10000 8000 6000 4000
ancient China
If we go back to ancient times, we'll see how popular they really were.
ANCIENT CHINA 10000–6000 BCE
BOOK OF ODES
The first instances we see of pickles in ancient history are in poems! That's how loved they were.
The *Book of Odes* collects poems from some of the oldest times documented in China, including the pickling of gourds to offer to ancestors.

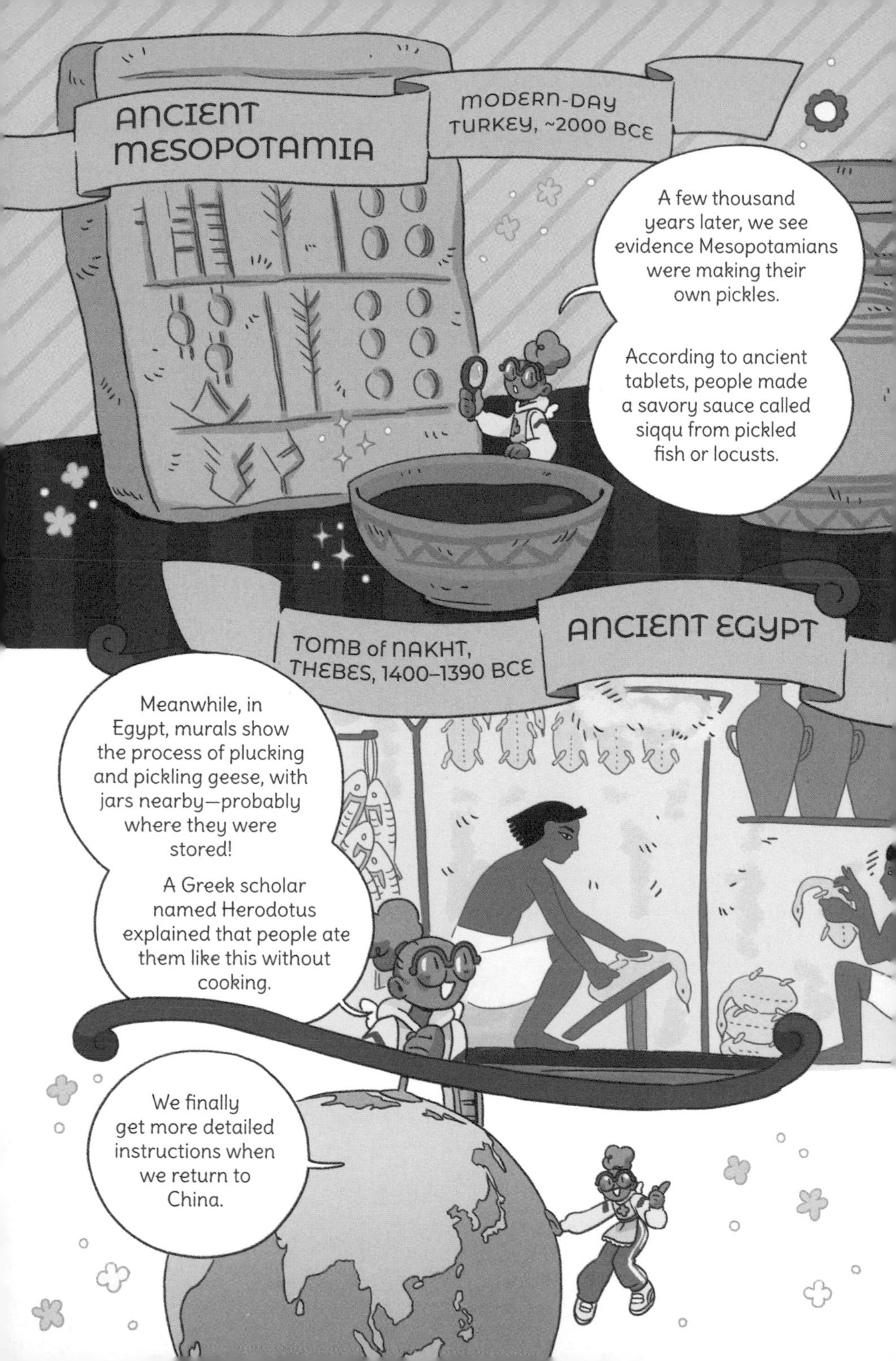
ANCIENT MESOPOTAMIA
MODERN-DAY TURKEY, ~2000 BCE
A few thousand years later, we see evidence Mesopotamians were making their own pickles.
According to ancient tablets, people made a savory sauce called siqqu from pickled fish or locusts.
ANCIENT EGYPT
TOMB of NAKHT, THEBES, 1400–1390 BCE
Meanwhile, in Egypt, murals show the process of plucking and pickling geese, with jars nearby—probably where they were stored!
A Greek scholar named Herodotus explained that people ate them like this without cooking.
We finally get more detailed instructions when we return to China.

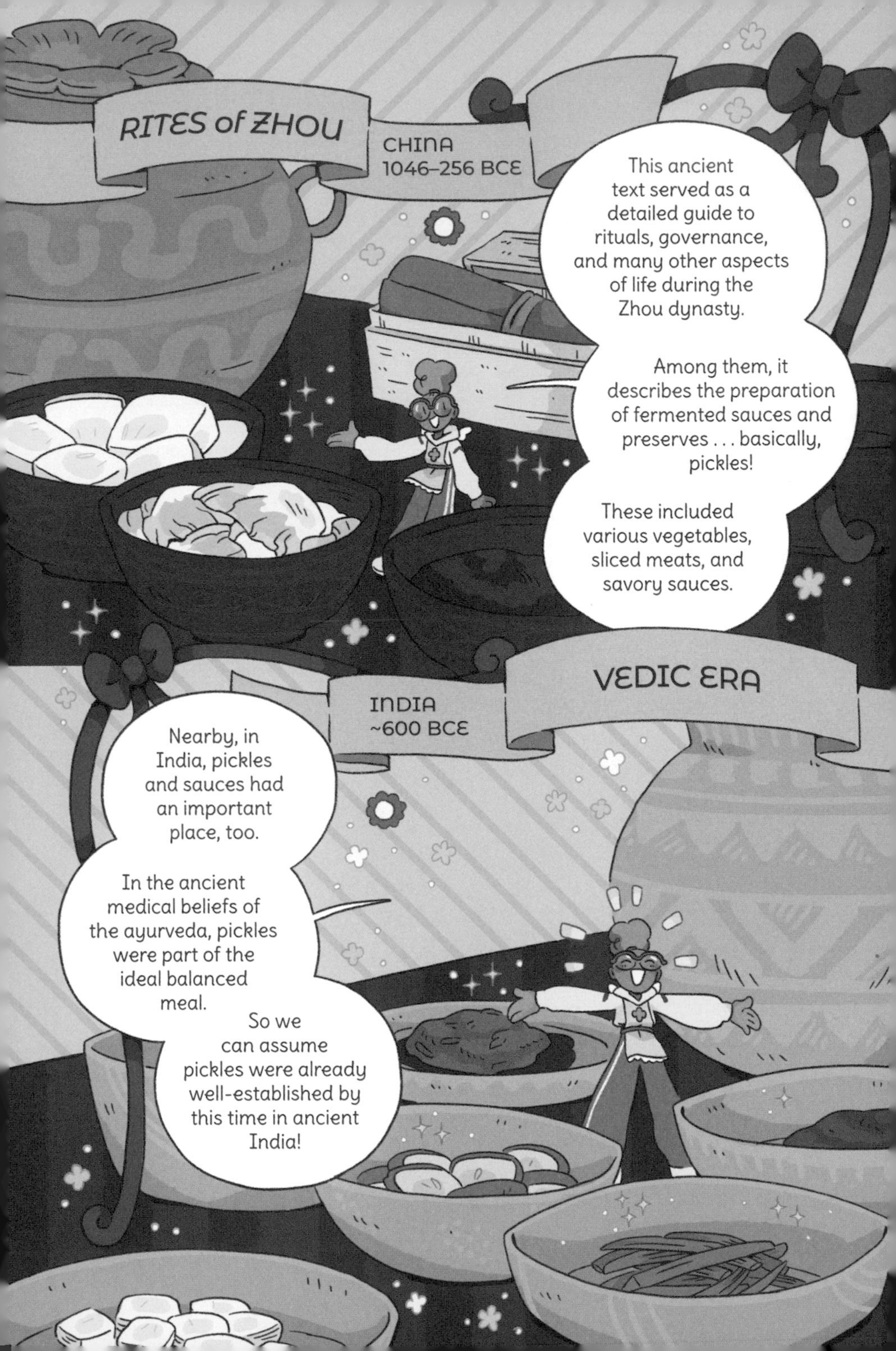
RITES of ZHOU
CHINA 1046–256 BCE
This ancient text served as a detailed guide to rituals, governance, and many other aspects of life during the Zhou dynasty.
Among them, it describes the preparation of fermented sauces and preserves . . . basically, pickles!
These included various vegetables, sliced meats, and savory sauces.
VEDIC ERA
INDIA ~600 BCE
Nearby, in India, pickles and sauces had an important place, too.
In the ancient medical beliefs of the ayurveda, pickles were part of the ideal balanced meal.
So we can assume pickles were already well-established by this time in ancient India!

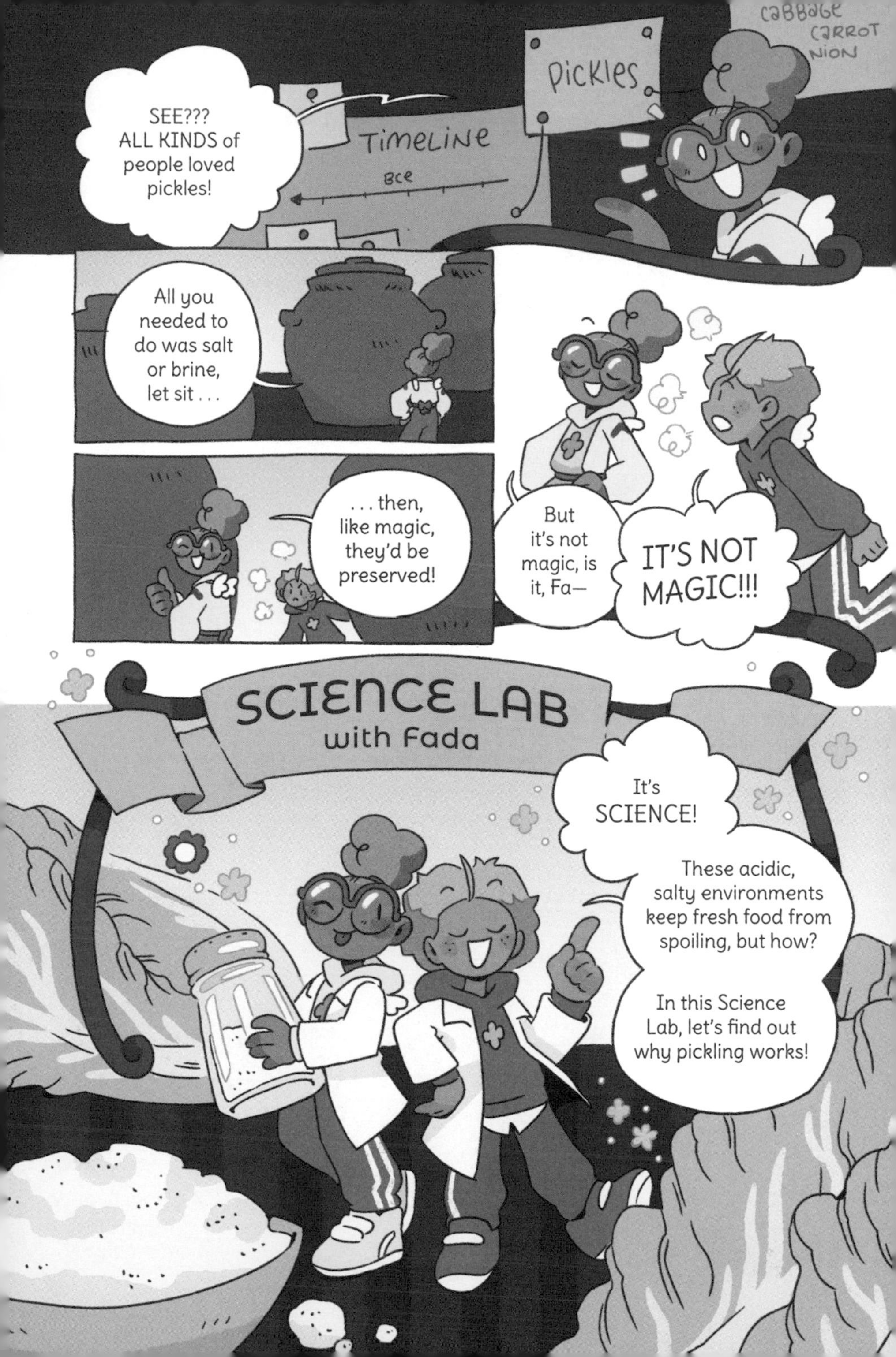
CABBAGE
CARROT
NION
PICKLES
TIMELINE
BCE
SEE??? ALL KINDS of people loved pickles!
All you needed to do was salt or brine, let sit . . .
. . . then, like magic, they'd be preserved!
But it's not magic, is it, Fa—
IT'S NOT MAGIC!!!
SCIENCE LAB with Fada
It's SCIENCE!
These acidic, salty environments keep fresh food from spoiling, but how?
In this Science Lab, let's find out why pickling works!

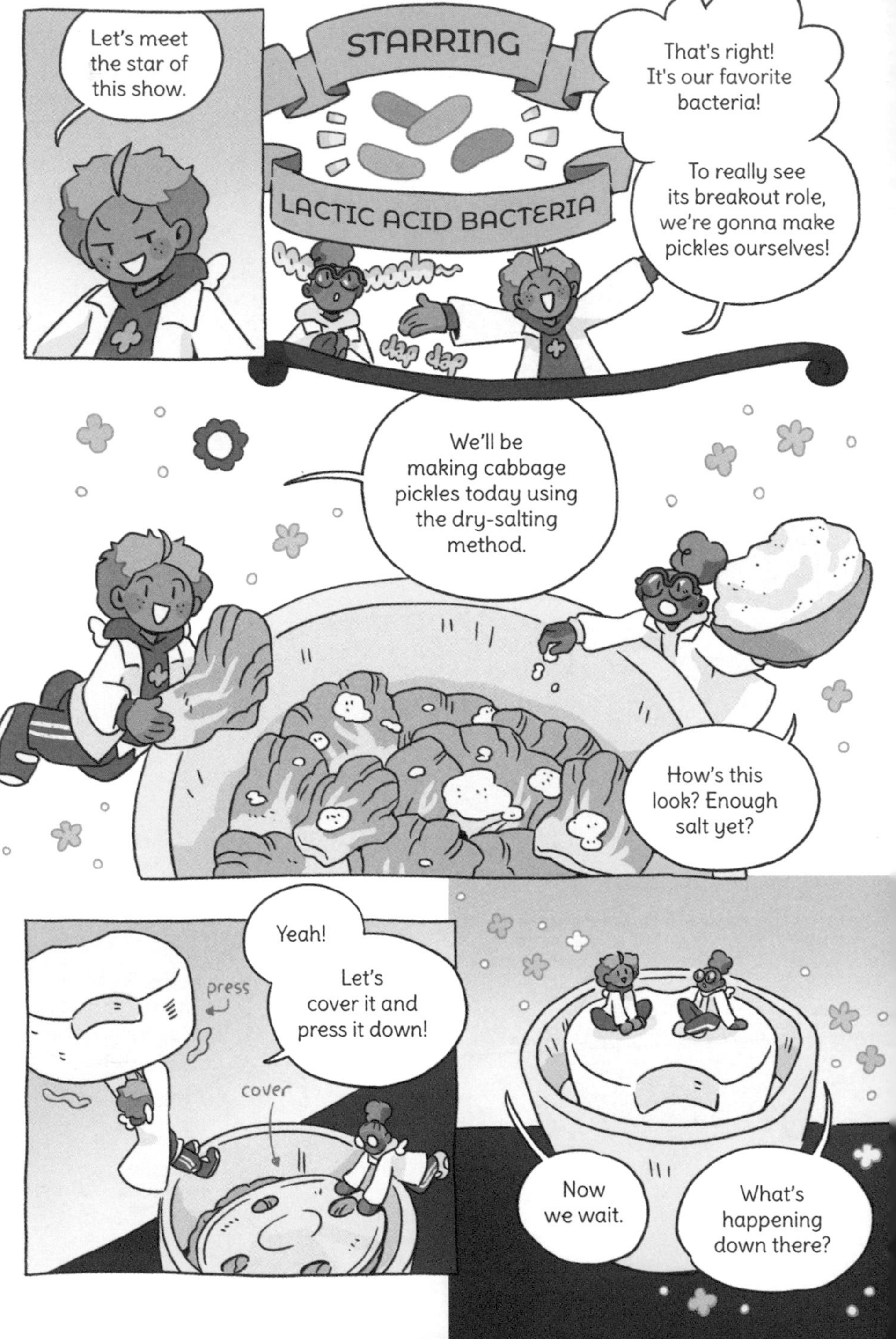
Let's meet the star of this show.
STARRING
LACTIC ACID BACTERIA
That's right! It's our favorite bacteria!
To really see its breakout role, we're gonna make pickles ourselves!
clap clap
We'll be making cabbage pickles today using the dry-salting method.
How's this look? Enough salt yet?
Yeah!
Let's cover it and press it down!
press
cover
Now we wait.
What's happening down there?

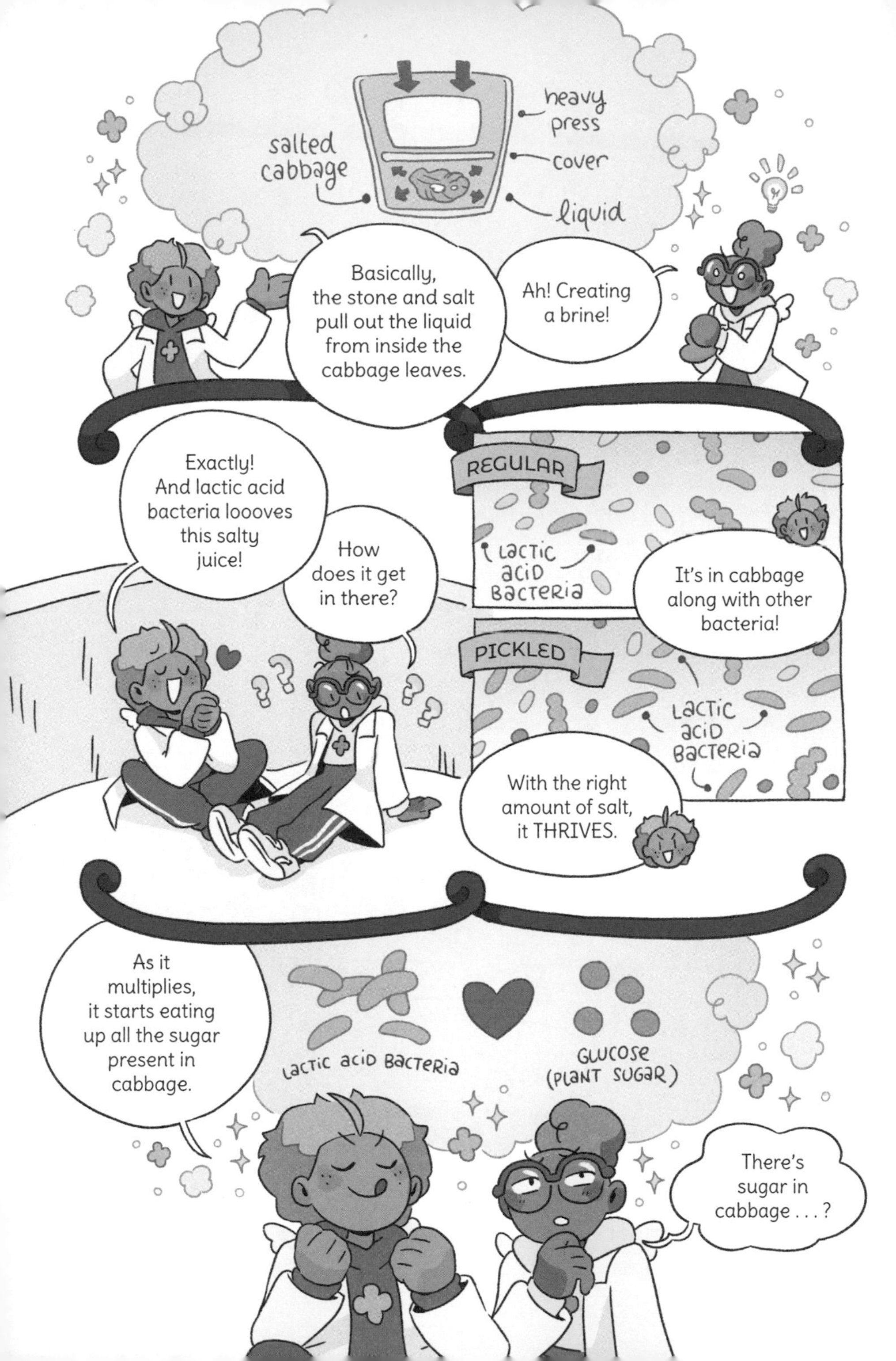
heavy press
cover
salted cabbage
liquid
Basically, the stone and salt pull out the liquid from inside the cabbage leaves.
Ah! Creating a brine!
Exactly! And lactic acid bacteria loooves this salty juice!
How does it get in there?
REGULAR
LACTIC ACID BACTERIA
It's in cabbage along with other bacteria!
PICKLED
LACTIC ACID BACTERIA
With the right amount of salt, it THRIVES.
As it multiplies, it starts eating up all the sugar present in cabbage.
LACTIC ACID BACTERIA
GLUCOSE (PLANT SUGAR)
There's sugar in cabbage . . . ?

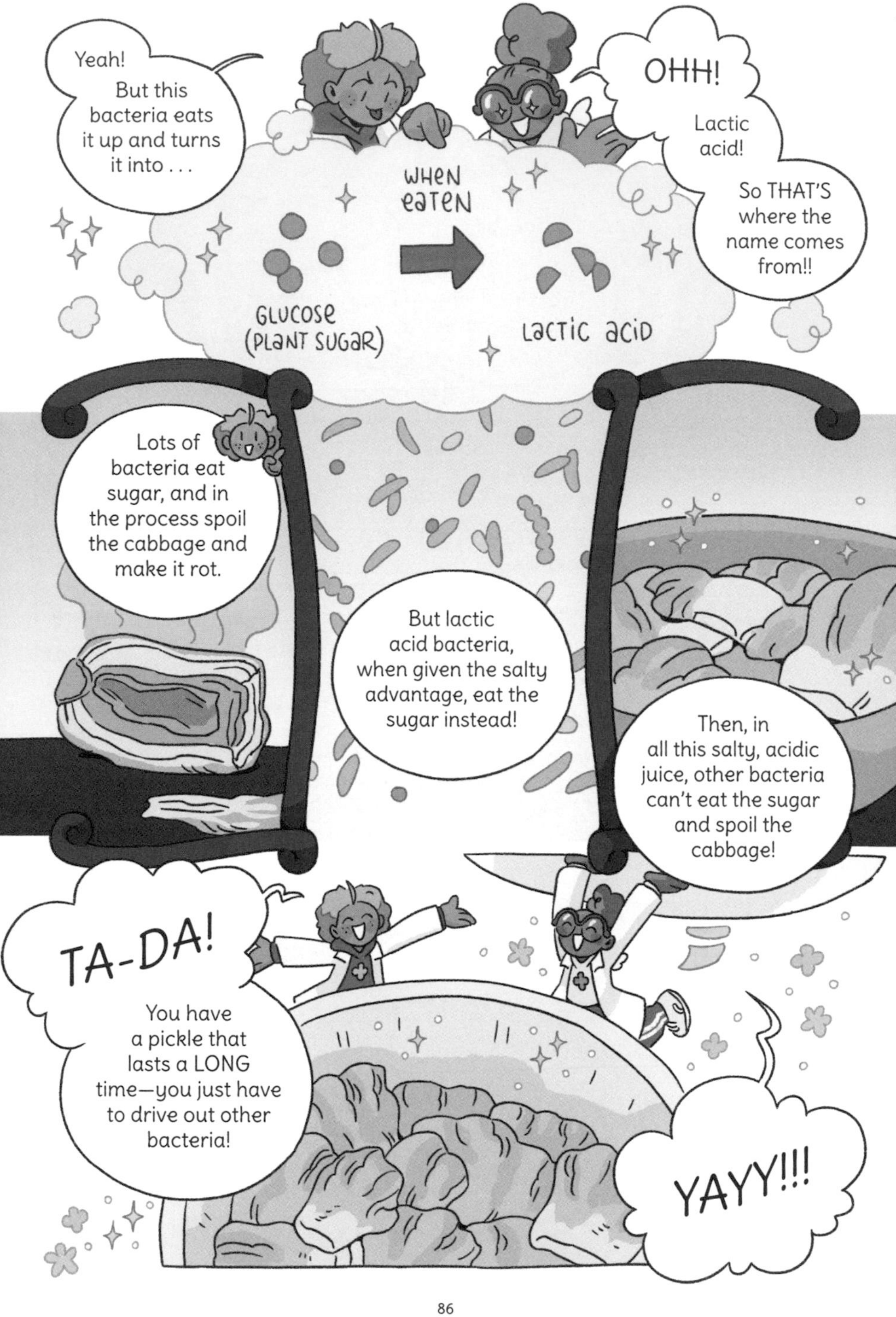
Yeah! But this bacteria eats it up and turns it into . . .
OHH! Lactic acid!
So THAT'S where the name comes from!!
WHEN EATEN
GLUCOSE (PLANT SUGAR)
LACTIC ACID
Lots of bacteria eat sugar, and in the process spoil the cabbage and make it rot.
But lactic acid bacteria, when given the salty advantage, eat the sugar instead!
Then, in all this salty, acidic juice, other bacteria can't eat the sugar and spoil the cabbage!
TA-DA!
You have a pickle that lasts a LONG time—you just have to drive out other bacteria!
YAYY!!!

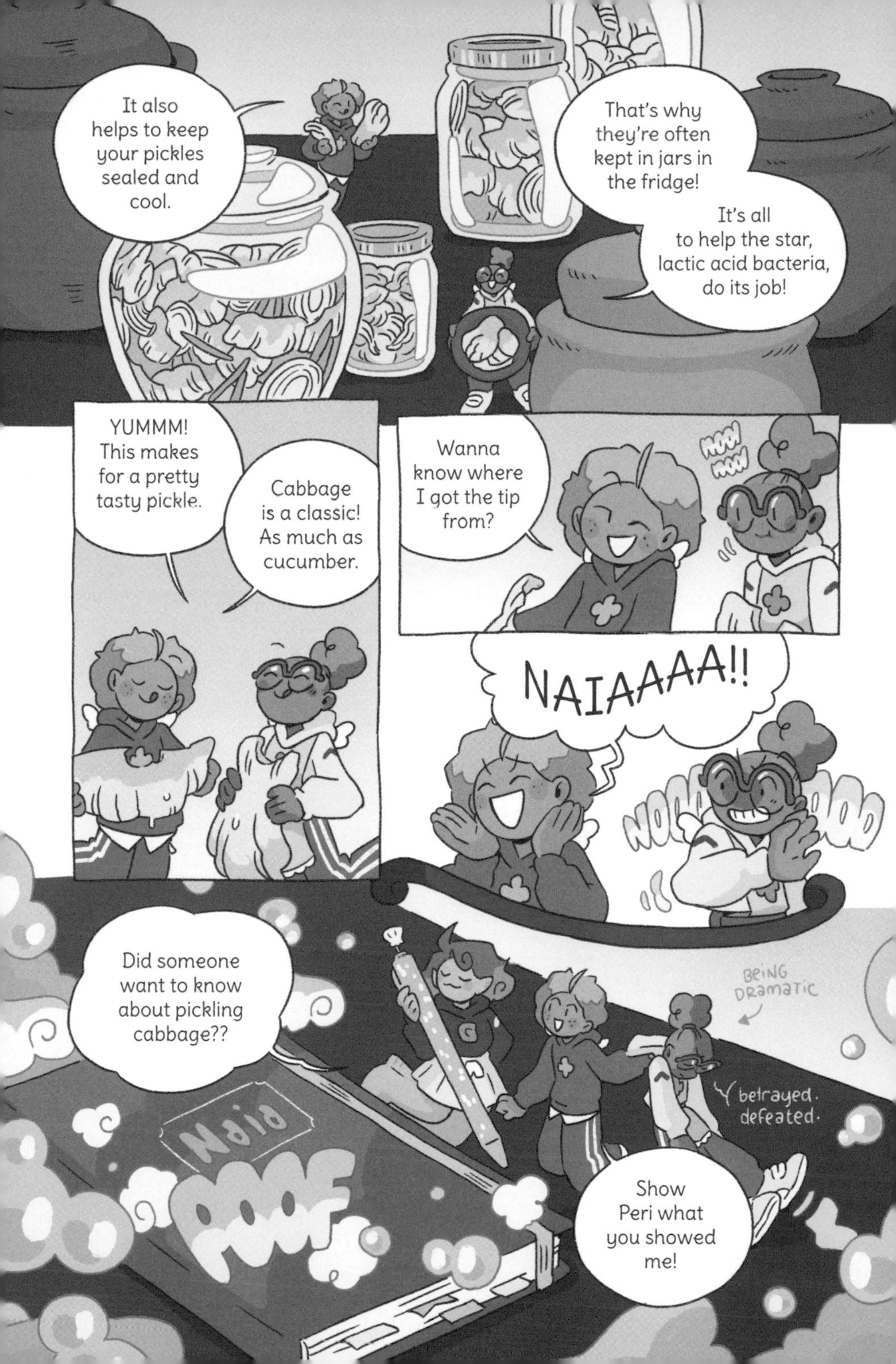
It also helps to keep your pickles sealed and cool.
That's why they're often kept in jars in the fridge!
It's all to help the star, lactic acid bacteria, do its job!
YUMMM! This makes for a pretty tasty pickle.
Cabbage is a classic! As much as cucumber.
Wanna know where I got the tip from?
NOM NOM
NAIAAAA!!
Did someone want to know about pickling cabbage??
Naia
POOF
BEING DRAMATIC
betrayed. defeated.
Show Peri what you showed me!

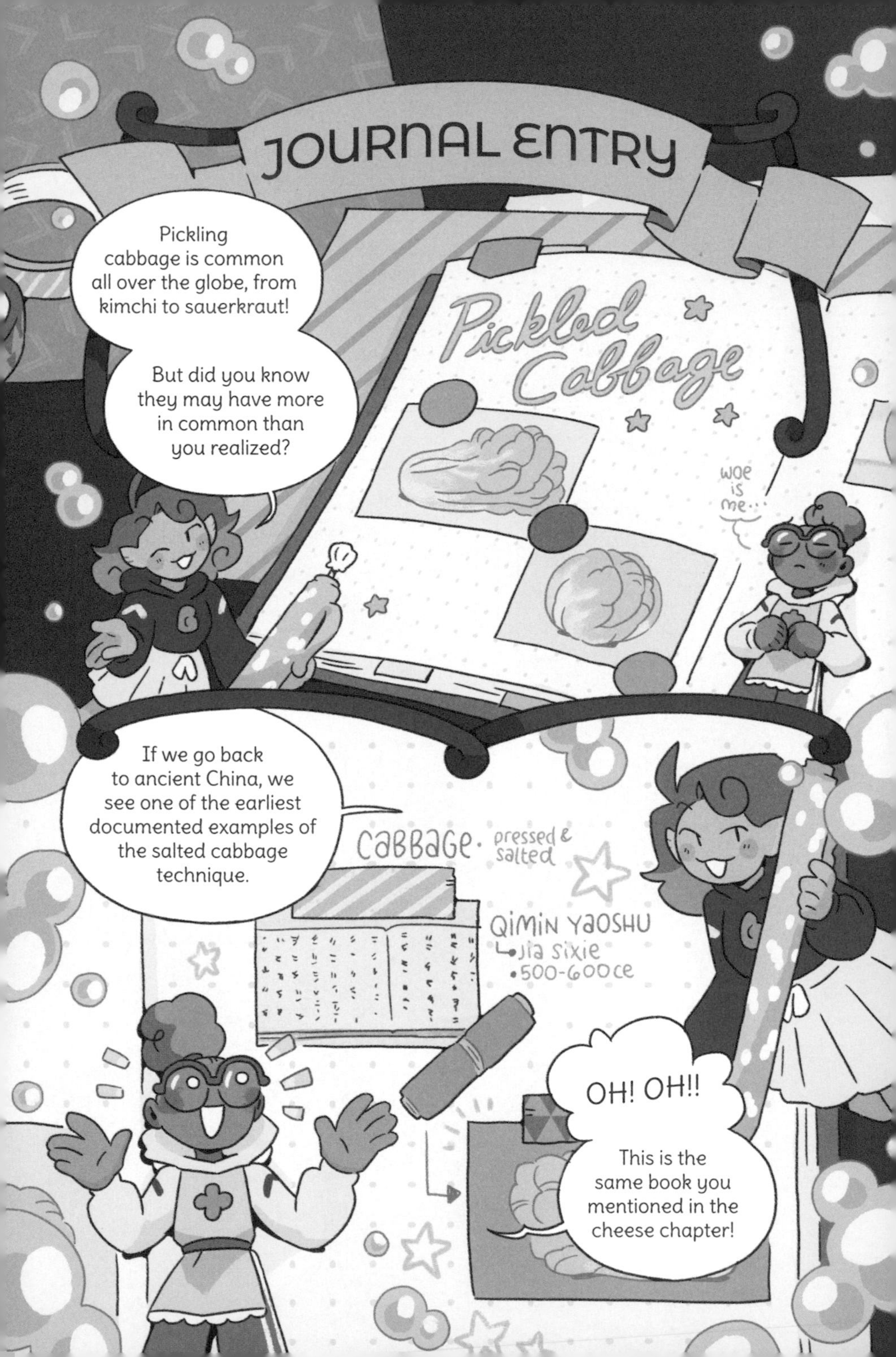
JOURNAL ENTRY
Pickling cabbage is common all over the globe, from kimchi to sauerkraut!
But did you know they may have more in common than you realized?
Pickled Cabbage
woe is me...
If we go back to ancient China, we see one of the earliest documented examples of the salted cabbage technique.
CABBAGE · pressed & salted
QIMIN YAOSHU
Jia Sixie
500-600 CE
OH! OH!!
This is the same book you mentioned in the cheese chapter!

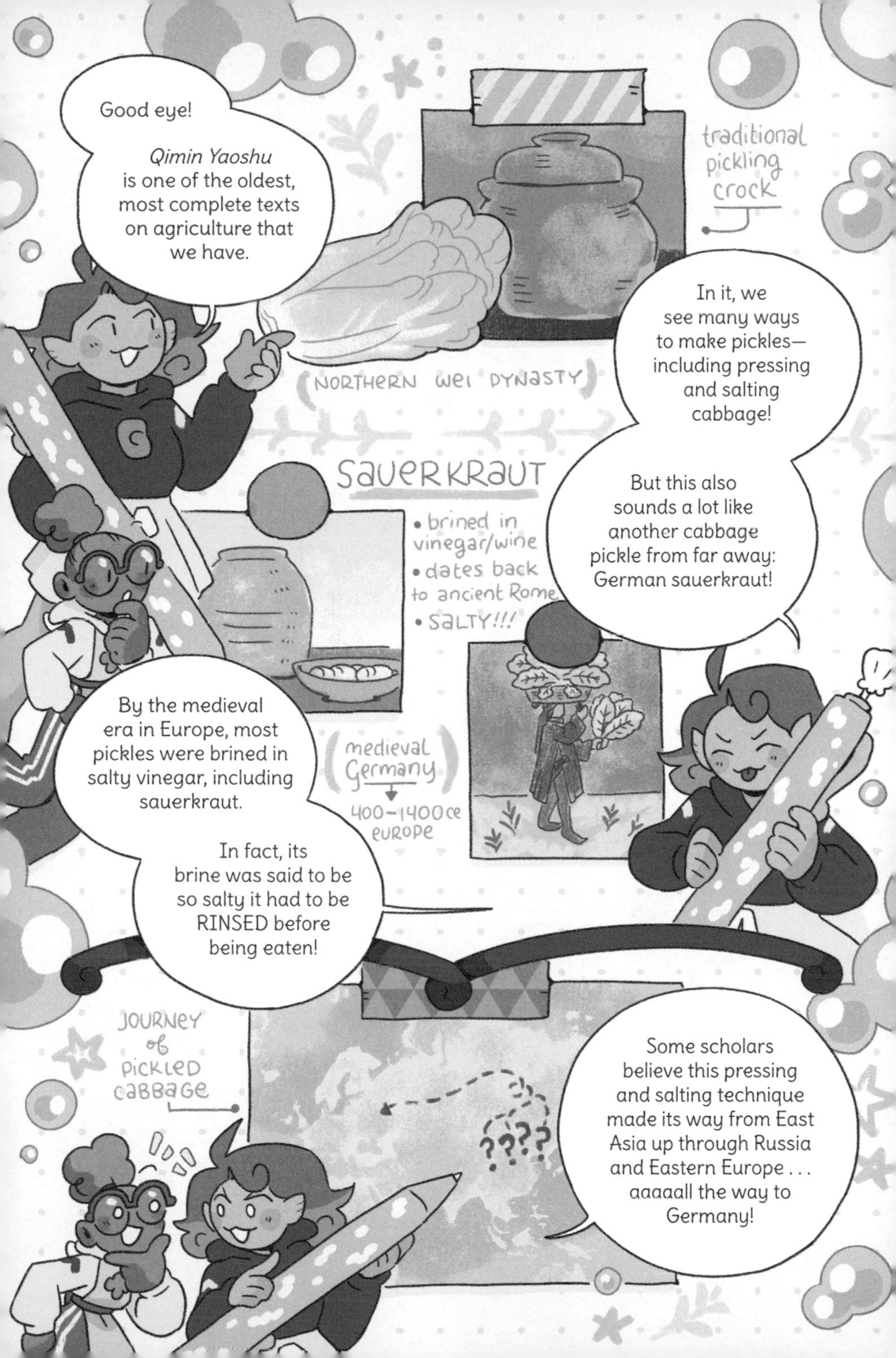

Good eye!
*Qimin Yaoshu* is one of the oldest, most complete texts on agriculture that we have.
traditional pickling crock
In it, we see many ways to make pickles—including pressing and salting cabbage!
(NORTHERN WEI DYNASTY)
SAUERKRAUT
• brined in vinegar/wine
• dates back to ancient Rome
• SALTY!!!
But this also sounds a lot like another cabbage pickle from far away: German sauerkraut!
By the medieval era in Europe, most pickles were brined in salty vinegar, including sauerkraut.
(medieval Germany)
400–1400 CE EUROPE
In fact, its brine was said to be so salty it had to be RINSED before being eaten!
JOURNEY of PICKLED CABBAGE
????
Some scholars believe this pressing and salting technique made its way from East Asia up through Russia and Eastern Europe . . . aaaaall the way to Germany!

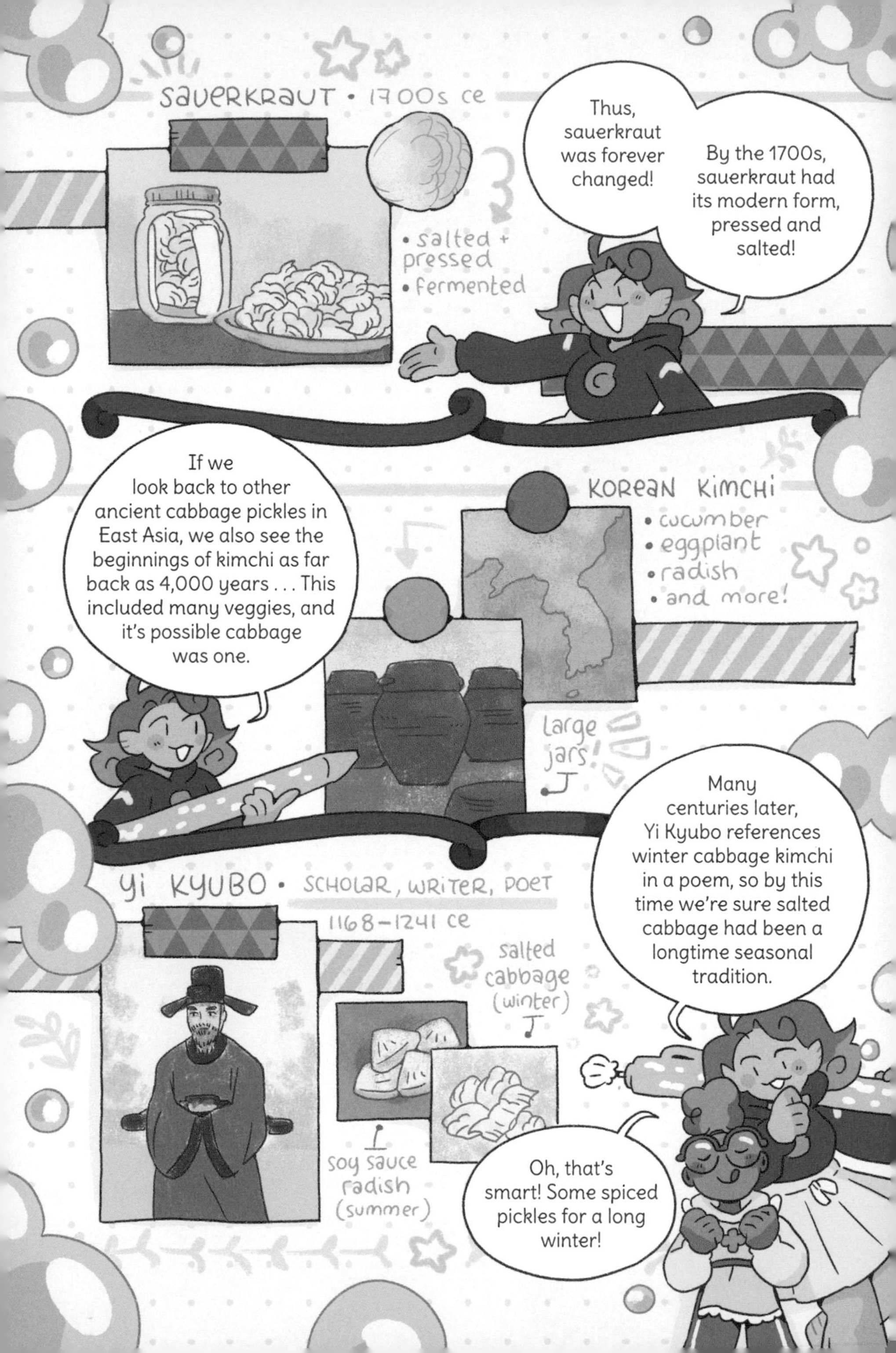
SAUERKRAUT • 1700s CE
• salted + pressed
• fermented
Thus, sauerkraut was forever changed!
By the 1700s, sauerkraut had its modern form, pressed and salted!
If we look back to other ancient cabbage pickles in East Asia, we also see the beginnings of kimchi as far back as 4,000 years . . . This included many veggies, and it's possible cabbage was one.
KOREAN KIMCHI
• cucumber
• eggplant
• radish
• and more!
large jars!
YI KYUBO • SCHOLAR, WRITER, POET
1168–1241 CE
salted cabbage (winter)
soy sauce radish (summer)
Many centuries later, Yi Kyubo references winter cabbage kimchi in a poem, so by this time we're sure salted cabbage had been a longtime seasonal tradition.
Oh, that's smart! Some spiced pickles for a long winter!

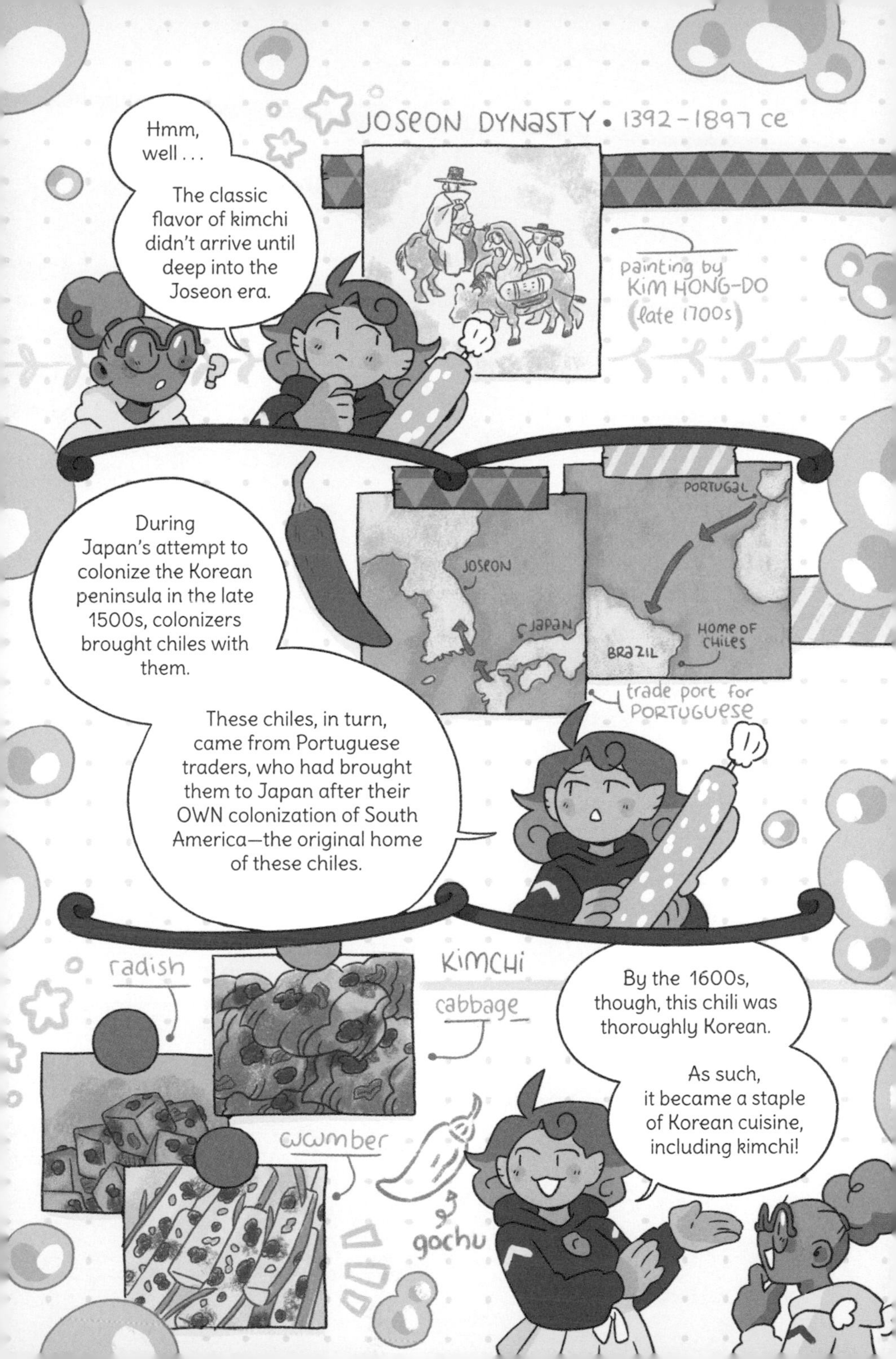
JOSEON DYNASTY • 1392–1897 CE
Hmm, well . . .
The classic flavor of kimchi didn't arrive until deep into the Joseon era.
painting by KIM HONG-DO (late 1700s)
During Japan's attempt to colonize the Korean peninsula in the late 1500s, colonizers brought chiles with them.
JOSEON
JAPAN
trade port for PORTUGUESE
PORTUGAL
BRAZIL
HOME OF CHILES
These chiles, in turn, came from Portuguese traders, who had brought them to Japan after their OWN colonization of South America—the original home of these chiles.
radish
KIMCHI
cabbage
cucumber
By the 1600s, though, this chili was thoroughly Korean.
As such, it became a staple of Korean cuisine, including kimchi!
고추
gochu

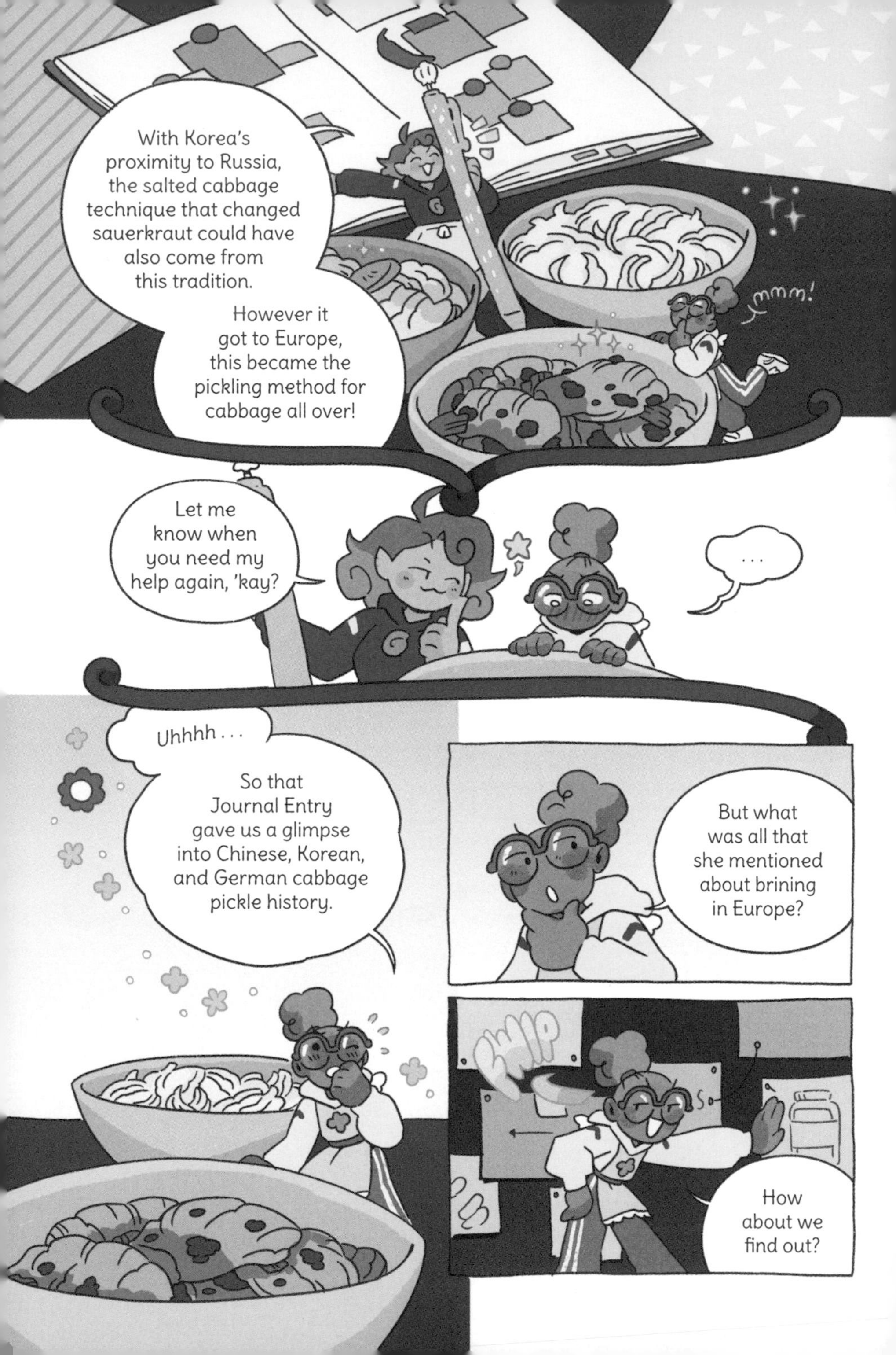
With Korea's proximity to Russia, the salted cabbage technique that changed sauerkraut could have also come from this tradition.
However it got to Europe, this became the pickling method for cabbage all over!
mmm!
Let me know when you need my help again, 'kay?
. . .
Uhhhh . . .
So that Journal Entry gave us a glimpse into Chinese, Korean, and German cabbage pickle history.
But what was all that she mentioned about brining in Europe?
SWIP
How about we find out?

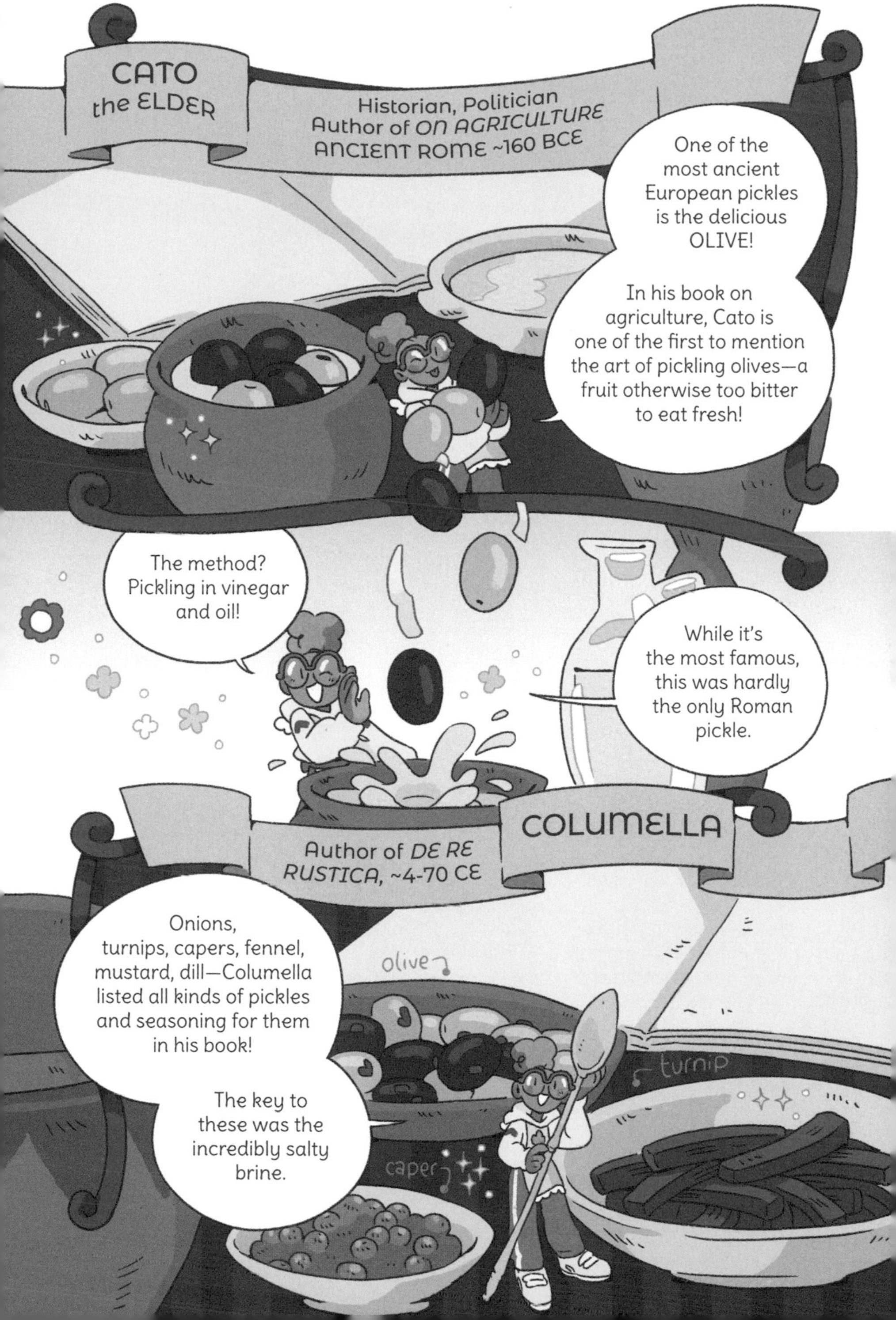
CATO the ELDER
Historian, Politician Author of ON AGRICULTURE ANCIENT ROME ~160 BCE
One of the most ancient European pickles is the delicious OLIVE!
In his book on agriculture, Cato is one of the first to mention the art of pickling olives—a fruit otherwise too bitter to eat fresh!
The method? Pickling in vinegar and oil!
While it's the most famous, this was hardly the only Roman pickle.
COLUMELLA
Author of DE RE RUSTICA, ~4-70 CE
Onions, turnips, capers, fennel, mustard, dill—Columella listed all kinds of pickles and seasoning for them in his book!
olive
turnip
The key to these was the incredibly salty brine.
caper

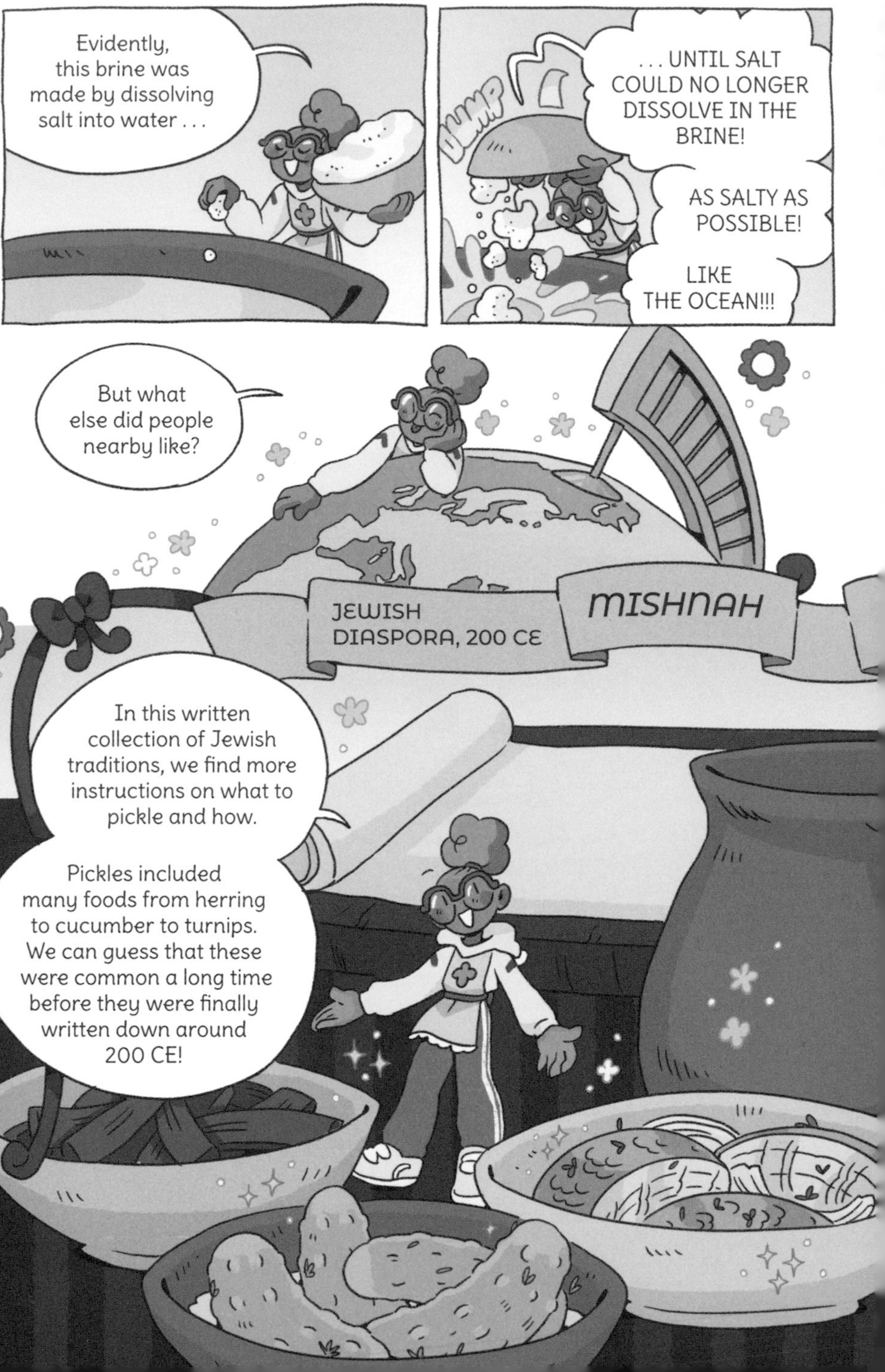

Evidently, this brine was made by dissolving salt into water . . .
. . . UNTIL SALT COULD NO LONGER DISSOLVE IN THE BRINE!
AS SALTY AS POSSIBLE!
LIKE THE OCEAN!!!
But what else did people nearby like?
JEWISH DIASPORA, 200 CE
MISHNAH
In this written collection of Jewish traditions, we find more instructions on what to pickle and how.
Pickles included many foods from herring to cucumber to turnips. We can guess that these were common a long time before they were finally written down around 200 CE!

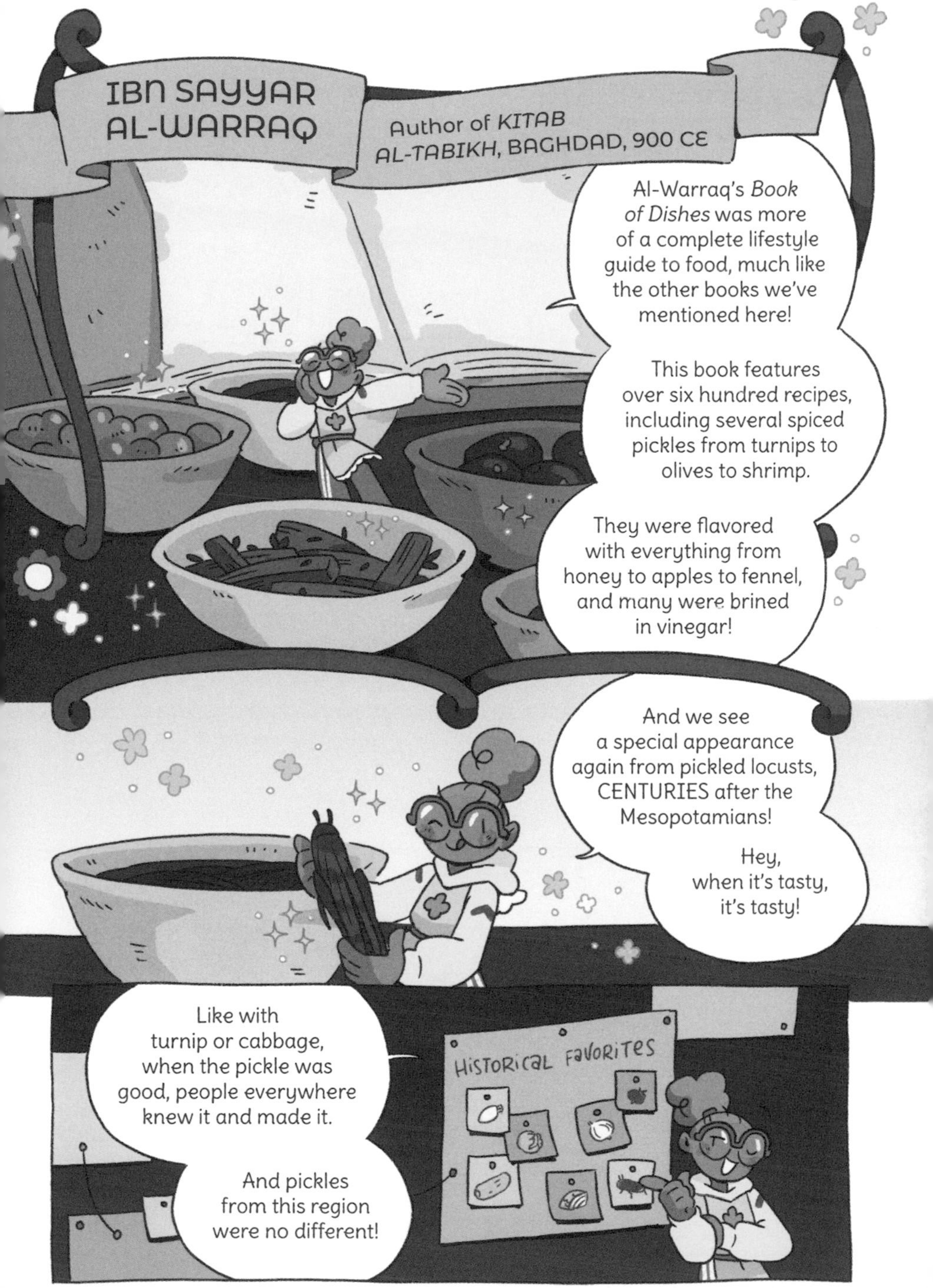
IBN SAYYAR AL-WARRAQ
Author of *KITAB AL-TABIKH*, BAGHDAD, 900 CE
Al-Warraq's *Book of Dishes* was more of a complete lifestyle guide to food, much like the other books we've mentioned here!
This book features over six hundred recipes, including several spiced pickles from turnips to olives to shrimp.
They were flavored with everything from honey to apples to fennel, and many were brined in vinegar!
And we see a special appearance again from pickled locusts, CENTURIES after the Mesopotamians!
Hey, when it's tasty, it's tasty!
Like with turnip or cabbage, when the pickle was good, people everywhere knew it and made it.
HISTORICAL FAVORITES
And pickles from this region were no different!

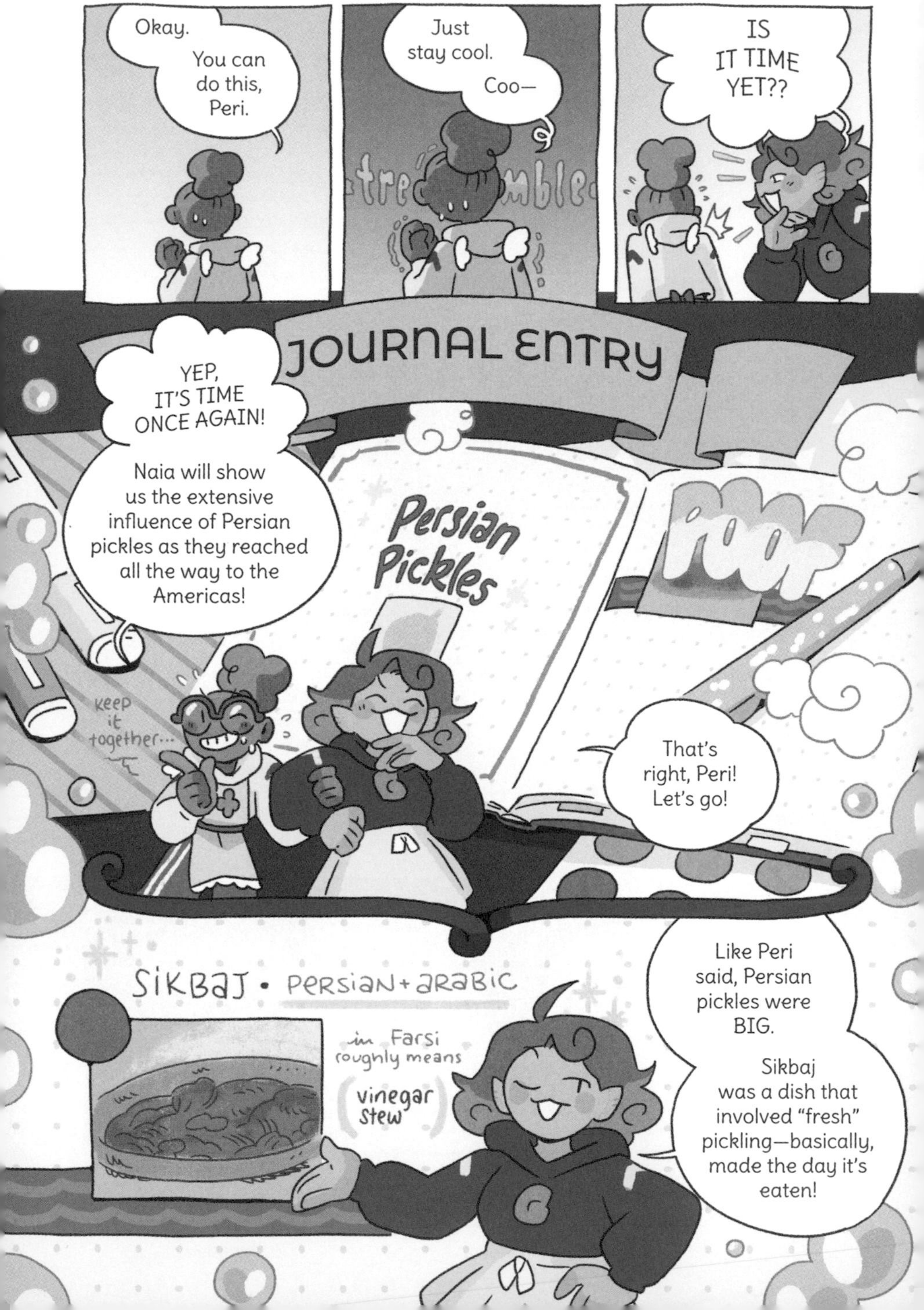

Okay.
You can do this, Peri.
Just stay cool.
Coo—
tremble
IS IT TIME YET??
JOURNAL ENTRY
YEP, IT'S TIME ONCE AGAIN!
Naia will show us the extensive influence of Persian pickles as they reached all the way to the Americas!
Persian Pickles
POOF
keep it together...
That's right, Peri! Let's go!
SIKBAJ • PERSIAN + ARABIC
in Farsi roughly means
(vinegar stew)
Like Peri said, Persian pickles were BIG.
Sikbaj was a dish that involved "fresh" pickling—basically, made the day it's eaten!

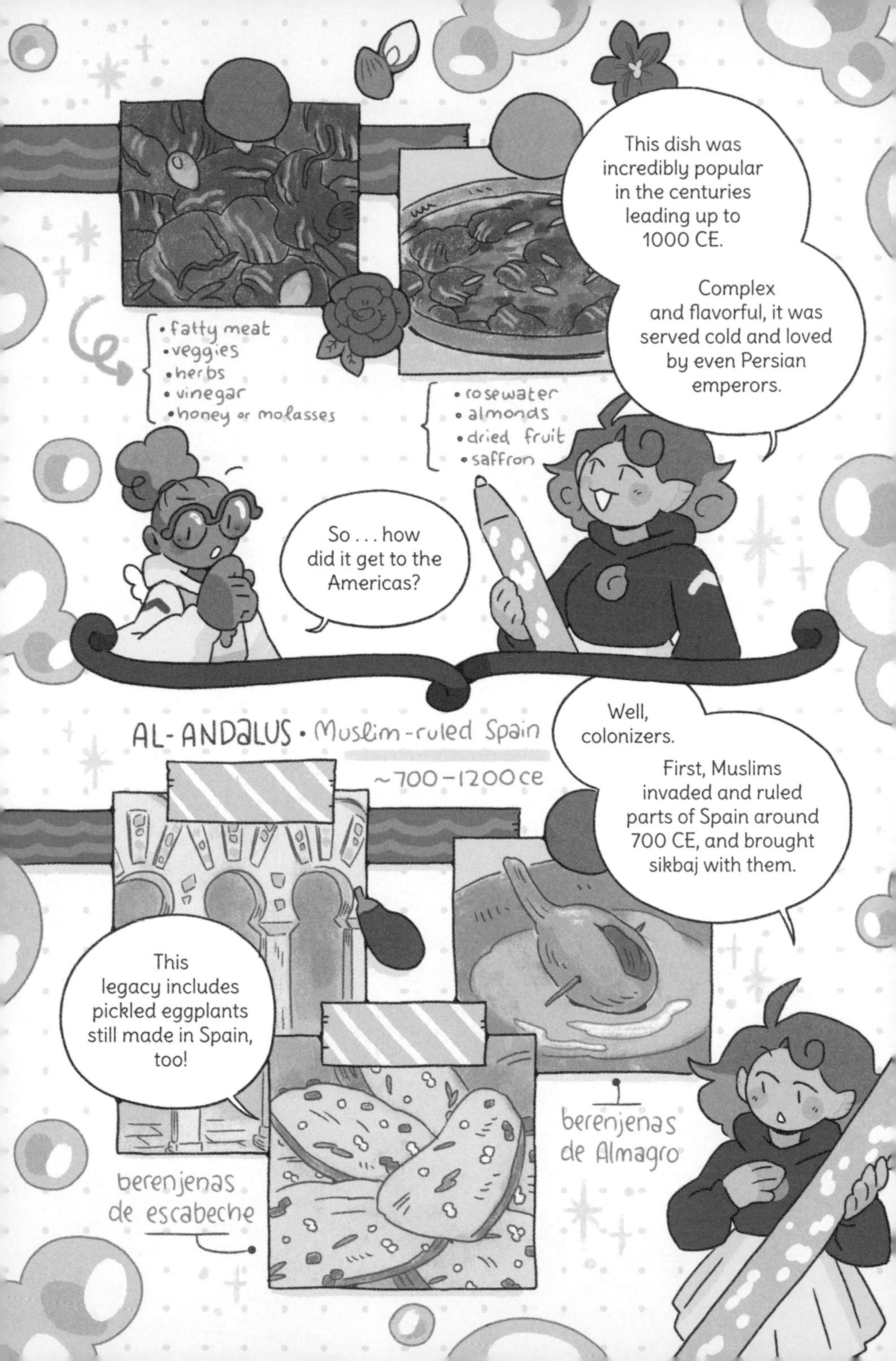
• fatty meat
• veggies
• herbs
• vinegar
• honey or molasses
• rosewater
• almonds
• dried fruit
• saffron
This dish was incredibly popular in the centuries leading up to 1000 CE.
Complex and flavorful, it was served cold and loved by even Persian emperors.
So . . . how did it get to the Americas?
Well, colonizers.
First, Muslims invaded and ruled parts of Spain around 700 CE, and brought sikbaj with them.
AL-ANDALUS • Muslim-ruled Spain
~700–1200 CE
This legacy includes pickled eggplants still made in Spain, too!
berenjenas de escabeche
berenjenas de Almagro

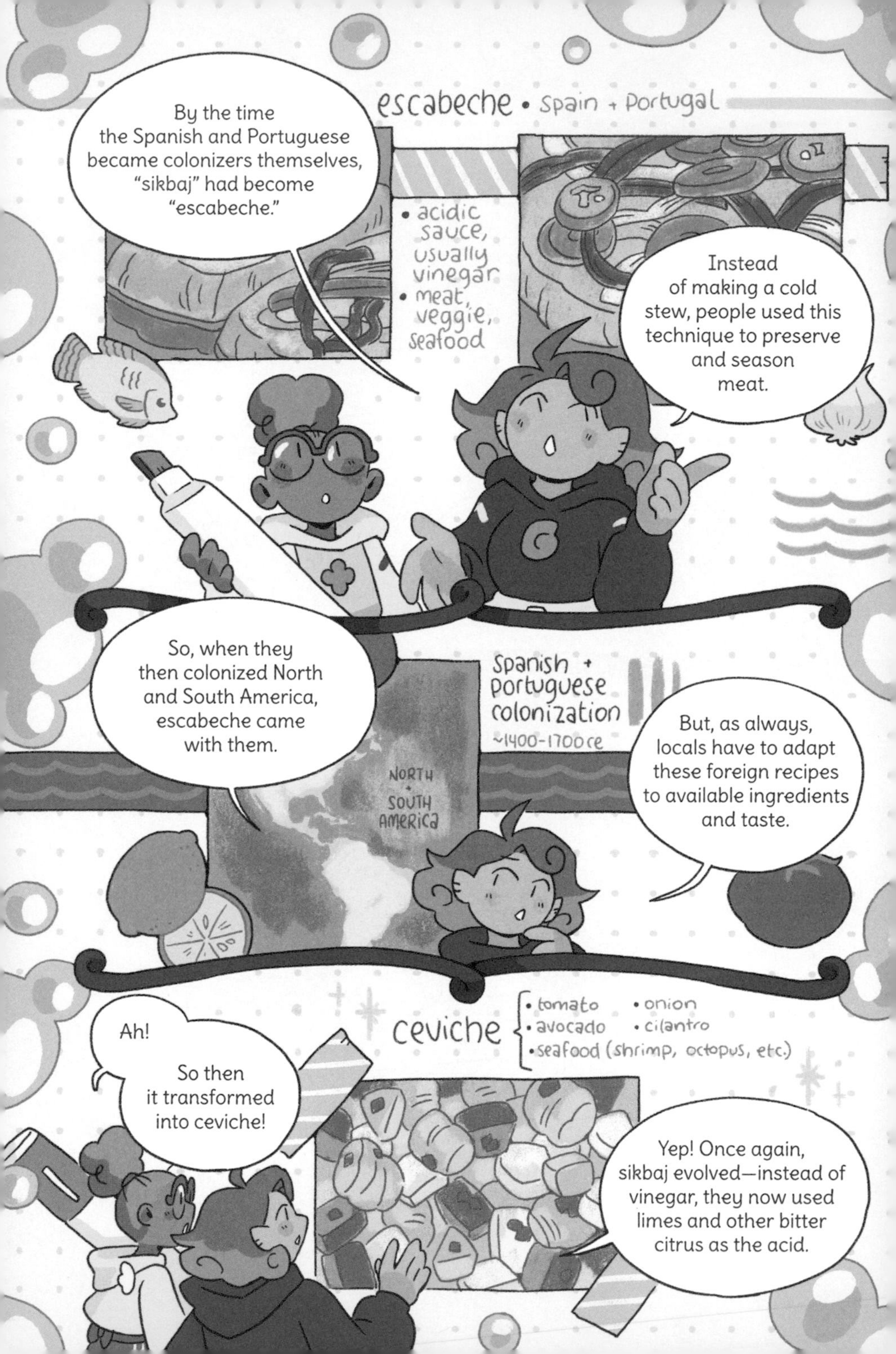
By the time the Spanish and Portuguese became colonizers themselves, "sikbaj" had become "escabeche."
escabeche • Spain + Portugal
• acidic sauce, usually vinegar
• meat, veggie, seafood
Instead of making a cold stew, people used this technique to preserve and season meat.
So, when they then colonized North and South America, escabeche came with them.
Spanish + Portuguese colonization
~1400-1700 CE
NORTH + SOUTH AMERICA
But, as always, locals have to adapt these foreign recipes to available ingredients and taste.
ceviche
• tomato
• onion
• avocado
• cilantro
• seafood (shrimp, octopus, etc.)
Ah!
So then it transformed into ceviche!
Yep! Once again, sikbaj evolved—instead of vinegar, they now used limes and other bitter citrus as the acid.

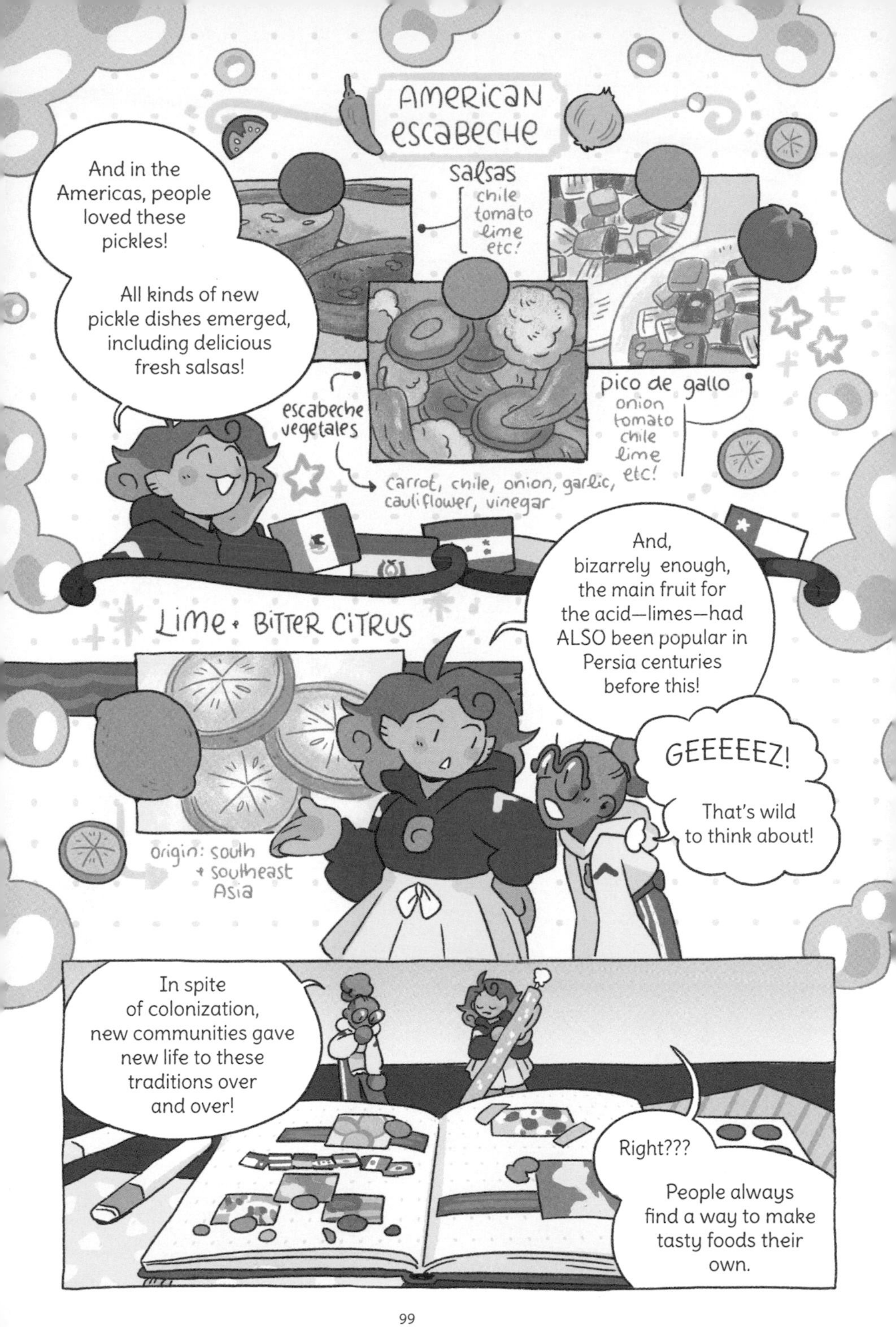
American escabeche
And in the Americas, people loved these pickles!
All kinds of new pickle dishes emerged, including delicious fresh salsas!
salsas
chile tomato lime etc!
escabeche vegetales
carrot, chile, onion, garlic, cauliflower, vinegar
pico de gallo
onion tomato chile lime etc!
Lime + Bitter Citrus
origin: south + southeast Asia
And, bizarrely enough, the main fruit for the acid—limes—had ALSO been popular in Persia centuries before this!
GEEEEEZ!
That's wild to think about!
In spite of colonization, new communities gave new life to these traditions over and over!
Right???
People always find a way to make tasty foods their own.

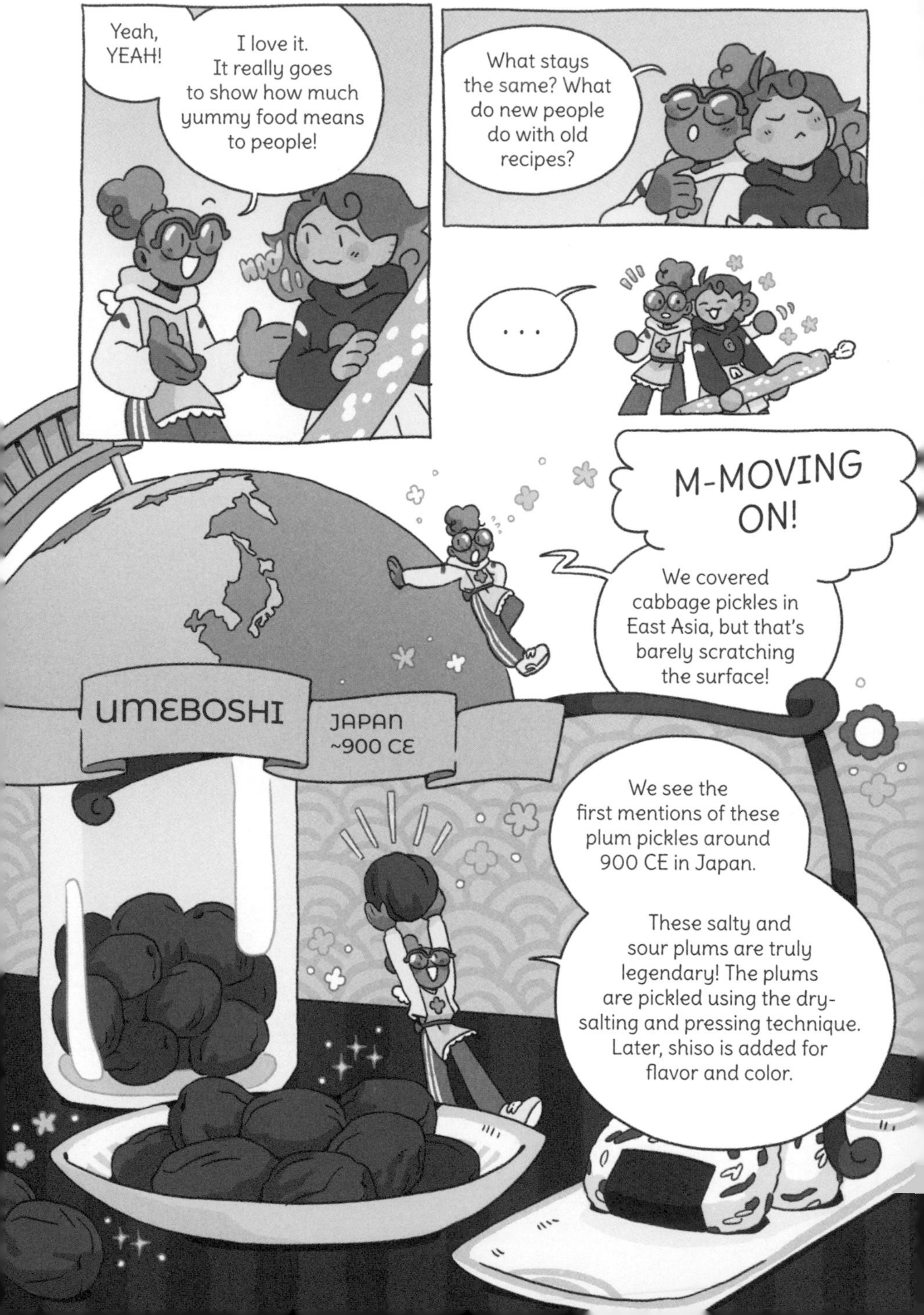
Yeah, YEAH!
I love it. It really goes to show how much yummy food means to people!
What stays the same? What do new people do with old recipes?
. . .
M-MOVING ON!
We covered cabbage pickles in East Asia, but that's barely scratching the surface!
UMEBOSHI
JAPAN ~900 CE
We see the first mentions of these plum pickles around 900 CE in Japan.
These salty and sour plums are truly legendary! The plums are pickled using the dry-salting and pressing technique. Later, shiso is added for flavor and color.

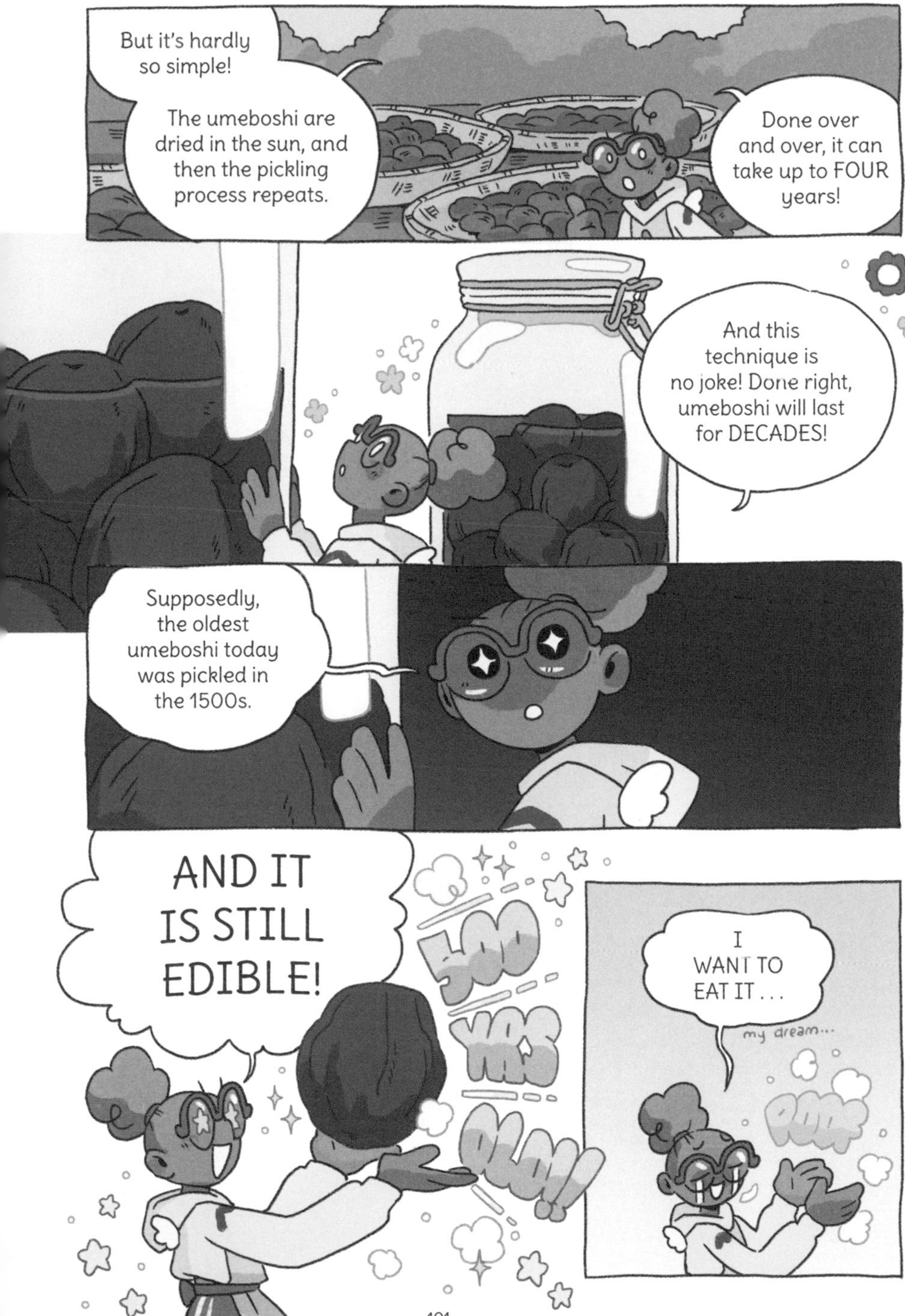
But it's hardly so simple!
The umeboshi are dried in the sun, and then the pickling process repeats.
Done over and over, it can take up to FOUR years!
And this technique is no joke! Done right, umeboshi will last for DECADES!
Supposedly, the oldest umeboshi today was pickled in the 1500s.
AND IT IS STILL EDIBLE!
500 YRS OLD!!
I WANT TO EAT IT . . .
my dream...
POOF

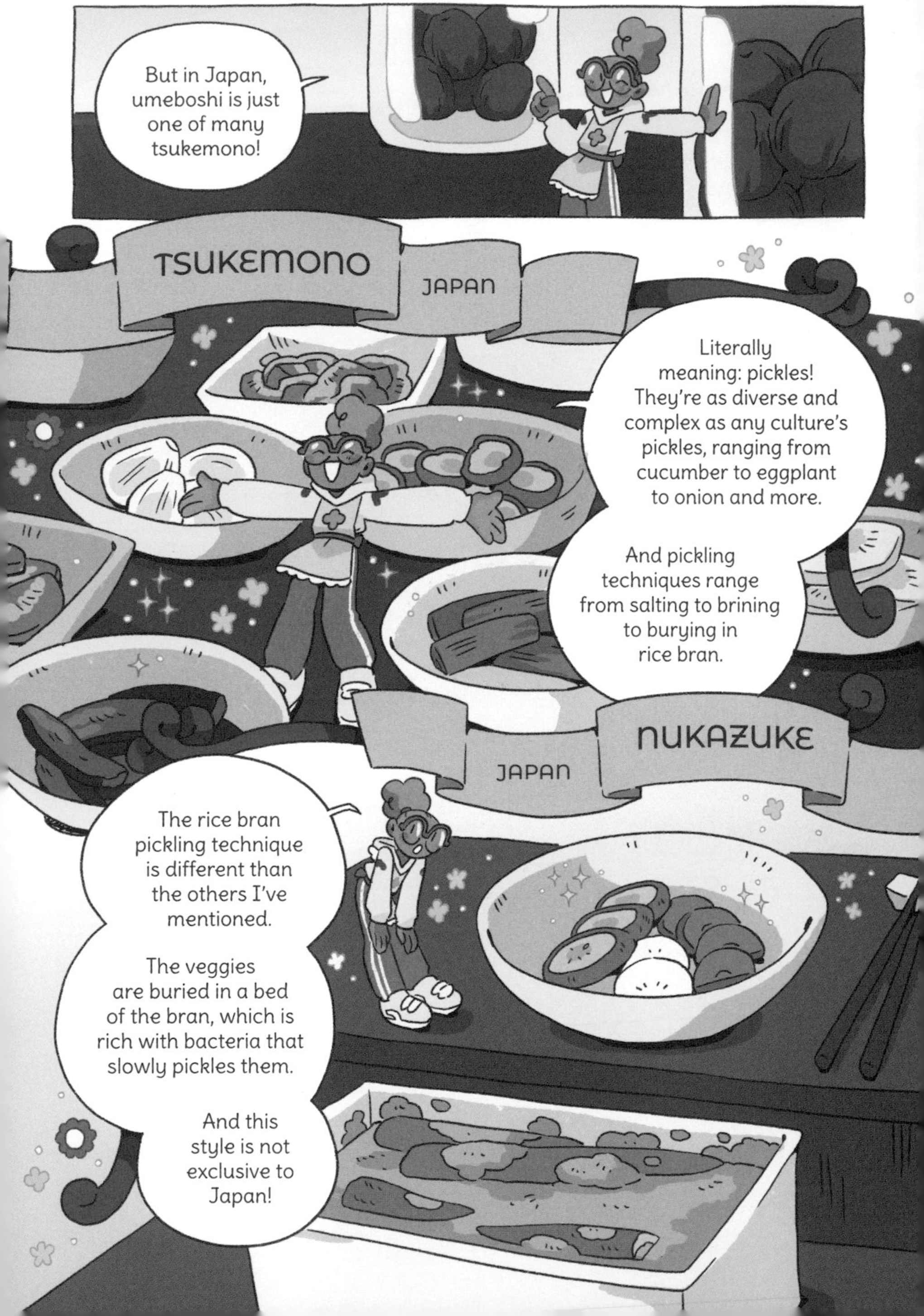

But in Japan, umeboshi is just one of many tsukemono!
TSUKEMONO
JAPAN
Literally meaning: pickles! They're as diverse and complex as any culture's pickles, ranging from cucumber to eggplant to onion and more.
And pickling techniques range from salting to brining to burying in rice bran.
NUKAZUKE
JAPAN
The rice bran pickling technique is different than the others I've mentioned.
The veggies are buried in a bed of the bran, which is rich with bacteria that slowly pickles them.
And this style is not exclusive to Japan!

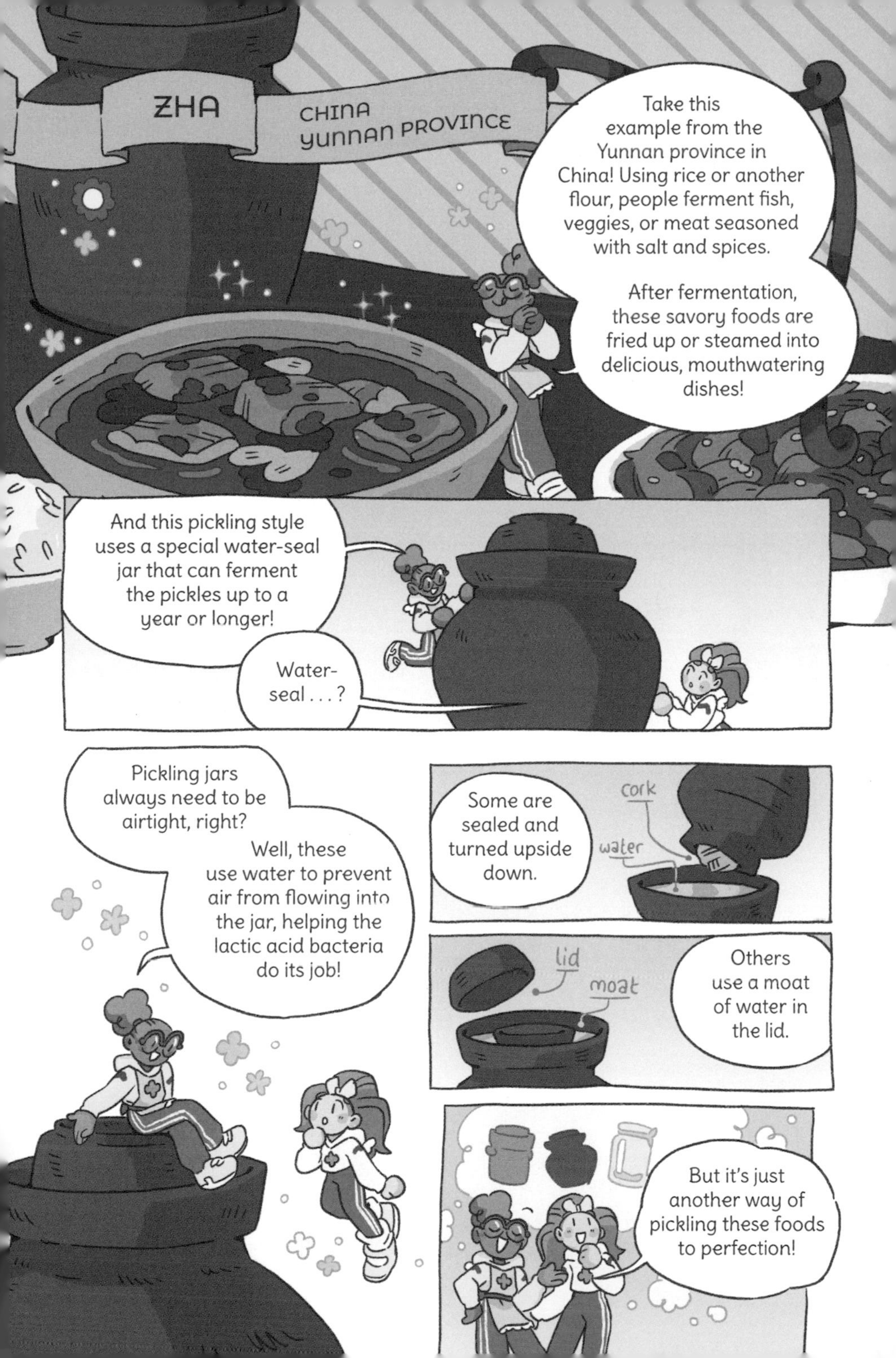
ZHA
CHINA YUNNAN PROVINCE
Take this example from the Yunnan province in China! Using rice or another flour, people ferment fish, veggies, or meat seasoned with salt and spices.
After fermentation, these savory foods are fried up or steamed into delicious, mouthwatering dishes!
And this pickling style uses a special water-seal jar that can ferment the pickles up to a year or longer!
Water-seal . . . ?
Pickling jars always need to be airtight, right?
Well, these use water to prevent air from flowing into the jar, helping the lactic acid bacteria do its job!
Some are sealed and turned upside down.
cork
water
lid
moat
Others use a moat of water in the lid.
But it's just another way of pickling these foods to perfection!

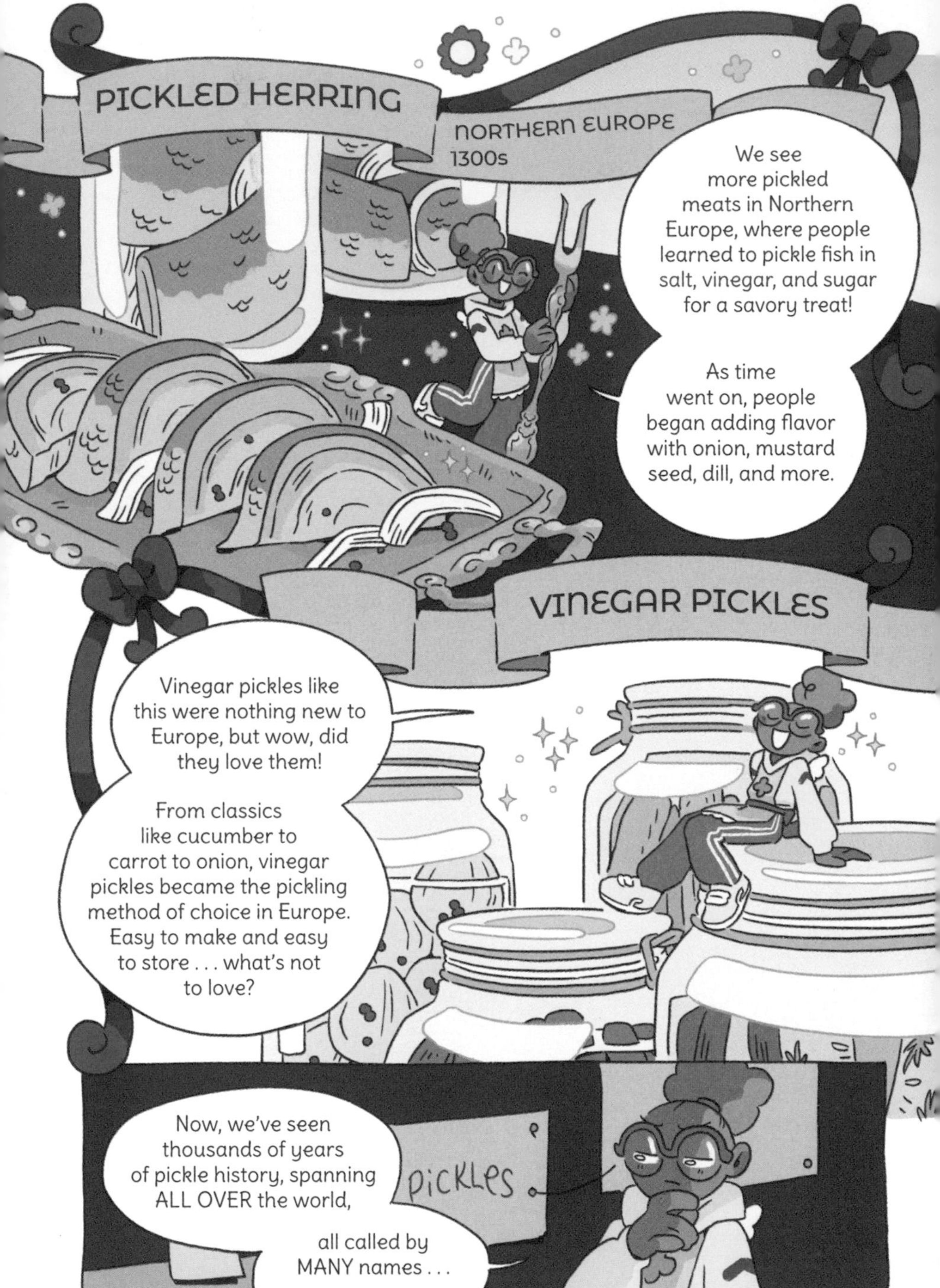

PICKLED HERRING
NORTHERN EUROPE 1300s
We see more pickled meats in Northern Europe, where people learned to pickle fish in salt, vinegar, and sugar for a savory treat!
As time went on, people began adding flavor with onion, mustard seed, dill, and more.
VINEGAR PICKLES
Vinegar pickles like this were nothing new to Europe, but wow, did they love them!
From classics like cucumber to carrot to onion, vinegar pickles became the pickling method of choice in Europe. Easy to make and easy to store . . . what's not to love?
Now, we've seen thousands of years of pickle history, spanning ALL OVER the world,
PiCKLES
all called by MANY names . . .

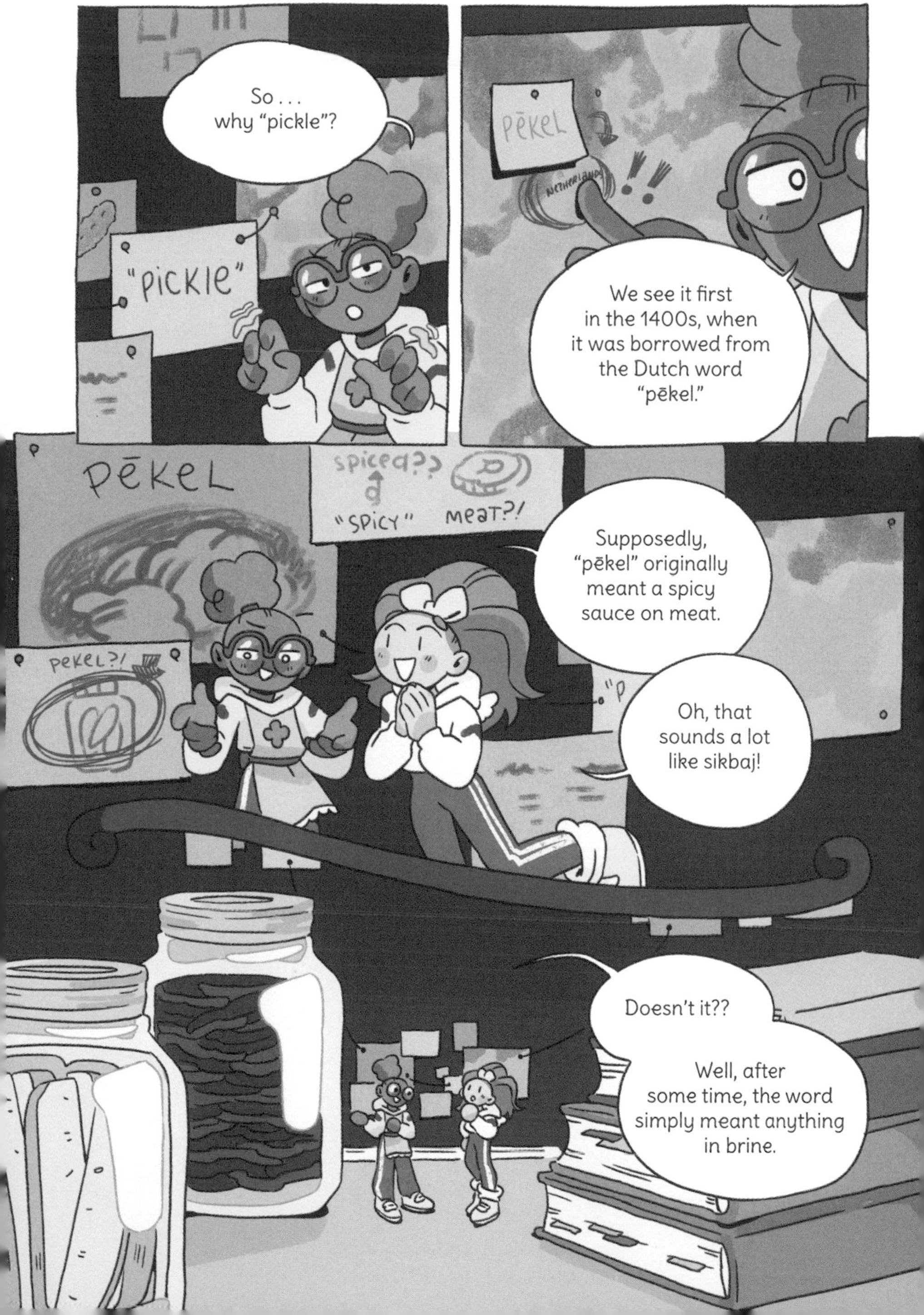

"pickle"
So . . . why "pickle"?
pēkel
NETHERLANDS
We see it first in the 1400s, when it was borrowed from the Dutch word "pēkel."
pēkel
spiced?? "spicy" meat?!
pekel?!
Supposedly, "pēkel" originally meant a spicy sauce on meat.
Oh, that sounds a lot like sikbaj!
Doesn't it??
Well, after some time, the word simply meant anything in brine.

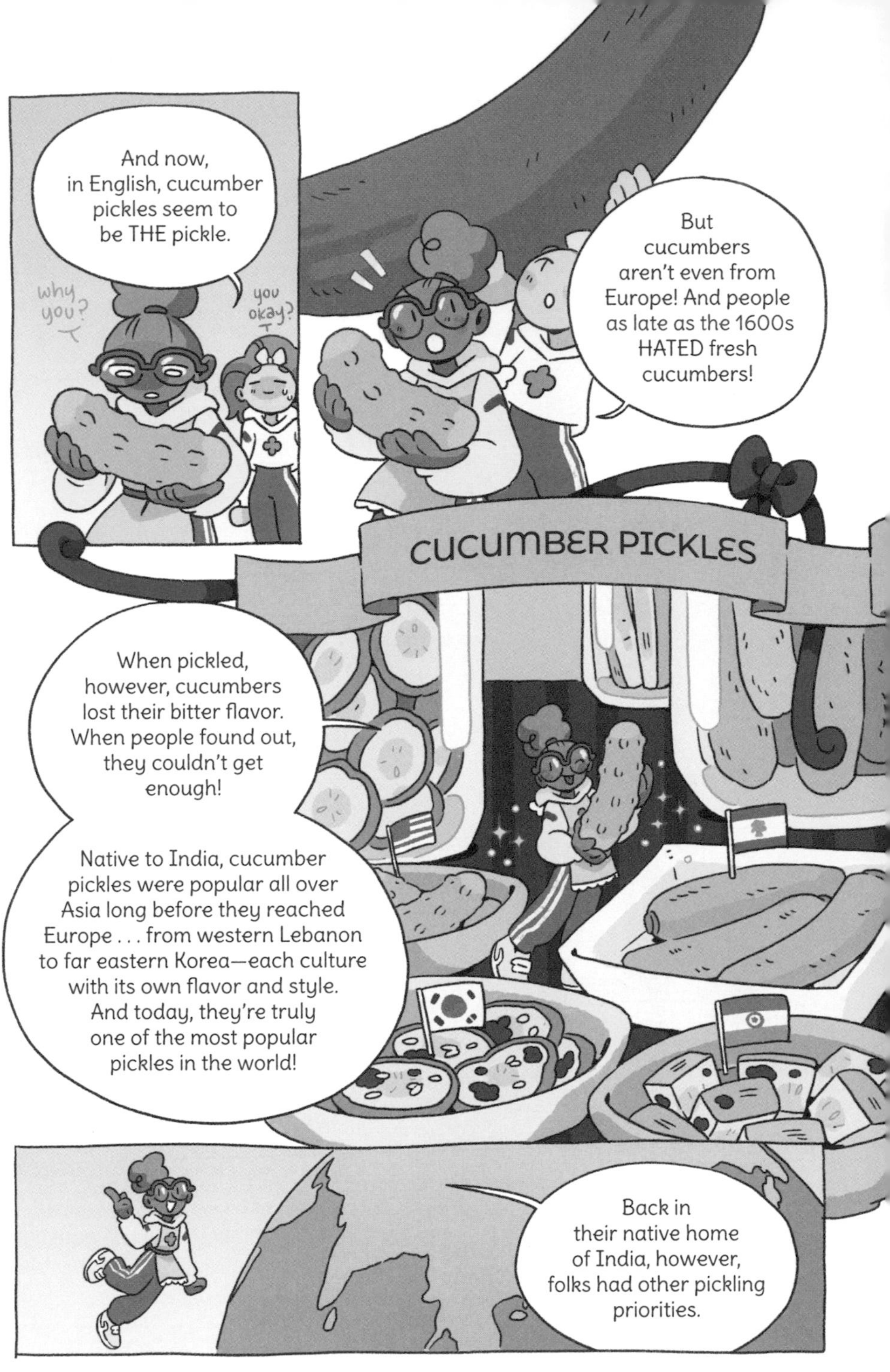
And now, in English, cucumber pickles seem to be THE pickle.
why you?
you okay?
But cucumbers aren't even from Europe! And people as late as the 1600s HATED fresh cucumbers!
CUCUMBER PICKLES
When pickled, however, cucumbers lost their bitter flavor. When people found out, they couldn't get enough!
Native to India, cucumber pickles were popular all over Asia long before they reached Europe . . . from western Lebanon to far eastern Korea—each culture with its own flavor and style. And today, they're truly one of the most popular pickles in the world!
Back in their native home of India, however, folks had other pickling priorities.

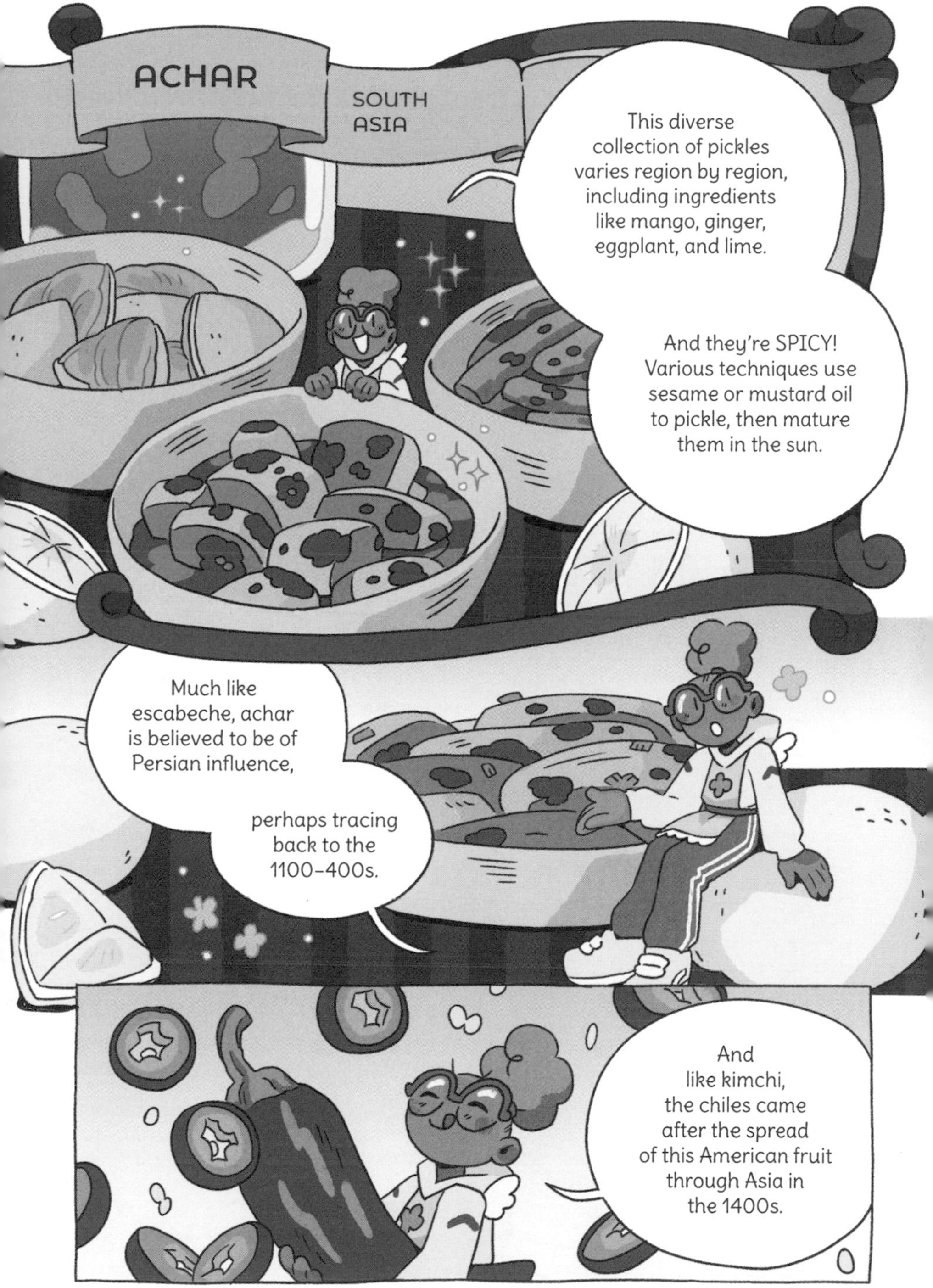
ACHAR
SOUTH ASIA
This diverse collection of pickles varies region by region, including ingredients like mango, ginger, eggplant, and lime.
And they're SPICY! Various techniques use sesame or mustard oil to pickle, then mature them in the sun.
Much like escabeche, achar is believed to be of Persian influence,
perhaps tracing back to the 1100–400s.
And like kimchi, the chiles came after the spread of this American fruit through Asia in the 1400s.

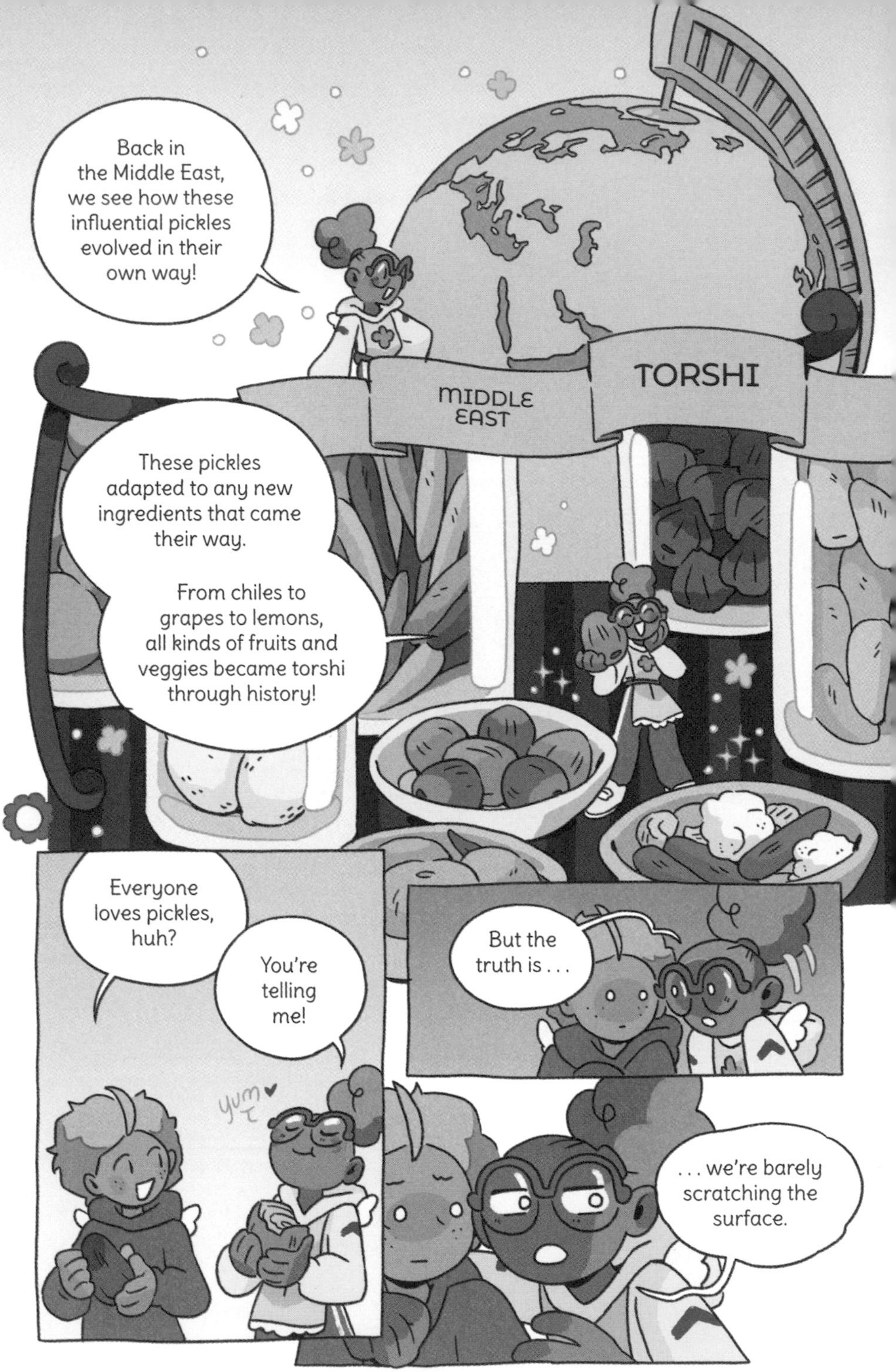
Back in the Middle East, we see how these influential pickles evolved in their own way!
MIDDLE EAST
TORSHI
These pickles adapted to any new ingredients that came their way.
From chiles to grapes to lemons, all kinds of fruits and veggies became torshi through history!
Everyone loves pickles, huh?
You're telling me!
yum
But the truth is . . .
. . . we're barely scratching the surface.

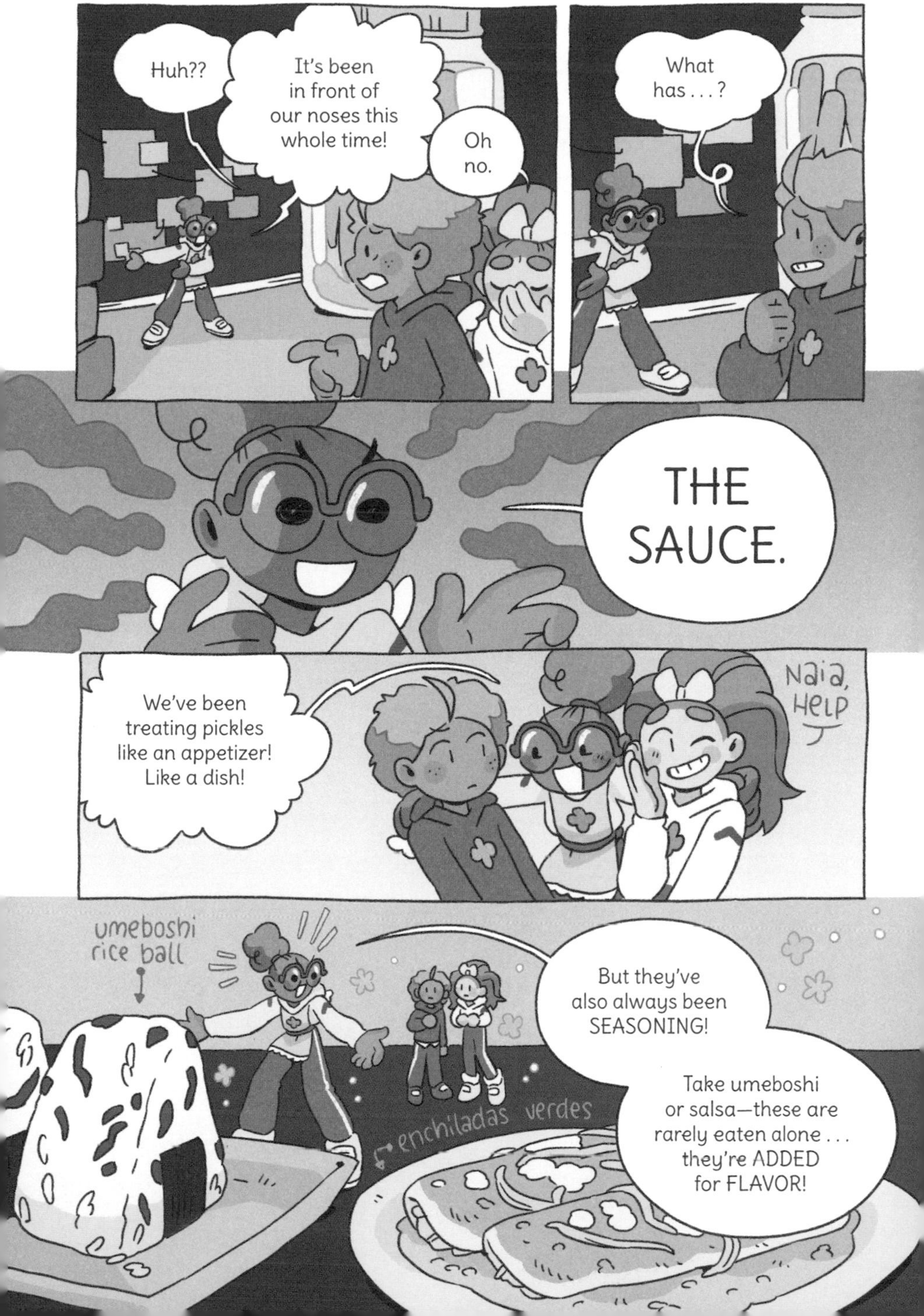
Huh??
It's been in front of our noses this whole time!
Oh no.
What has . . . ?
THE SAUCE.
We've been treating pickles like an appetizer! Like a dish!
Naia, HELP
umeboshi rice ball
But they've also always been SEASONING!
enchiladas verdes
Take umeboshi or salsa—these are rarely eaten alone . . . they're ADDED for FLAVOR!

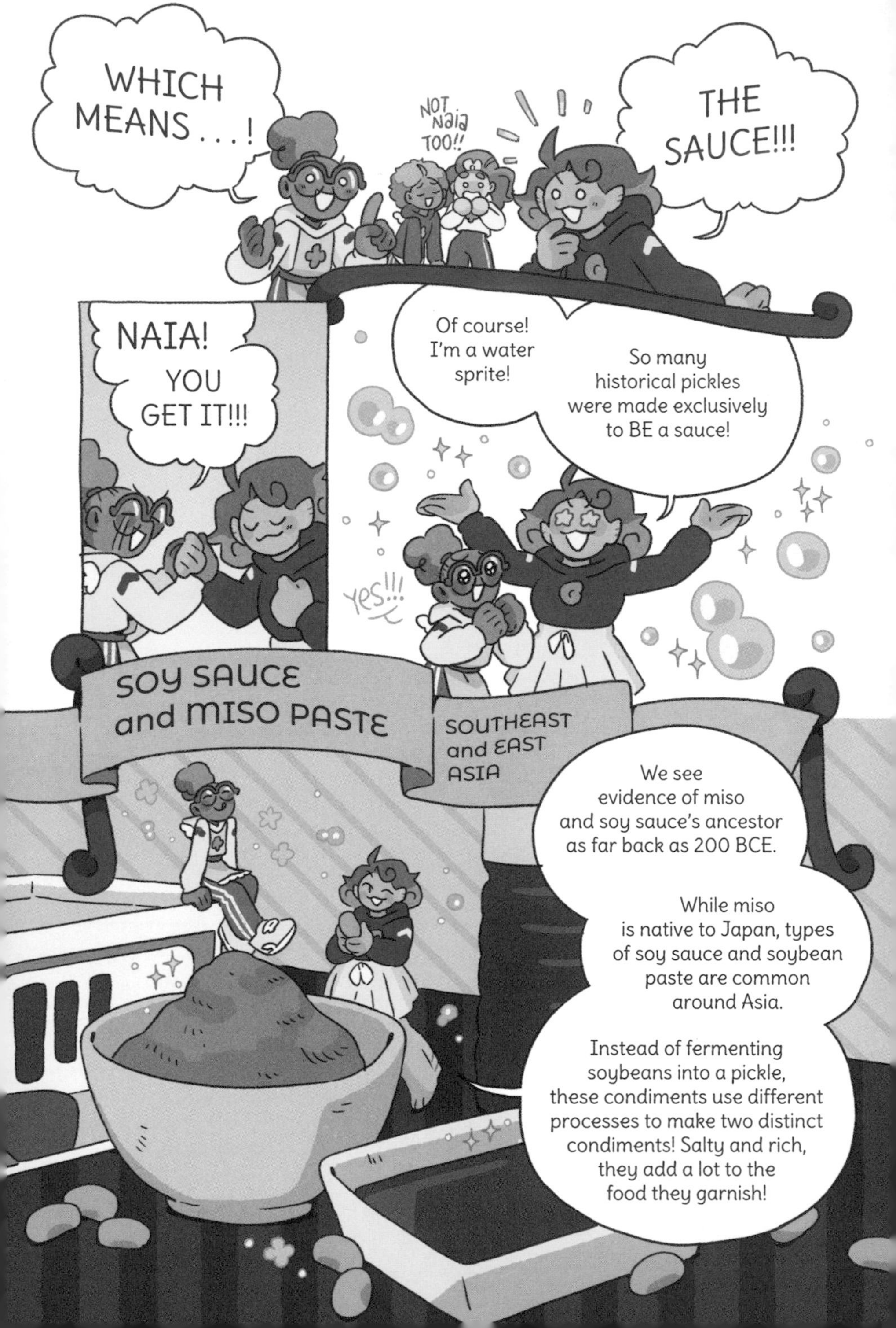
WHICH MEANS . . . !
NOT Naia TOO!!
THE SAUCE!!!
NAIA! YOU GET IT!!!
Of course! I'm a water sprite!
So many historical pickles were made exclusively to BE a sauce!
YES!!!
SOY SAUCE and MISO PASTE
SOUTHEAST and EAST ASIA
We see evidence of miso and soy sauce's ancestor as far back as 200 BCE.
While miso is native to Japan, types of soy sauce and soybean paste are common around Asia.
Instead of fermenting soybeans into a pickle, these condiments use different processes to make two distinct condiments! Salty and rich, they add a lot to the food they garnish!

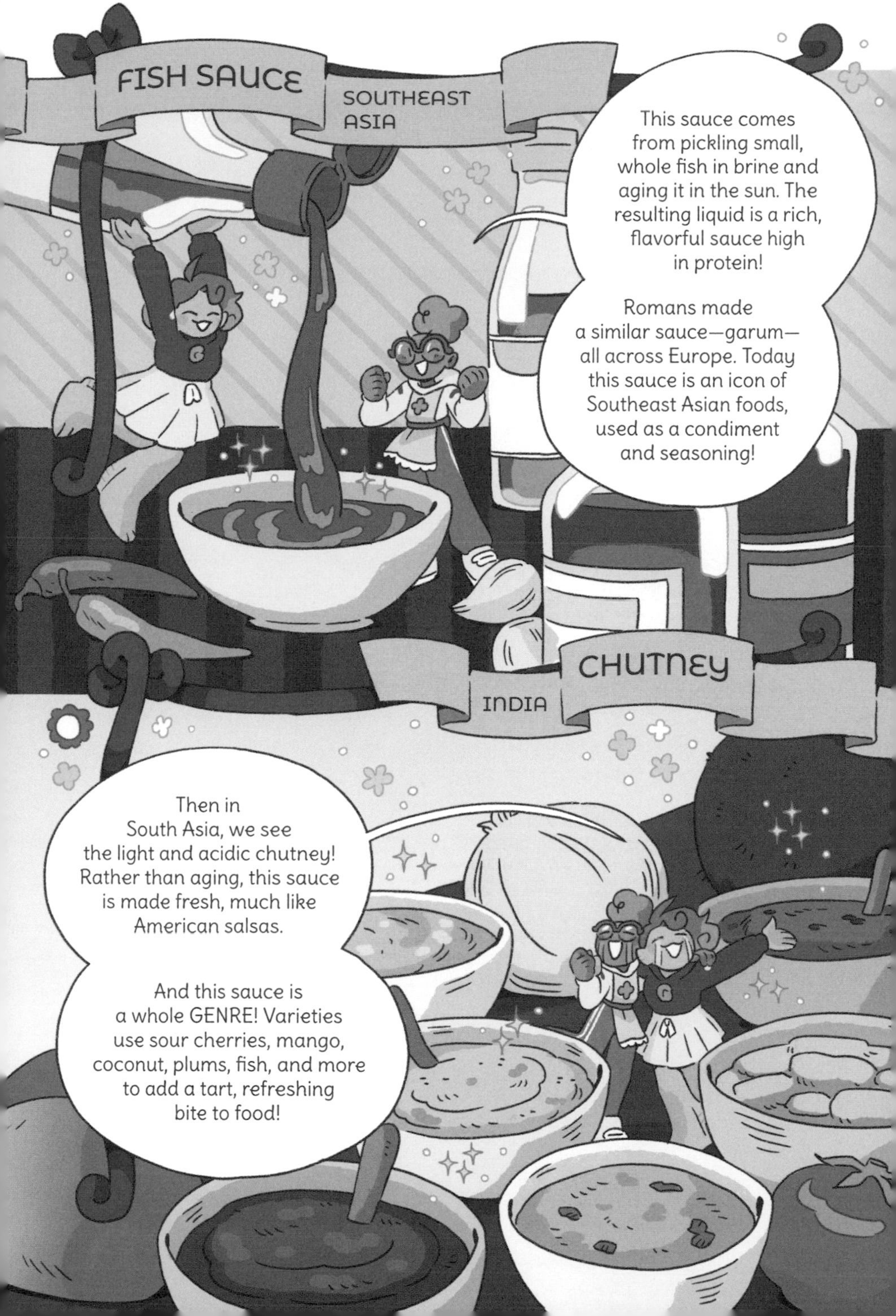
FISH SAUCE
SOUTHEAST ASIA
This sauce comes from pickling small, whole fish in brine and aging it in the sun. The resulting liquid is a rich, flavorful sauce high in protein!
Romans made a similar sauce—garum—all across Europe. Today this sauce is an icon of Southeast Asian foods, used as a condiment and seasoning!
CHUTNEY
INDIA
Then in South Asia, we see the light and acidic chutney! Rather than aging, this sauce is made fresh, much like American salsas.
And this sauce is a whole GENRE! Varieties use sour cherries, mango, coconut, plums, fish, and more to add a tart, refreshing bite to food!

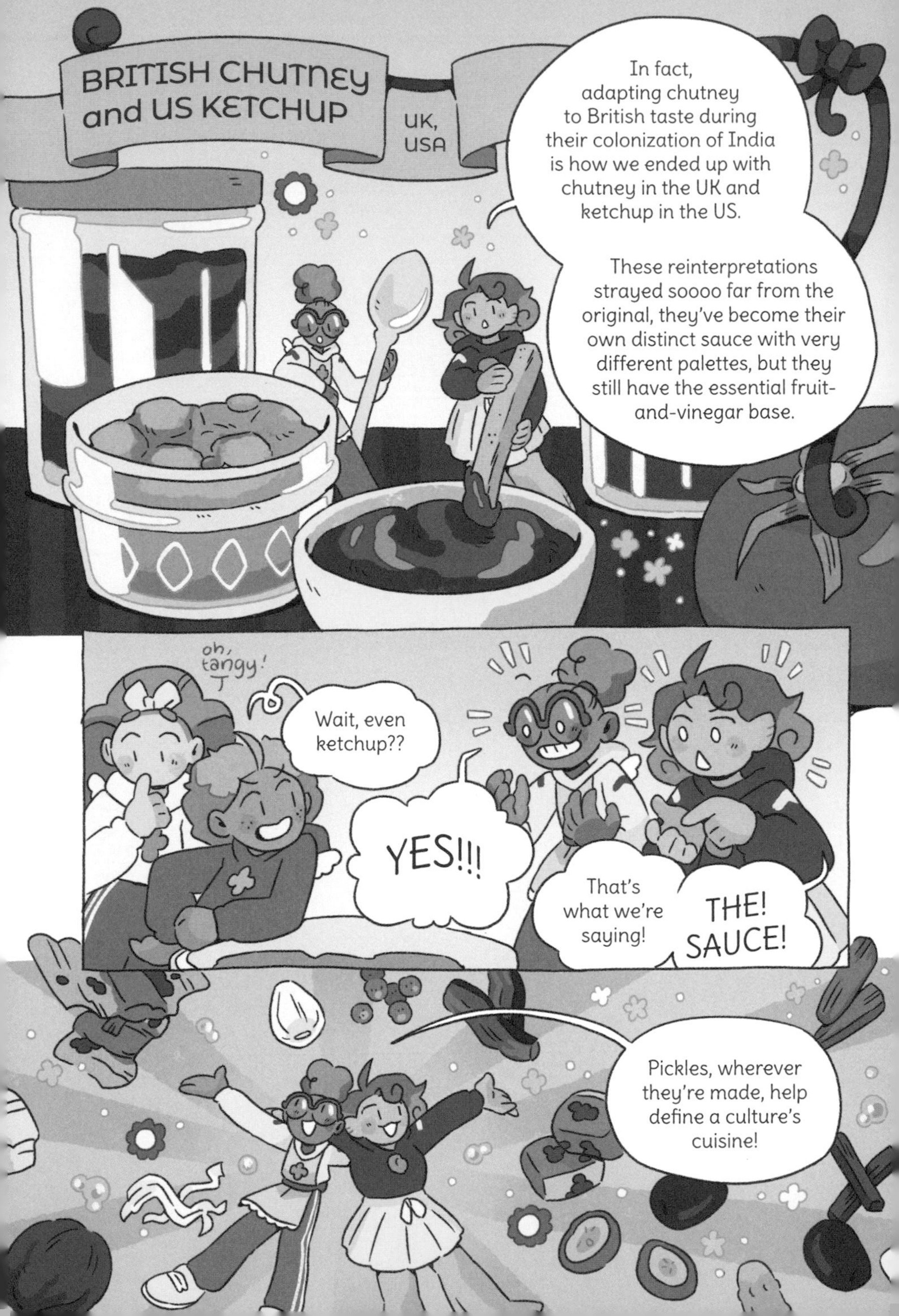
BRITISH CHUTNEY and US KETCHUP
UK, USA
In fact, adapting chutney to British taste during their colonization of India is how we ended up with chutney in the UK and ketchup in the US.
These reinterpretations strayed soooo far from the original, they've become their own distinct sauce with very different palettes, but they still have the essential fruit-and-vinegar base.
oh, tangy!
Wait, even ketchup??
YES!!!
That's what we're saying!
THE! SAUCE!
Pickles, wherever they're made, help define a culture's cuisine!

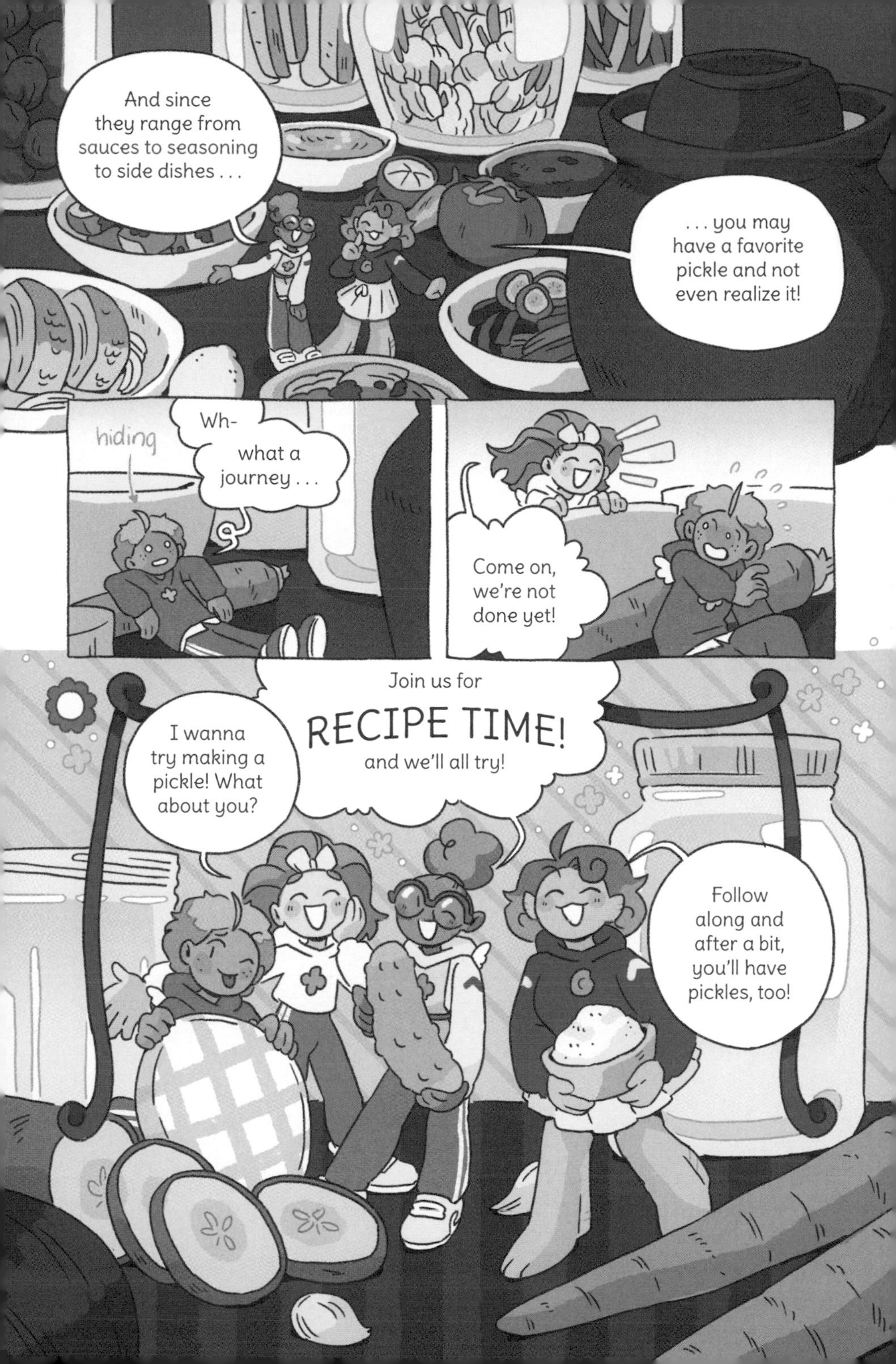
And since they range from sauces to seasoning to side dishes . . .
. . . you may have a favorite pickle and not even realize it!
hiding
Wh- what a journey . . .
Come on, we're not done yet!
Join us for RECIPE TIME! and we'll all try!
I wanna try making a pickle! What about you?
Follow along and after a bit, you'll have pickles, too!

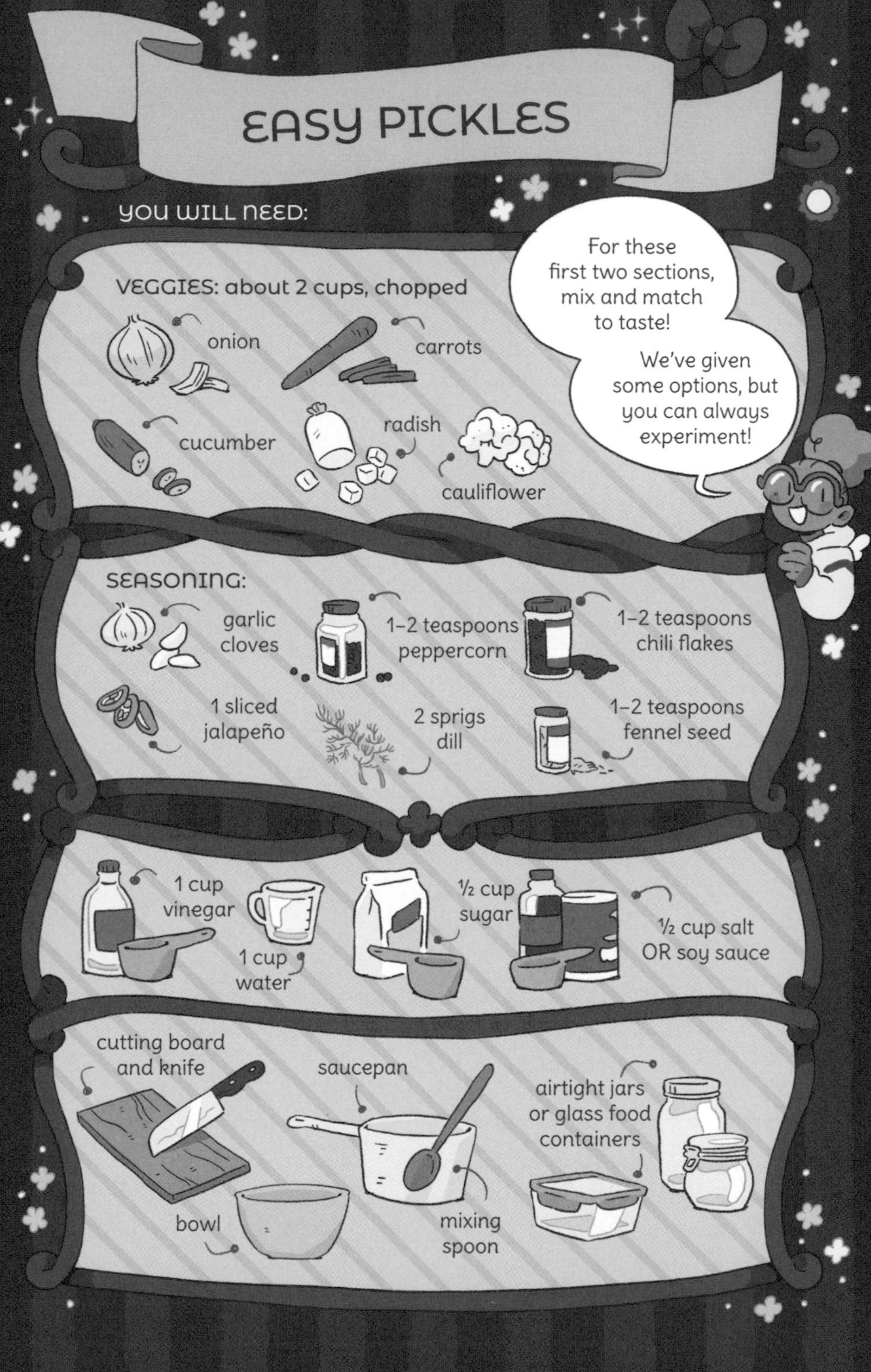

EASY PICKLES
YOU WILL NEED:
For these first two sections, mix and match to taste!
We've given some options, but you can always experiment!
VEGGIES: about 2 cups, chopped
onion
carrots
cucumber
radish
cauliflower
SEASONING:
garlic cloves
1–2 teaspoons peppercorn
1–2 teaspoons chili flakes
1 sliced jalapeño
2 sprigs dill
1–2 teaspoons fennel seed
1 cup vinegar
1 cup water
½ cup sugar
½ cup salt OR soy sauce
cutting board and knife
saucepan
airtight jars or glass food containers
bowl
mixing spoon

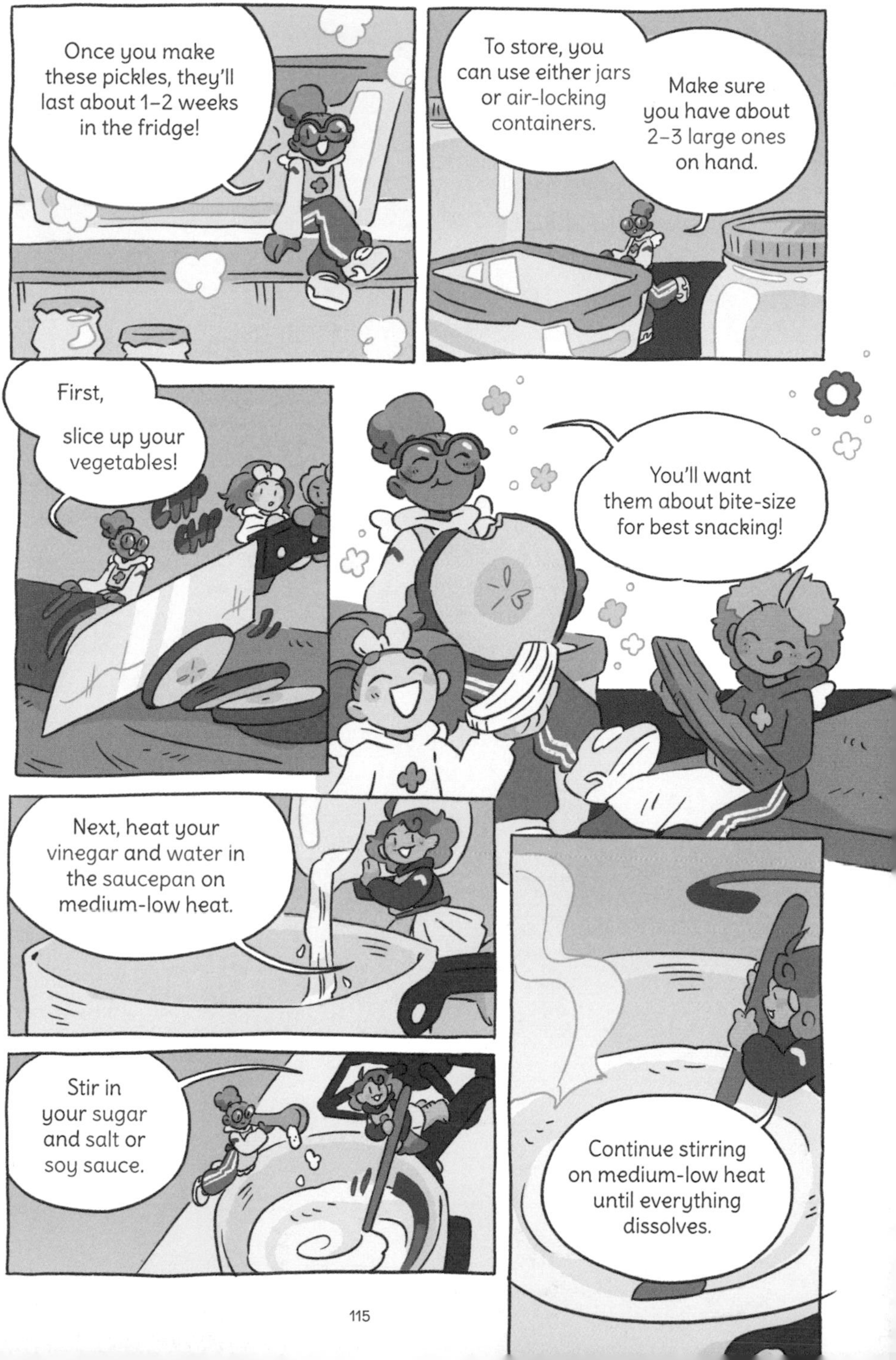
Once you make these pickles, they'll last about 1–2 weeks in the fridge!
To store, you can use either jars or air-locking containers.
Make sure you have about 2–3 large ones on hand.
First,
slice up your vegetables!
CHIP CHIP
You'll want them about bite-size for best snacking!
Next, heat your vinegar and water in the saucepan on medium-low heat.
Stir in your sugar and salt or soy sauce.
Continue stirring on medium-low heat until everything dissolves.

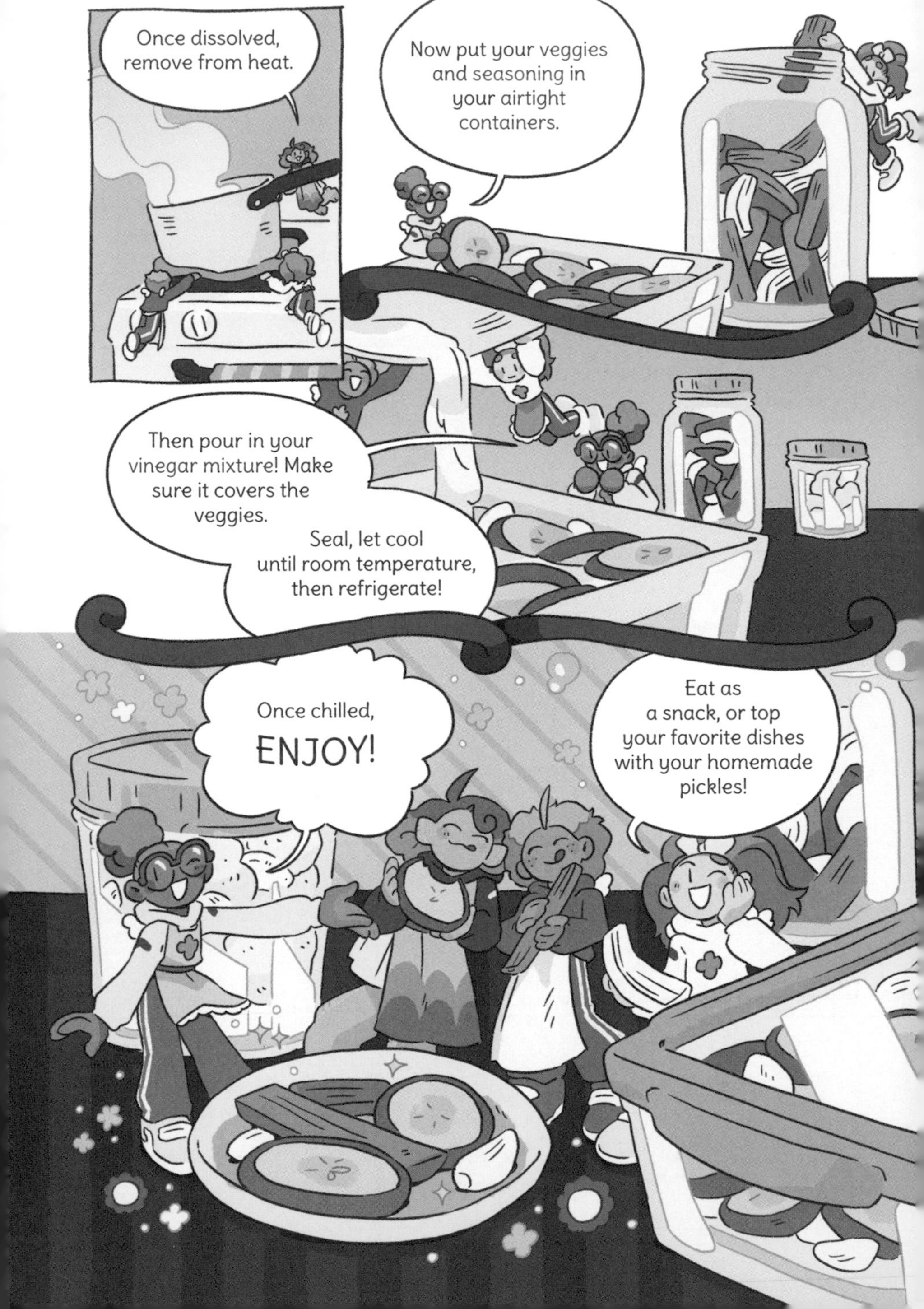
Once dissolved,
remove from heat.
Now put your veggies
and seasoning in
your airtight
containers.
Then pour in your
vinegar mixture! Make
sure it covers the
veggies.
Seal, let cool
until room temperature,
then refrigerate!
Once chilled,
ENJOY!
Eat as
a snack, or top
your favorite dishes
with your homemade
pickles!

# The Abridged
# Atlas of Soda History

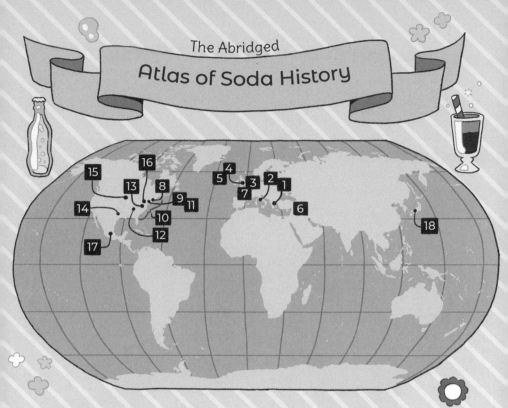

1. Greek Physician Hippocrates
2. Italian Physician Giacomo de Dondi
3. Swiss and German Mineral Water Experiments
4. British Scientist William Brownrigg
5. Early Soda Devices
6. Persian Sharbat
7. European Spritzers
8. Summer of Soda Wars
9. Robert McCay Green's Ice Cream Soda
10. American New Soda Experiments
11. Philadelphia Root Beer
12. Atlanta Coca-Cola
13. North Carolina Pepsi-Cola
14. Texas Dr Pepper
15. St. Louis 7UP
16. William Painter's Bottle Cap
17. Mexican Jarritos
18. Japanese Ramuné

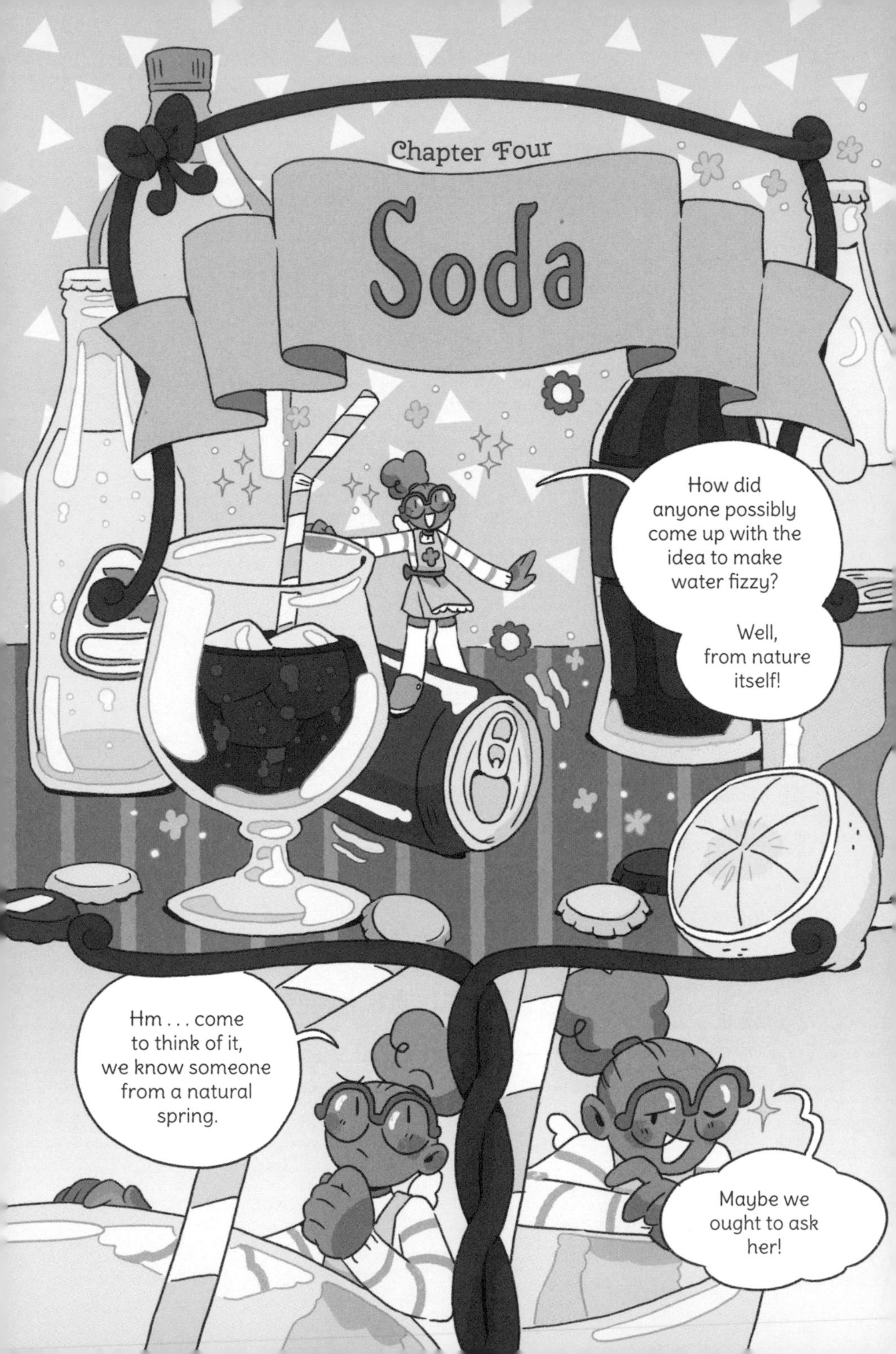
Chapter Four
Soda
How did anyone possibly come up with the idea to make water fizzy?
Well, from nature itself!
Hm . . . come to think of it, we know someone from a natural spring.
Maybe we ought to ask her!

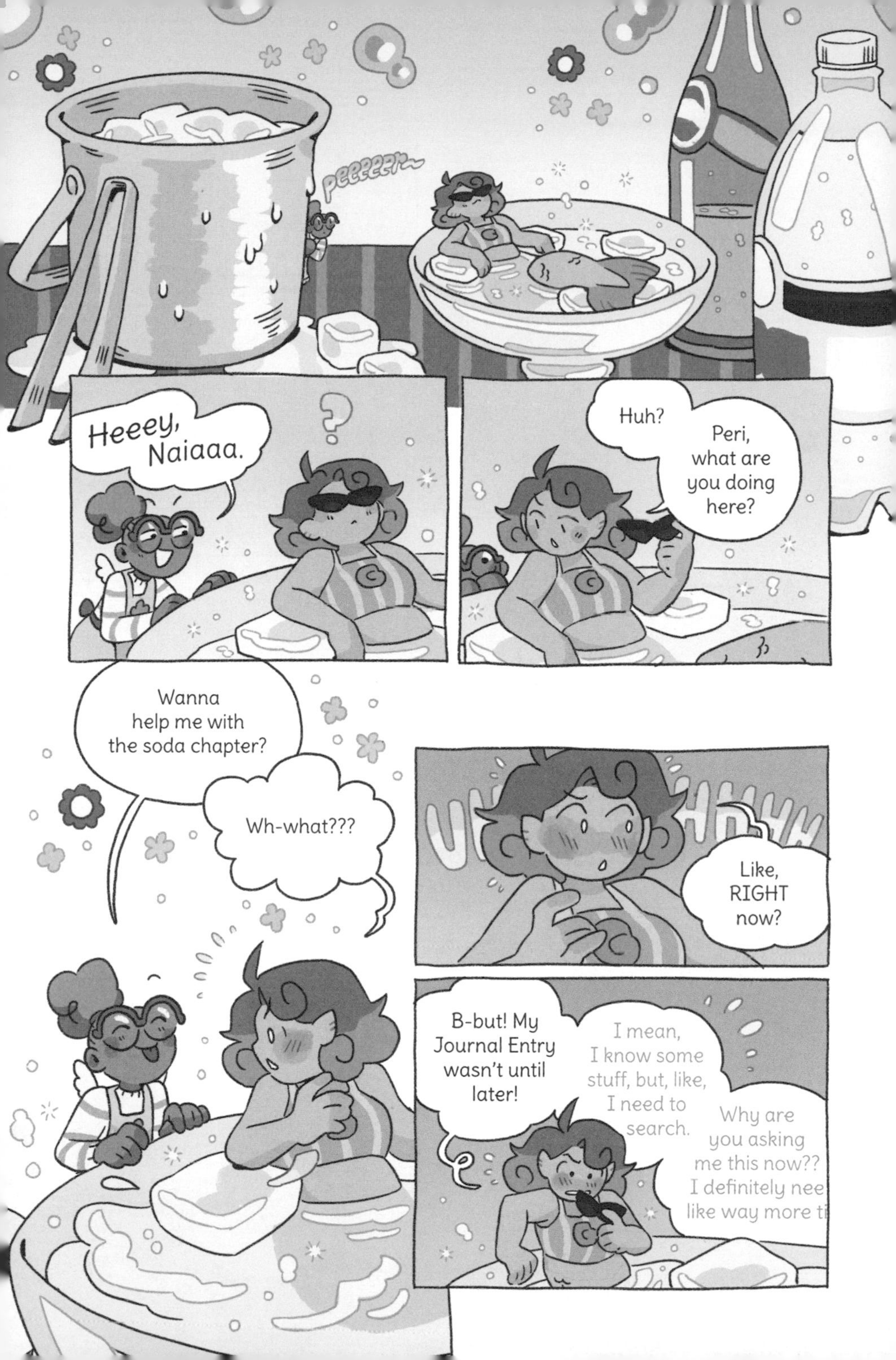
peeeeer~
Heeey, Naiaaa.
Huh?
Peri, what are you doing here?
Wanna help me with the soda chapter?
Wh-what???
Like, RIGHT now?
B-but! My Journal Entry wasn't until later!
I mean, I know some stuff, but, like, I need to search.
Why are you asking me this now??

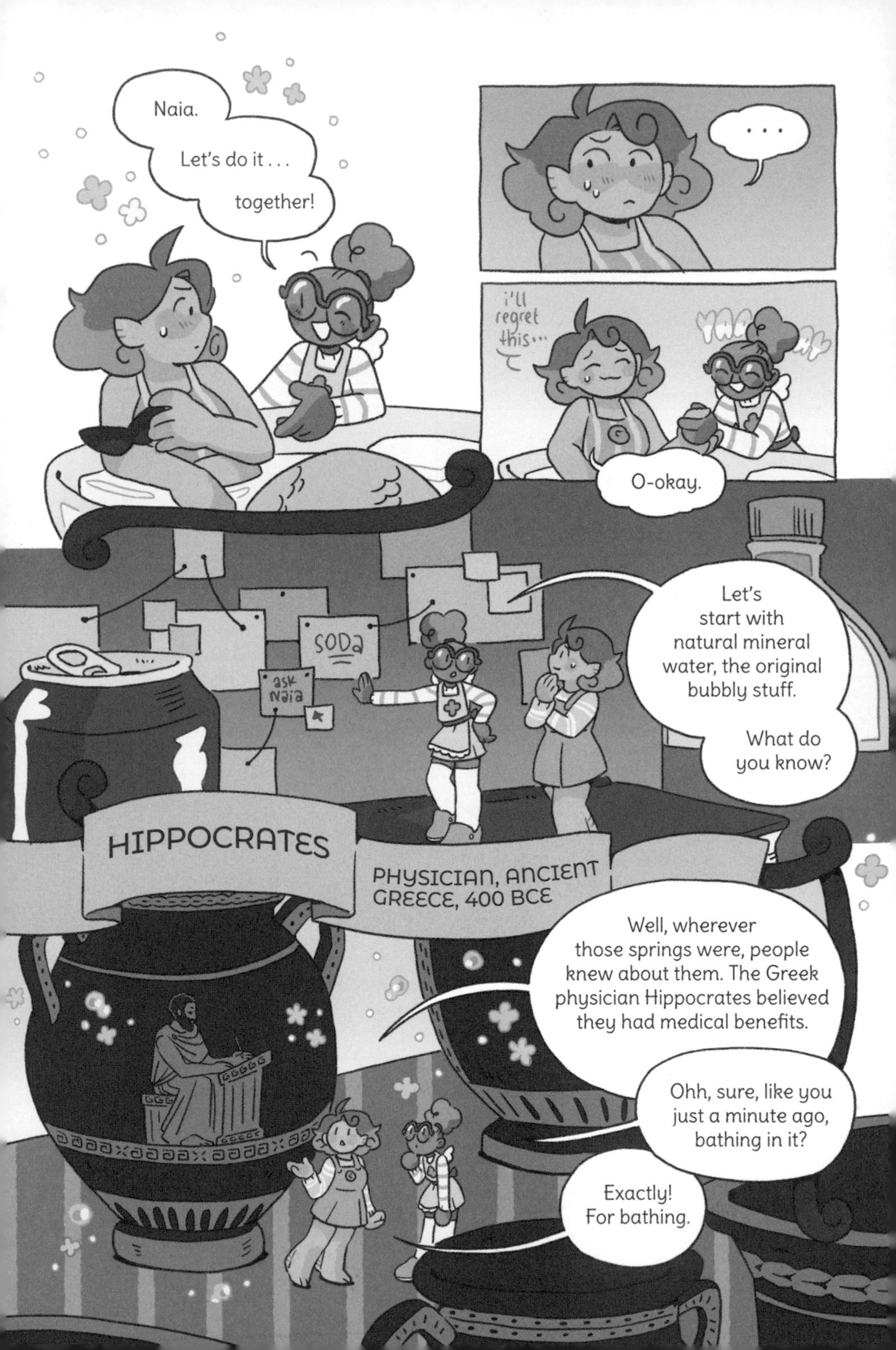

Naia.
Let's do it . . .
together!
. . .
i'll regret this...
O-okay.
SODa
ask Naia
Let's start with natural mineral water, the original bubbly stuff.
What do you know?
HIPPOCRATES
PHYSICIAN, ANCIENT GREECE, 400 BCE
Well, wherever those springs were, people knew about them. The Greek physician Hippocrates believed they had medical benefits.
Ohh, sure, like you just a minute ago, bathing in it?
Exactly! For bathing.

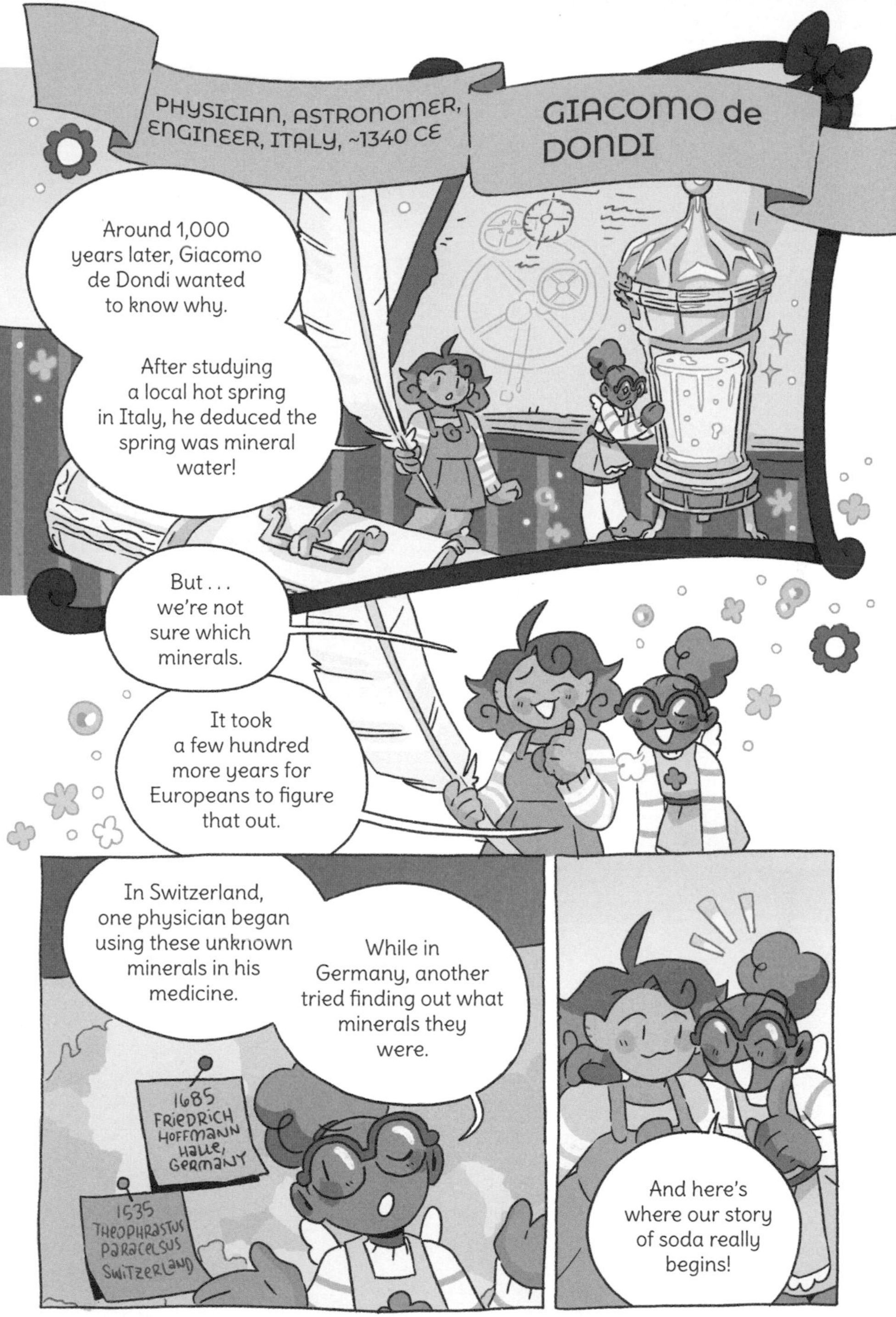
PHYSICIAN, ASTRONOMER, ENGINEER, ITALY, ~1340 CE
GIACOMO de DONDI
Around 1,000 years later, Giacomo de Dondi wanted to know why.
After studying a local hot spring in Italy, he deduced the spring was mineral water!
But . . . we're not sure which minerals.
It took a few hundred more years for Europeans to figure that out.
In Switzerland, one physician began using these unknown minerals in his medicine.
While in Germany, another tried finding out what minerals they were.
1685 FRIEDRICH HOFFMANN HALLE, GERMANY
1535 THEOPHRASTUS PARACELSUS SWITZERLAND
And here's where our story of soda really begins!

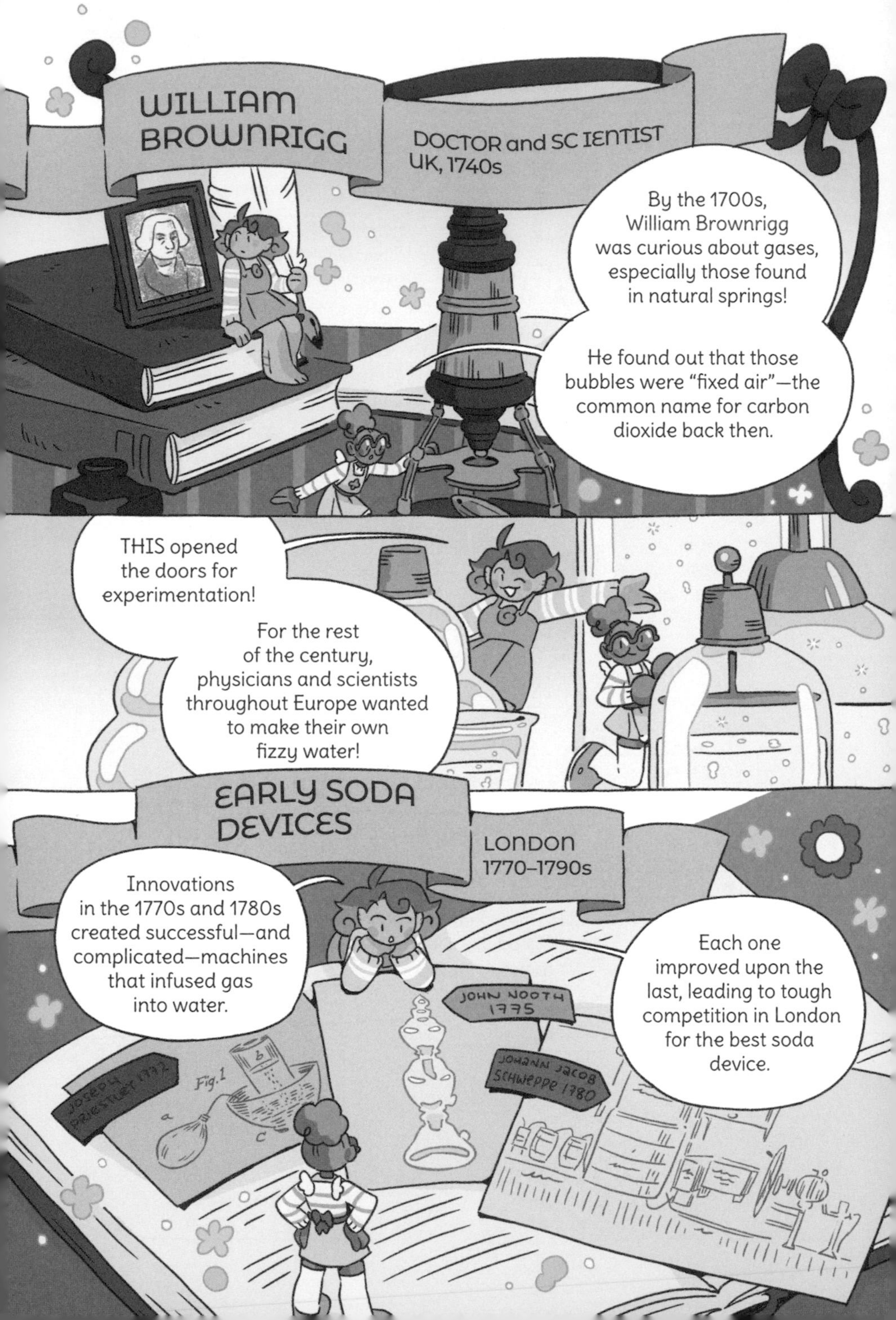
WILLIAM BROWNRIGG
DOCTOR and SCIENTIST UK, 1740s
By the 1700s, William Brownrigg was curious about gases, especially those found in natural springs!
He found out that those bubbles were "fixed air"—the common name for carbon dioxide back then.
THIS opened the doors for experimentation!
For the rest of the century, physicians and scientists throughout Europe wanted to make their own fizzy water!
EARLY SODA DEVICES
LONDON 1770–1790s
Innovations in the 1770s and 1780s created successful—and complicated—machines that infused gas into water.
Each one improved upon the last, leading to tough competition in London for the best soda device.
JOHN NOOTH 1775
JOSEPH PRIESTLEY 1772
Fig. 1
JOHANN JACOB SCHWEPPE 1780

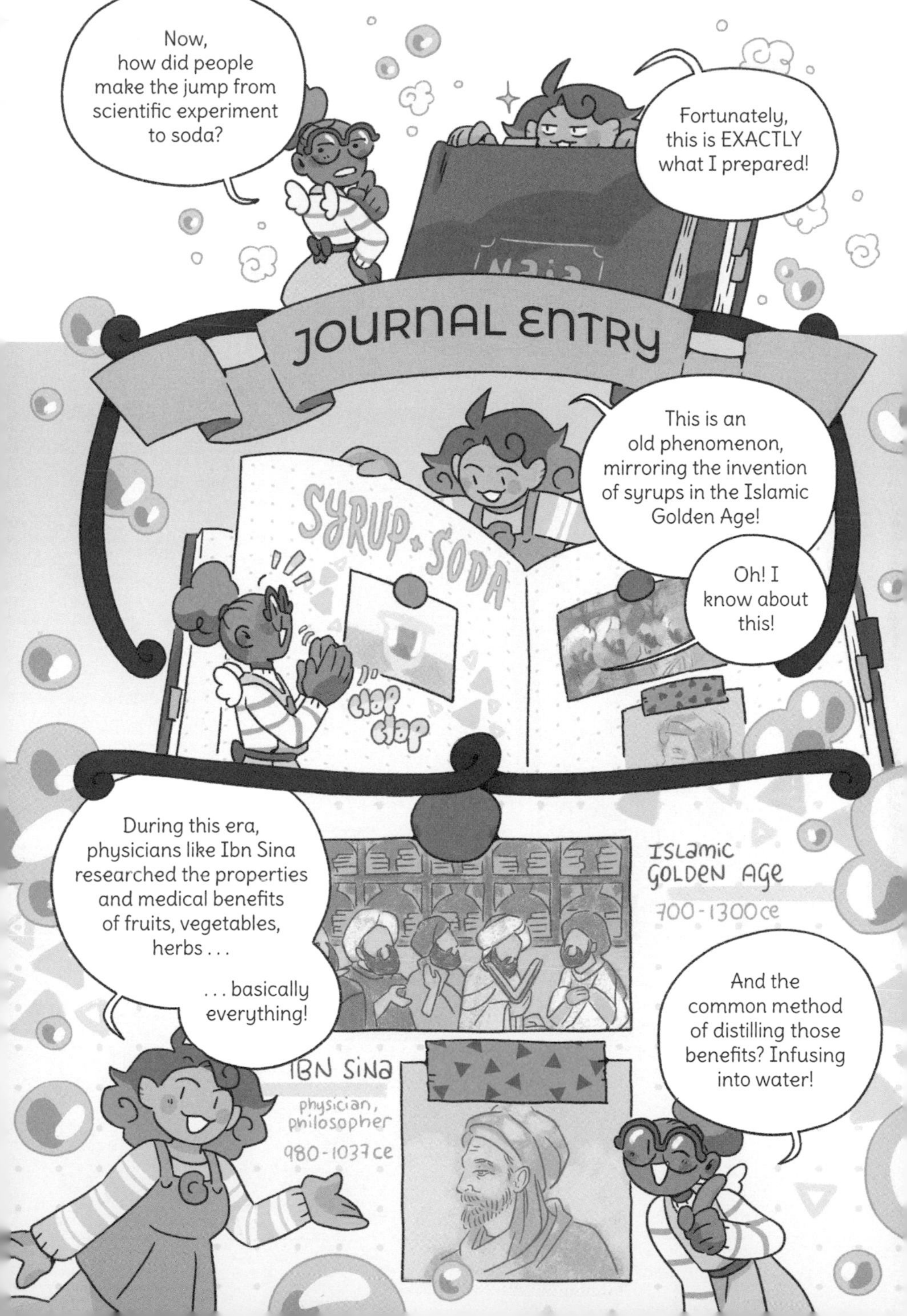

Now, how did people make the jump from scientific experiment to soda?
Fortunately, this is EXACTLY what I prepared!
JOURNAL ENTRY
This is an old phenomenon, mirroring the invention of syrups in the Islamic Golden Age!
SYRUP + SODA
Oh! I know about this!
clap clap
During this era, physicians like Ibn Sina researched the properties and medical benefits of fruits, vegetables, herbs . . .
. . . basically everything!
ISLAMIC GOLDEN AGE
700-1300 CE
IBN SINA
physician, philosopher
980-1037 CE
And the common method of distilling those benefits? Infusing into water!

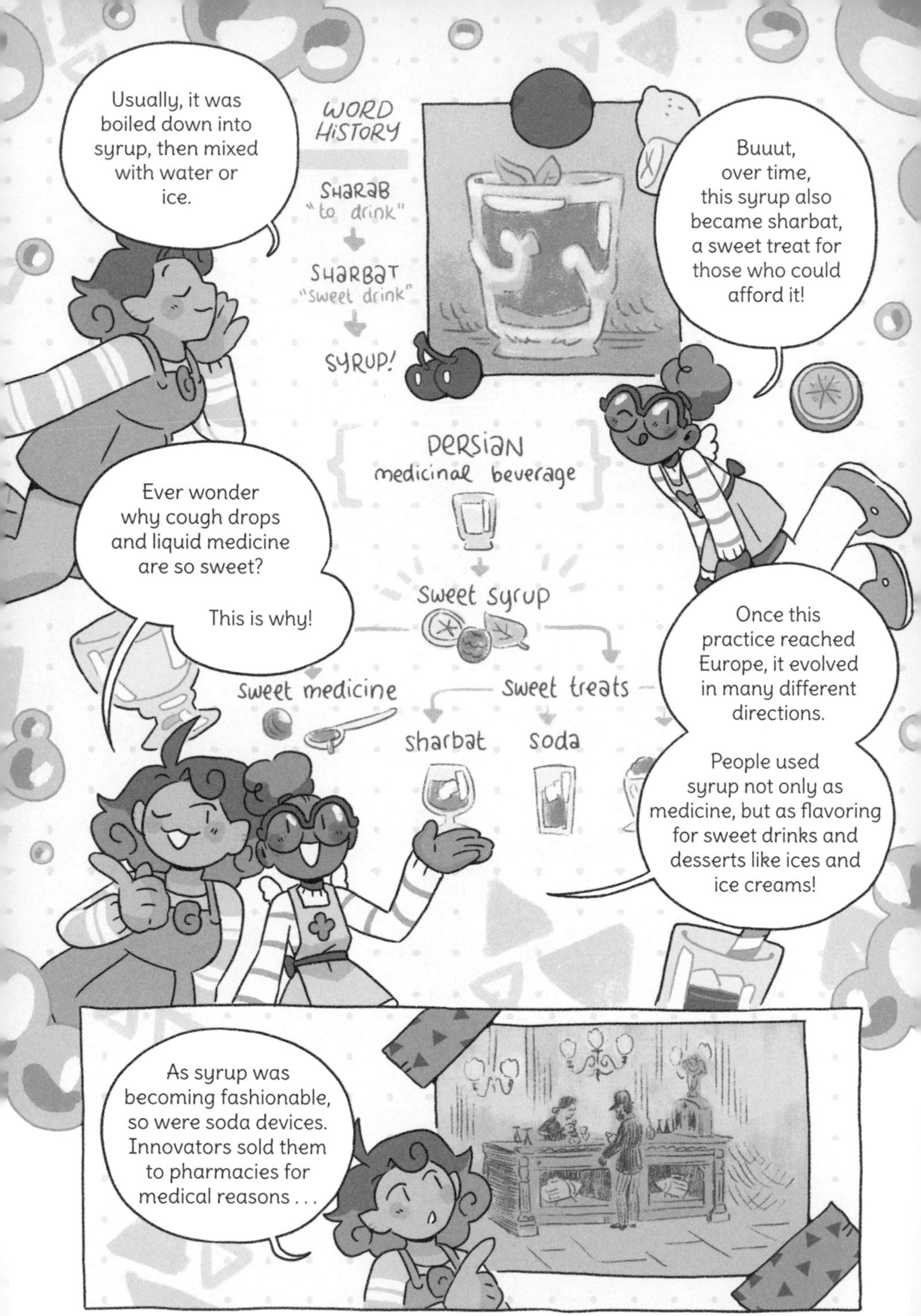
Usually, it was boiled down into syrup, then mixed with water or ice.
WORD HISTORY
SHARAB "to drink"
SHARBAT "sweet drink"
SYRUP!
Buuut, over time, this syrup also became sharbat, a sweet treat for those who could afford it!
PERSIAN medicinal beverage
Ever wonder why cough drops and liquid medicine are so sweet?
This is why!
sweet syrup
sweet medicine
sweet treats
sharbat
soda
Once this practice reached Europe, it evolved in many different directions.
People used syrup not only as medicine, but as flavoring for sweet drinks and desserts like ices and ice creams!
As syrup was becoming fashionable, so were soda devices. Innovators sold them to pharmacies for medical reasons . . .

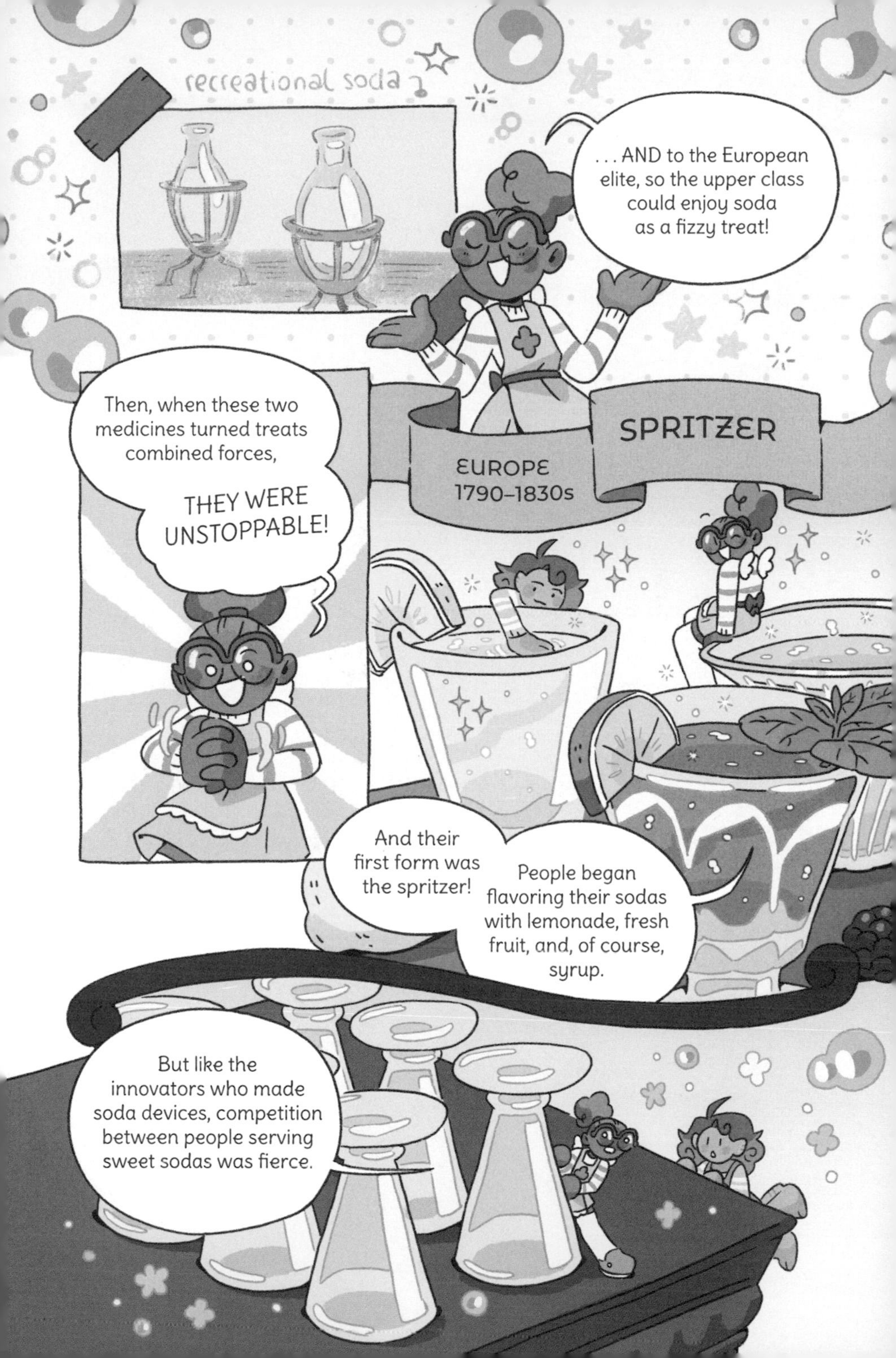
recreational soda
. . . AND to the European elite, so the upper class could enjoy soda as a fizzy treat!
Then, when these two medicines turned treats combined forces,
THEY WERE UNSTOPPABLE!
SPRITZER
EUROPE 1790–1830s
And their first form was the spritzer!
People began flavoring their sodas with lemonade, fresh fruit, and, of course, syrup.
But like the innovators who made soda devices, competition between people serving sweet sodas was fierce.

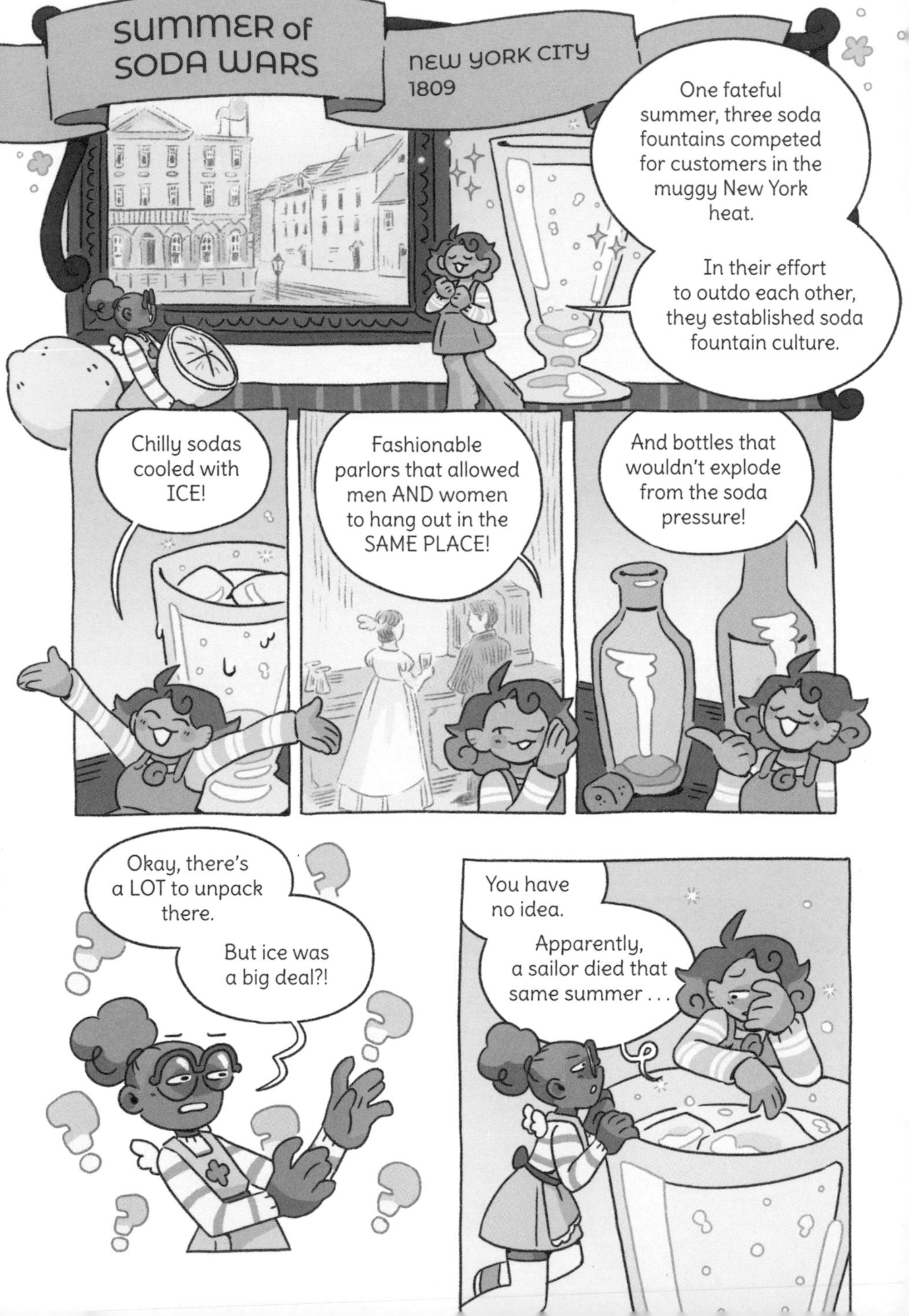
SUMMER of SODA WARS
NEW YORK CITY 1809
One fateful summer, three soda fountains competed for customers in the muggy New York heat.
In their effort to outdo each other, they established soda fountain culture.
Chilly sodas cooled with ICE!
Fashionable parlors that allowed men AND women to hang out in the SAME PLACE!
And bottles that wouldn't explode from the soda pressure!
Okay, there's a LOT to unpack there.
But ice was a big deal?!
You have no idea.
Apparently, a sailor died that same summer . . .

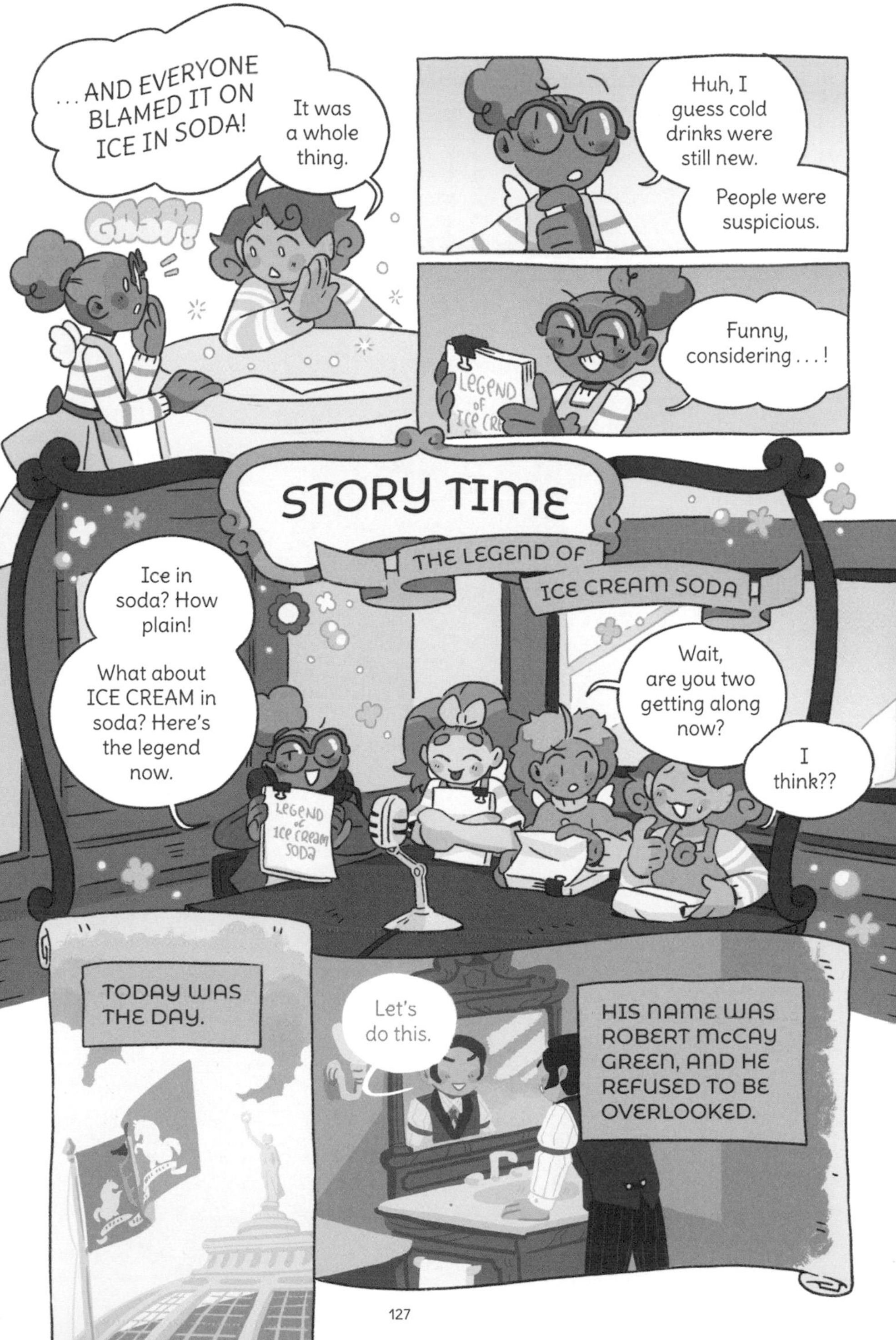
. . . AND EVERYONE BLAMED IT ON ICE IN SODA!
It was a whole thing.
GASP!
Huh, I guess cold drinks were still new.
People were suspicious.
Funny, considering . . . !
LEGEND of ICE CR
STORY TIME
THE LEGEND OF ICE CREAM SODA
Ice in soda? How plain!
What about ICE CREAM in soda? Here's the legend now.
LEGEND of ICE CREAM SODA
Wait, are you two getting along now?
I think??
TODAY WAS THE DAY.
Let's do this.
HIS NAME WAS ROBERT McCAY GREEN, AND HE REFUSED TO BE OVERLOOKED.

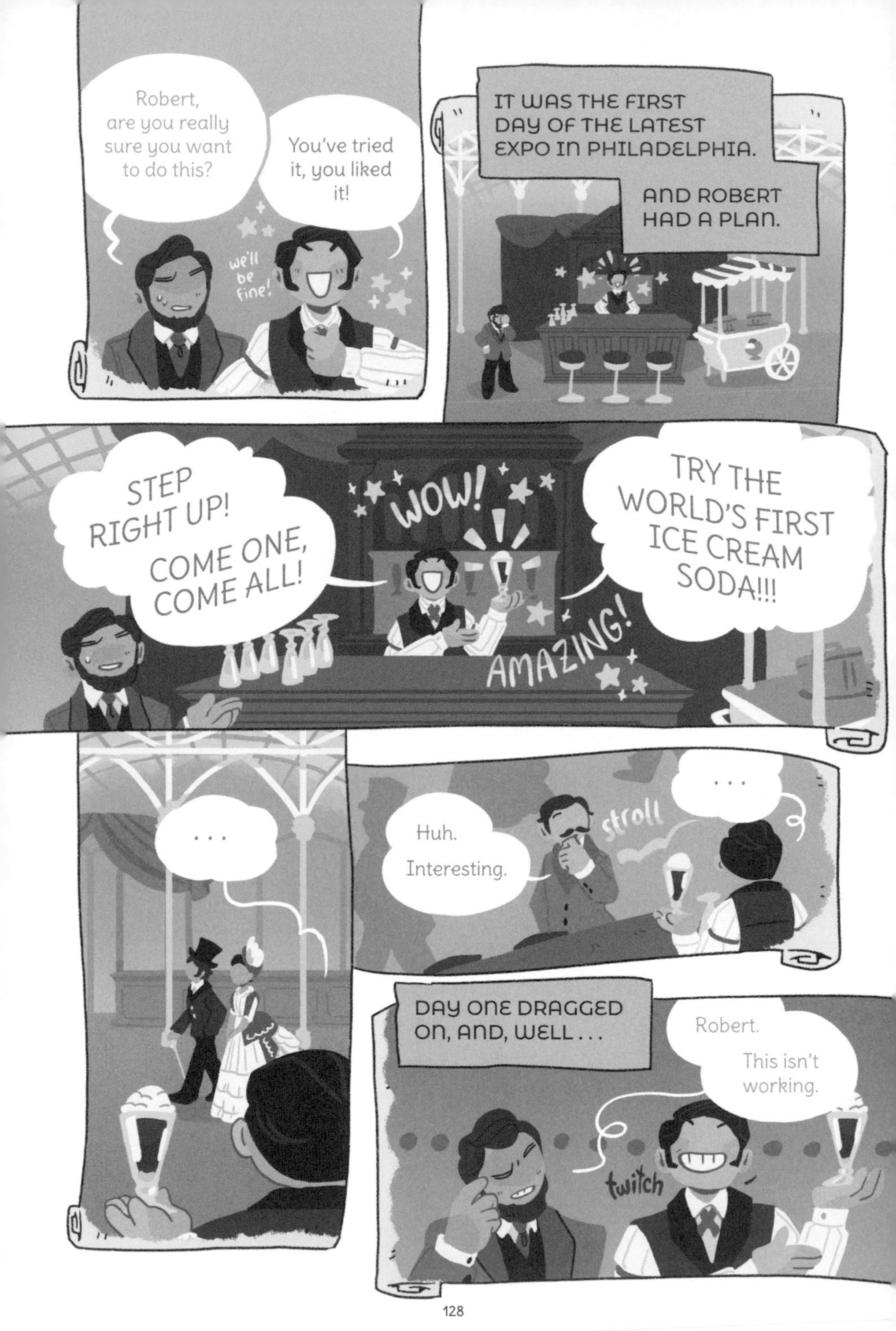

Robert, are you really sure you want to do this?
You've tried it, you liked it!
we'll be fine!
IT WAS THE FIRST DAY OF THE LATEST EXPO IN PHILADELPHIA.
AND ROBERT HAD A PLAN.
STEP RIGHT UP!
COME ONE, COME ALL!
WOW!
TRY THE WORLD'S FIRST ICE CREAM SODA!!!
AMAZING!
. . .
Huh.
Interesting.
stroll
. . .
DAY ONE DRAGGED ON, AND, WELL . . .
Robert.
This isn't working.
twitch

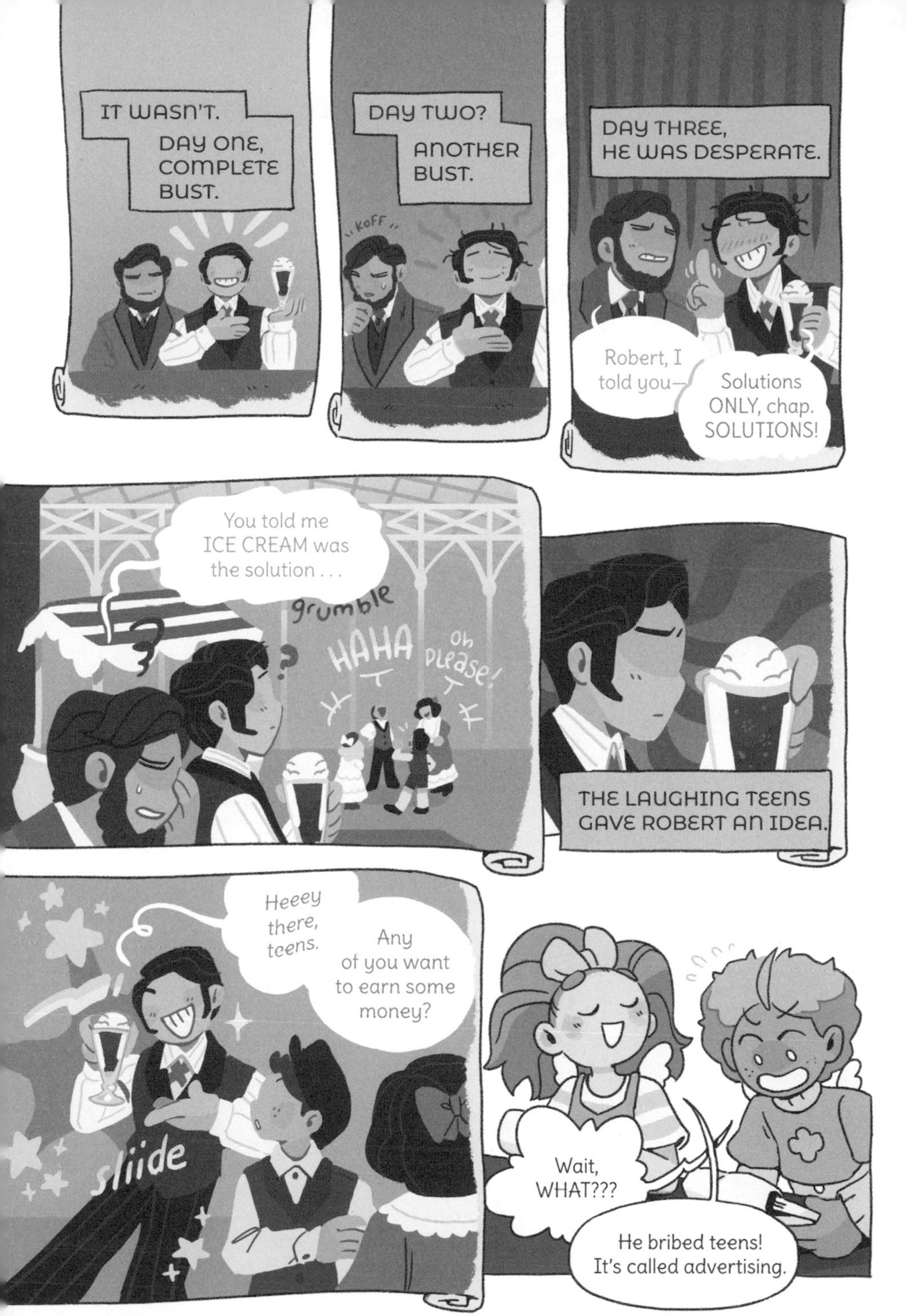

IT WASN'T.
DAY ONE, COMPLETE BUST.
DAY TWO?
ANOTHER BUST.
KOFF
DAY THREE, HE WAS DESPERATE.
Robert, I told you—
Solutions ONLY, chap. SOLUTIONS!
You told me ICE CREAM was the solution . . .
grumble
HAHA
Oh please!
THE LAUGHING TEENS GAVE ROBERT AN IDEA.
Heeey there, teens.
Any of you want to earn some money?
sliide
Wait, WHAT???
He bribed teens! It's called advertising.

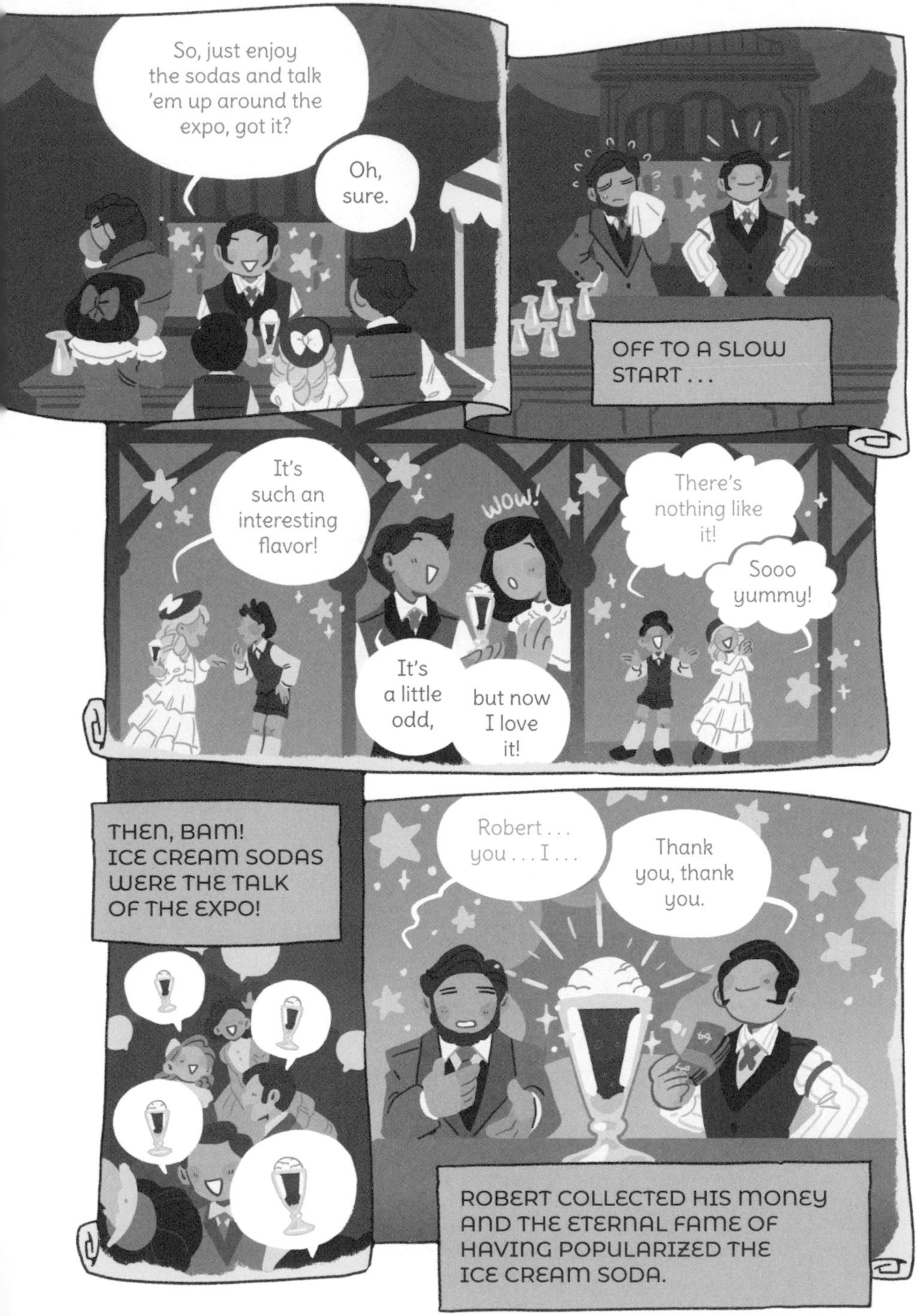
So, just enjoy the sodas and talk 'em up around the expo, got it?
Oh, sure.
OFF TO A SLOW START . . .
It's such an interesting flavor!
WOW!
It's a little odd,
but now I love it!
There's nothing like it!
Sooo yummy!
THEN, BAM! ICE CREAM SODAS WERE THE TALK OF THE EXPO!
Robert . . . you . . . I . . .
Thank you, thank you.
ROBERT COLLECTED HIS MONEY AND THE ETERNAL FAME OF HAVING POPULARIZED THE ICE CREAM SODA.

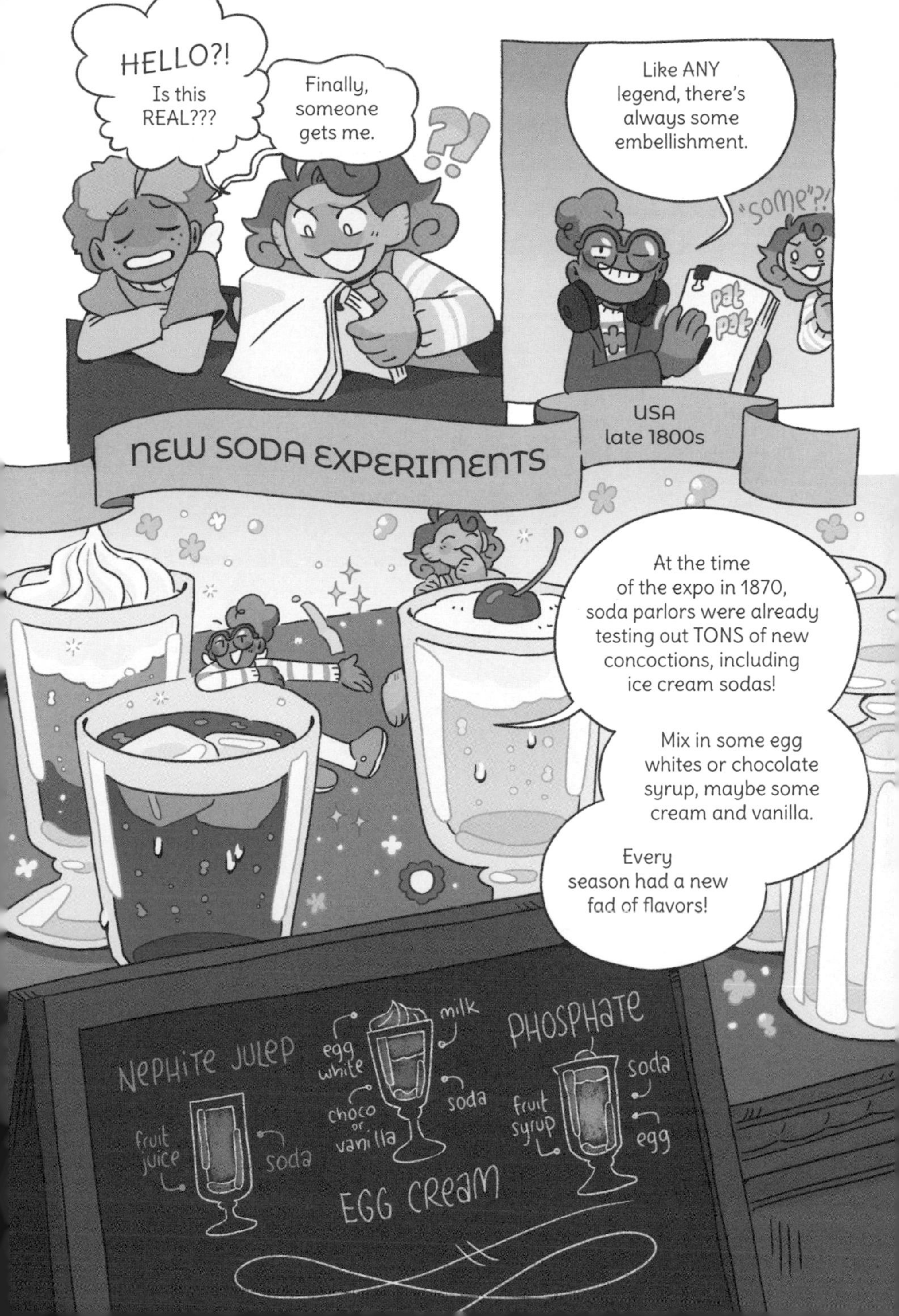
HELLO?! Is this REAL???
Finally, someone gets me.
?!
Like ANY legend, there's always some embellishment.
"some"?!
pat pat
NEW SODA EXPERIMENTS
USA late 1800s
At the time of the expo in 1870, soda parlors were already testing out TONS of new concoctions, including ice cream sodas!
Mix in some egg whites or chocolate syrup, maybe some cream and vanilla.
Every season had a new fad of flavors!
NEPHITE JULEP
fruit juice
soda
egg white
milk
choco or vanilla
soda
EGG CREAM
PHOSPHATE
fruit syrup
soda
egg

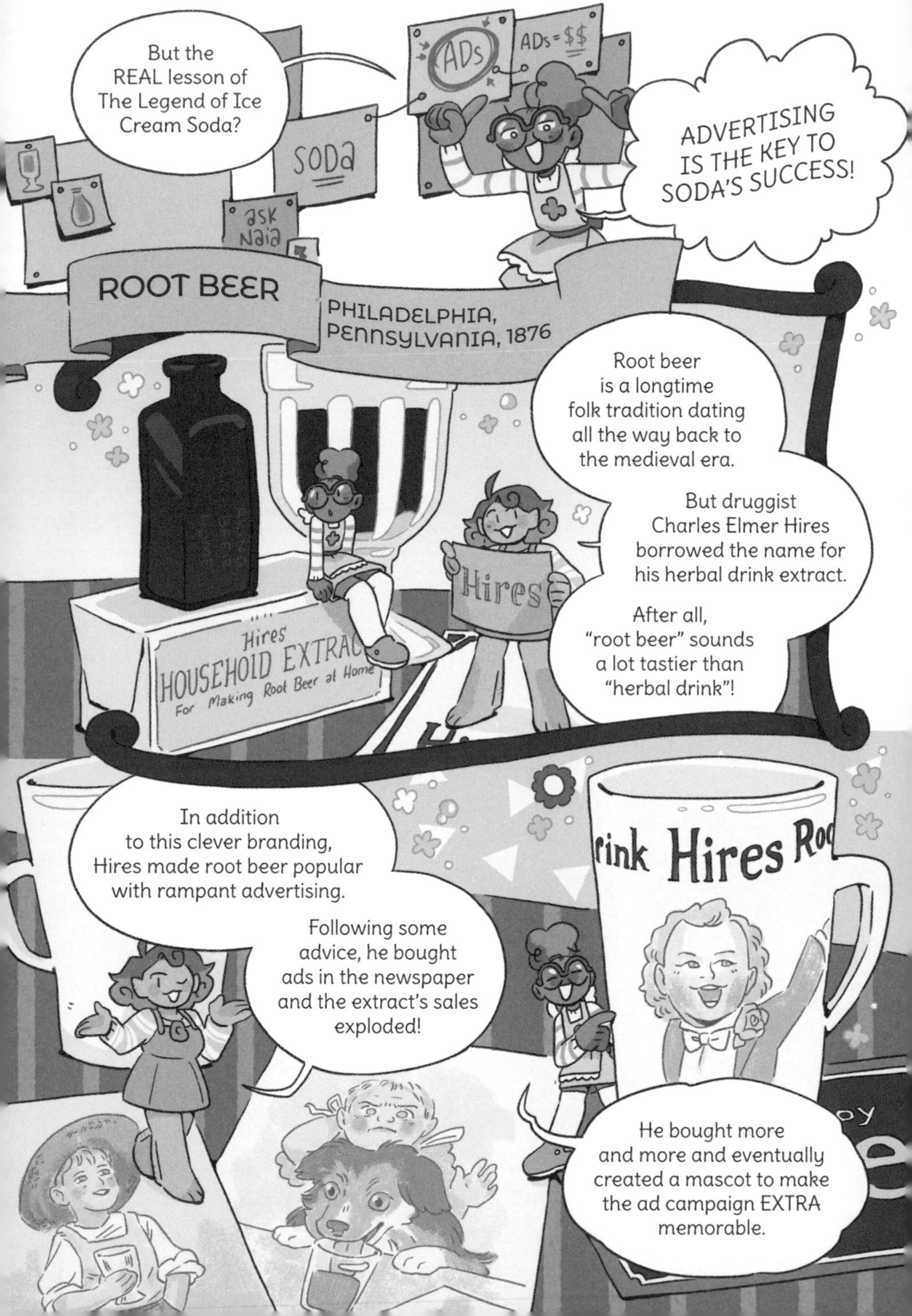

But the REAL lesson of The Legend of Ice Cream Soda?
ADs
ADs = $$
SODA
ask Naia
ADVERTISING IS THE KEY TO SODA'S SUCCESS!
ROOT BEER
PHILADELPHIA, PENNSYLVANIA, 1876
Root beer is a longtime folk tradition dating all the way back to the medieval era.
But druggist Charles Elmer Hires borrowed the name for his herbal drink extract.
After all, "root beer" sounds a lot tastier than "herbal drink"!
Hires
Hires HOUSEHOLD EXTRAC
For Making Root Beer at Home
In addition to this clever branding, Hires made root beer popular with rampant advertising.
Following some advice, he bought ads in the newspaper and the extract's sales exploded!
rink Hires Ro
He bought more and more and eventually created a mascot to make the ad campaign EXTRA memorable.

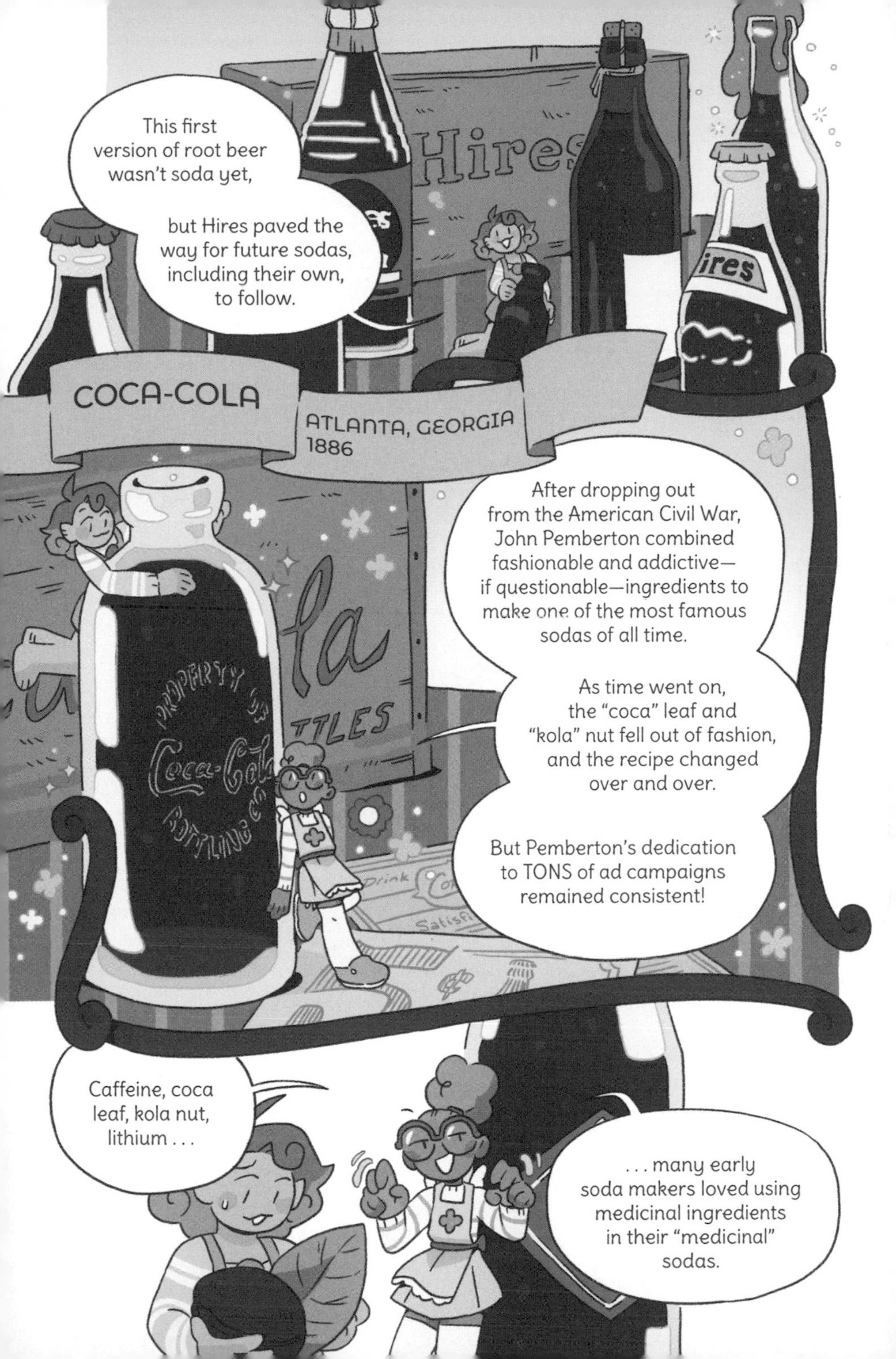
This first version of root beer wasn't soda yet,
but Hires paved the way for future sodas, including their own, to follow.
Hires
COCA-COLA
ATLANTA, GEORGIA 1886
After dropping out from the American Civil War, John Pemberton combined fashionable and addictive—if questionable—ingredients to make one of the most famous sodas of all time.
As time went on, the "coca" leaf and "kola" nut fell out of fashion, and the recipe changed over and over.
But Pemberton's dedication to TONS of ad campaigns remained consistent!
PROPERTY OF Coca-Cola BOTTLING CO
Caffeine, coca leaf, kola nut, lithium . . .
. . . many early soda makers loved using medicinal ingredients in their "medicinal" sodas.

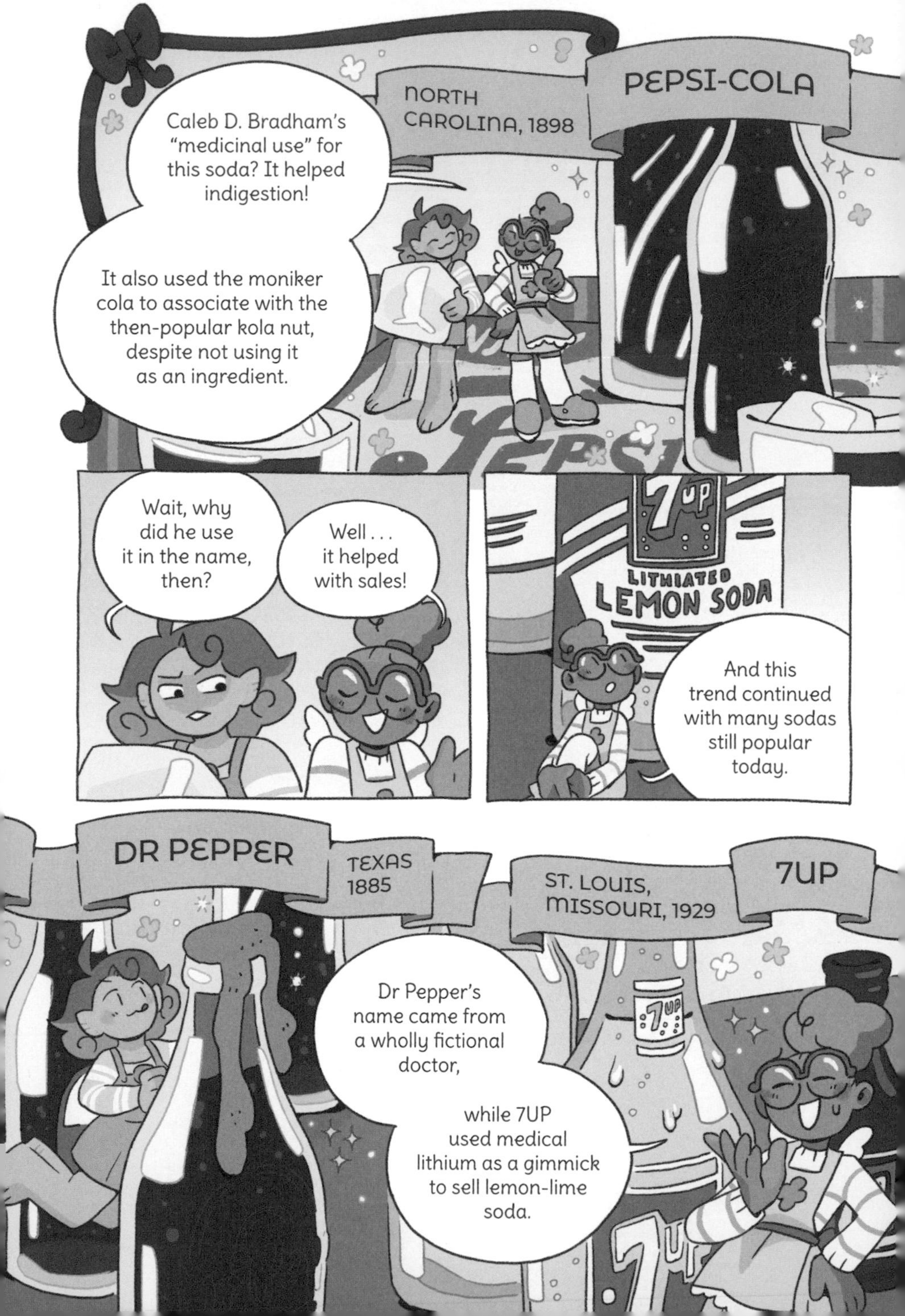
NORTH CAROLINA, 1898
PEPSI-COLA
Caleb D. Bradham's "medicinal use" for this soda? It helped indigestion!
It also used the moniker cola to associate with the then-popular kola nut, despite not using it as an ingredient.
Wait, why did he use it in the name, then?
Well . . . it helped with sales!
7UP
LITHIATED LEMON SODA
And this trend continued with many sodas still popular today.
DR PEPPER
TEXAS 1885
ST. LOUIS, MISSOURI, 1929
7UP
Dr Pepper's name came from a wholly fictional doctor,
while 7UP used medical lithium as a gimmick to sell lemon-lime soda.

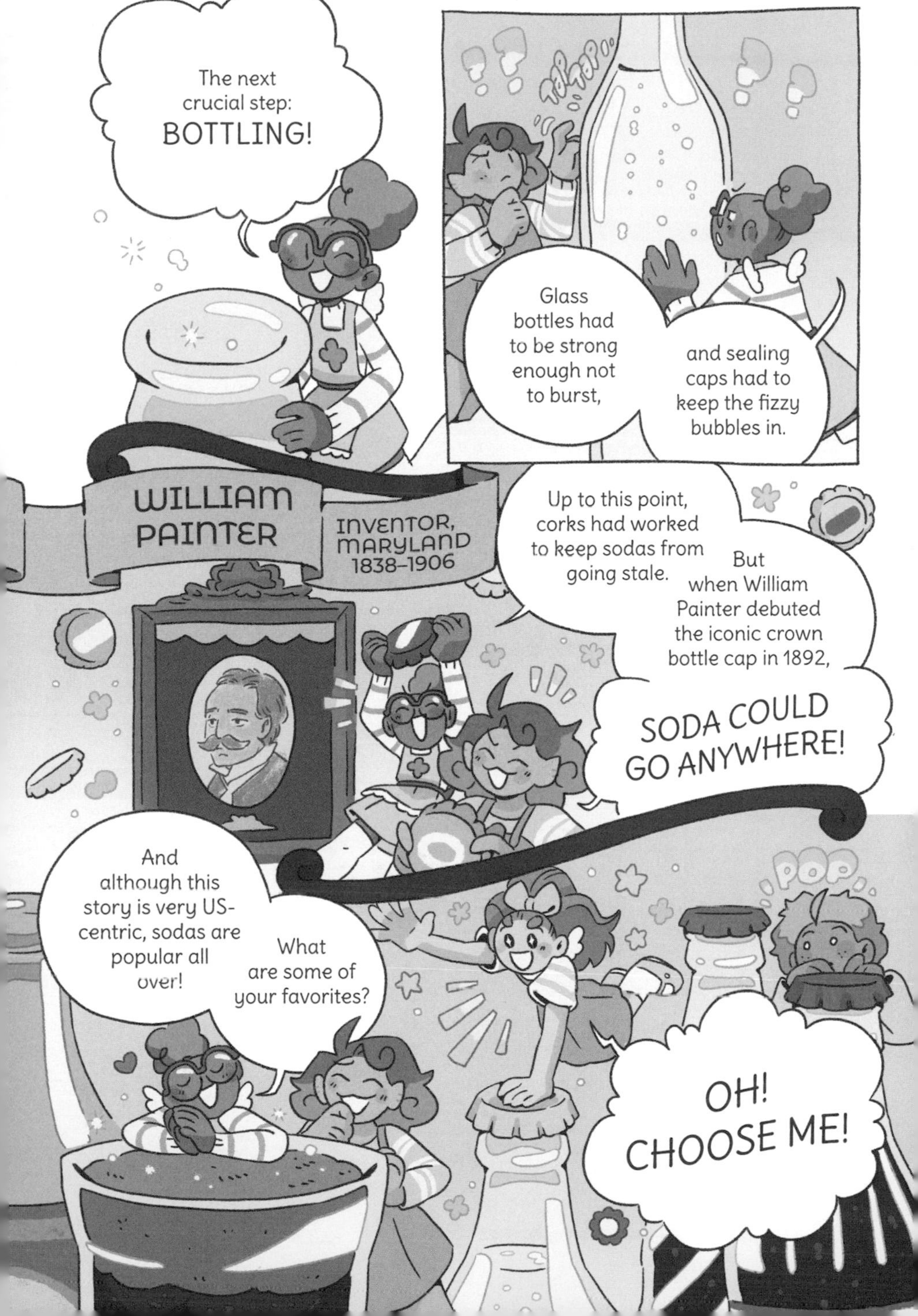

The next crucial step: BOTTLING!
TAP TAP
Glass bottles had to be strong enough not to burst,
and sealing caps had to keep the fizzy bubbles in.
WILLIAM PAINTER
INVENTOR, MARYLAND 1838–1906
Up to this point, corks had worked to keep sodas from going stale.
But when William Painter debuted the iconic crown bottle cap in 1892,
SODA COULD GO ANYWHERE!
And although this story is very US-centric, sodas are popular all over!
What are some of your favorites?
POP
OH! CHOOSE ME!

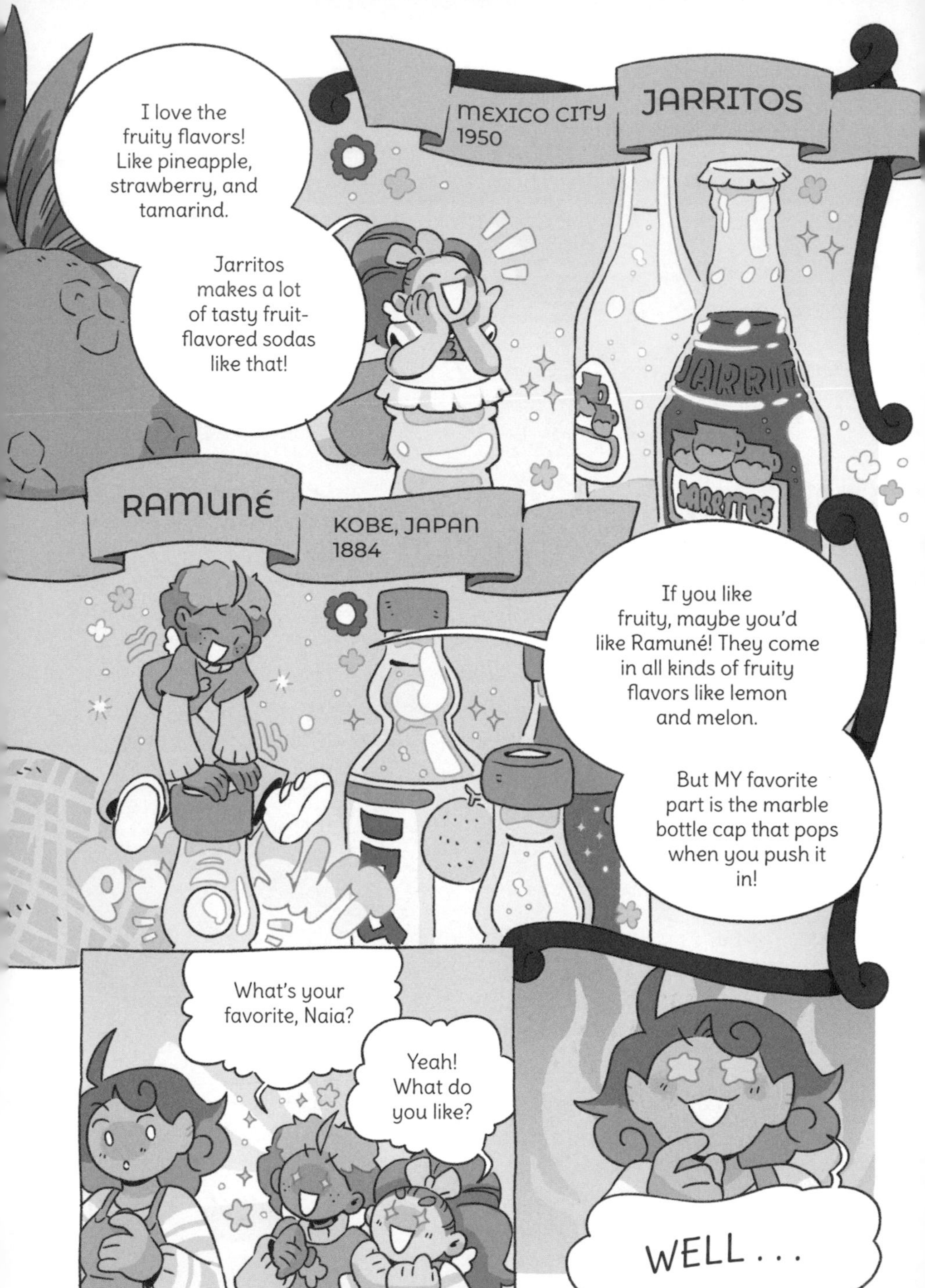
MEXICO CITY 1950
JARRITOS
I love the fruity flavors! Like pineapple, strawberry, and tamarind.
Jarritos makes a lot of tasty fruit-flavored sodas like that!
JARRITOS
RAMUNÉ
KOBE, JAPAN 1884
If you like fruity, maybe you'd like Ramuné! They come in all kinds of fruity flavors like lemon and melon.
But MY favorite part is the marble bottle cap that pops when you push it in!
What's your favorite, Naia?
Yeah! What do you like?
WELL . . .

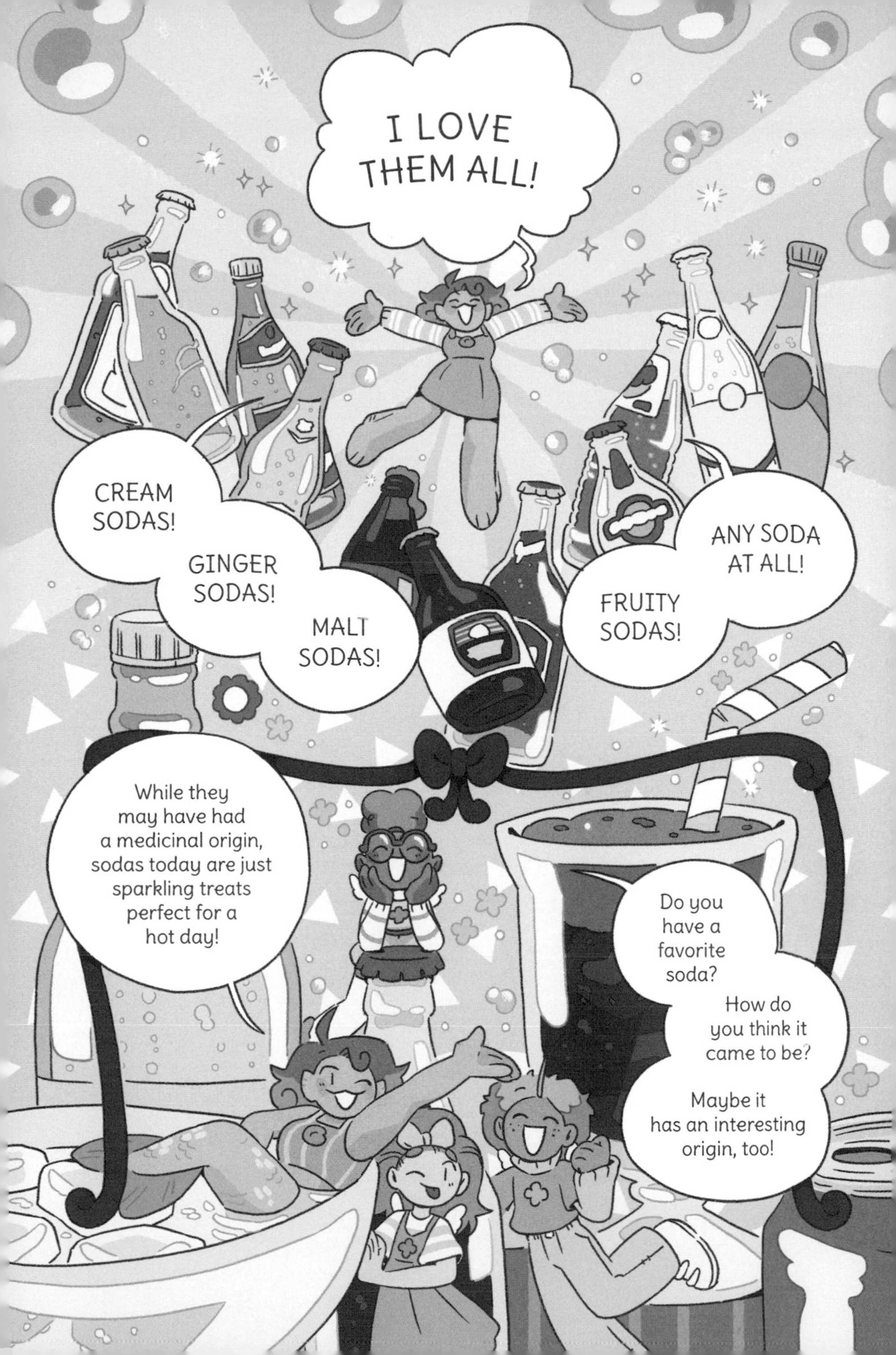
I LOVE THEM ALL!
CREAM SODAS!
GINGER SODAS!
MALT SODAS!
FRUITY SODAS!
ANY SODA AT ALL!
While they may have had a medicinal origin, sodas today are just sparkling treats perfect for a hot day!
Do you have a favorite soda?
How do you think it came to be?
Maybe it has an interesting origin, too!

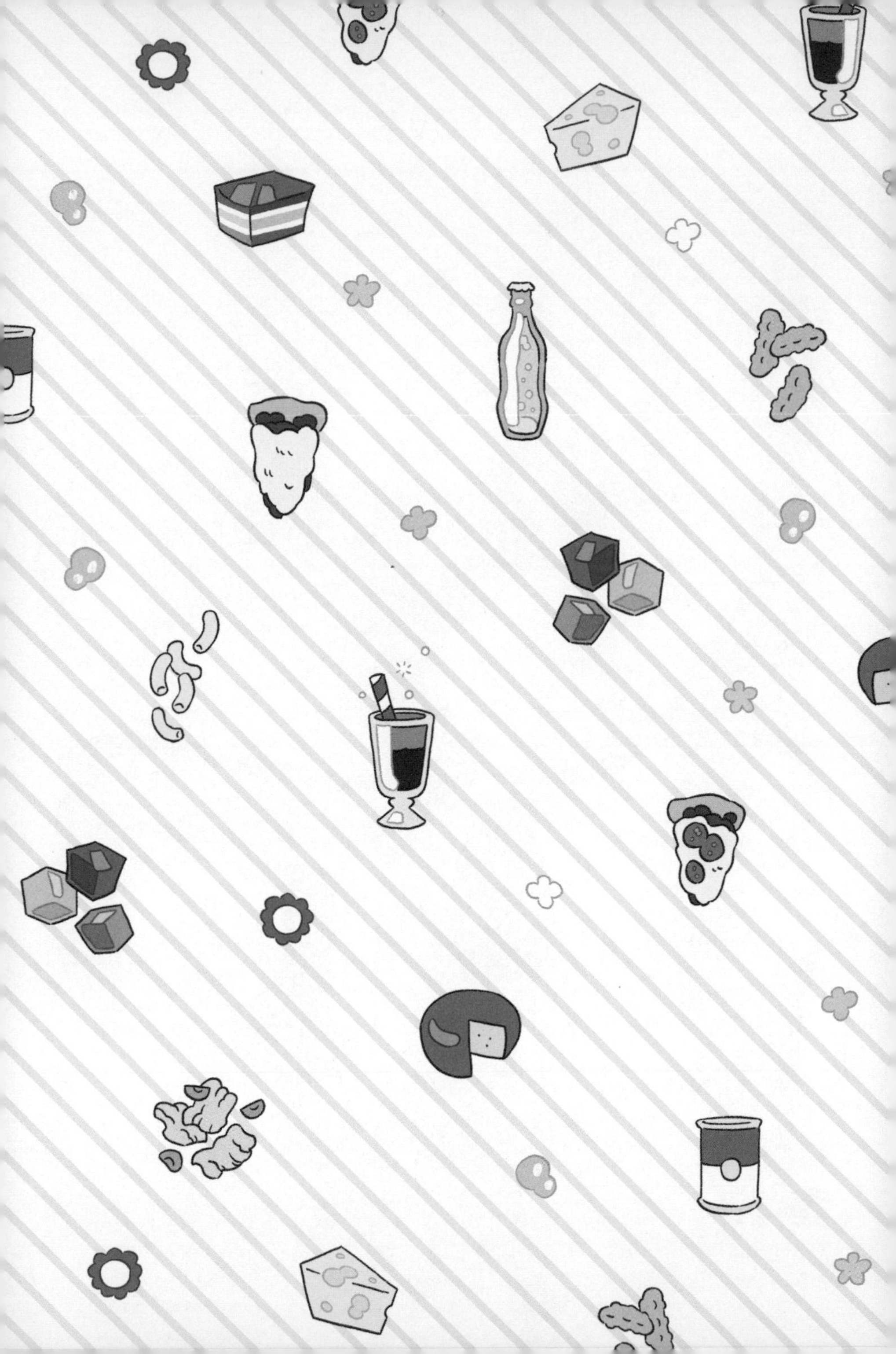

# The Abridged
# Atlas of Easy Food History

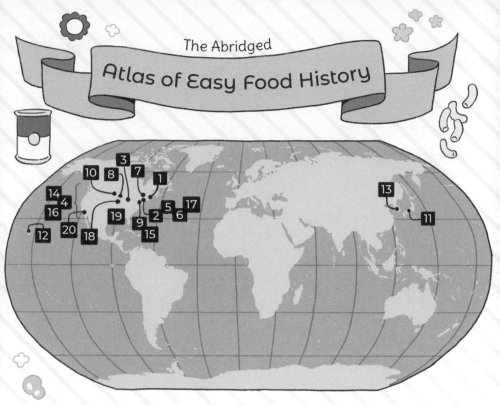

1. Boston Cooking-School
2. *Royal Baking Powder Cookbook*
3. Marion Harris Neil's *The Story of Crisco*
4. American Canned Food
5. Philadelphia Cream Cheese
6. Velveeta
7. James Heming's Macaroni Pie
8. Kraft Macaroni & Cheese
9. Campbell's Condensed Soups
10. Hormel's Spam
11. Momofuku Ando's Instant Ramen

12. Barbara Funamura's Spam Musubi
13. Korean Budae Jjigae
14. American Frozen Food
15. Dorcas Reilly's Green Bean Casserole
16. American Cake Mixes
17. Freda DeKnight's *A Date with a Dish*
18. St. Louis Gooey Butter Cake
19. Southern Ambrosia Salad
20. Julia Child's *Mastering the Art of French Cooking*

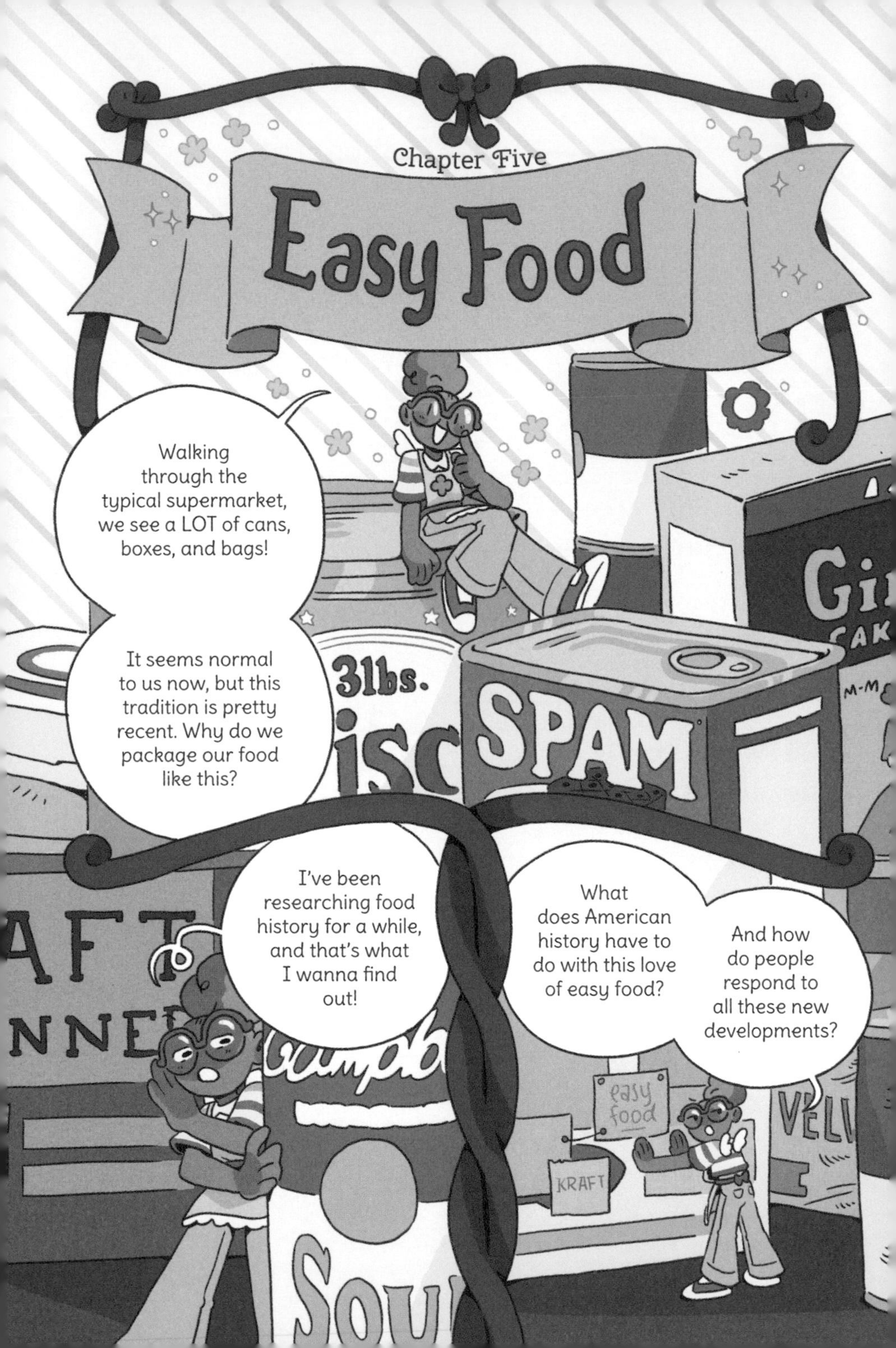
Chapter Five
Easy Food
Walking through the typical supermarket, we see a LOT of cans, boxes, and bags!
It seems normal to us now, but this tradition is pretty recent. Why do we package our food like this?
3lbs.
SPAM
I've been researching food history for a while, and that's what I wanna find out!
What does American history have to do with this love of easy food?
And how do people respond to all these new developments?
easy food
KRAFT

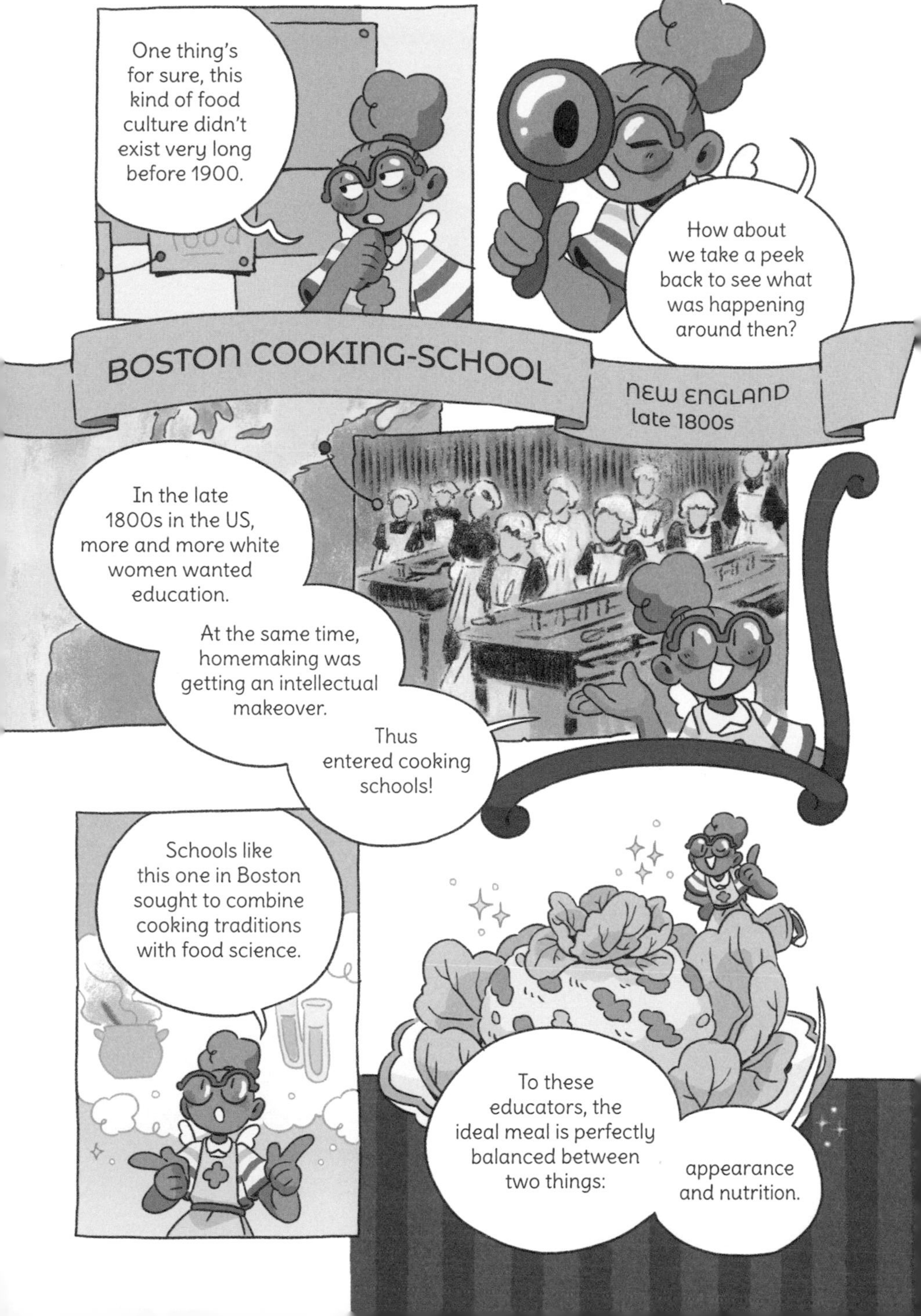
One thing's for sure, this kind of food culture didn't exist very long before 1900.
How about we take a peek back to see what was happening around then?
BOSTON COOKING-SCHOOL
NEW ENGLAND late 1800s
In the late 1800s in the US, more and more white women wanted education.
At the same time, homemaking was getting an intellectual makeover.
Thus entered cooking schools!
Schools like this one in Boston sought to combine cooking traditions with food science.
To these educators, the ideal meal is perfectly balanced between two things:
appearance and nutrition.

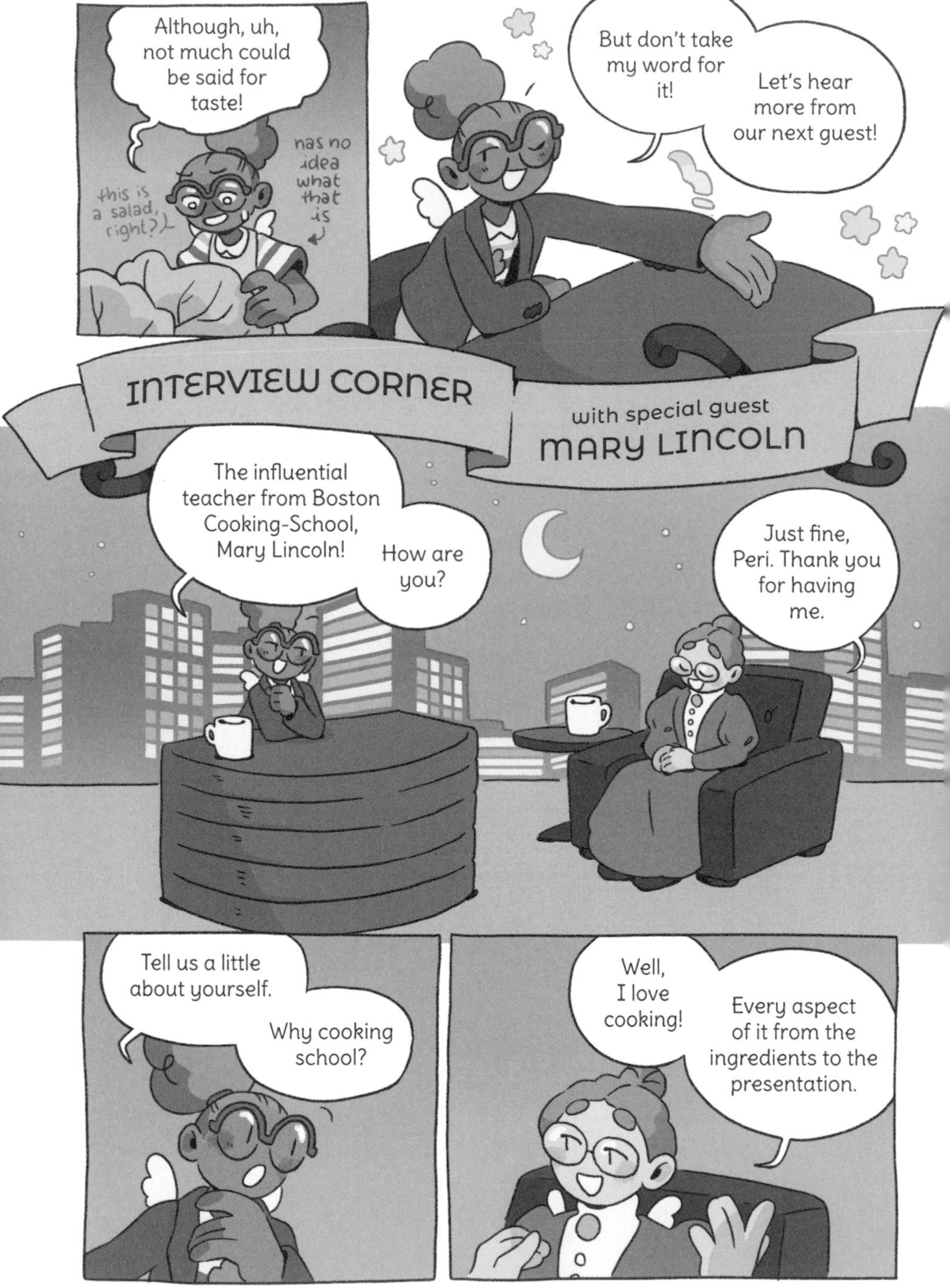
Although, uh, not much could be said for taste!
this is a salad, right?
has no idea what that is
But don't take my word for it!
Let's hear more from our next guest!
INTERVIEW CORNER
with special guest
MARY LINCOLN
The influential teacher from Boston Cooking-School, Mary Lincoln!
How are you?
Just fine, Peri. Thank you for having me.
Tell us a little about yourself.
Why cooking school?
Well, I love cooking!
Every aspect of it from the ingredients to the presentation.

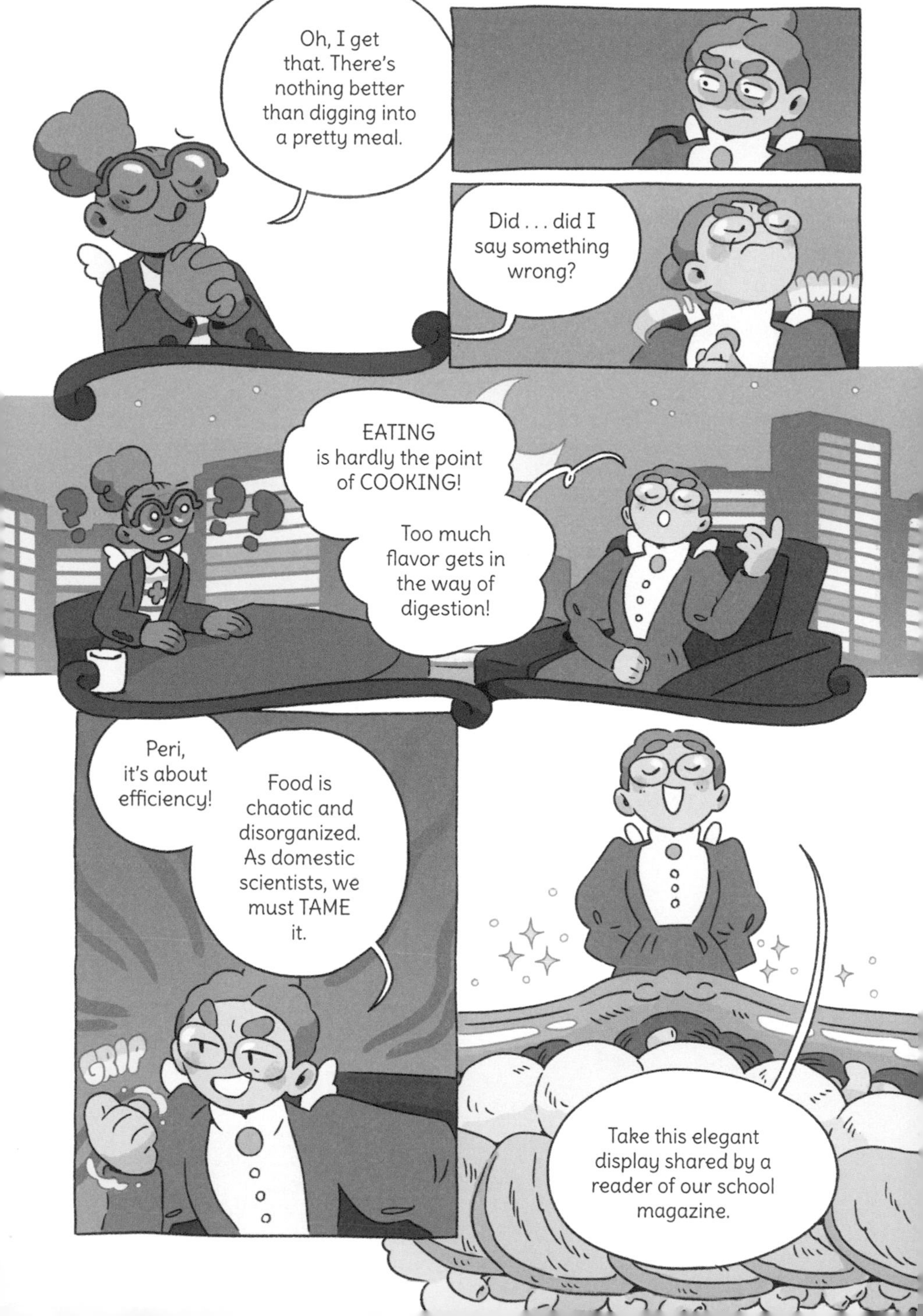

Oh, I get that. There's nothing better than digging into a pretty meal.
Did . . . did I say something wrong?
HMPH
EATING is hardly the point of COOKING!
Too much flavor gets in the way of digestion!
Peri, it's about efficiency!
Food is chaotic and disorganized. As domestic scientists, we must TAME it.
GRIP
Take this elegant display shared by a reader of our school magazine.

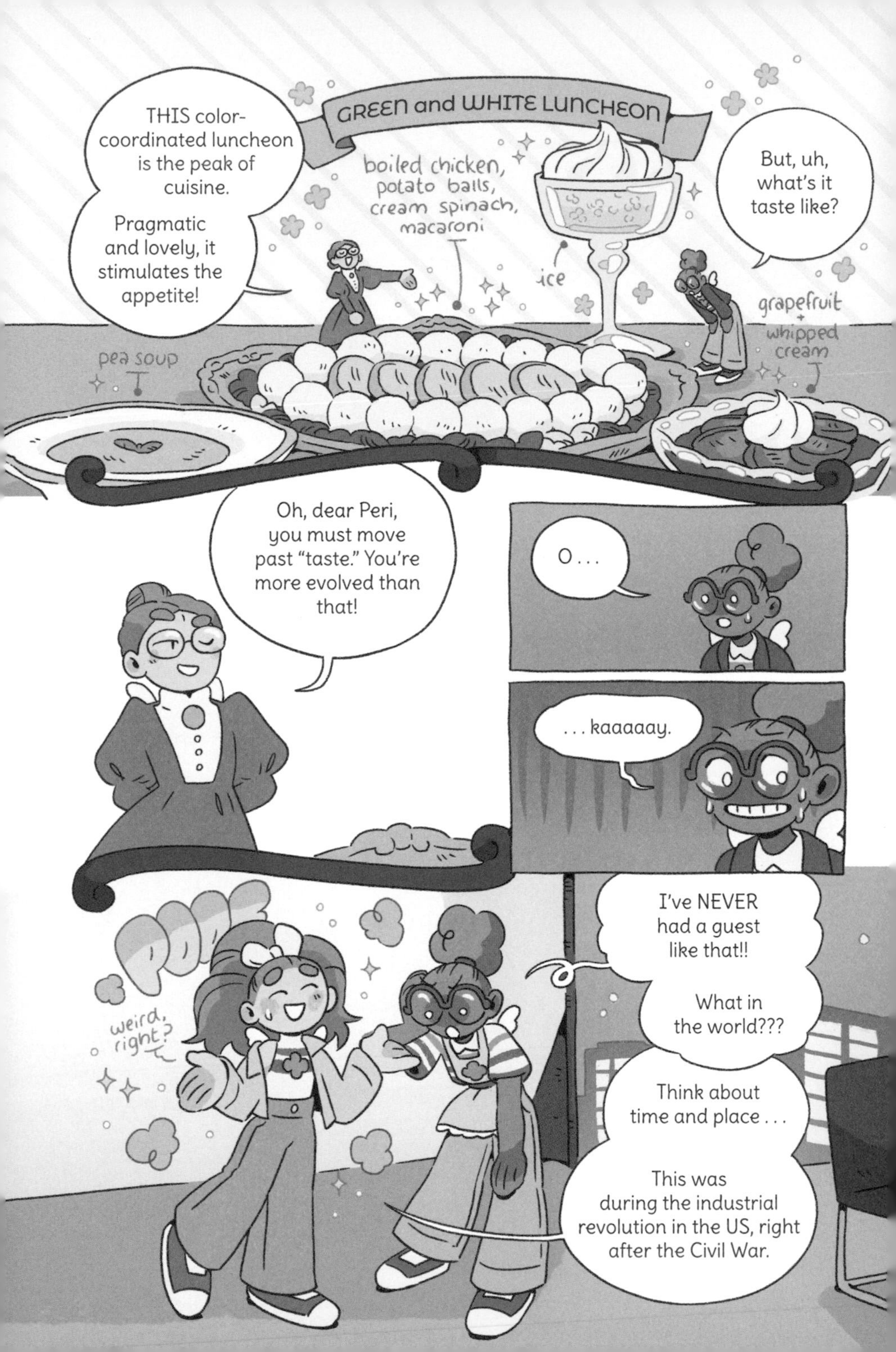
GREEN and WHITE LUNCHEON
THIS color-coordinated luncheon is the peak of cuisine.
Pragmatic and lovely, it stimulates the appetite!
boiled chicken, potato balls, cream spinach, macaroni
ice
But, uh, what's it taste like?
grapefruit + whipped cream
pea soup
Oh, dear Peri, you must move past "taste." You're more evolved than that!
O . . .
. . . kaaaaay.
weird, right?
I've NEVER had a guest like that!!
What in the world???
Think about time and place . . .
This was during the industrial revolution in the US, right after the Civil War.

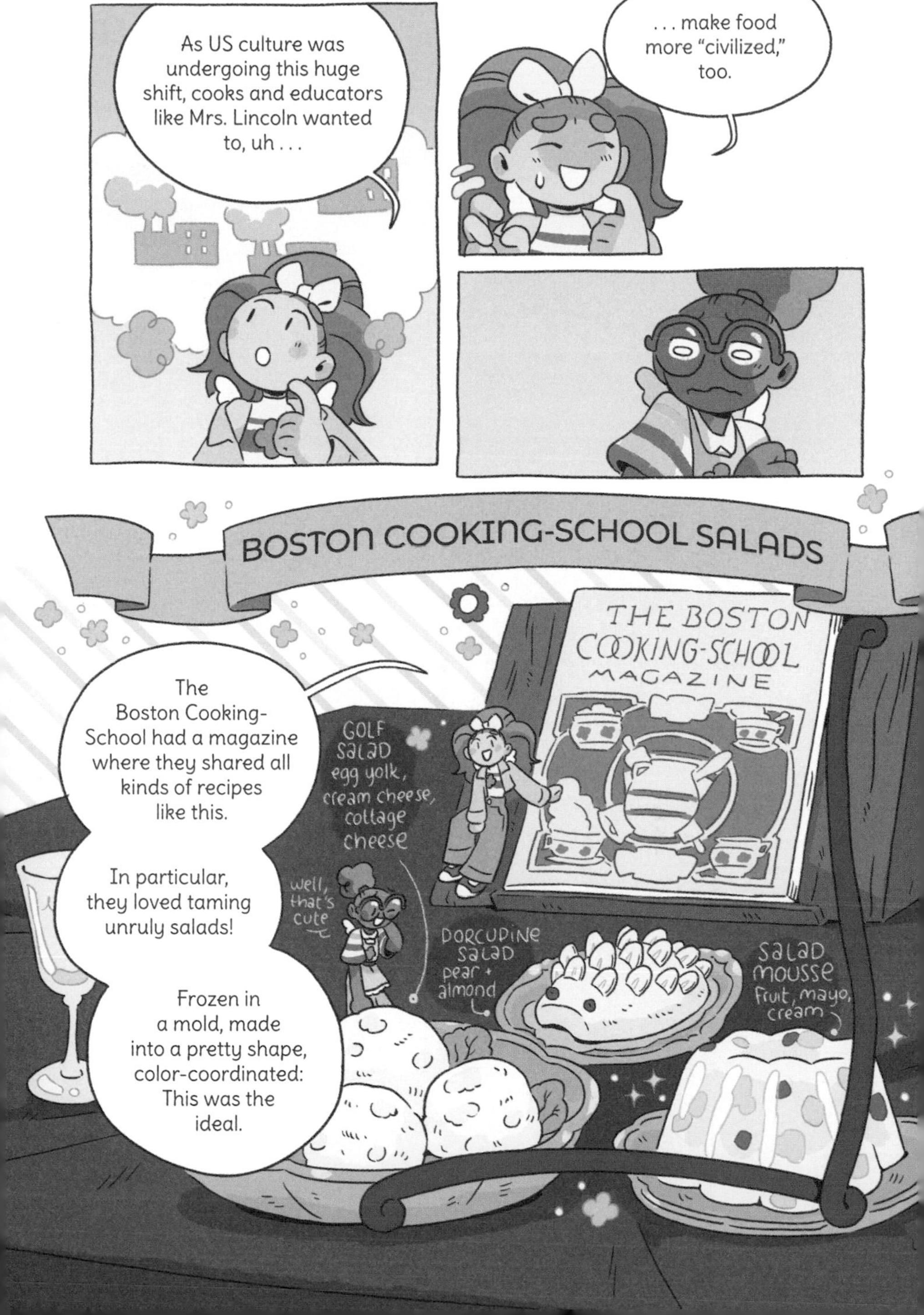
As US culture was undergoing this huge shift, cooks and educators like Mrs. Lincoln wanted to, uh . . .
. . . make food more "civilized," too.
BOSTON COOKING-SCHOOL SALADS
THE BOSTON COOKING-SCHOOL MAGAZINE
The Boston Cooking-School had a magazine where they shared all kinds of recipes like this.
GOLF SALAD egg yolk, cream cheese, cottage cheese
In particular, they loved taming unruly salads!
well, that's cute
PORCUPINE SALAD pear + almond
SALAD MOUSSE Fruit, mayo, cream
Frozen in a mold, made into a pretty shape, color-coordinated: This was the ideal.

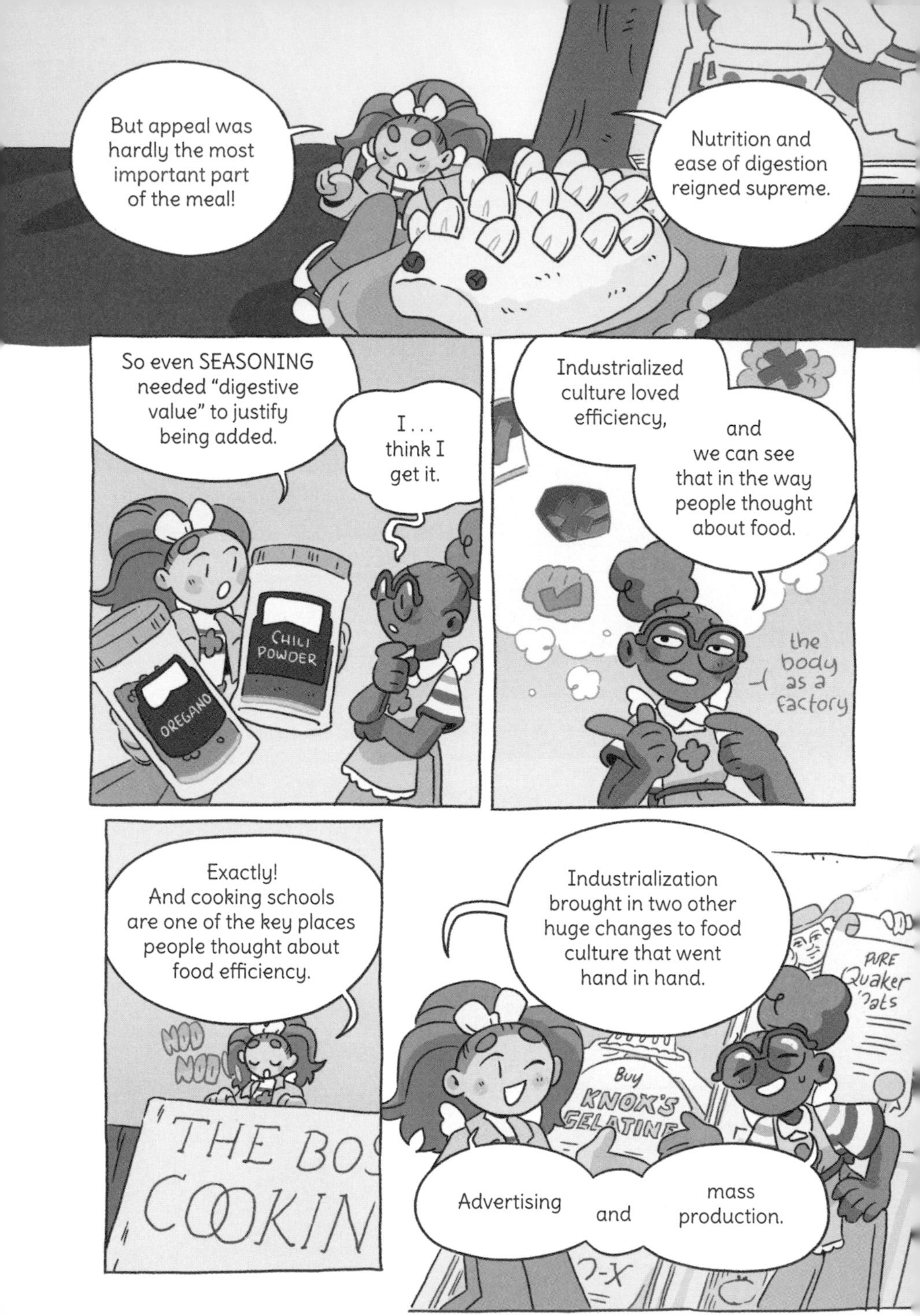
But appeal was hardly the most important part of the meal!
Nutrition and ease of digestion reigned supreme.
So even SEASONING needed "digestive value" to justify being added.
I... think I get it.
CHILI POWDER
OREGANO
Industrialized culture loved efficiency,
and we can see that in the way people thought about food.
the body as a factory
Exactly! And cooking schools are one of the key places people thought about food efficiency.
NOD NOD
THE BOS
COOKIN
Industrialization brought in two other huge changes to food culture that went hand in hand.
PURE Quaker Oats
Buy KNOX'S GELATINE
Advertising
and
mass production.

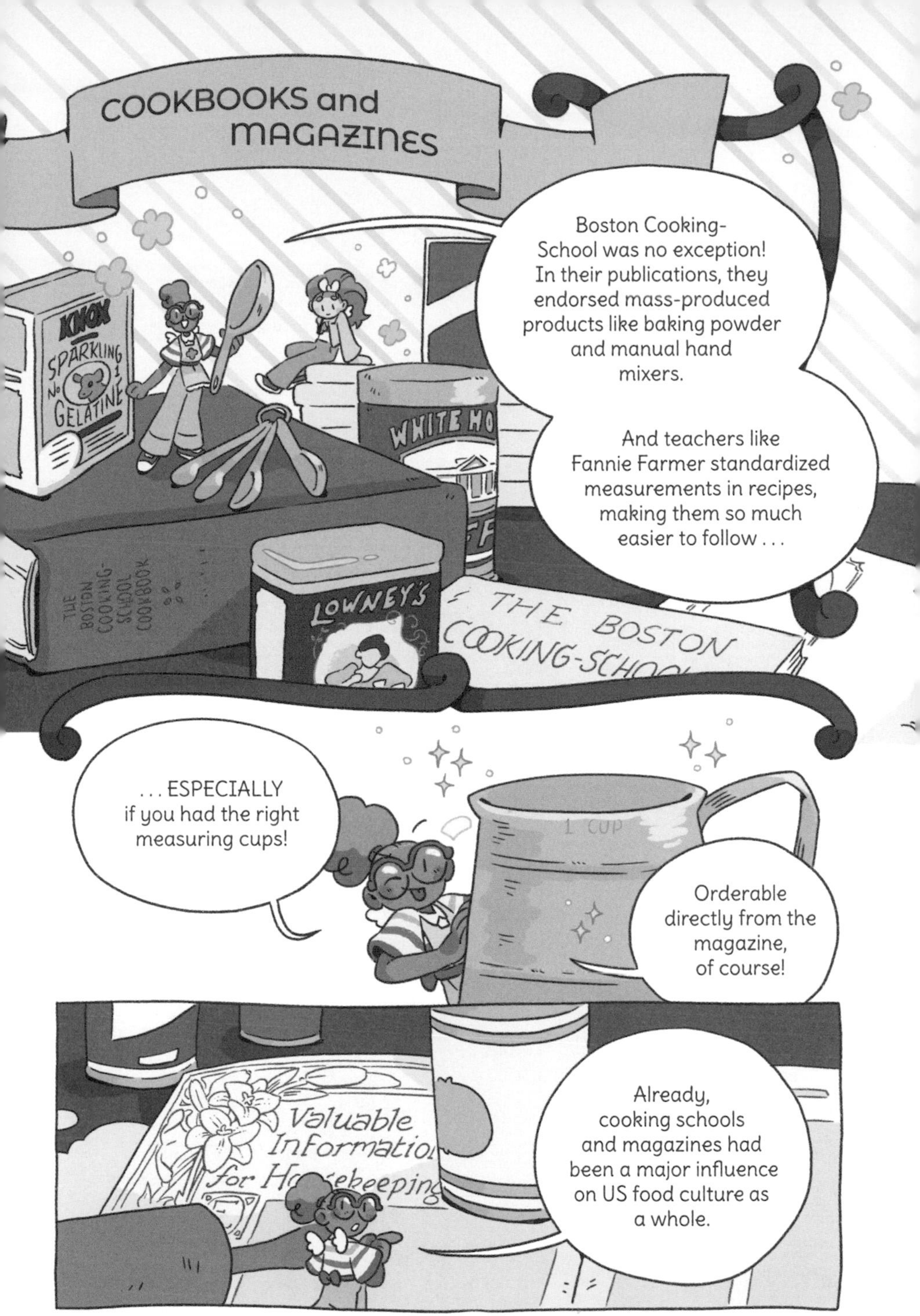
COOKBOOKS and MAGAZINES
KNOX SPARKLING GELATINE
WHITE HO
THE BOSTON COOKING-SCHOOL COOKBOOK
LOWNEY'S
THE BOSTON COOKING-SCHO
Boston Cooking-School was no exception! In their publications, they endorsed mass-produced products like baking powder and manual hand mixers.
And teachers like Fannie Farmer standardized measurements in recipes, making them so much easier to follow . . .
. . . ESPECIALLY if you had the right measuring cups!
1 CUP
Orderable directly from the magazine, of course!
Valuable Informatio for Ho ekeeping
Already, cooking schools and magazines had been a major influence on US food culture as a whole.

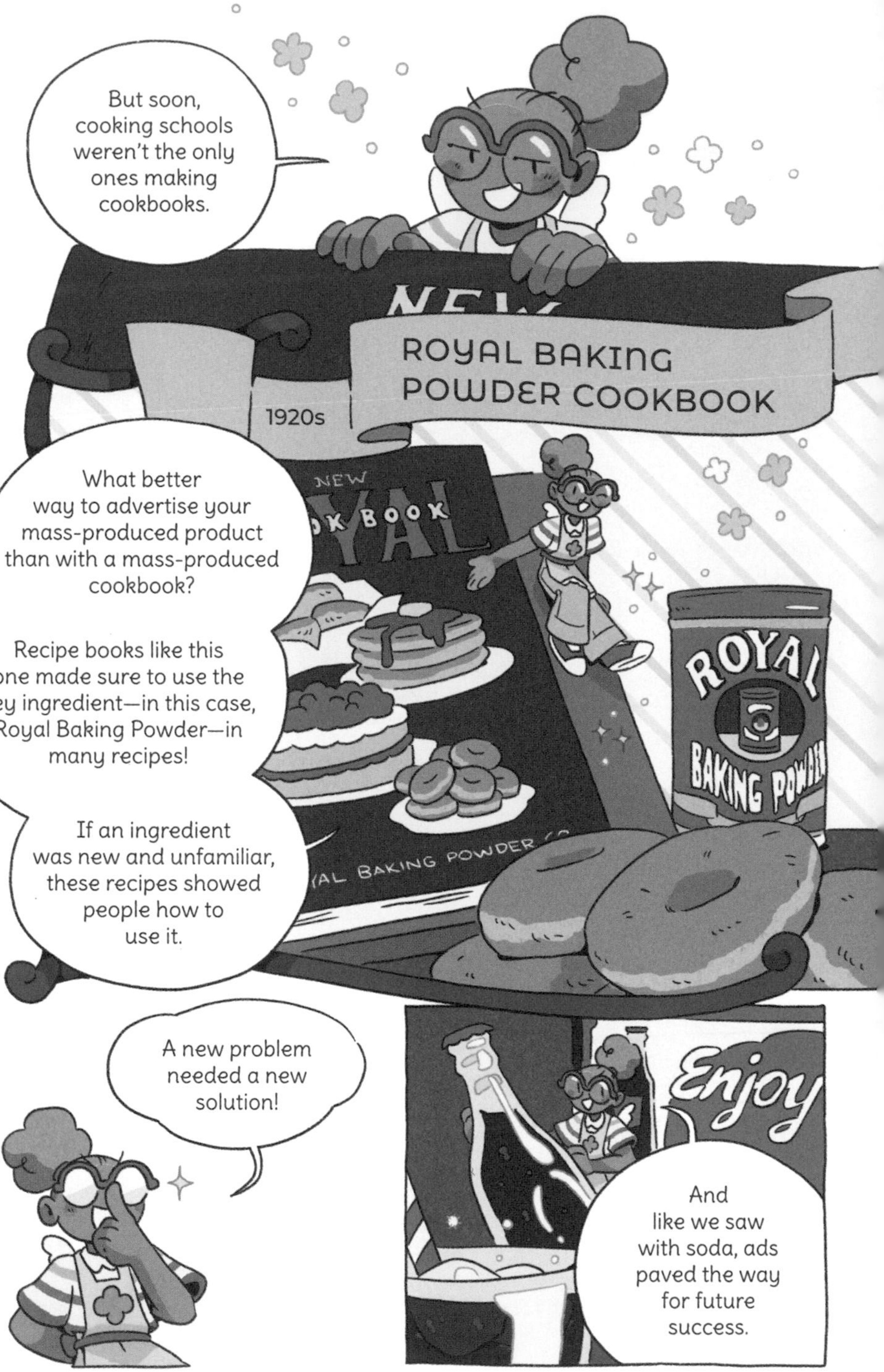
But soon, cooking schools weren't the only ones making cookbooks.
NEW
ROYAL BAKING POWDER COOKBOOK
1920s
NEW
OK BOOK
YAL
YAL BAKING POWDER C
ROYAL
BAKING POWDER
What better way to advertise your mass-produced product than with a mass-produced cookbook?
Recipe books like this one made sure to use the key ingredient—in this case, Royal Baking Powder—in many recipes!
If an ingredient was new and unfamiliar, these recipes showed people how to use it.
A new problem needed a new solution!
Enjoy
And like we saw with soda, ads paved the way for future success.

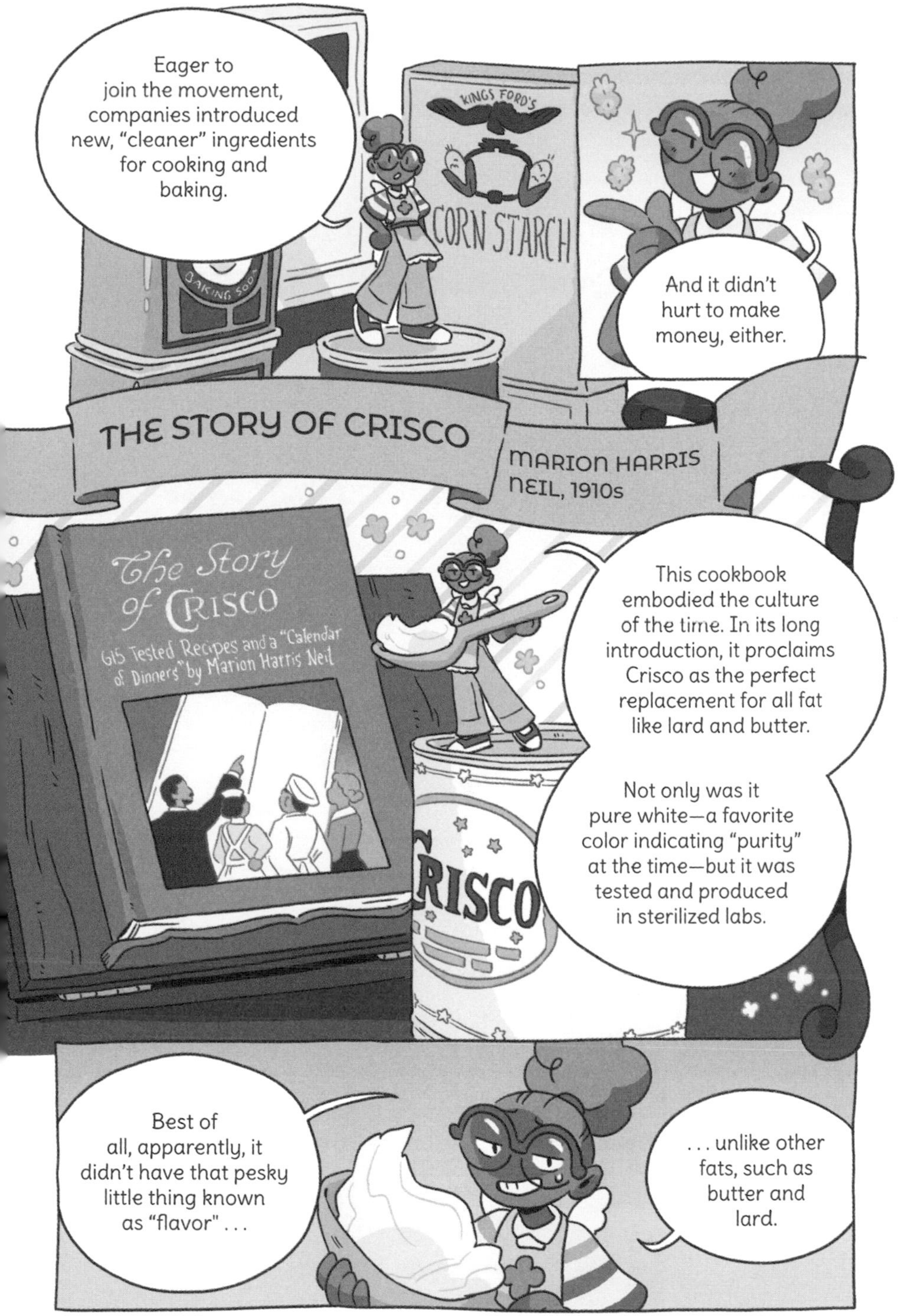

Eager to join the movement, companies introduced new, "cleaner" ingredients for cooking and baking.
KINGS FORD'S
CORN STARCH
BAKING SODA
And it didn't hurt to make money, either.
THE STORY OF CRISCO
MARION HARRIS NEIL, 1910s
The Story of Crisco
615 Tested Recipes and a "Calendar of Dinners" by Marion Harris Neil
This cookbook embodied the culture of the time. In its long introduction, it proclaims Crisco as the perfect replacement for all fat like lard and butter.
CRISCO
Not only was it pure white—a favorite color indicating "purity" at the time—but it was tested and produced in sterilized labs.
Best of all, apparently, it didn't have that pesky little thing known as "flavor" . . .
. . . unlike other fats, such as butter and lard.

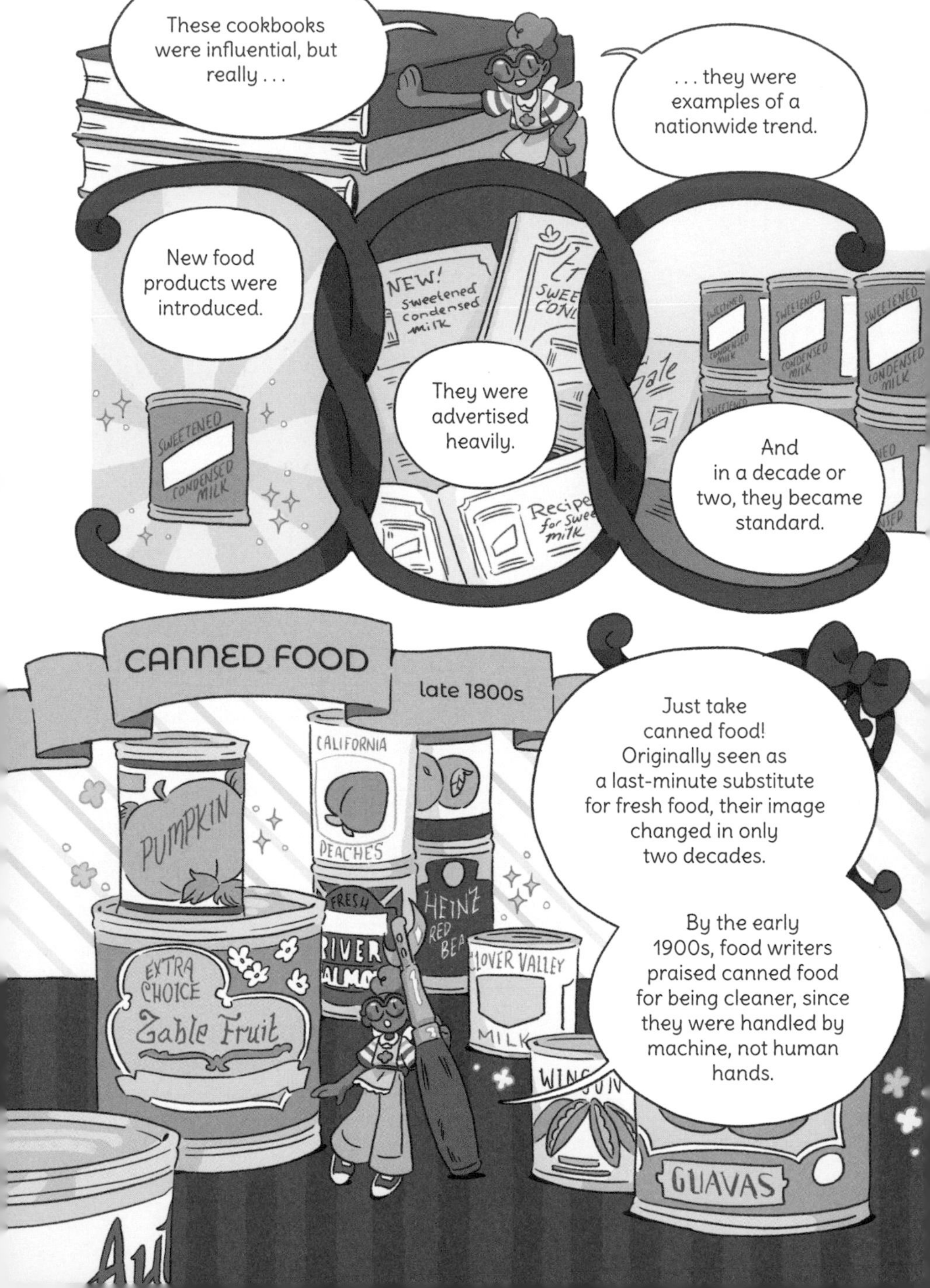
These cookbooks were influential, but really . . .
. . . they were examples of a nationwide trend.
New food products were introduced.
NEW! Sweetened Condensed milk
SWEETENED CONDENSED MILK
They were advertised heavily.
And in a decade or two, they became standard.
CANNED FOOD
late 1800s
Just take canned food! Originally seen as a last-minute substitute for fresh food, their image changed in only two decades.
By the early 1900s, food writers praised canned food for being cleaner, since they were handled by machine, not human hands.
PUMPKIN
CALIFORNIA
PEACHES
FRESH
HEINZ
CLOVER VALLEY
MILK
EXTRA CHOICE Table Fruit
GUAVAS

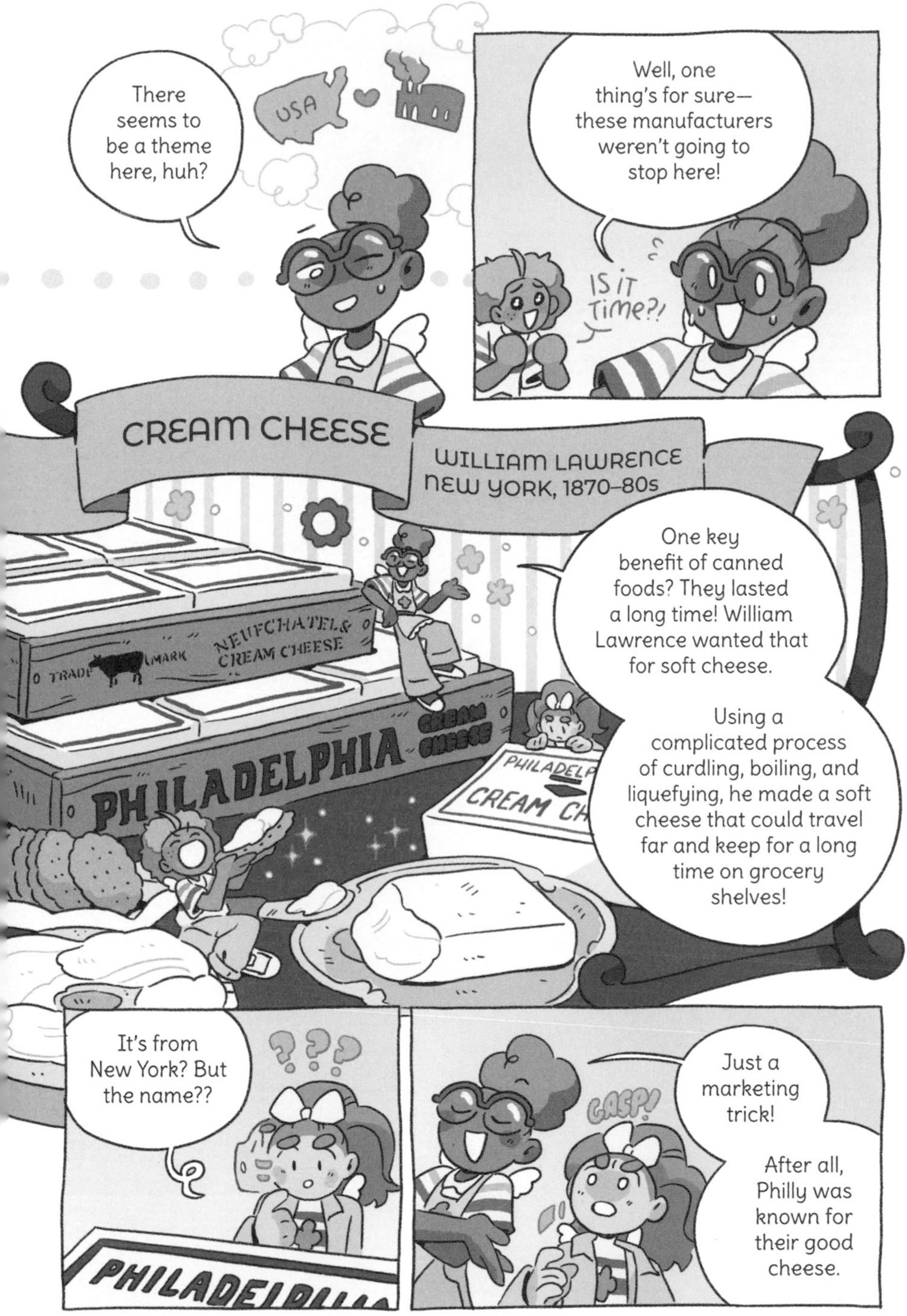
There seems to be a theme here, huh?
USA
Well, one thing's for sure— these manufacturers weren't going to stop here!
IS IT TIME?!
CREAM CHEESE
WILLIAM LAWRENCE
NEW YORK, 1870–80s
NEUFCHATEL & CREAM CHEESE
TRADE MARK
PHILADELPHIA
CREAM CHEESE
One key benefit of canned foods? They lasted a long time! William Lawrence wanted that for soft cheese.
Using a complicated process of curdling, boiling, and liquefying, he made a soft cheese that could travel far and keep for a long time on grocery shelves!
It's from New York? But the name??
Just a marketing trick!
GASP!
After all, Philly was known for their good cheese.

Fada doesn't seem to care.

Nope!

MORE!!! MORE EASY CHEESE!!!

LONG LIVE THE CHEESE!

Okay, OKAY!

The scientists at Kraft Foods wanted more easy cheese, too!

By the 1920s, they'd made a soft, blended cheese that didn't even require refrigeration.

Even after thousands of years making cheese, people found yet another way to make it!

1920s

VELVEETA

KRAFT

VELVEET

THE ...US CHEESE FOOD

And Fada's favorite cheese dish would soon enter the spotlight.

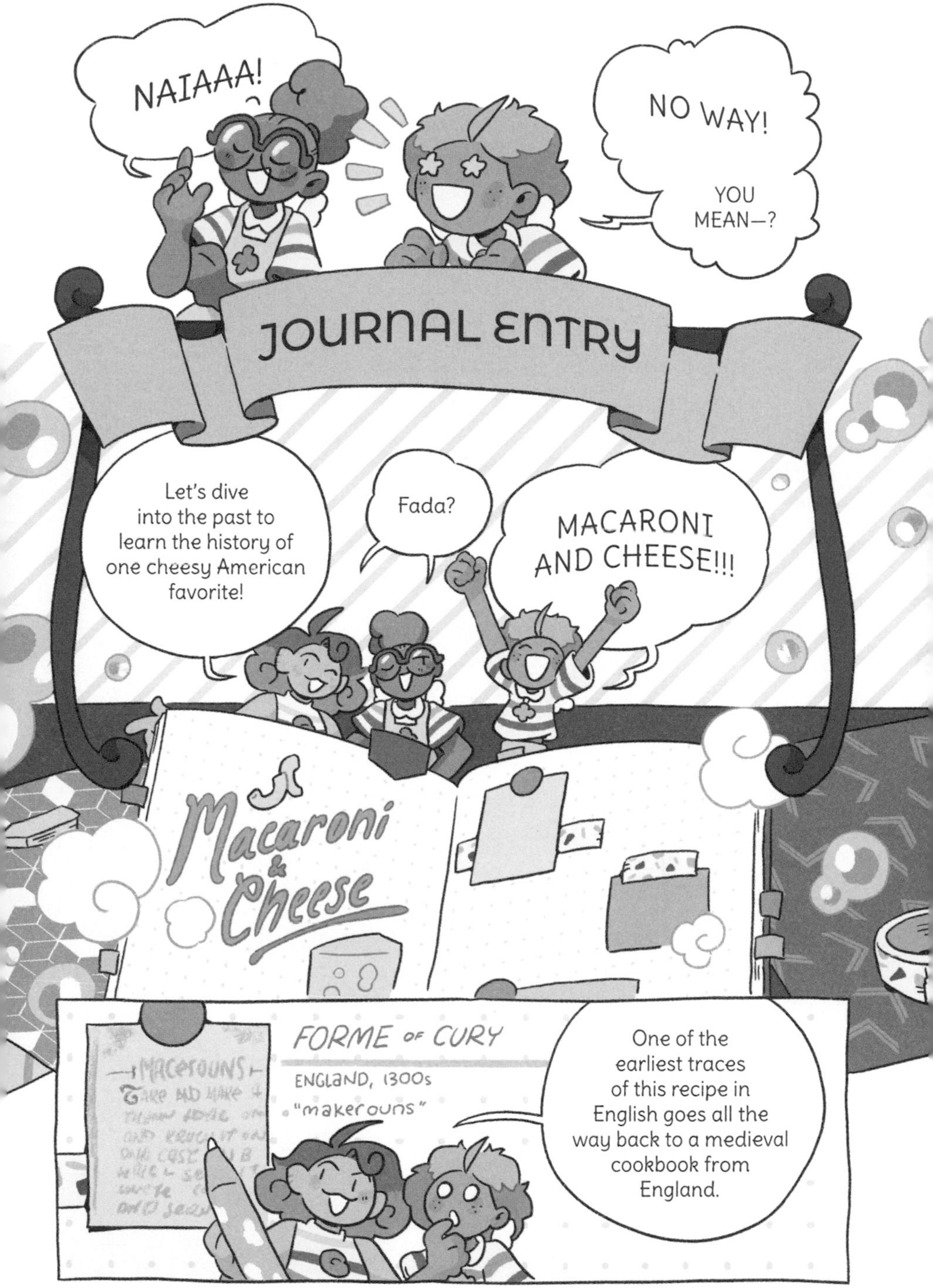
NAIAAA!
NO WAY!
YOU MEAN—?
JOURNAL ENTRY
Let's dive into the past to learn the history of one cheesy American favorite!
Fada?
MACARONI AND CHEESE!!!
Macaroni & Cheese
MACEROUNS
FORME OF CURY
ENGLAND, 1300s
"makerouns"
One of the earliest traces of this recipe in English goes all the way back to a medieval cookbook from England.

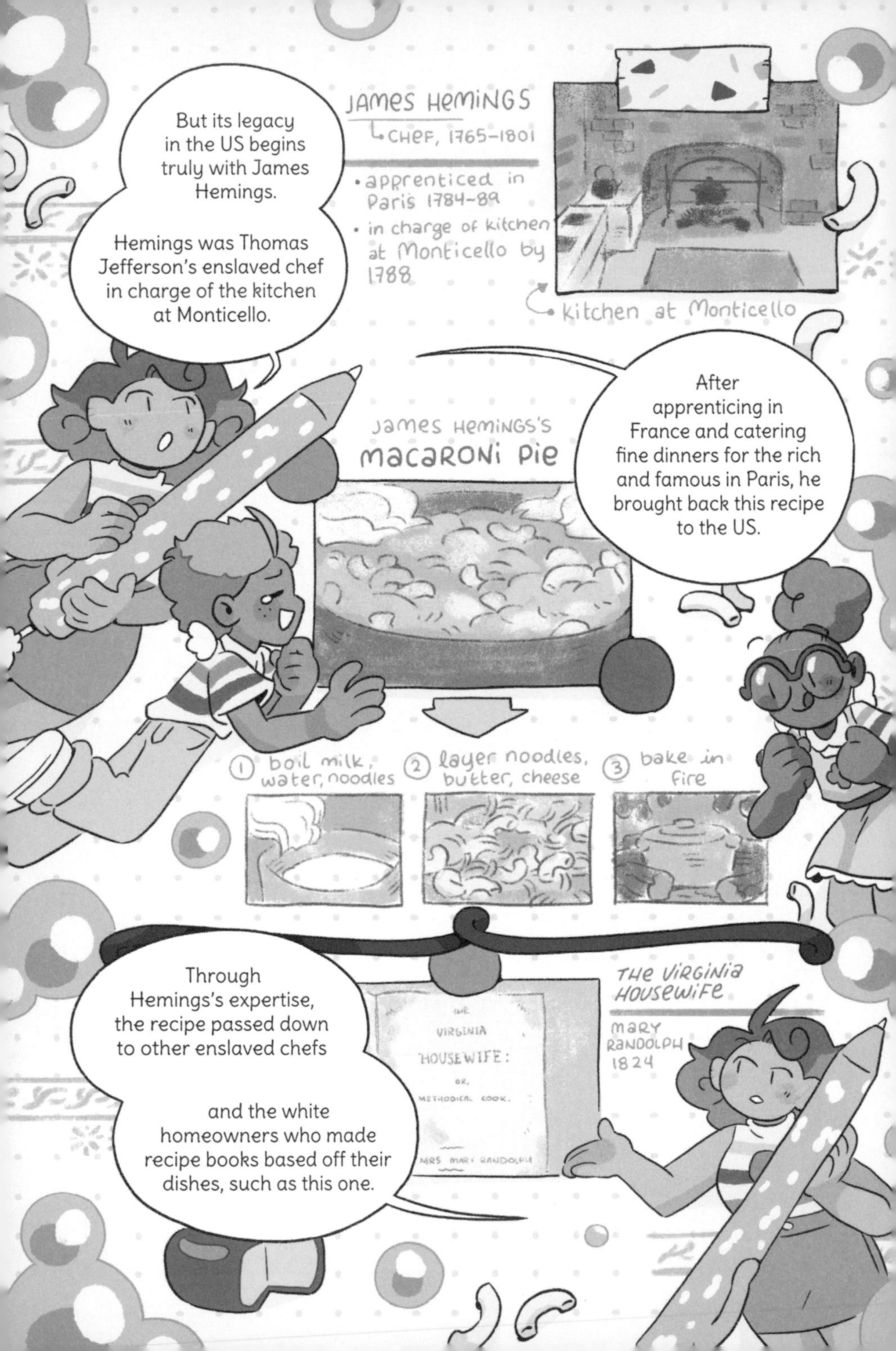
But its legacy in the US begins truly with James Hemings.
Hemings was Thomas Jefferson's enslaved chef in charge of the kitchen at Monticello.
JAMES HEMINGS
CHEF, 1765–1801
• apprenticed in Paris 1784–89
• in charge of kitchen at Monticello by 1788
kitchen at Monticello
After apprenticing in France and catering fine dinners for the rich and famous in Paris, he brought back this recipe to the US.
JAMES HEMINGS'S
MACARONI PIE
1 boil milk, water, noodles
2 layer noodles, butter, cheese
3 bake in fire
Through Hemings's expertise, the recipe passed down to other enslaved chefs
and the white homeowners who made recipe books based off their dishes, such as this one.
THE VIRGINIA HOUSEWIFE
MARY RANDOLPH
1824
THE VIRGINIA HOUSEWIFE: OR, METHODICAL COOK.
MRS MARY RANDOLPH

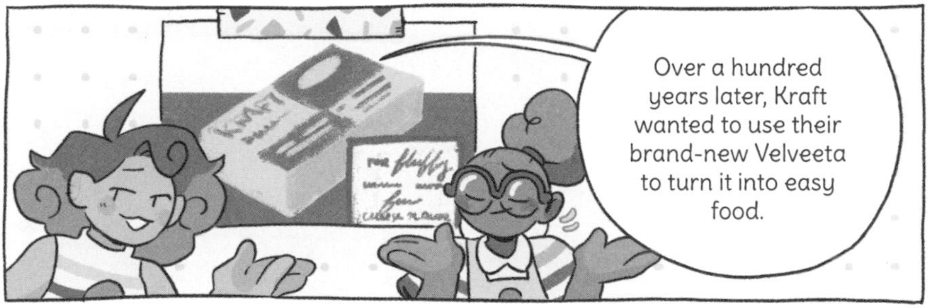
Over a hundred years later, Kraft wanted to use their brand-new Velveeta to turn it into easy food.

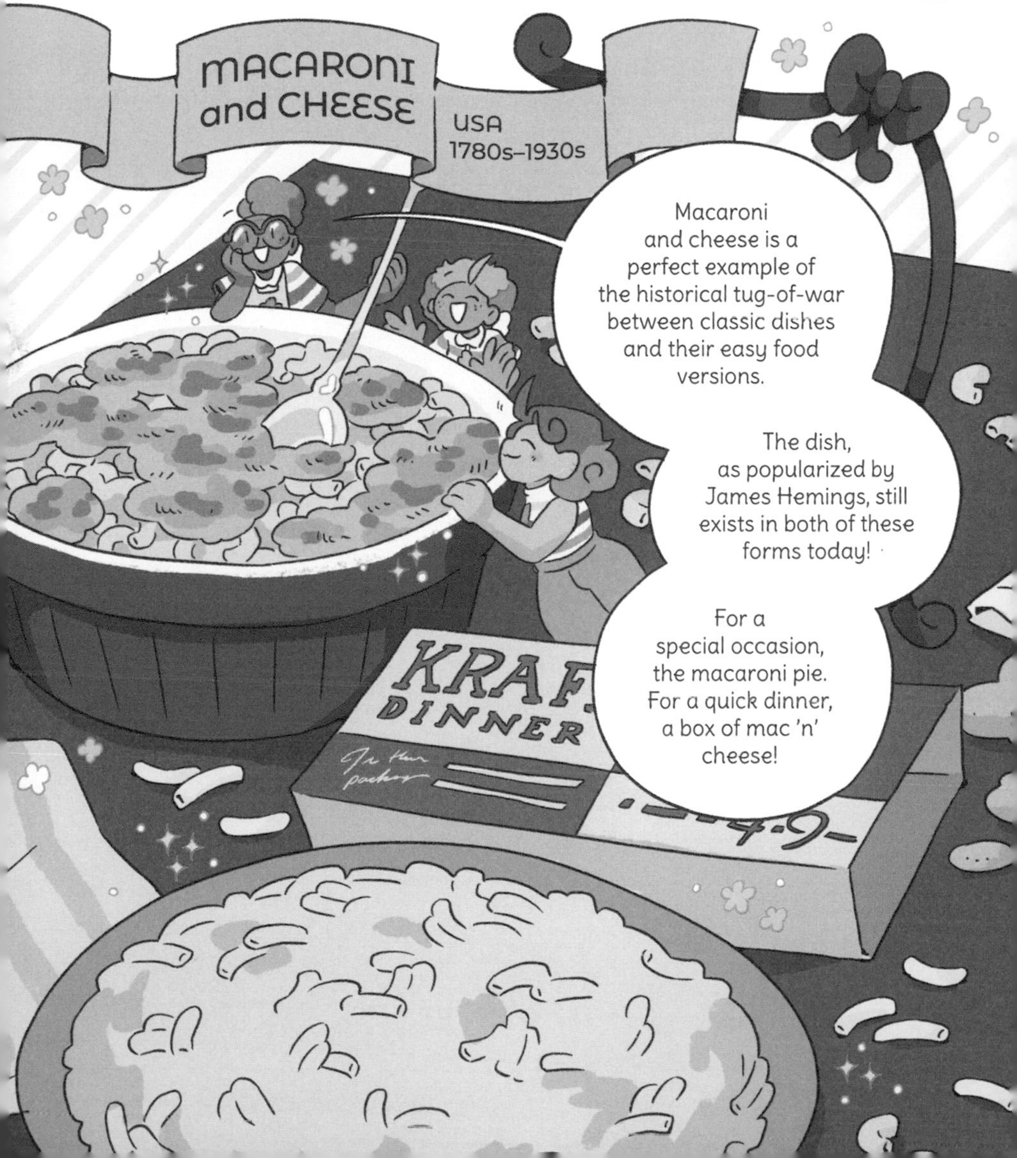
MACARONI and CHEESE
USA
1780s–1930s
Macaroni and cheese is a perfect example of the historical tug-of-war between classic dishes and their easy food versions.
The dish, as popularized by James Hemings, still exists in both of these forms today!
For a special occasion, the macaroni pie. For a quick dinner, a box of mac 'n' cheese!
DINNER

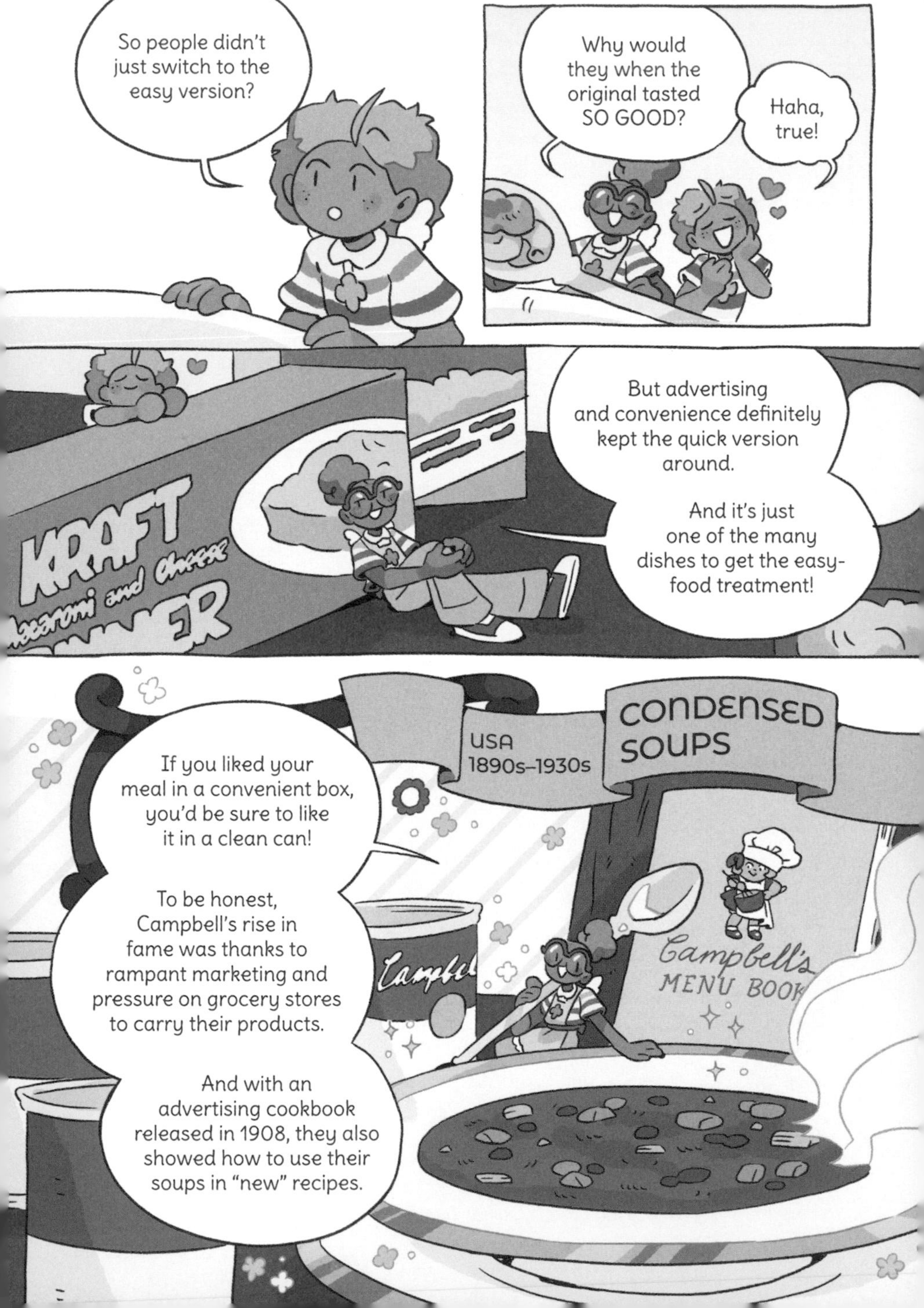
So people didn't just switch to the easy version?
Why would they when the original tasted SO GOOD?
Haha, true!
KRAFT Macaroni and Cheese DINNER
But advertising and convenience definitely kept the quick version around.
And it's just one of the many dishes to get the easy-food treatment!
USA 1890s–1930s
CONDENSED SOUPS
If you liked your meal in a convenient box, you'd be sure to like it in a clean can!
To be honest, Campbell's rise in fame was thanks to rampant marketing and pressure on grocery stores to carry their products.
And with an advertising cookbook released in 1908, they also showed how to use their soups in "new" recipes.
Campbell's MENU BOOK

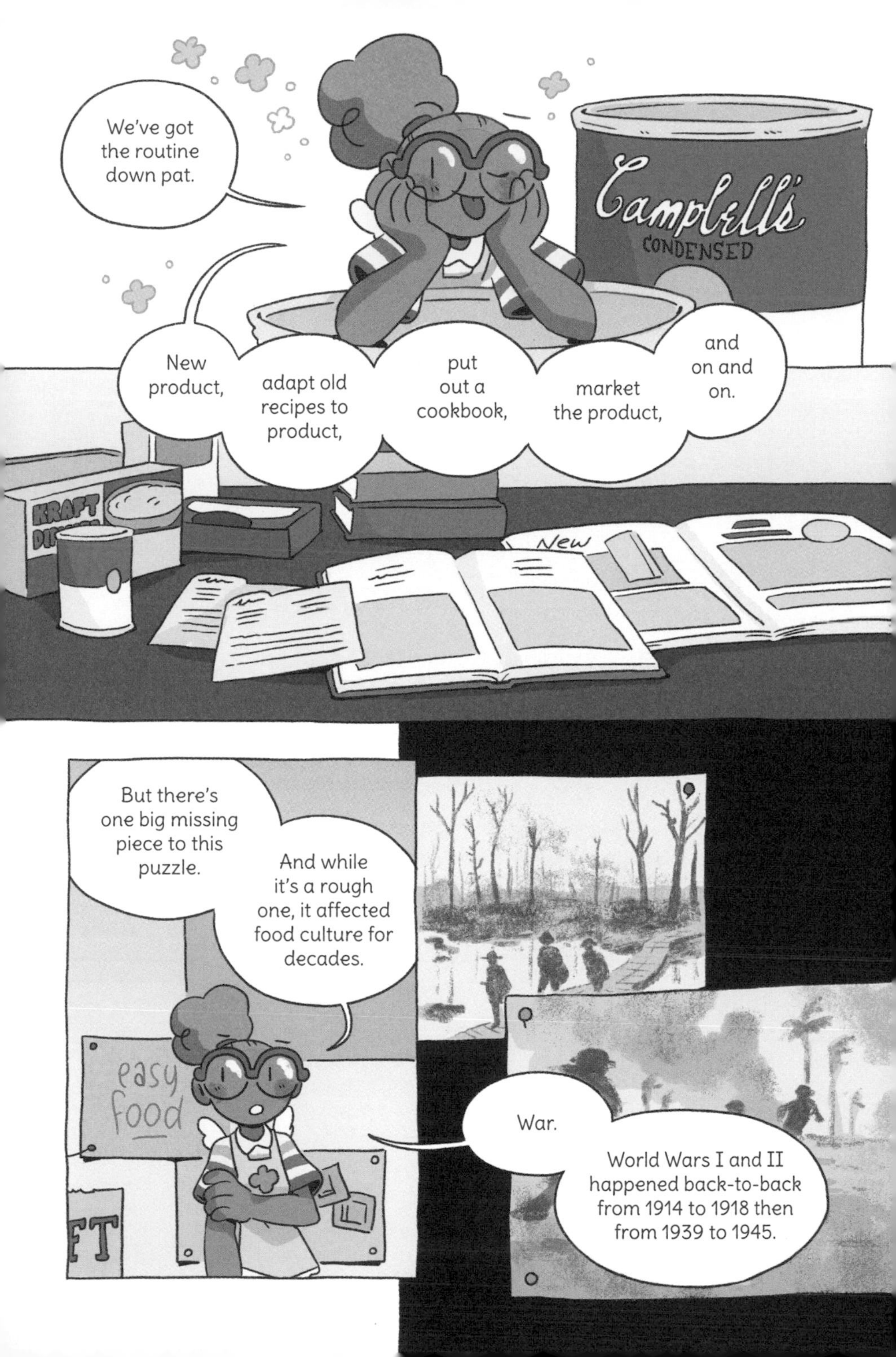

We've got the routine down pat.
Campbell's
CONDENSED
New product,
adapt old recipes to product,
put out a cookbook,
market the product,
and on and on.
KRAFT
New
But there's one big missing piece to this puzzle.
And while it's a rough one, it affected food culture for decades.
easy food
War.
World Wars I and II happened back-to-back from 1914 to 1918 then from 1939 to 1945.

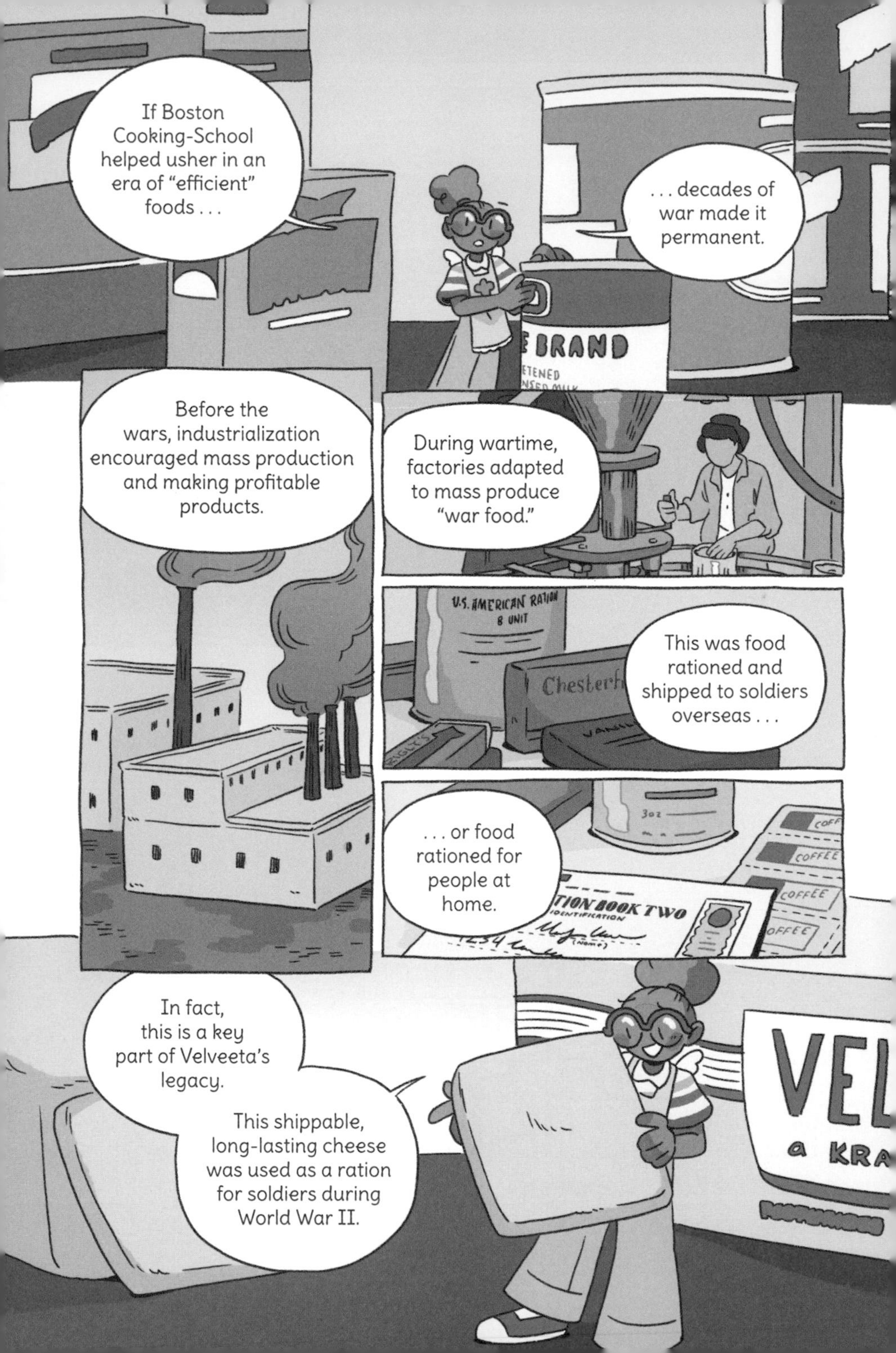
If Boston Cooking-School helped usher in an era of "efficient" foods . . .
. . . decades of war made it permanent.
Before the wars, industrialization encouraged mass production and making profitable products.
During wartime, factories adapted to mass produce "war food."
U.S. AMERICAN RATION
B UNIT
This was food rationed and shipped to soldiers overseas . . .
. . . or food rationed for people at home.
COFFEE
COFFEE
In fact, this is a key part of Velveeta's legacy.
This shippable, long-lasting cheese was used as a ration for soldiers during World War II.

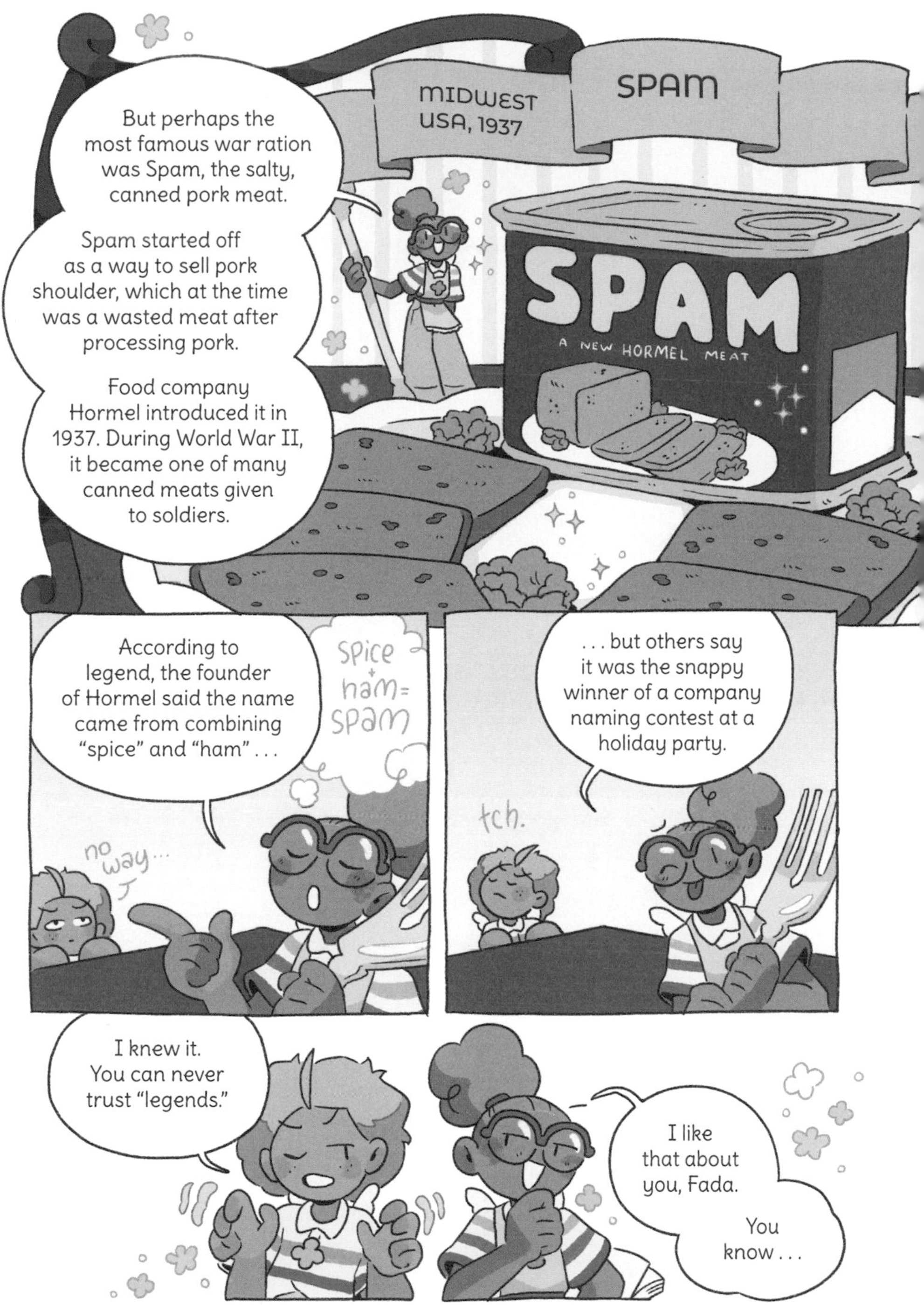
MIDWEST USA, 1937
SPAM
But perhaps the most famous war ration was Spam, the salty, canned pork meat.
Spam started off as a way to sell pork shoulder, which at the time was a wasted meat after processing pork.
Food company Hormel introduced it in 1937. During World War II, it became one of many canned meats given to soldiers.
SPAM
A NEW HORMEL MEAT
According to legend, the founder of Hormel said the name came from combining "spice" and "ham" . . .
spice + ham = spam
no way...
. . . but others say it was the snappy winner of a company naming contest at a holiday party.
tch.
I knew it. You can never trust "legends."
I like that about you, Fada.
You know . . .

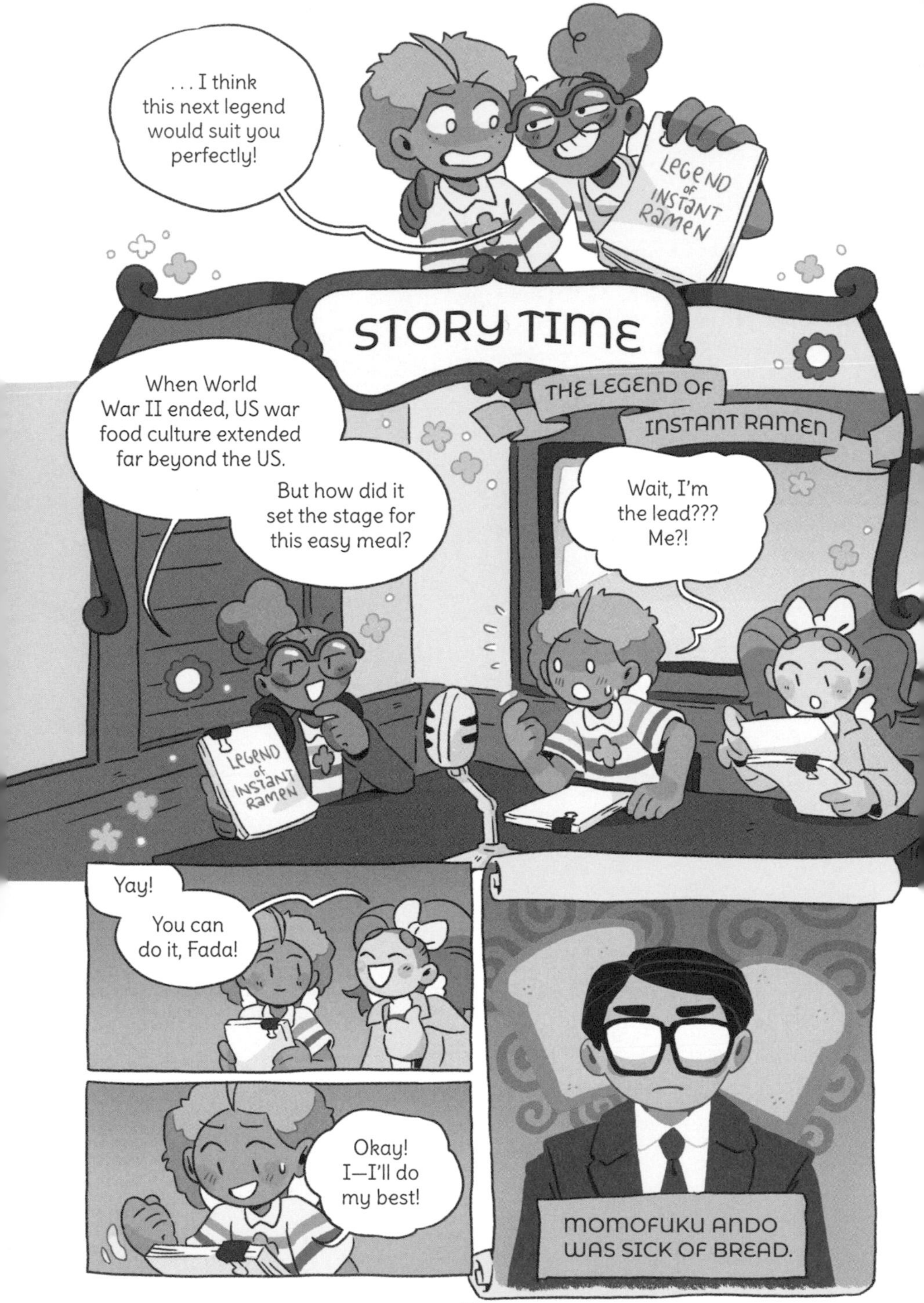
. . . I think this next legend would suit you perfectly!
LEGEND of INSTANT RAMEN
STORY TIME
THE LEGEND OF INSTANT RAMEN
When World War II ended, US war food culture extended far beyond the US.
But how did it set the stage for this easy meal?
Wait, I'm the lead??? Me?!
LEGEND of INSTANT RAMEN
Yay!
You can do it, Fada!
Okay! I—I'll do my best!
MOMOFUKU ANDO WAS SICK OF BREAD.

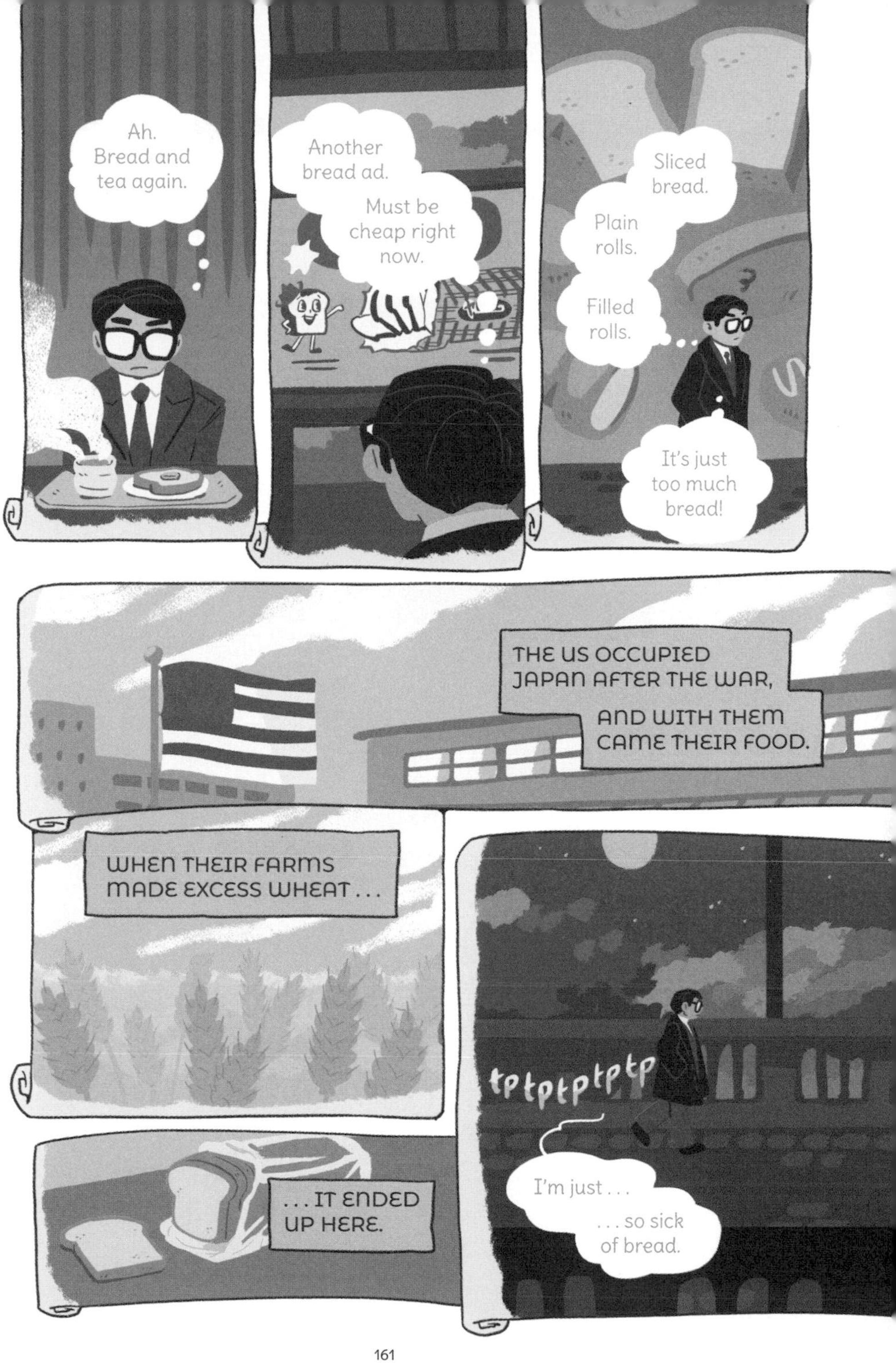
Ah. Bread and tea again.
Another bread ad.
Must be cheap right now.
Sliced bread.
Plain rolls.
Filled rolls.
It's just too much bread!
THE US OCCUPIED JAPAN AFTER THE WAR,
AND WITH THEM CAME THEIR FOOD.
WHEN THEIR FARMS MADE EXCESS WHEAT . . .
. . . IT ENDED UP HERE.
tptptptptp
I'm just . . .
. . . so sick of bread.

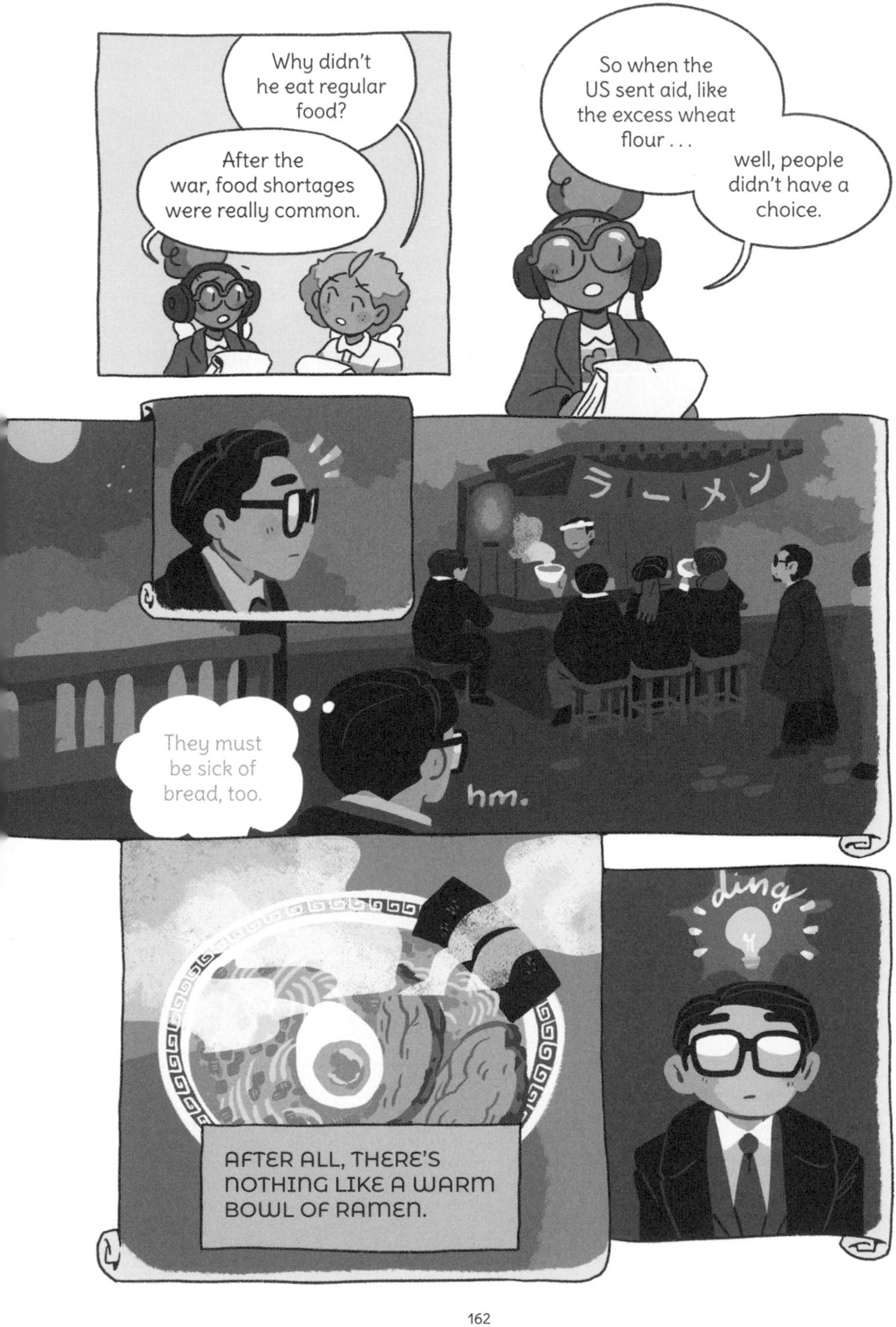

Why didn't he eat regular food?
After the war, food shortages were really common.
So when the US sent aid, like the excess wheat flour . . .
well, people didn't have a choice.
ラーメン
They must be sick of bread, too.
hm.
AFTER ALL, THERE'S NOTHING LIKE A WARM BOWL OF RAMEN.
ding

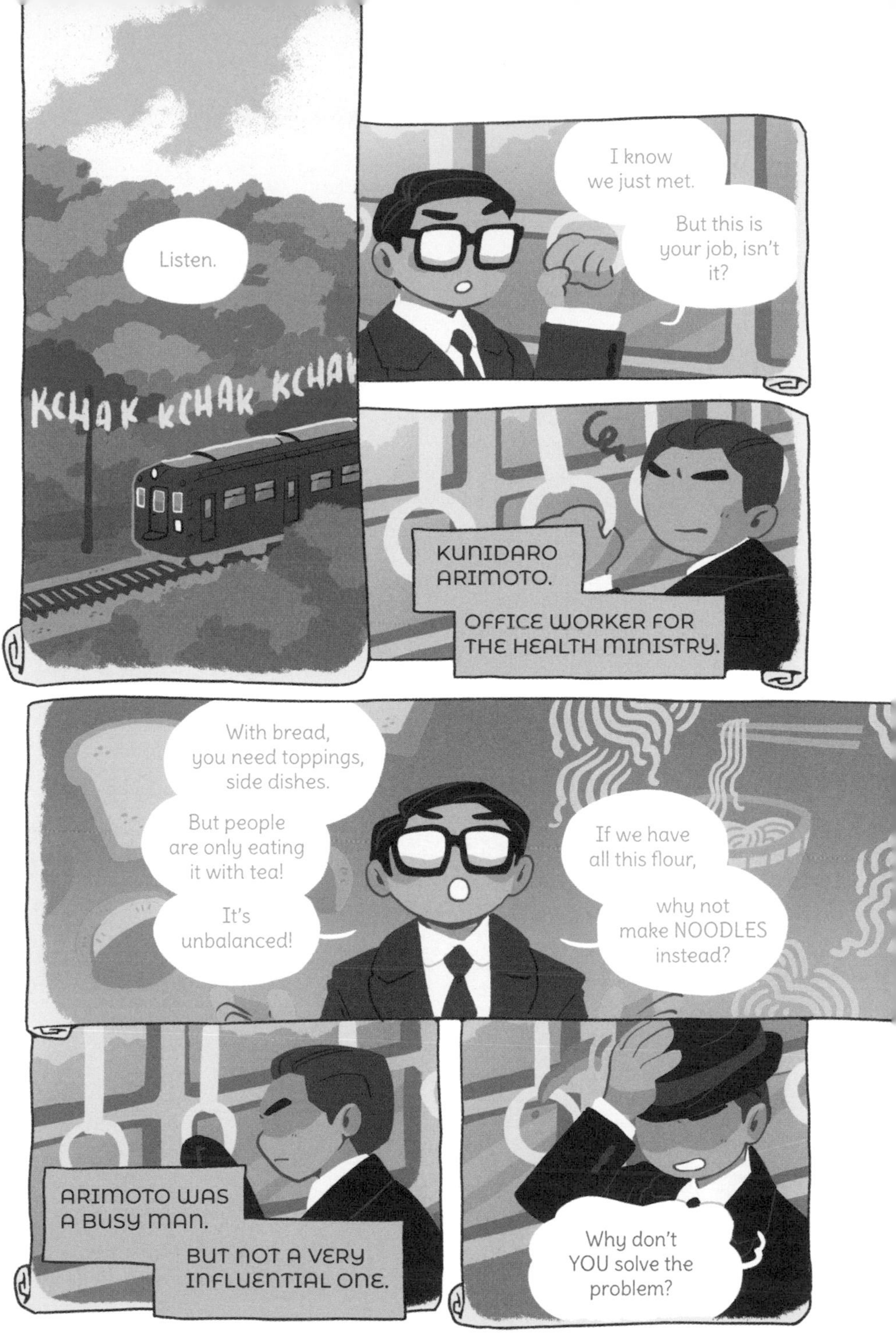
Listen.
KCHAK KCHAK KCHAK
I know we just met.
But this is your job, isn't it?
KUNIDARO ARIMOTO.
OFFICE WORKER FOR THE HEALTH MINISTRY.
With bread, you need toppings, side dishes.
But people are only eating it with tea!
It's unbalanced!
If we have all this flour,
why not make NOODLES instead?
ARIMOTO WAS A BUSY MAN.
BUT NOT A VERY INFLUENTIAL ONE.
Why don't YOU solve the problem?

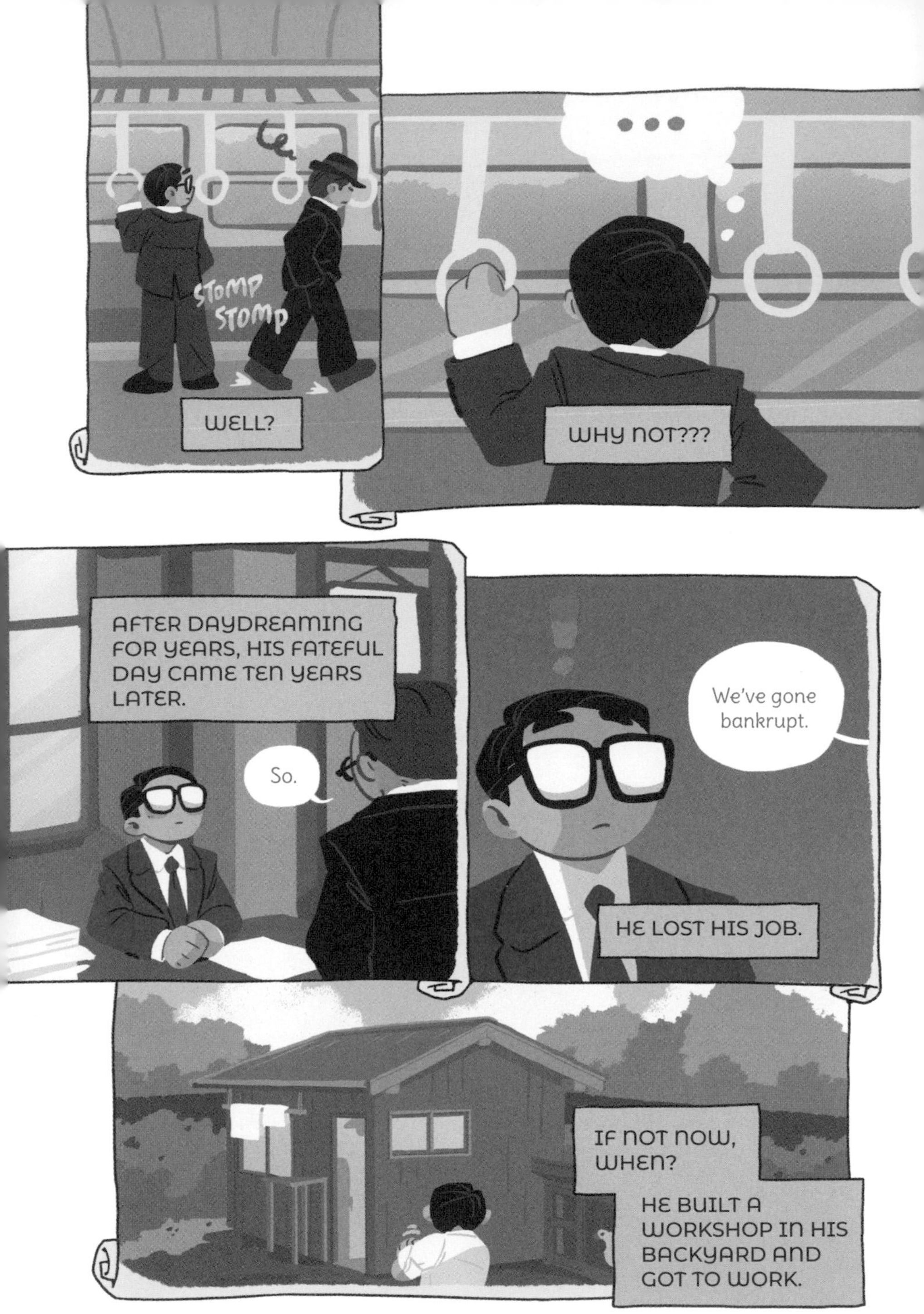
STOMP
STOMP
WELL?
...
WHY NOT???
AFTER DAYDREAMING FOR YEARS, HIS FATEFUL DAY CAME TEN YEARS LATER.
So.
We've gone bankrupt.
HE LOST HIS JOB.
IF NOT NOW, WHEN?
HE BUILT A WORKSHOP IN HIS BACKYARD AND GOT TO WORK.

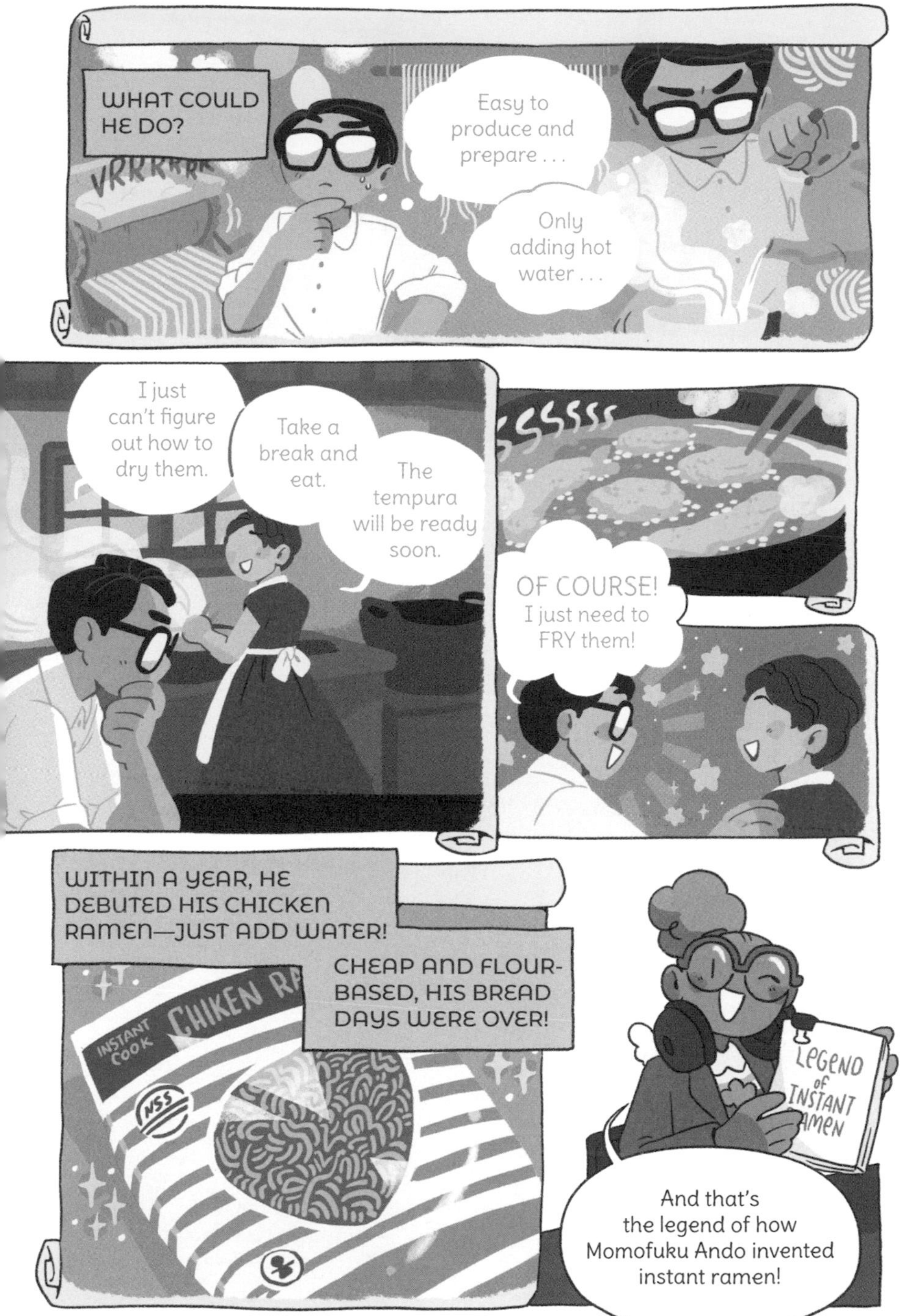

WHAT COULD HE DO?
VRRRRRR
Easy to produce and prepare . . .
Only adding hot water . . .
I just can't figure out how to dry them.
Take a break and eat.
The tempura will be ready soon.
SSSSSS
OF COURSE! I just need to FRY them!
WITHIN A YEAR, HE DEBUTED HIS CHICKEN RAMEN—JUST ADD WATER!
CHEAP AND FLOUR-BASED, HIS BREAD DAYS WERE OVER!
INSTANT COOK
CHIKEN RA
NSS
LEGEND of INSTANT AMEN
And that's the legend of how Momofuku Ando invented instant ramen!

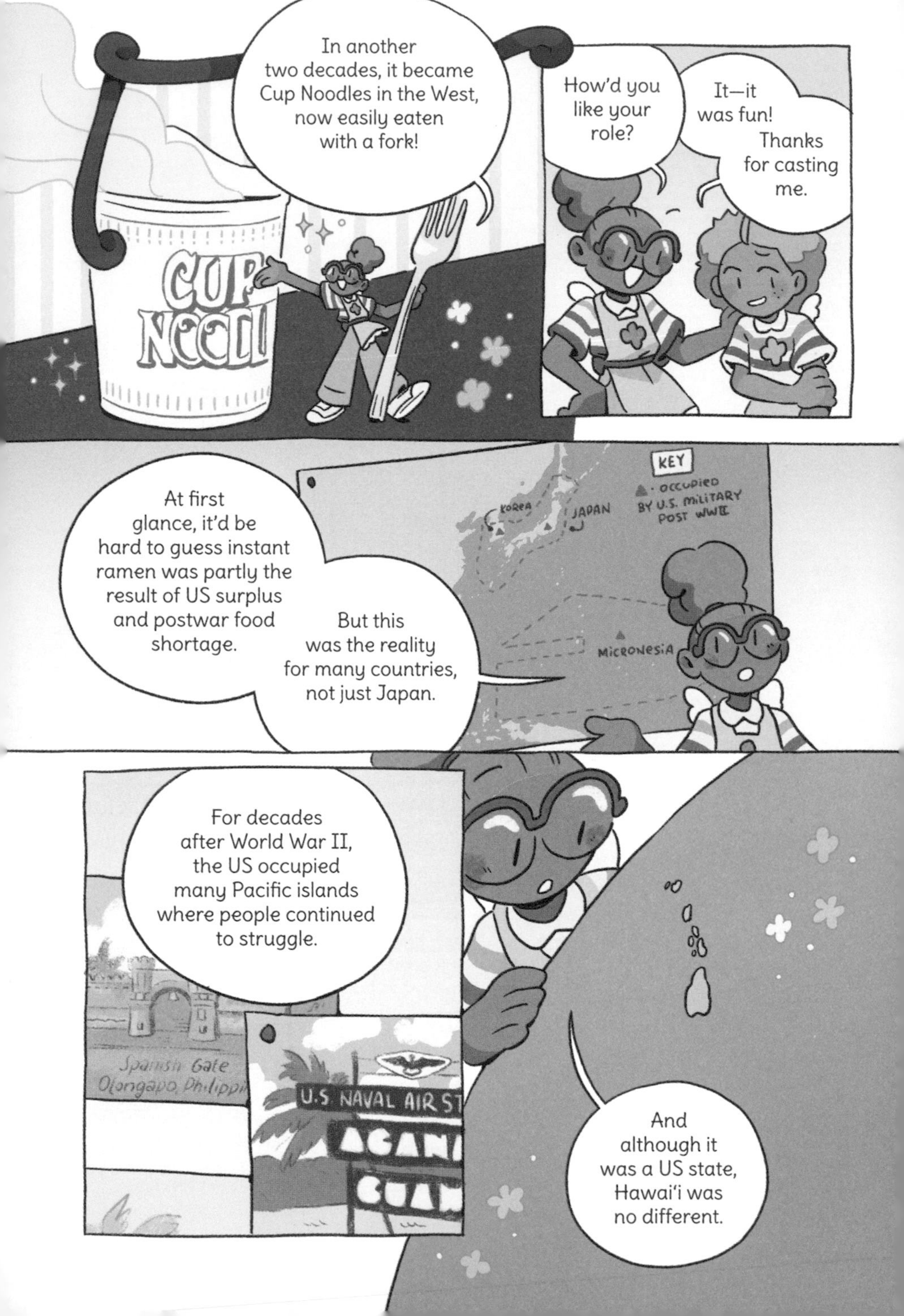
In another two decades, it became Cup Noodles in the West, now easily eaten with a fork!
CUP NOODL
How'd you like your role?
It—it was fun!
Thanks for casting me.
At first glance, it'd be hard to guess instant ramen was partly the result of US surplus and postwar food shortage.
But this was the reality for many countries, not just Japan.
KEY
▲ · OCCUPIED BY U.S. MILITARY POST WWII
KOREA
JAPAN
MICRONESIA
For decades after World War II, the US occupied many Pacific islands where people continued to struggle.
Spanish Gate Olongapo, Philippi
U.S NAVAL AIR ST
AGANA
GUAM
And although it was a US state, Hawai'i was no different.

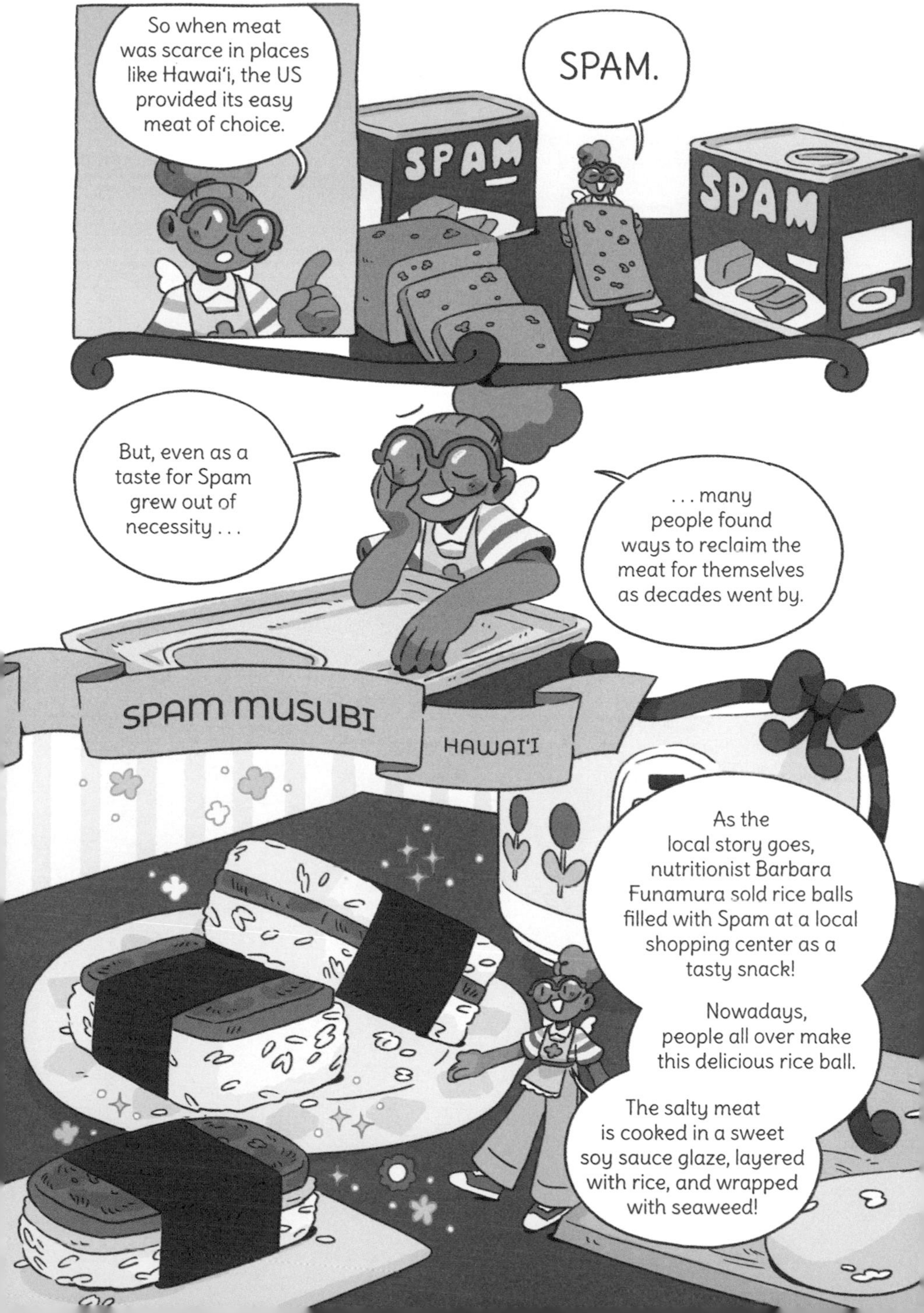
So when meat was scarce in places like Hawai'i, the US provided its easy meat of choice.
SPAM.
SPAM
SPAM
But, even as a taste for Spam grew out of necessity . . .
. . . many people found ways to reclaim the meat for themselves as decades went by.
SPAM MUSUBI
HAWAI'I
As the local story goes, nutritionist Barbara Funamura sold rice balls filled with Spam at a local shopping center as a tasty snack!
Nowadays, people all over make this delicious rice ball.
The salty meat is cooked in a sweet soy sauce glaze, layered with rice, and wrapped with seaweed!

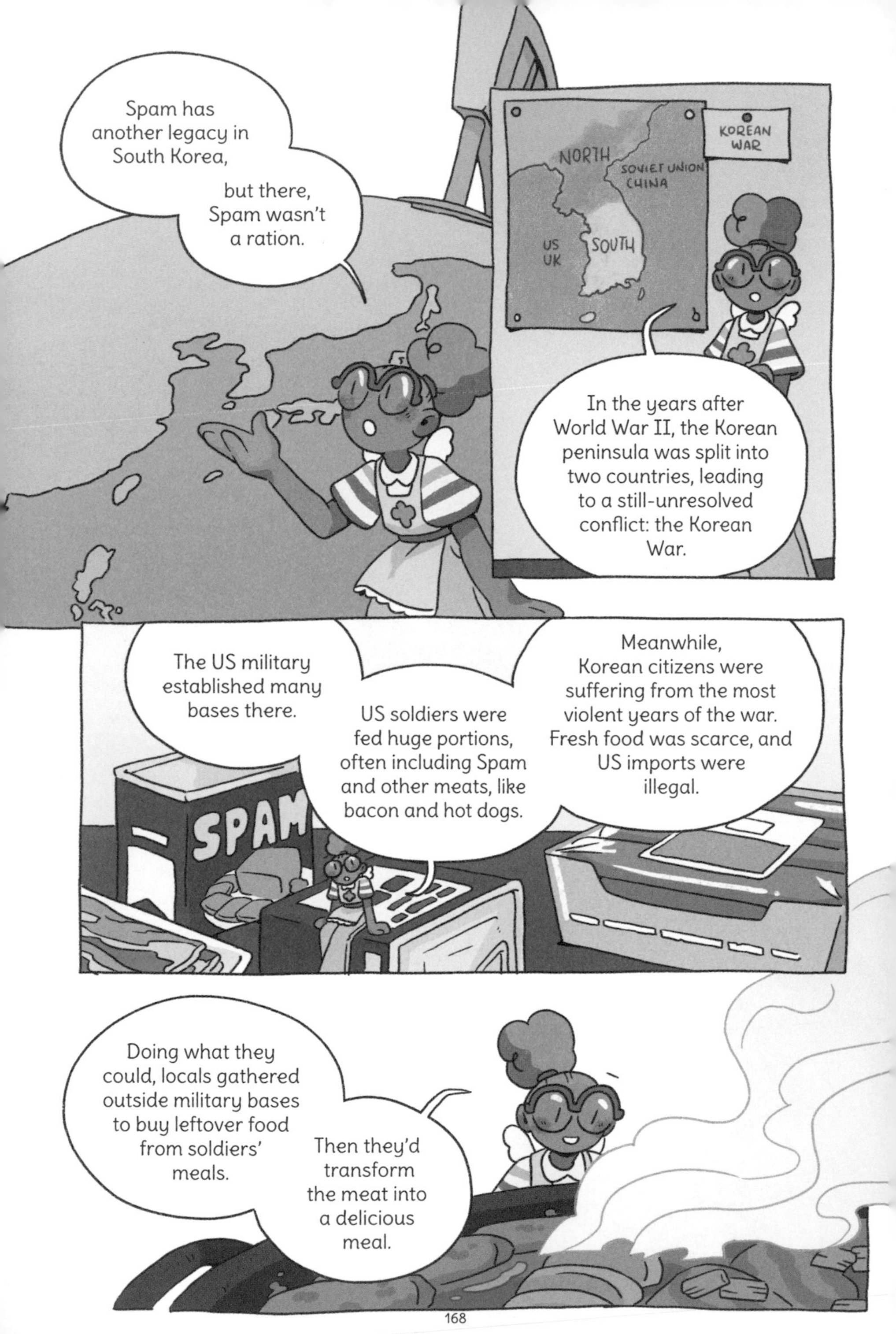

Spam has another legacy in South Korea,
but there, Spam wasn't a ration.
KOREAN WAR
NORTH
SOVIET UNION
CHINA
US
UK
SOUTH
In the years after World War II, the Korean peninsula was split into two countries, leading to a still-unresolved conflict: the Korean War.
The US military established many bases there.
US soldiers were fed huge portions, often including Spam and other meats, like bacon and hot dogs.
Meanwhile, Korean citizens were suffering from the most violent years of the war. Fresh food was scarce, and US imports were illegal.
SPAM
Doing what they could, locals gathered outside military bases to buy leftover food from soldiers' meals.
Then they'd transform the meat into a delicious meal.

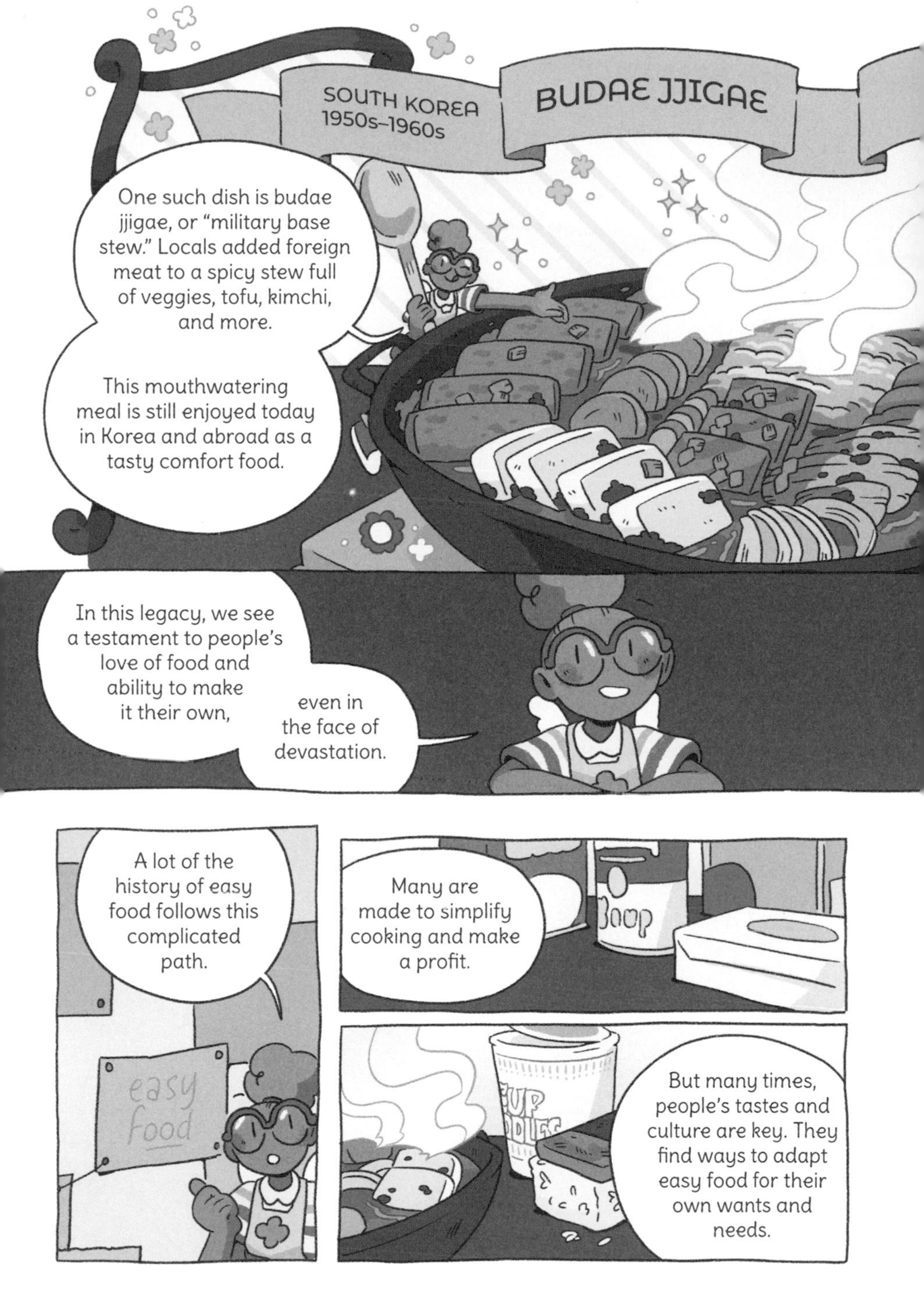
SOUTH KOREA
1950s–1960s
BUDAE JJIGAE
One such dish is budae jjigae, or "military base stew." Locals added foreign meat to a spicy stew full of veggies, tofu, kimchi, and more.
This mouthwatering meal is still enjoyed today in Korea and abroad as a tasty comfort food.
In this legacy, we see a testament to people's love of food and ability to make it their own,
even in the face of devastation.
A lot of the history of easy food follows this complicated path.
easy food
Many are made to simplify cooking and make a profit.
Boop
But many times, people's tastes and culture are key. They find ways to adapt easy food for their own wants and needs.

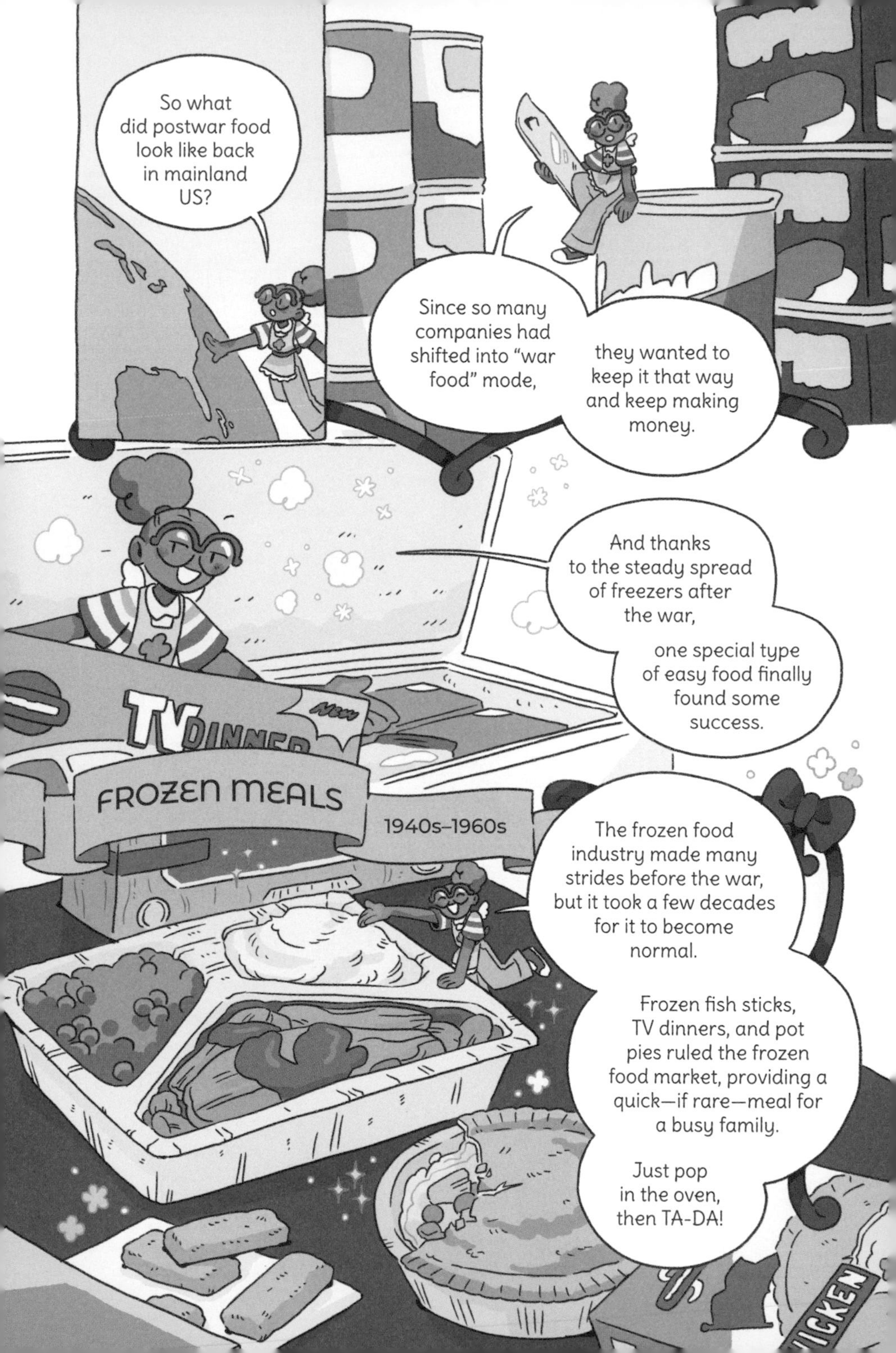
So what did postwar food look like back in mainland US?
Since so many companies had shifted into "war food" mode,
they wanted to keep it that way and keep making money.
And thanks to the steady spread of freezers after the war,
one special type of easy food finally found some success.
TV DINNER
New
FROZEN MEALS
1940s–1960s
The frozen food industry made many strides before the war, but it took a few decades for it to become normal.
Frozen fish sticks, TV dinners, and pot pies ruled the frozen food market, providing a quick—if rare—meal for a busy family.
Just pop in the oven, then TA-DA!
CHICKEN

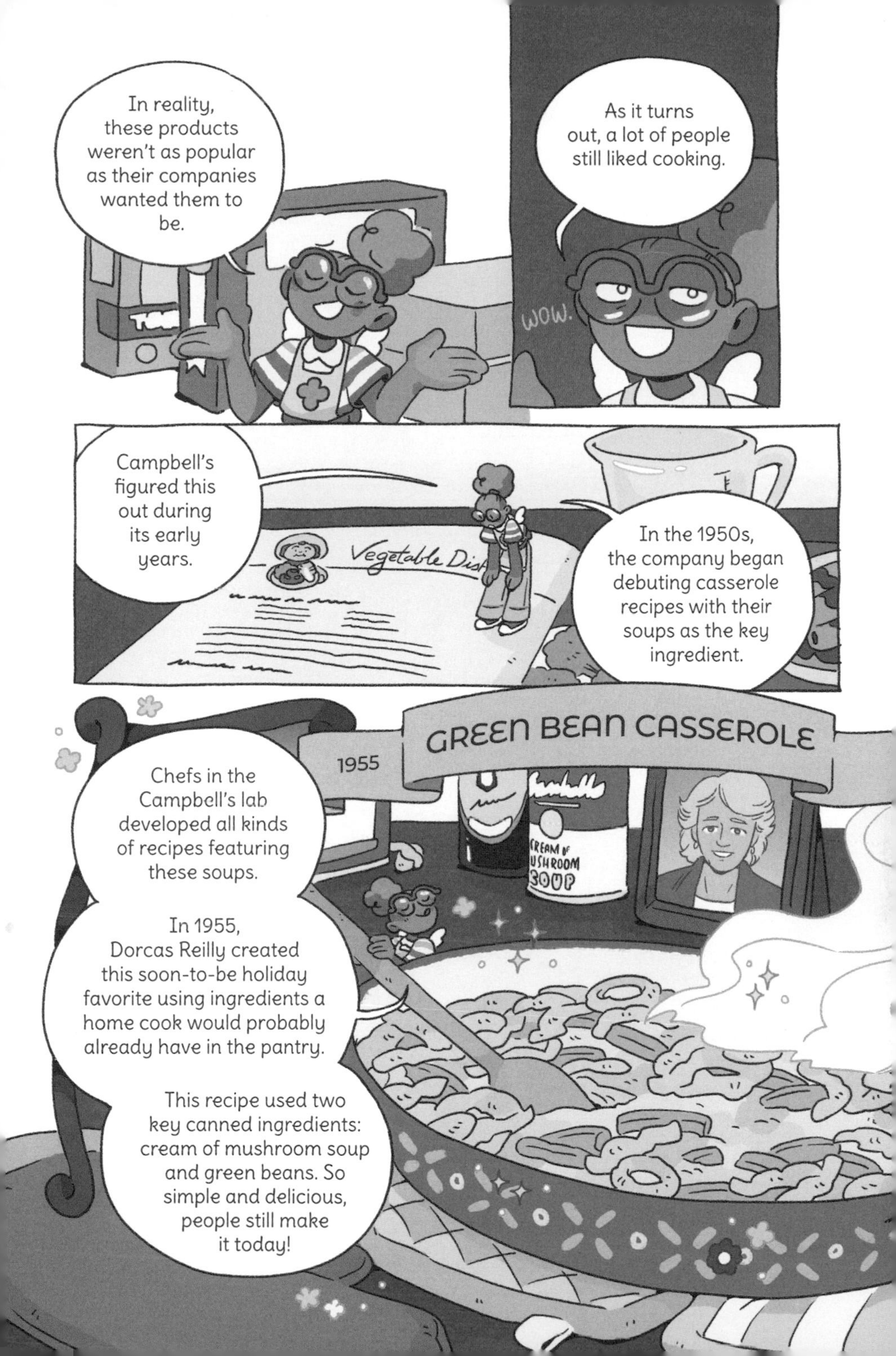

In reality, these products weren't as popular as their companies wanted them to be.
As it turns out, a lot of people still liked cooking.
WOW.
Campbell's figured this out during its early years.
Vegetable Dis
In the 1950s, the company began debuting casserole recipes with their soups as the key ingredient.
GREEN BEAN CASSEROLE
1955
CREAM OF
USHROOM
SOUP
Chefs in the Campbell's lab developed all kinds of recipes featuring these soups.
In 1955, Dorcas Reilly created this soon-to-be holiday favorite using ingredients a home cook would probably already have in the pantry.
This recipe used two key canned ingredients: cream of mushroom soup and green beans. So simple and delicious, people still make it today!

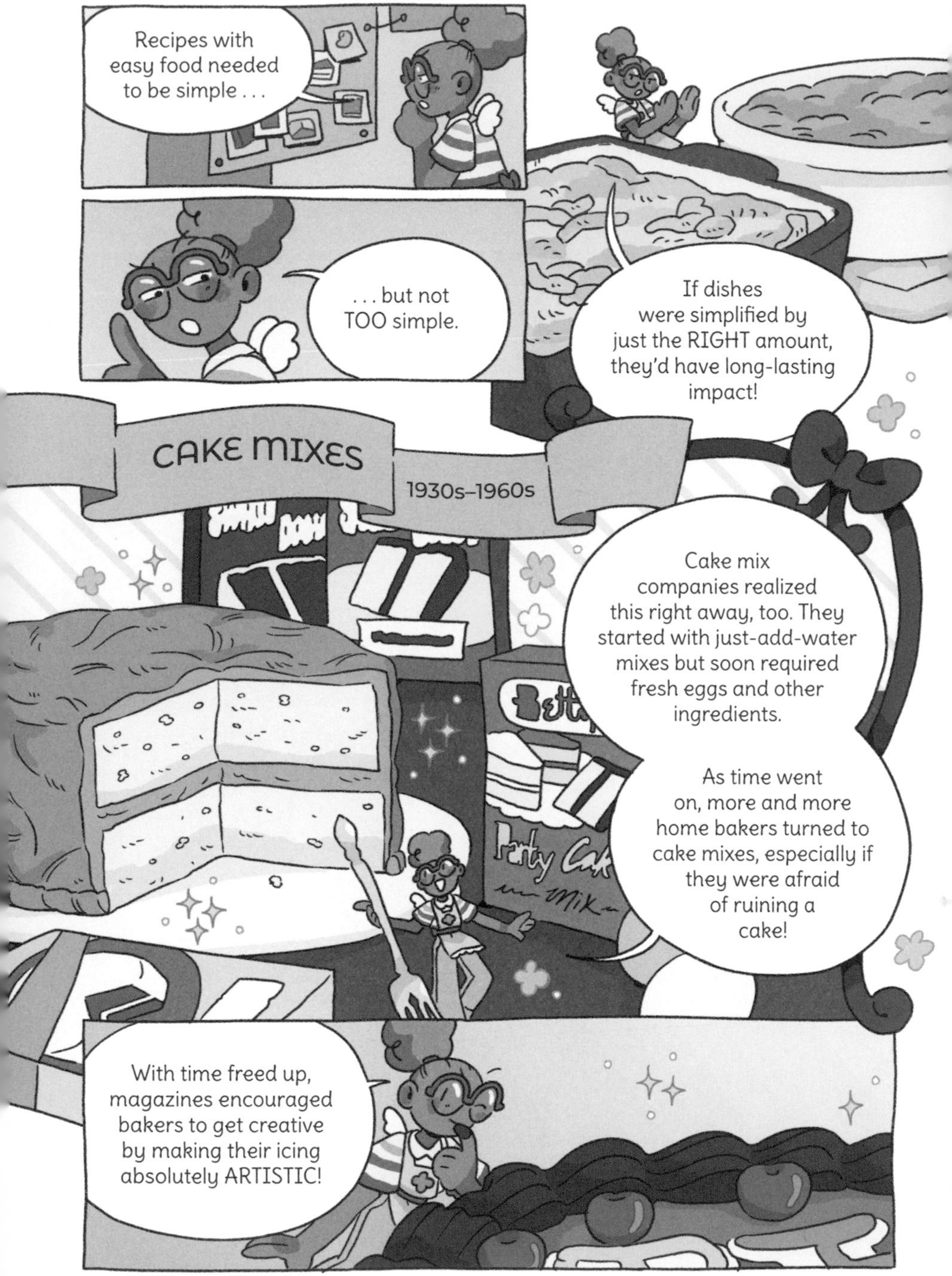

Recipes with easy food needed to be simple . . .
. . . but not TOO simple.
If dishes were simplified by just the RIGHT amount, they'd have long-lasting impact!
CAKE MIXES
1930s–1960s
Cake mix companies realized this right away, too. They started with just-add-water mixes but soon required fresh eggs and other ingredients.
As time went on, more and more home bakers turned to cake mixes, especially if they were afraid of ruining a cake!
With time freed up, magazines encouraged bakers to get creative by making their icing absolutely ARTISTIC!

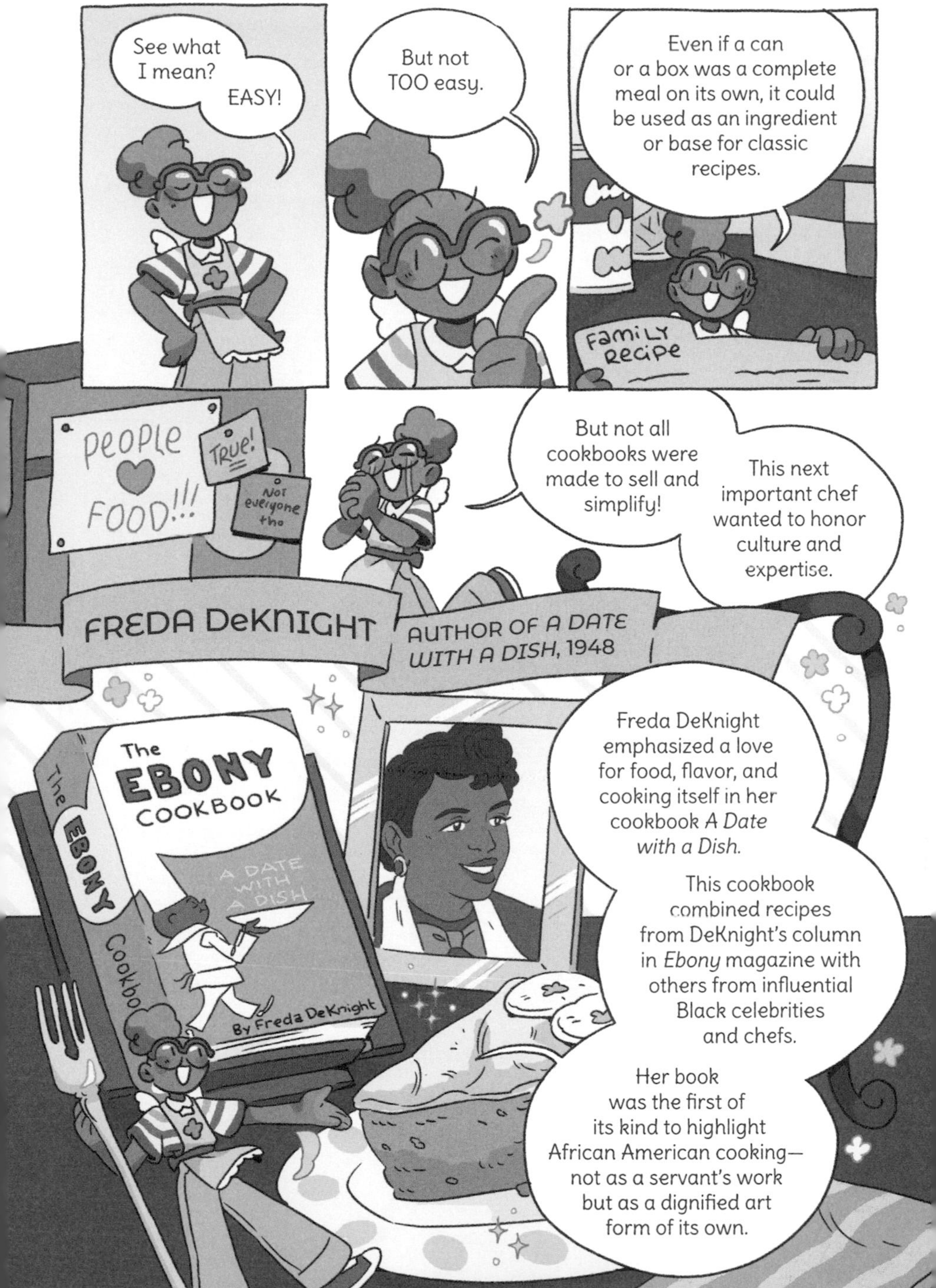
See what I mean? EASY!
But not TOO easy.
Even if a can or a box was a complete meal on its own, it could be used as an ingredient or base for classic recipes.
FAMILY RECIPE
PEOPLE ♥ FOOD!!!
TRUE!
NOT everyone tho
But not all cookbooks were made to sell and simplify!
This next important chef wanted to honor culture and expertise.
FREDA DeKNIGHT
AUTHOR OF *A DATE WITH A DISH*, 1948
The EBONY COOKBOOK
A DATE WITH A DISH
By Freda DeKnight
The EBONY Cookbo
Freda DeKnight emphasized a love for food, flavor, and cooking itself in her cookbook *A Date with a Dish*.
This cookbook combined recipes from DeKnight's column in *Ebony* magazine with others from influential Black celebrities and chefs.
Her book was the first of its kind to highlight African American cooking—not as a servant's work but as a dignified art form of its own.

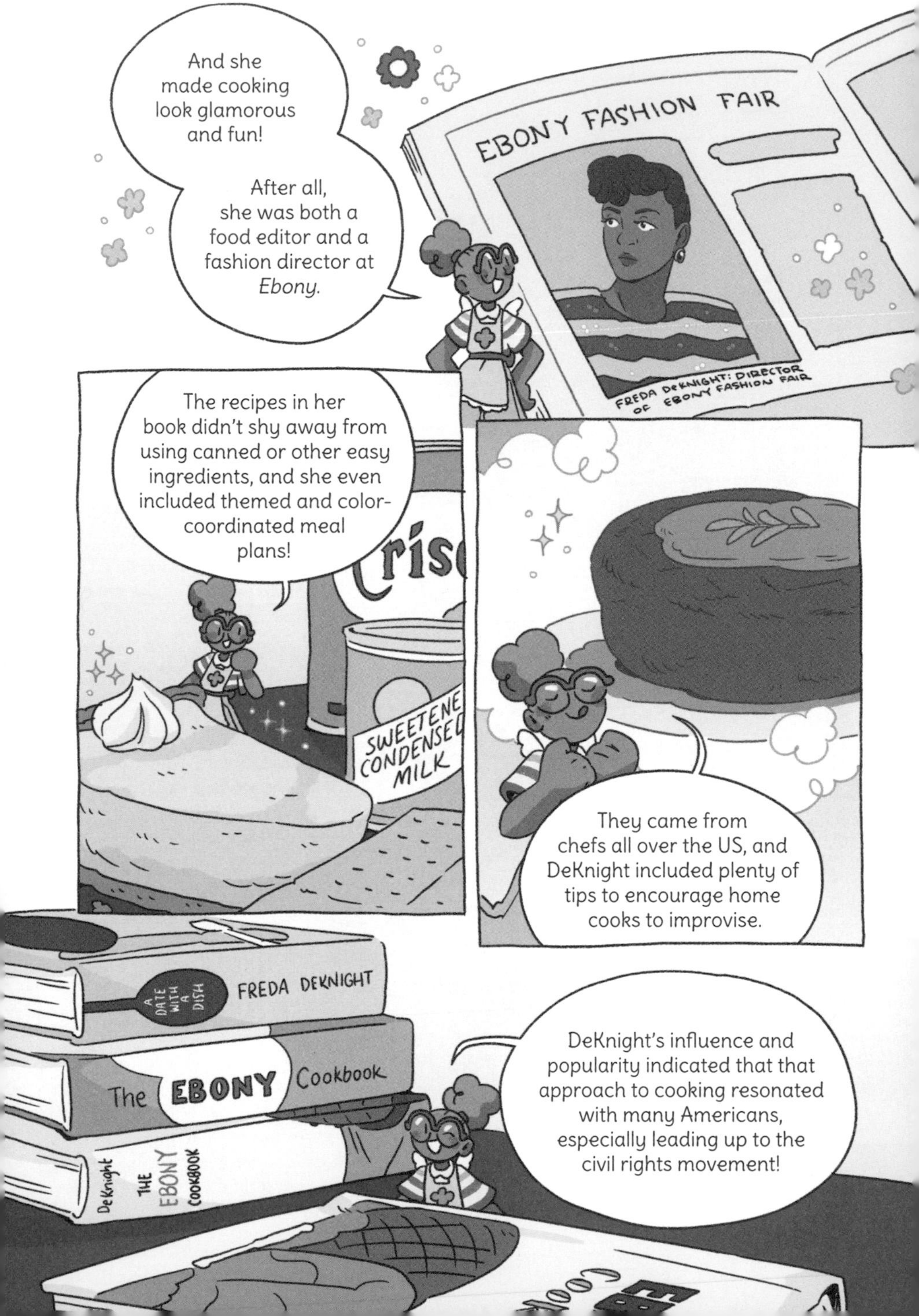
And she made cooking look glamorous and fun!
After all, she was both a food editor and a fashion director at *Ebony*.
EBONY FASHION FAIR
FREDA DeKNIGHT: DIRECTOR OF EBONY FASHION FAIR
The recipes in her book didn't shy away from using canned or other easy ingredients, and she even included themed and color-coordinated meal plans!
SWEETENED CONDENSED MILK
They came from chefs all over the US, and DeKnight included plenty of tips to encourage home cooks to improvise.
A DATE WITH A DISH
FREDA DEKNIGHT
The EBONY Cookbook
DeKnight THE EBONY COOKBOOK
DeKnight's influence and popularity indicated that that approach to cooking resonated with many Americans, especially leading up to the civil rights movement!

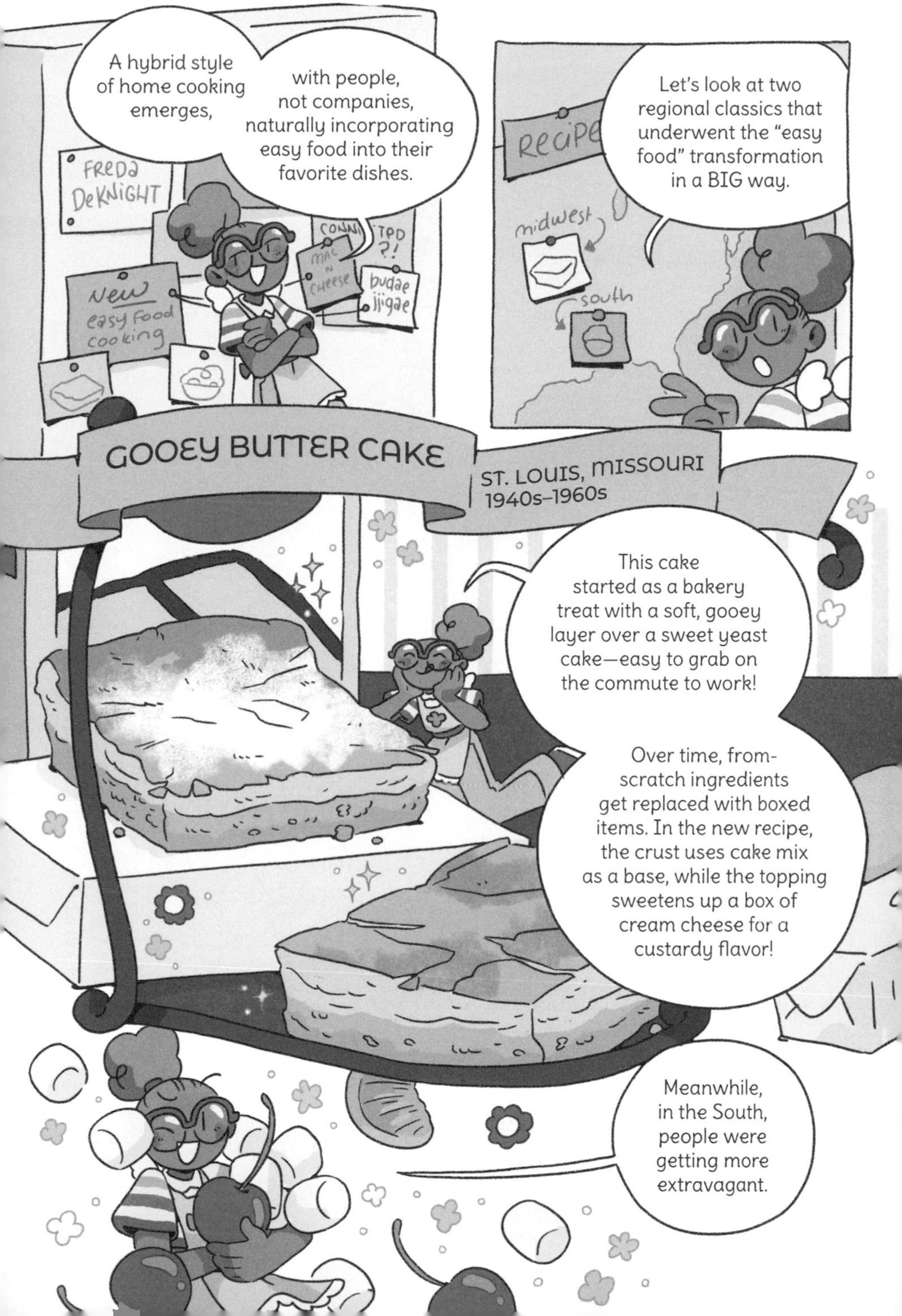
A hybrid style of home cooking emerges,
with people, not companies, naturally incorporating easy food into their favorite dishes.
Freda DeKnight
New easy food cooking
Mac n cheese
budae jjigae
Let's look at two regional classics that underwent the "easy food" transformation in a BIG way.
Recipe
midwest
south
GOOEY BUTTER CAKE
ST. LOUIS, MISSOURI 1940s–1960s
This cake started as a bakery treat with a soft, gooey layer over a sweet yeast cake—easy to grab on the commute to work!
Over time, from-scratch ingredients get replaced with boxed items. In the new recipe, the crust uses cake mix as a base, while the topping sweetens up a box of cream cheese for a custardy flavor!
Meanwhile, in the South, people were getting more extravagant.

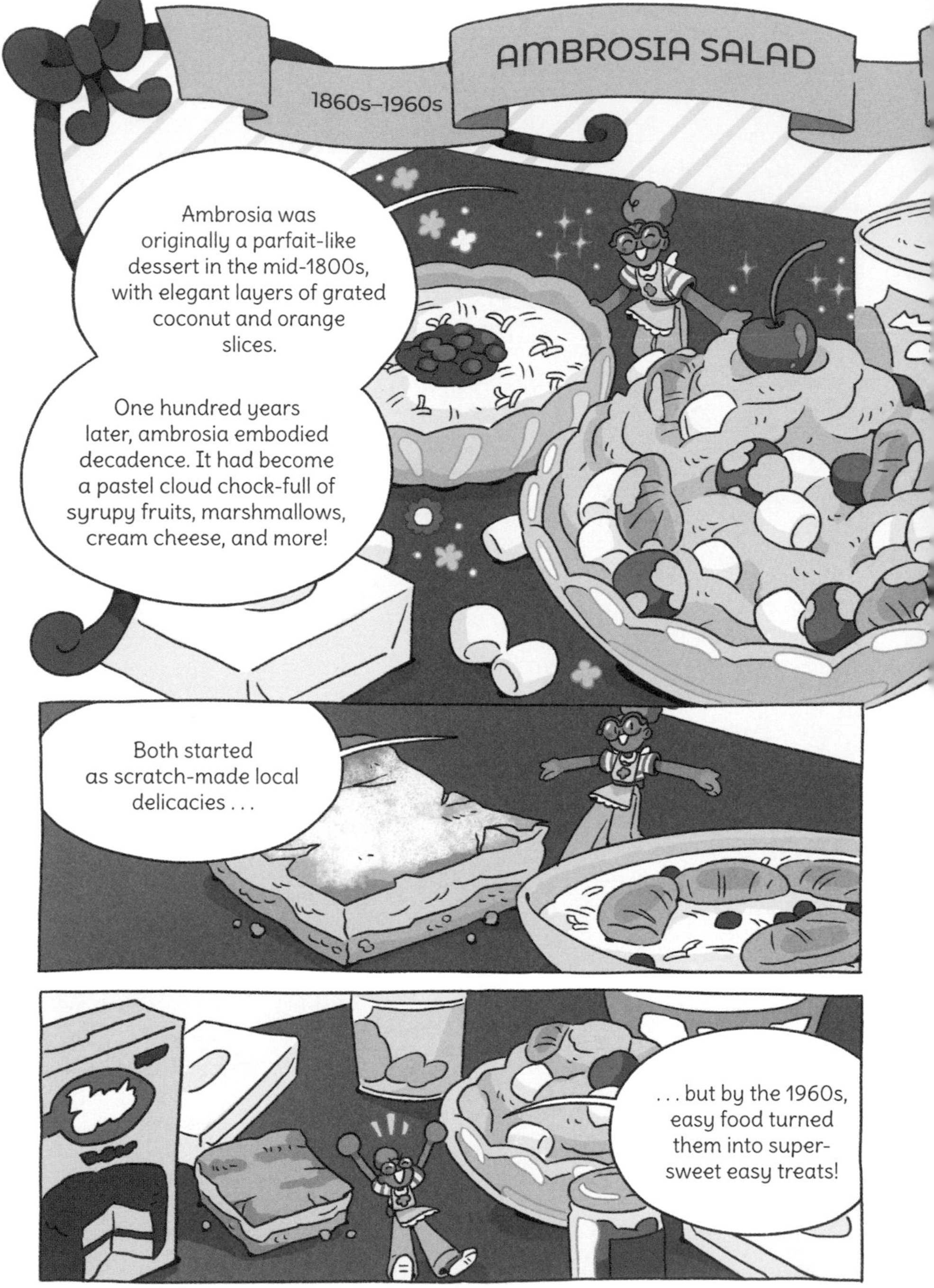
AMBROSIA SALAD
1860s–1960s
Ambrosia was originally a parfait-like dessert in the mid-1800s, with elegant layers of grated coconut and orange slices.
One hundred years later, ambrosia embodied decadence. It had become a pastel cloud chock-full of syrupy fruits, marshmallows, cream cheese, and more!
Both started as scratch-made local delicacies . . .
. . . but by the 1960s, easy food turned them into super-sweet easy treats!

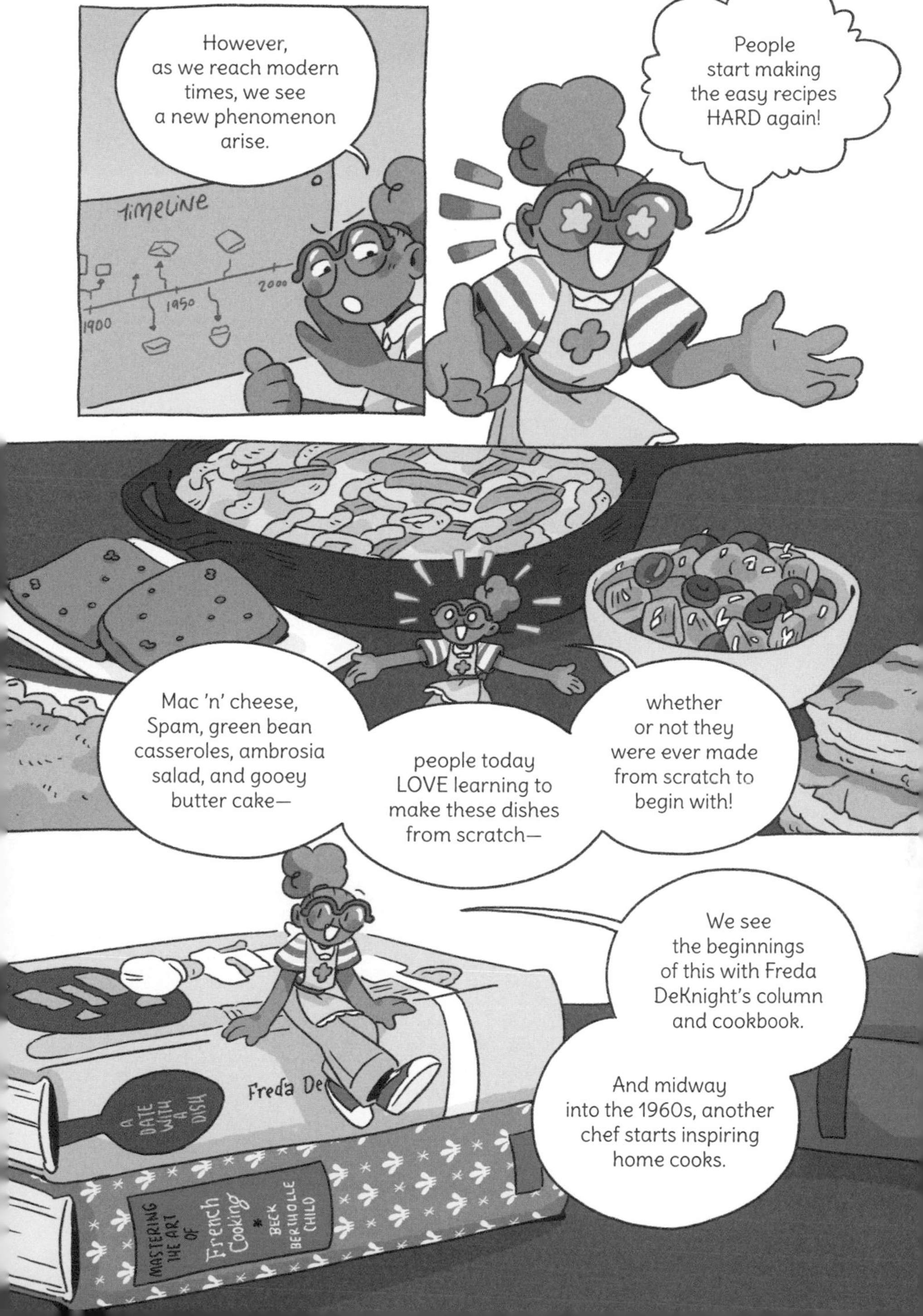
However, as we reach modern times, we see a new phenomenon arise.
TIMELINE
1900
1950
2000
People start making the easy recipes HARD again!
Mac 'n' cheese, Spam, green bean casseroles, ambrosia salad, and gooey butter cake—
people today LOVE learning to make these dishes from scratch—
whether or not they were ever made from scratch to begin with!
We see the beginnings of this with Freda DeKnight's column and cookbook.
And midway into the 1960s, another chef starts inspiring home cooks.
A DATE WITH A DISH
Freda De
MASTERING THE ART OF French Cooking
BECK BERTHOLLE CHILD

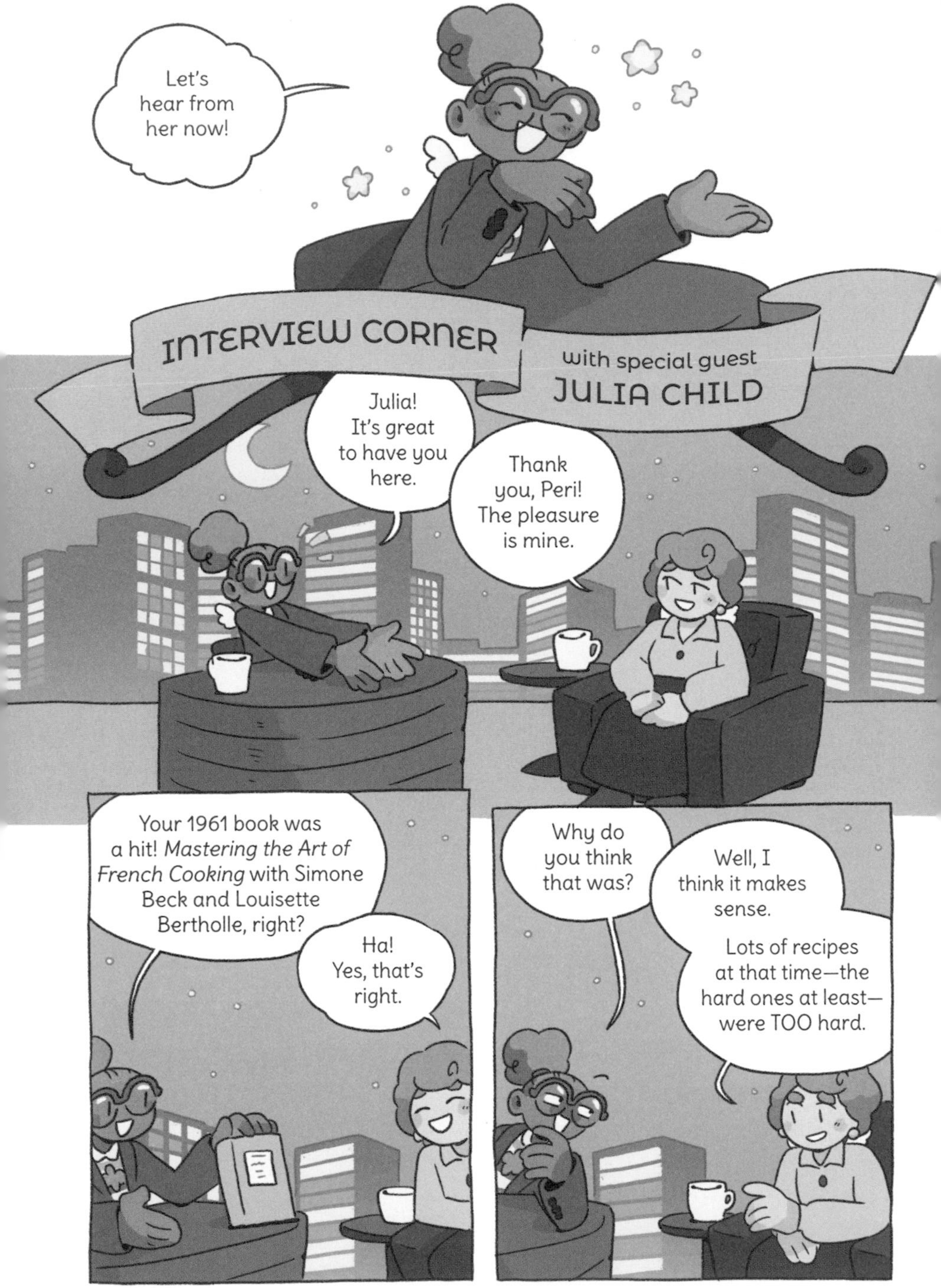
Let's hear from her now!
INTERVIEW CORNER
with special guest JULIA CHILD
Julia! It's great to have you here.
Thank you, Peri! The pleasure is mine.
Your 1961 book was a hit! *Mastering the Art of French Cooking* with Simone Beck and Louisette Bertholle, right?
Ha! Yes, that's right.
Why do you think that was?
Well, I think it makes sense.
Lots of recipes at that time—the hard ones at least—were TOO hard.

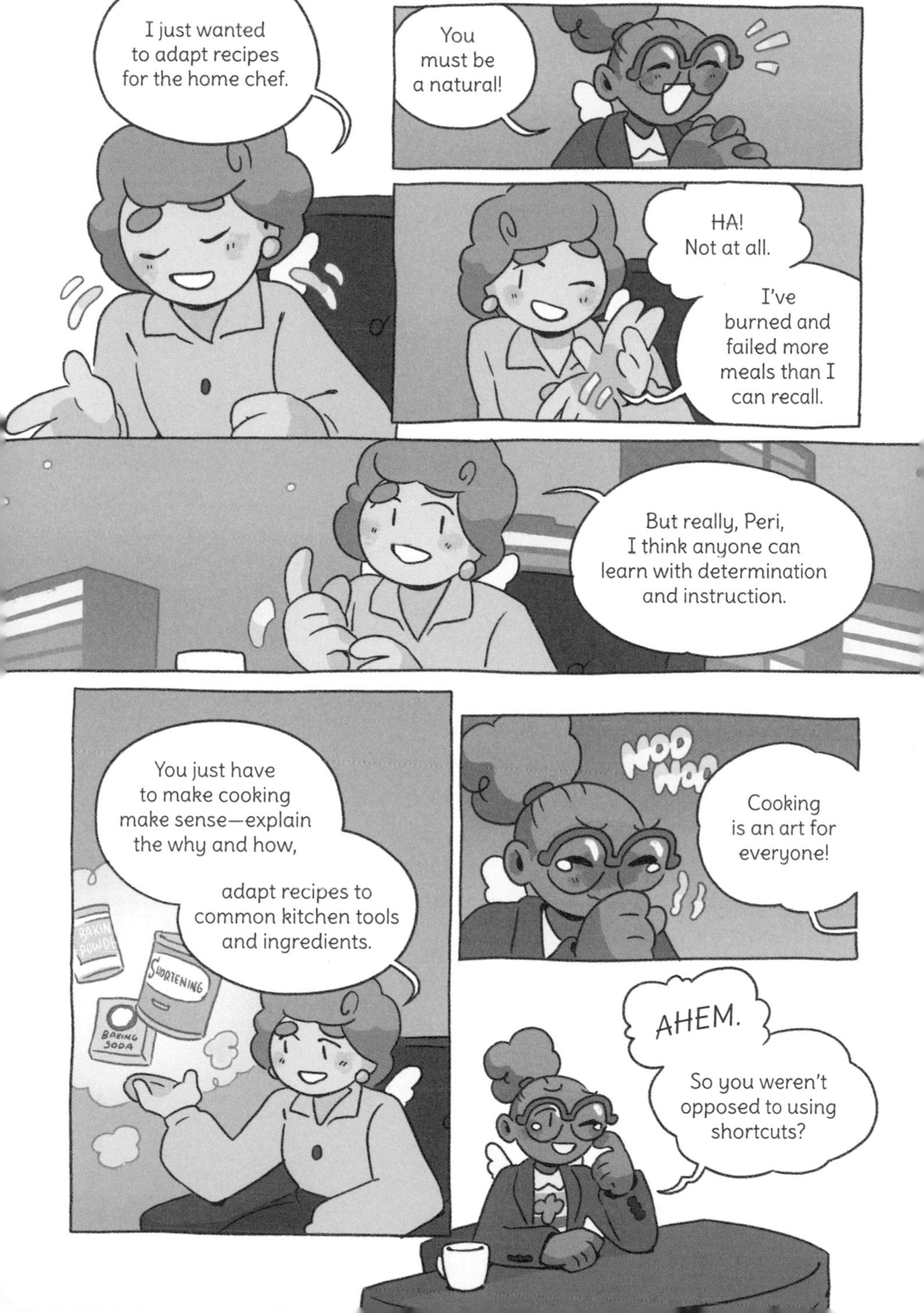
I just wanted to adapt recipes for the home chef.
You must be a natural!
HA! Not at all.
I've burned and failed more meals than I can recall.
But really, Peri, I think anyone can learn with determination and instruction.
You just have to make cooking make sense—explain the why and how,
adapt recipes to common kitchen tools and ingredients.
SHORTENING
BAKING SODA
NOD NOD
Cooking is an art for everyone!
AHEM.
So you weren't opposed to using shortcuts?

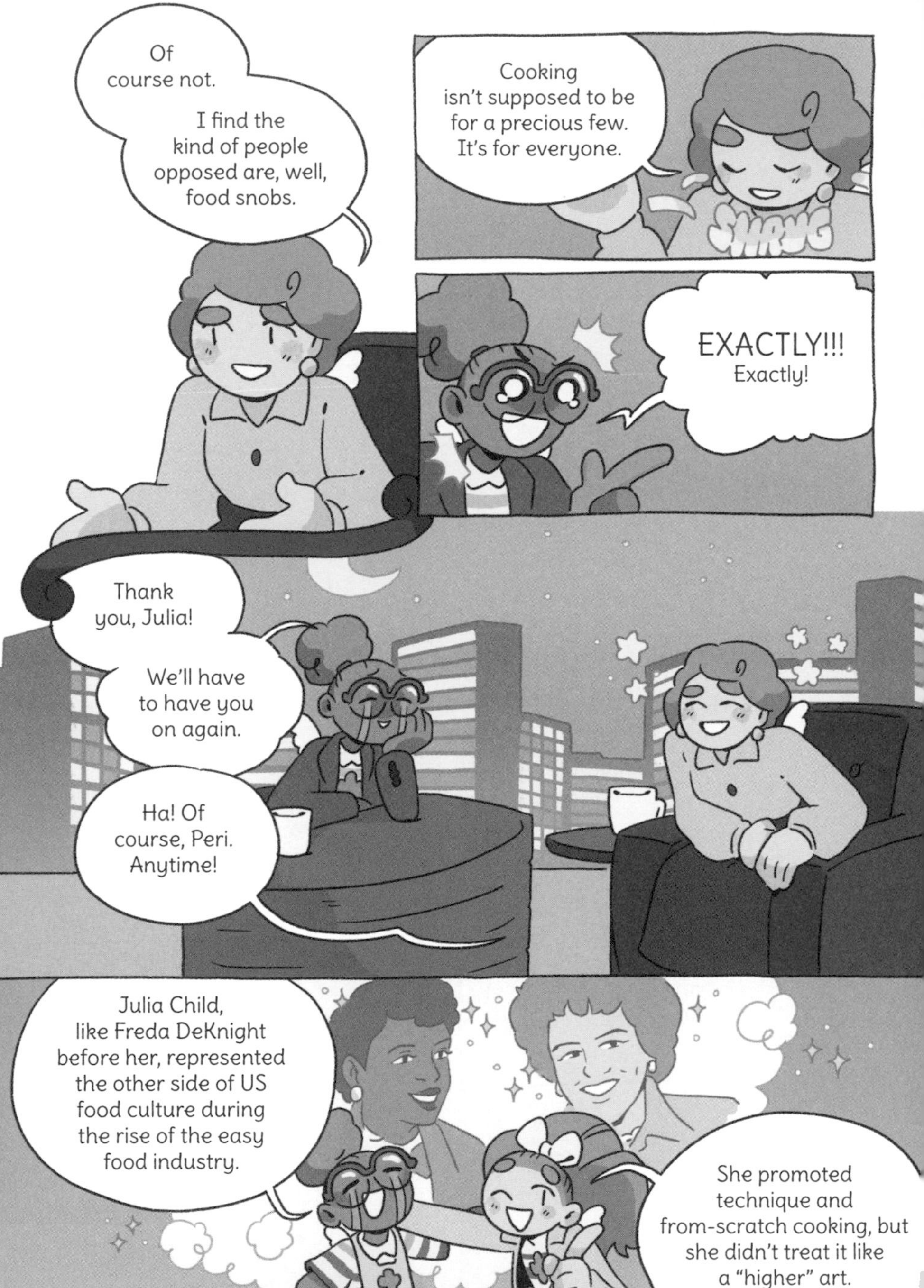
Of course not.
I find the kind of people opposed are, well, food snobs.
Cooking isn't supposed to be for a precious few. It's for everyone.
SHRUG
EXACTLY!!! Exactly!
Thank you, Julia!
We'll have to have you on again.
Ha! Of course, Peri. Anytime!
Julia Child, like Freda DeKnight before her, represented the other side of US food culture during the rise of the easy food industry.
She promoted technique and from-scratch cooking, but she didn't treat it like a "higher" art.

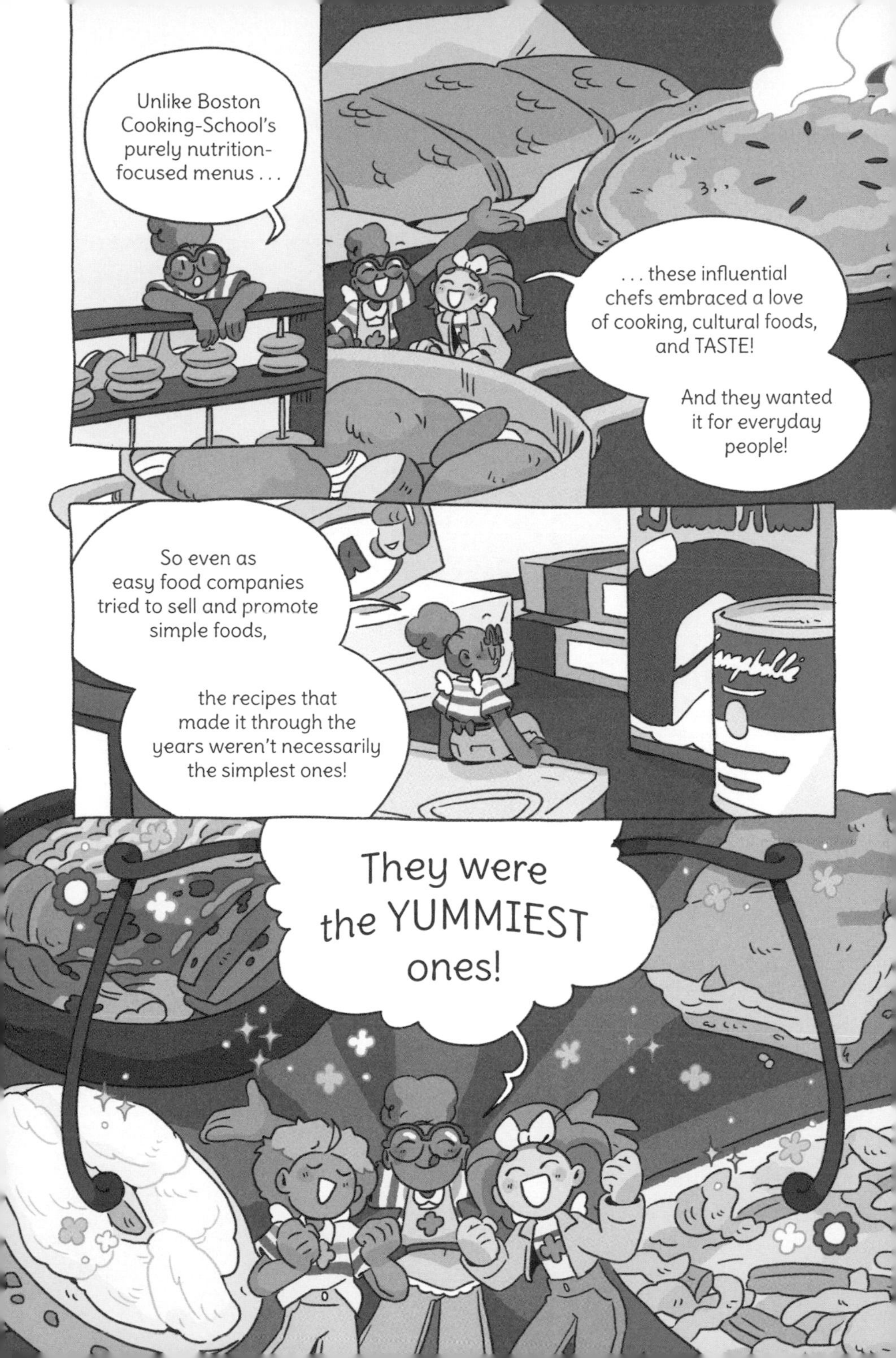
Unlike Boston Cooking-School's purely nutrition-focused menus . . .
. . . these influential chefs embraced a love of cooking, cultural foods, and TASTE!
And they wanted it for everyday people!
So even as easy food companies tried to sell and promote simple foods,
the recipes that made it through the years weren't necessarily the simplest ones!
They were the YUMMIEST ones!

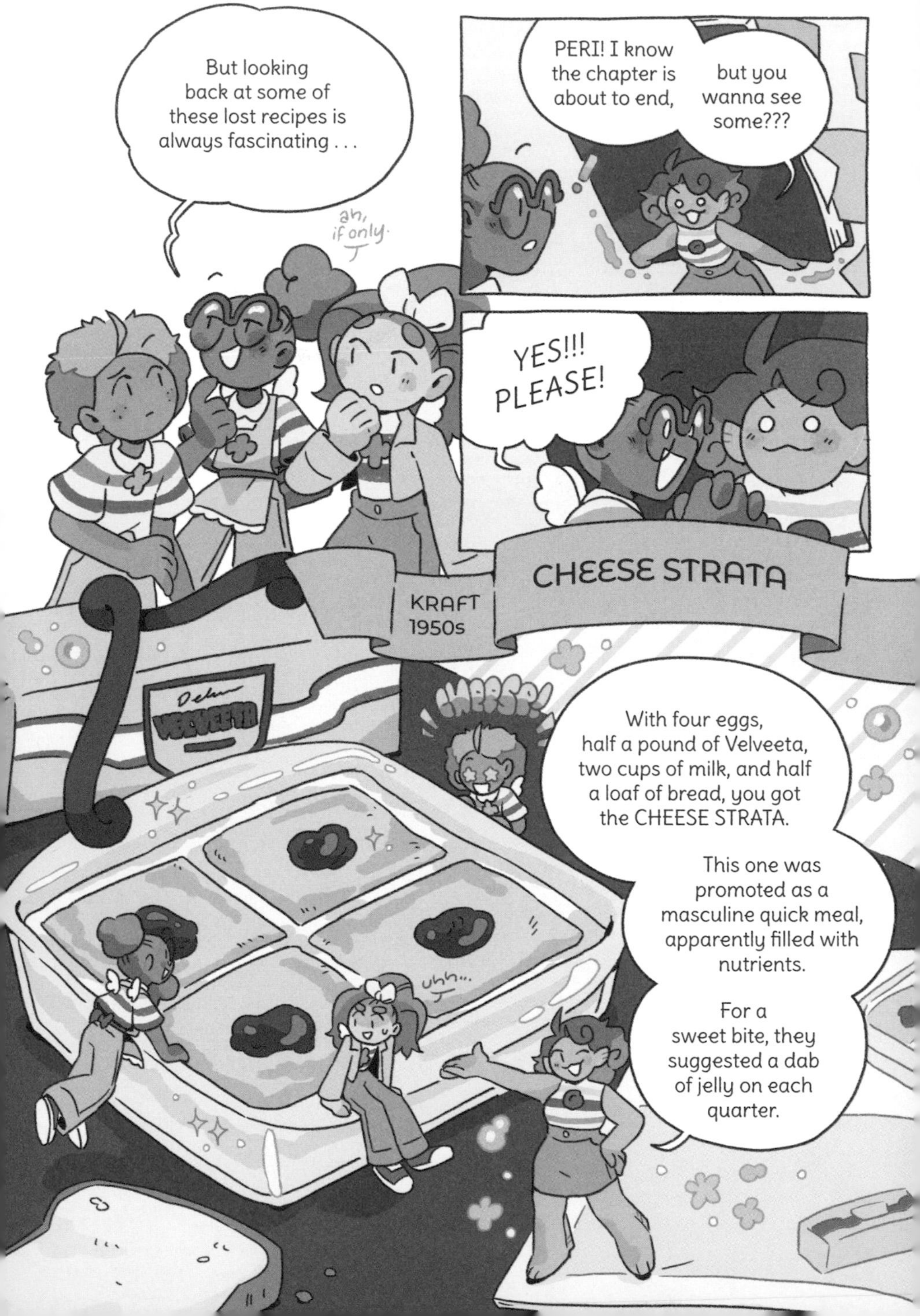

But looking back at some of these lost recipes is always fascinating . . .
ah, if only.
PERI! I know the chapter is about to end,
but you wanna see some???
YES!!! PLEASE!
KRAFT 1950s
CHEESE STRATA
With four eggs, half a pound of Velveeta, two cups of milk, and half a loaf of bread, you got the CHEESE STRATA.
This one was promoted as a masculine quick meal, apparently filled with nutrients.
For a sweet bite, they suggested a dab of jelly on each quarter.
uhh...

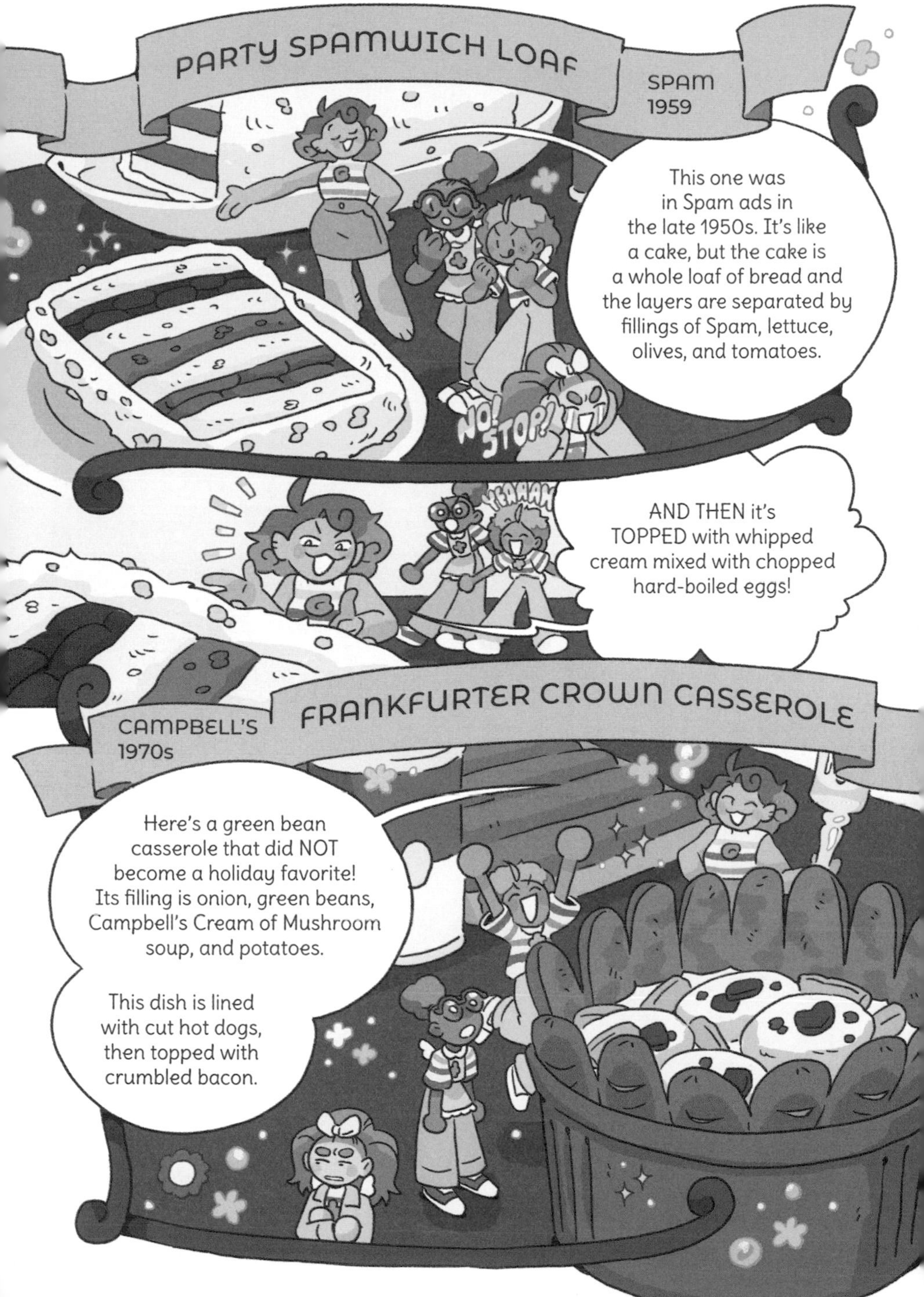
PARTY SPAMWICH LOAF
SPAM
1959
This one was in Spam ads in the late 1950s. It's like a cake, but the cake is a whole loaf of bread and the layers are separated by fillings of Spam, lettuce, olives, and tomatoes.
NO! STOP!
AND THEN it's TOPPED with whipped cream mixed with chopped hard-boiled eggs!
YEAAAAH
FRANKFURTER CROWN CASSEROLE
CAMPBELL'S
1970s
Here's a green bean casserole that did NOT become a holiday favorite! Its filling is onion, green beans, Campbell's Cream of Mushroom soup, and potatoes.
This dish is lined with cut hot dogs, then topped with crumbled bacon.

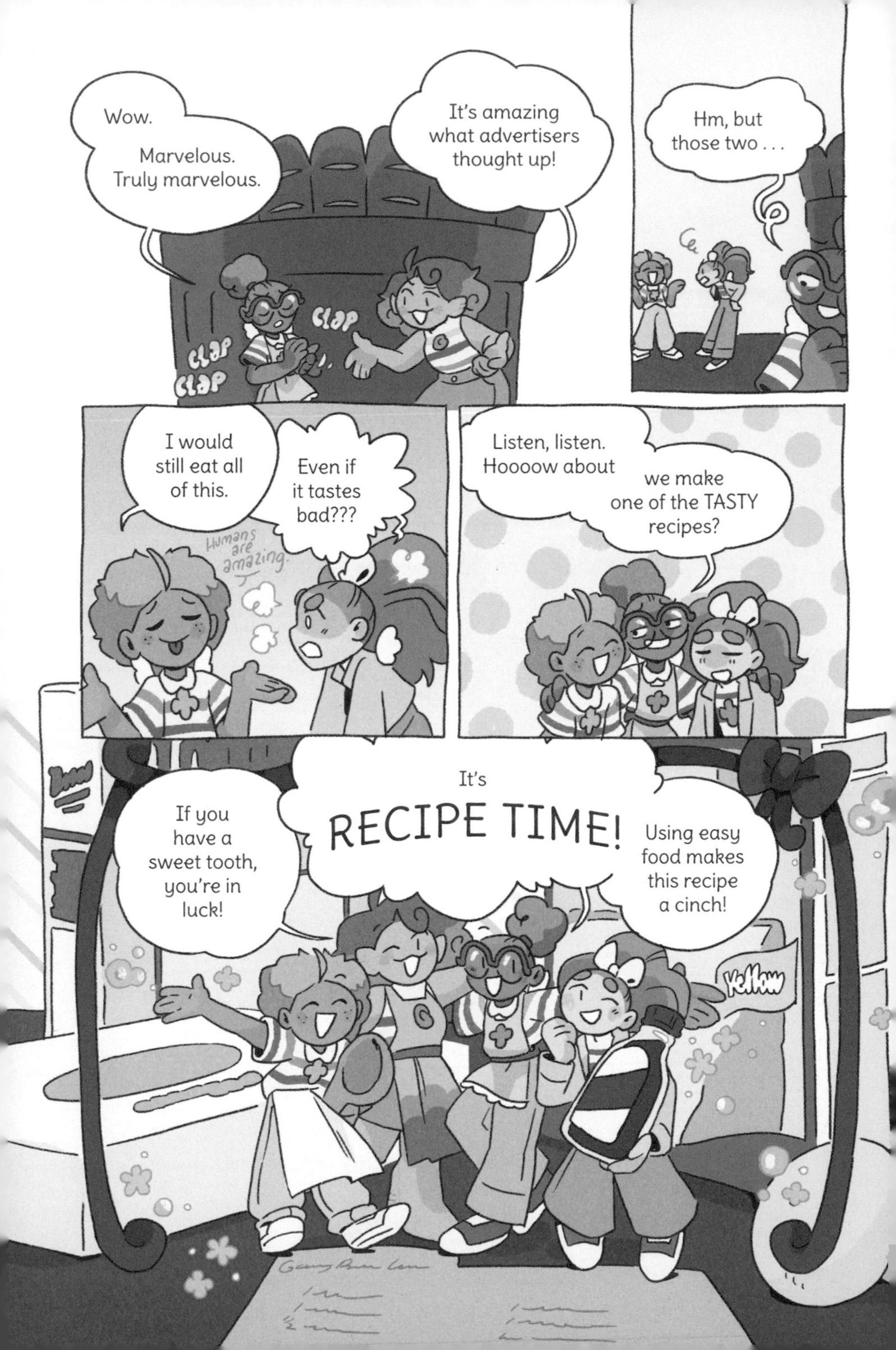
Wow.
Marvelous. Truly marvelous.
It's amazing what advertisers thought up!
CLAP
CLAP
CLAP
Hm, but those two . . .
I would still eat all of this.
Even if it tastes bad???
Humans are amazing.
Listen, listen. Hoooow about
we make one of the TASTY recipes?
It's
RECIPE TIME!
If you have a sweet tooth, you're in luck!
Using easy food makes this recipe a cinch!
Yellow

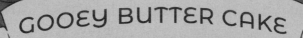

# GOOEY BUTTER CAKE

## YOU WILL NEED:

### CRUST

1 box yellow cake mix (15.25 oz)

1 stick butter (½ cup)

1 egg

This recipe uses ingredients in boxed amounts, but we've also given measurements if you need them!

### TOPPING

1 box cream cheese (8 oz)

2 eggs

1 box powdered sugar (16 oz)

1 stick butter (½ cup)

1 teaspoon vanilla extract

9x13-inch baking pan (can vary)

whisk and spatula

medium and large mixing bowls

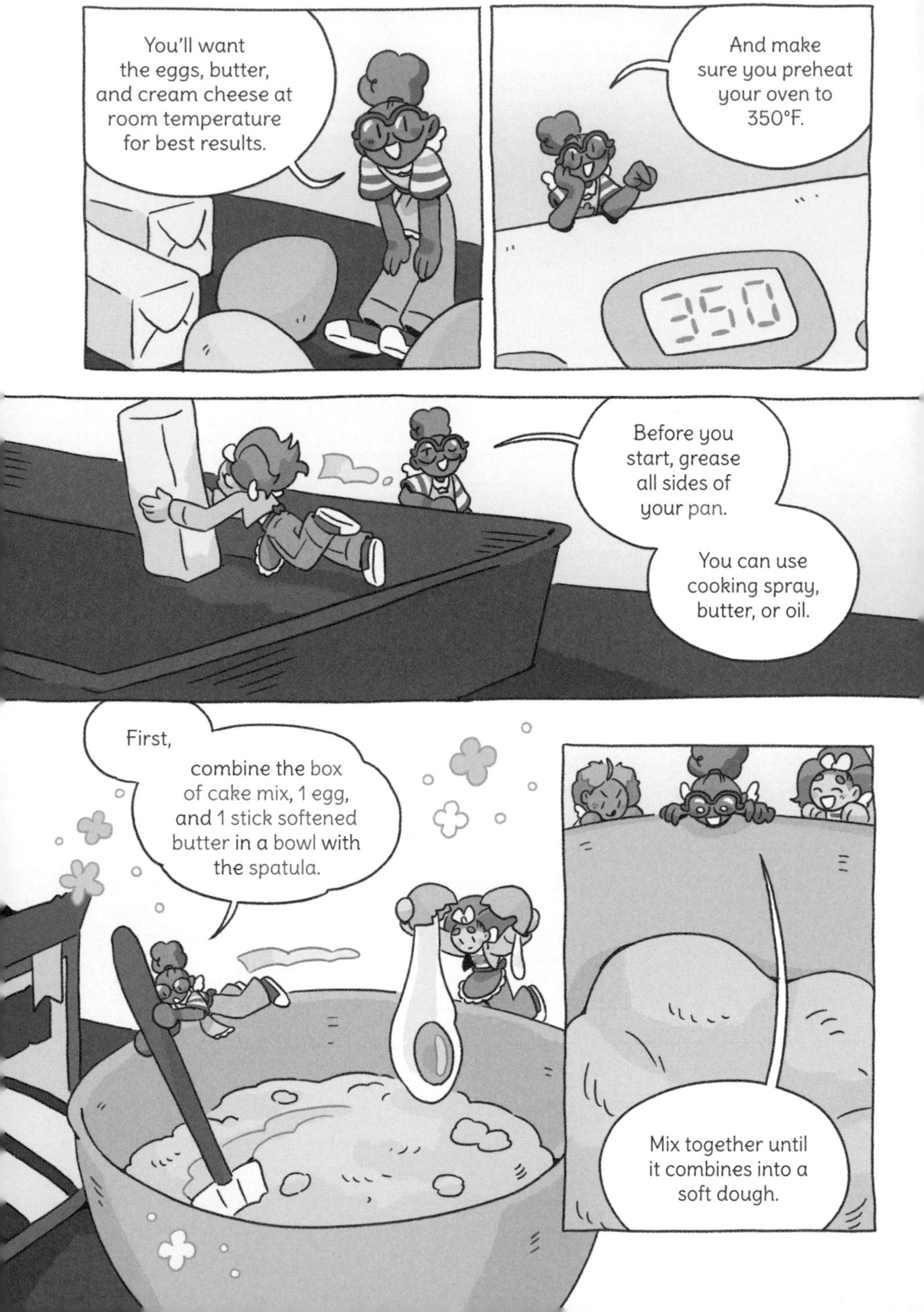
You'll want the eggs, butter, and cream cheese at room temperature for best results.
And make sure you preheat your oven to 350°F.
350
Before you start, grease all sides of your pan.
You can use cooking spray, butter, or oil.
First,
combine the box of cake mix, 1 egg, and 1 stick softened butter in a bowl with the spatula.
Mix together until it combines into a soft dough.

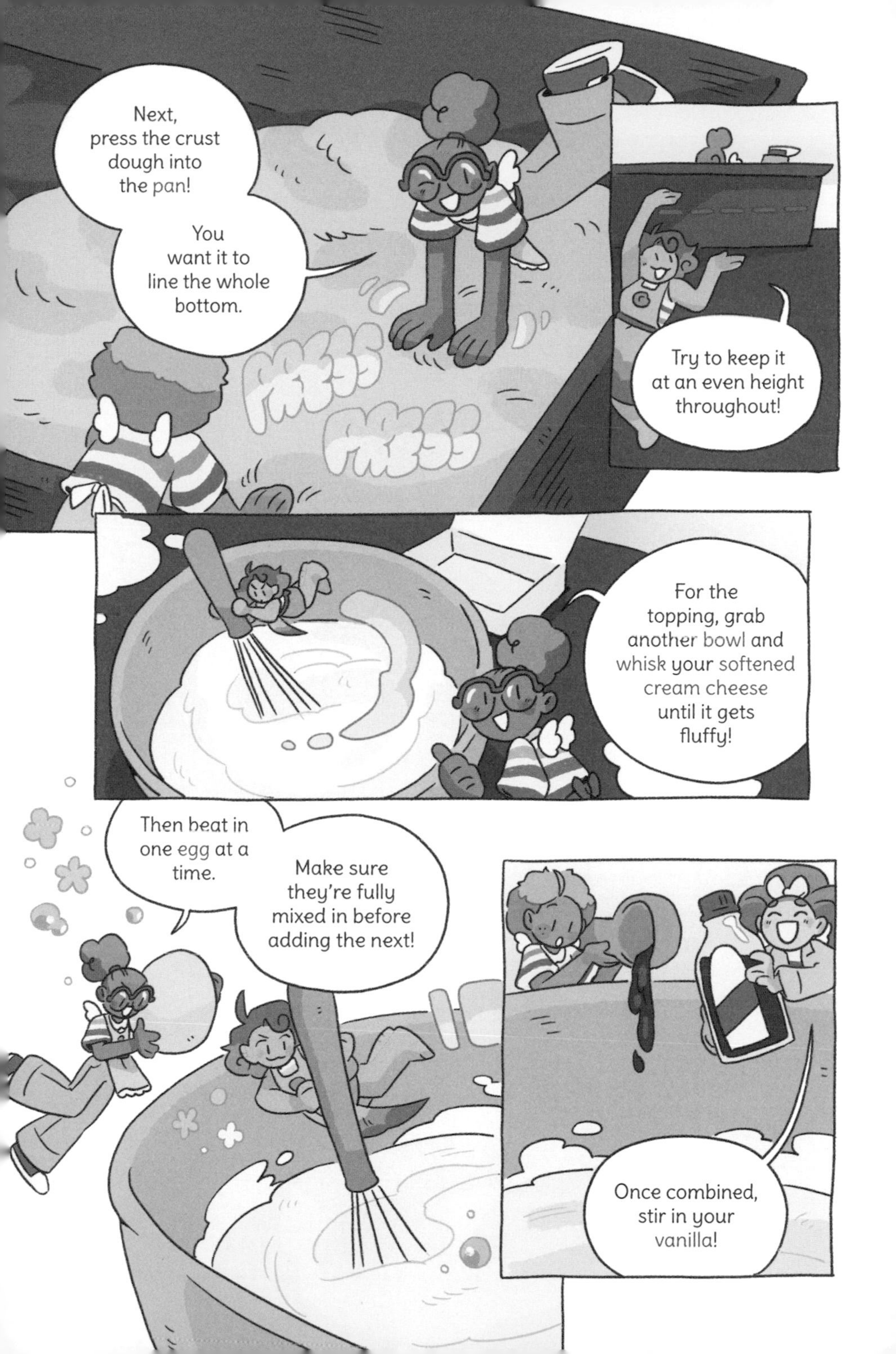
Next, press the crust dough into the pan!
You want it to line the whole bottom.
PRESS PRESS
Try to keep it at an even height throughout!
For the topping, grab another bowl and whisk your softened cream cheese until it gets fluffy!
Then beat in one egg at a time.
Make sure they're fully mixed in before adding the next!
Once combined, stir in your vanilla!

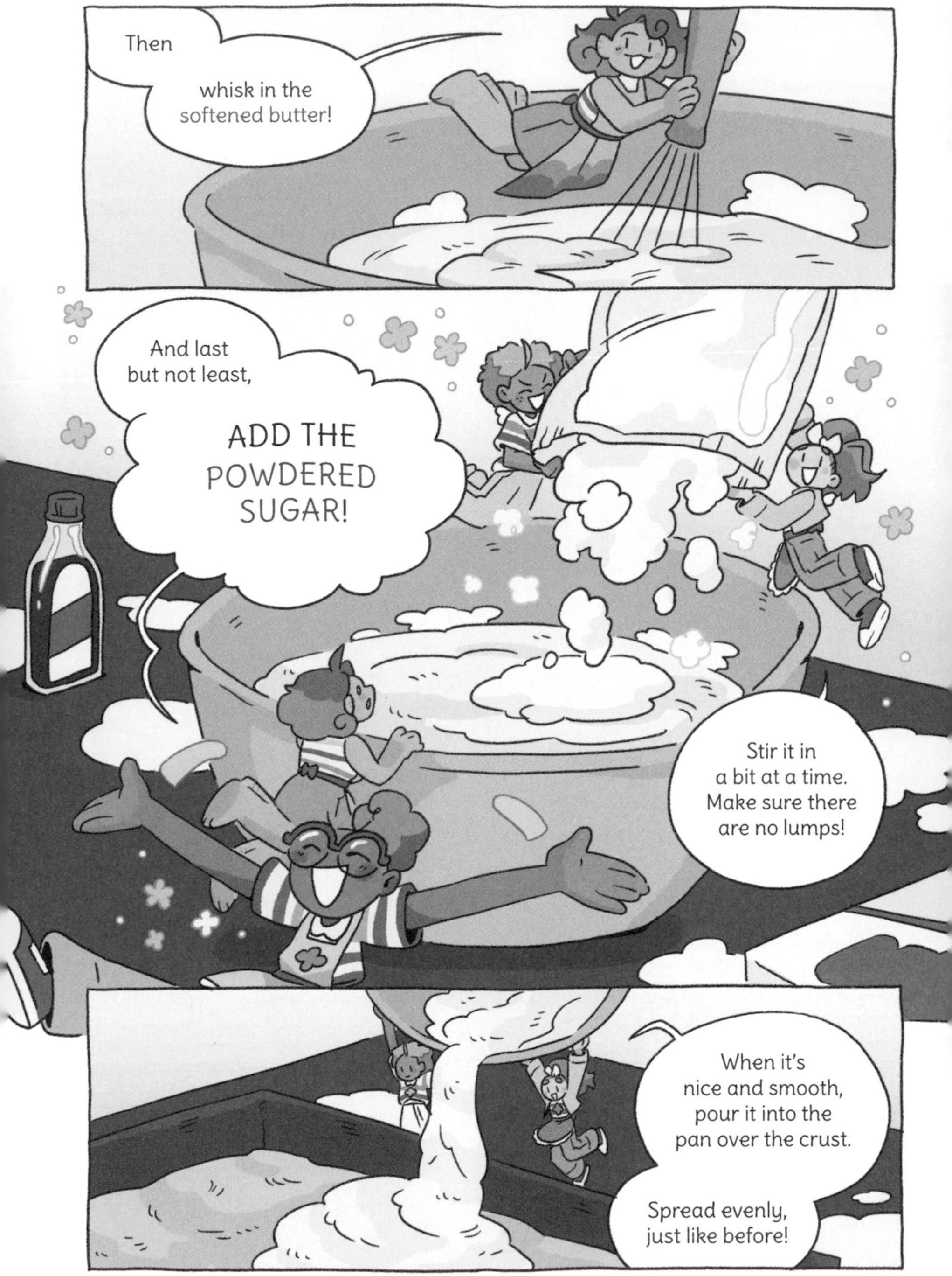
Then
whisk in the softened butter!
And last but not least,
ADD THE POWDERED SUGAR!
Stir it in a bit at a time. Make sure there are no lumps!
When it's nice and smooth, pour it into the pan over the crust.
Spread evenly, just like before!

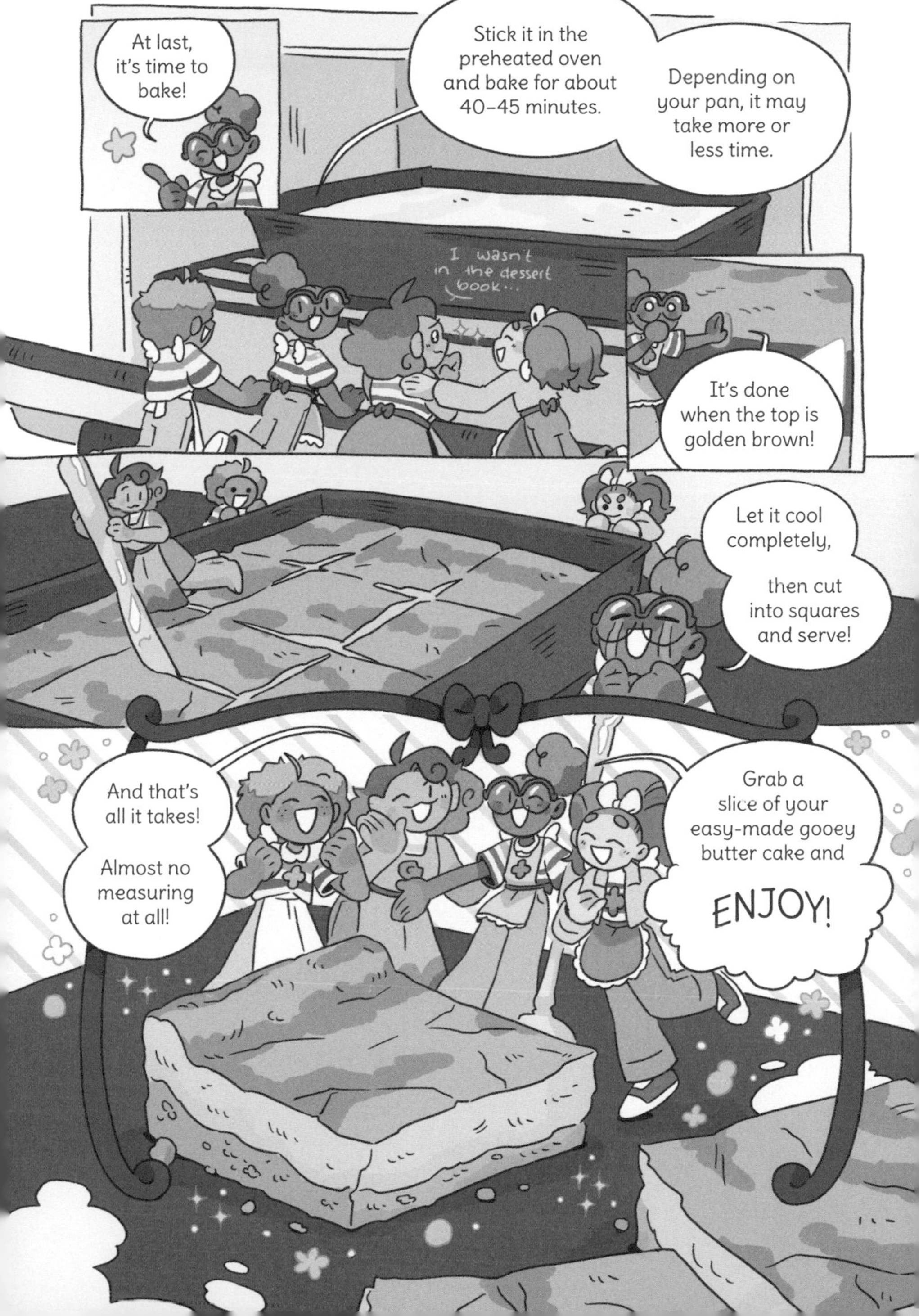
At last, it's time to bake!
Stick it in the preheated oven and bake for about 40–45 minutes.
Depending on your pan, it may take more or less time.
I wasn't in the dessert book...
It's done when the top is golden brown!
Let it cool completely,
then cut into squares and serve!
And that's all it takes!
Almost no measuring at all!
Grab a slice of your easy-made gooey butter cake and
ENJOY!

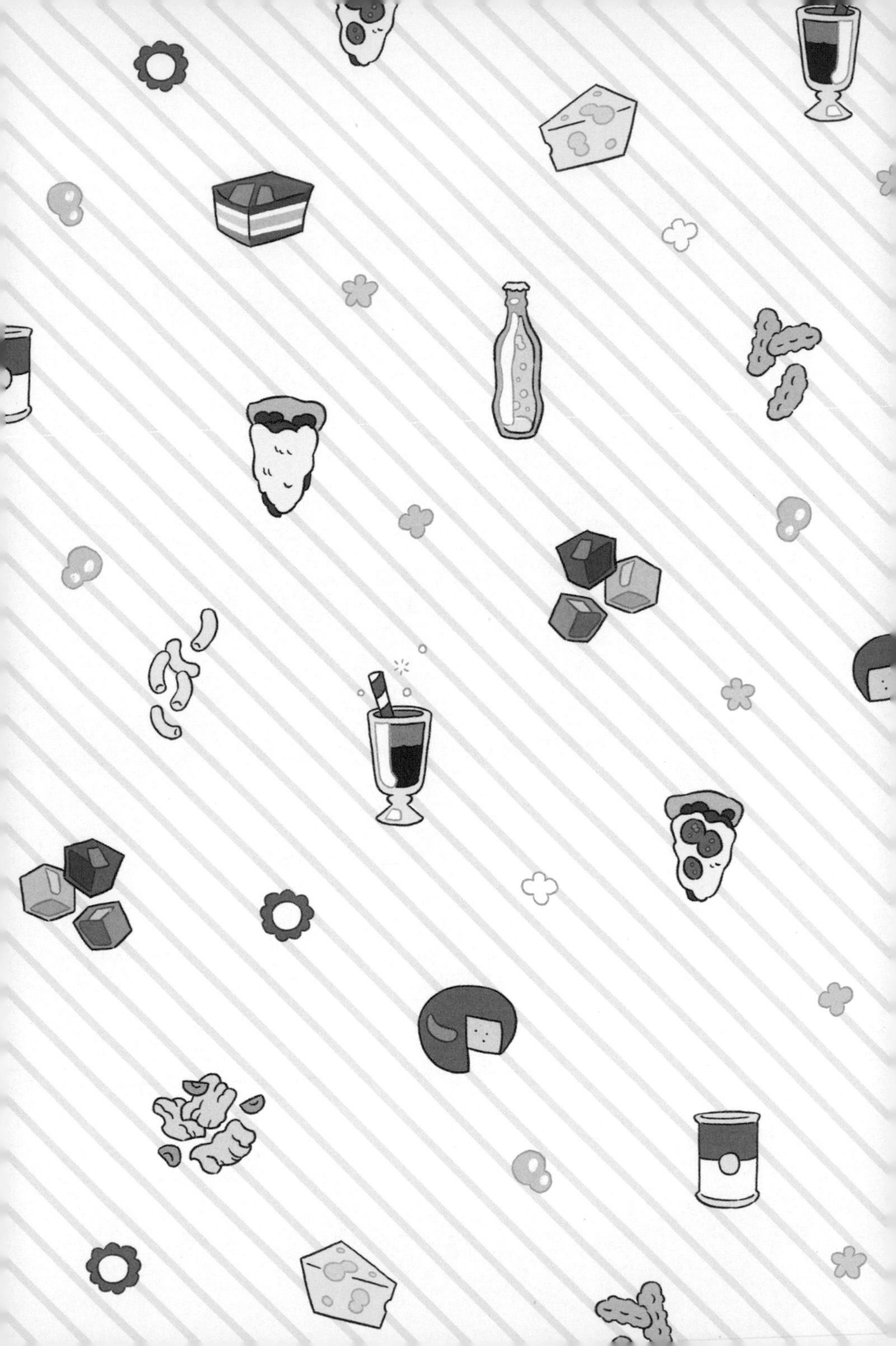

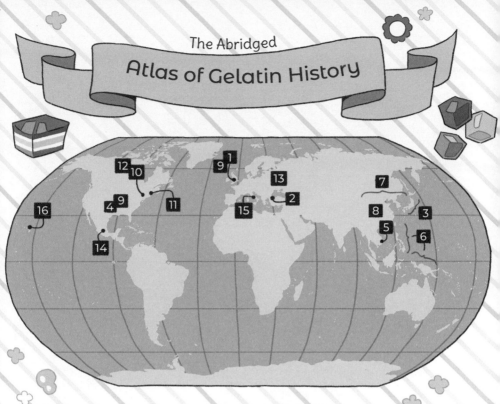

The Abridged
# Atlas of Gelatin History

1. Medieval British *The Forme of Cury*
2. Turkish Lokum
3. Japanese Yōkan
4. American Jelly Beans
5. Vietnamese Thạch
6. Southeast Asian Tapioca Pearls
7. East Asian Oxtail Soup
8. Chinese Ejiao Cake
9. Sheet and Powder Gelatin
10. Jell-O
11. Mrs. J. E. Cook's Perfection Salad
12. Jell-O Recipe Books
13. Eastern European Kholodets
14. Mexican Gelatina Mosaico and Gelatina Artistica
15. Italian Panna Cotta
16. Hawaiian Rainbow Jell-O

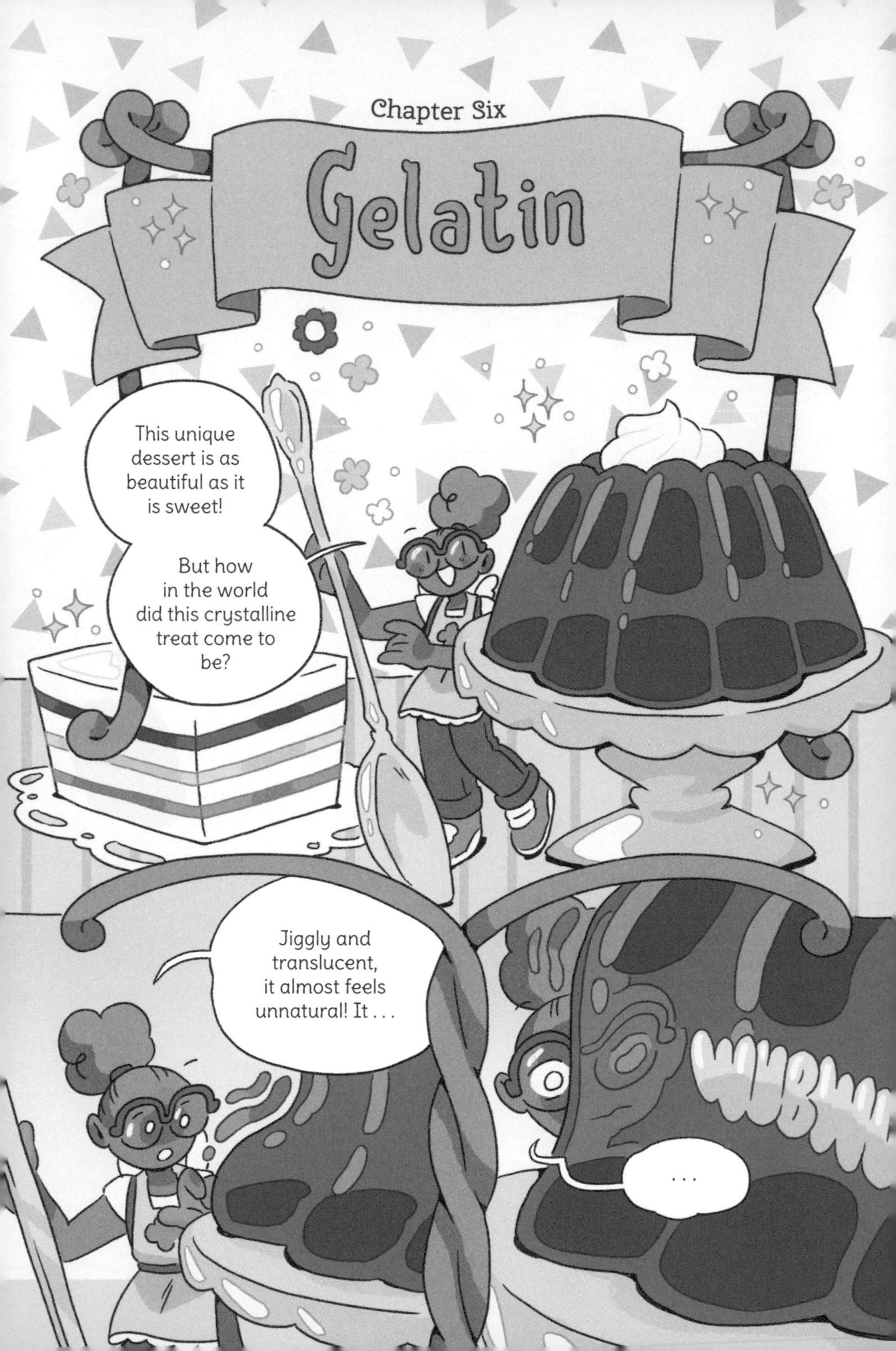
Chapter Six
Gelatin
This unique dessert is as beautiful as it is sweet!
But how in the world did this crystalline treat come to be?
Jiggly and translucent, it almost feels unnatural! It . . .
. . .

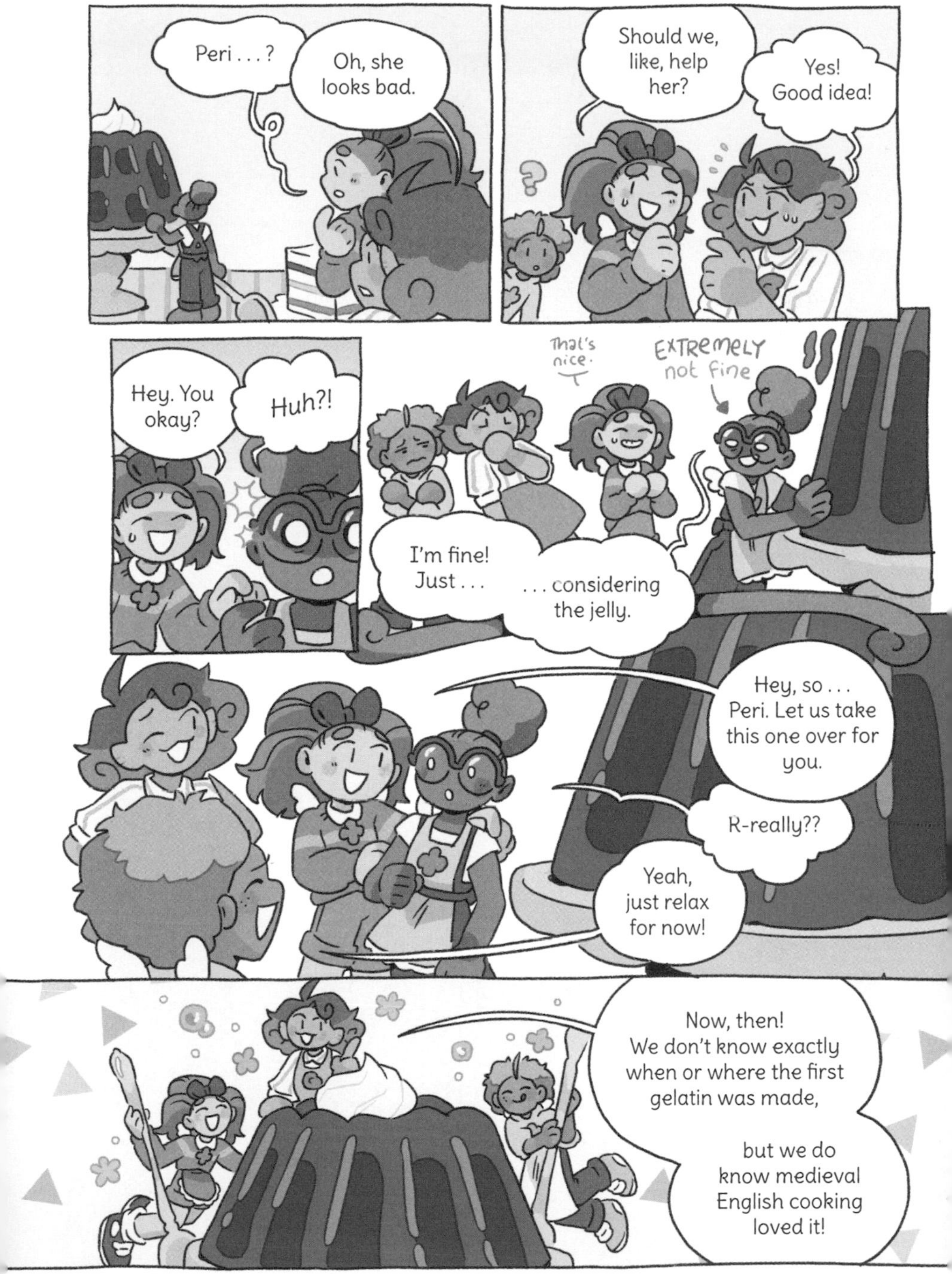
Peri . . . ?
Oh, she looks bad.
Should we, like, help her?
Yes! Good idea!
Hey. You okay?
Huh?!
That's nice.
EXTREMELY not fine
I'm fine! Just . . .
. . . considering the jelly.
Hey, so . . . Peri. Let us take this one over for you.
R-really??
Yeah, just relax for now!
Now, then! We don't know exactly when or where the first gelatin was made,
but we do know medieval English cooking loved it!

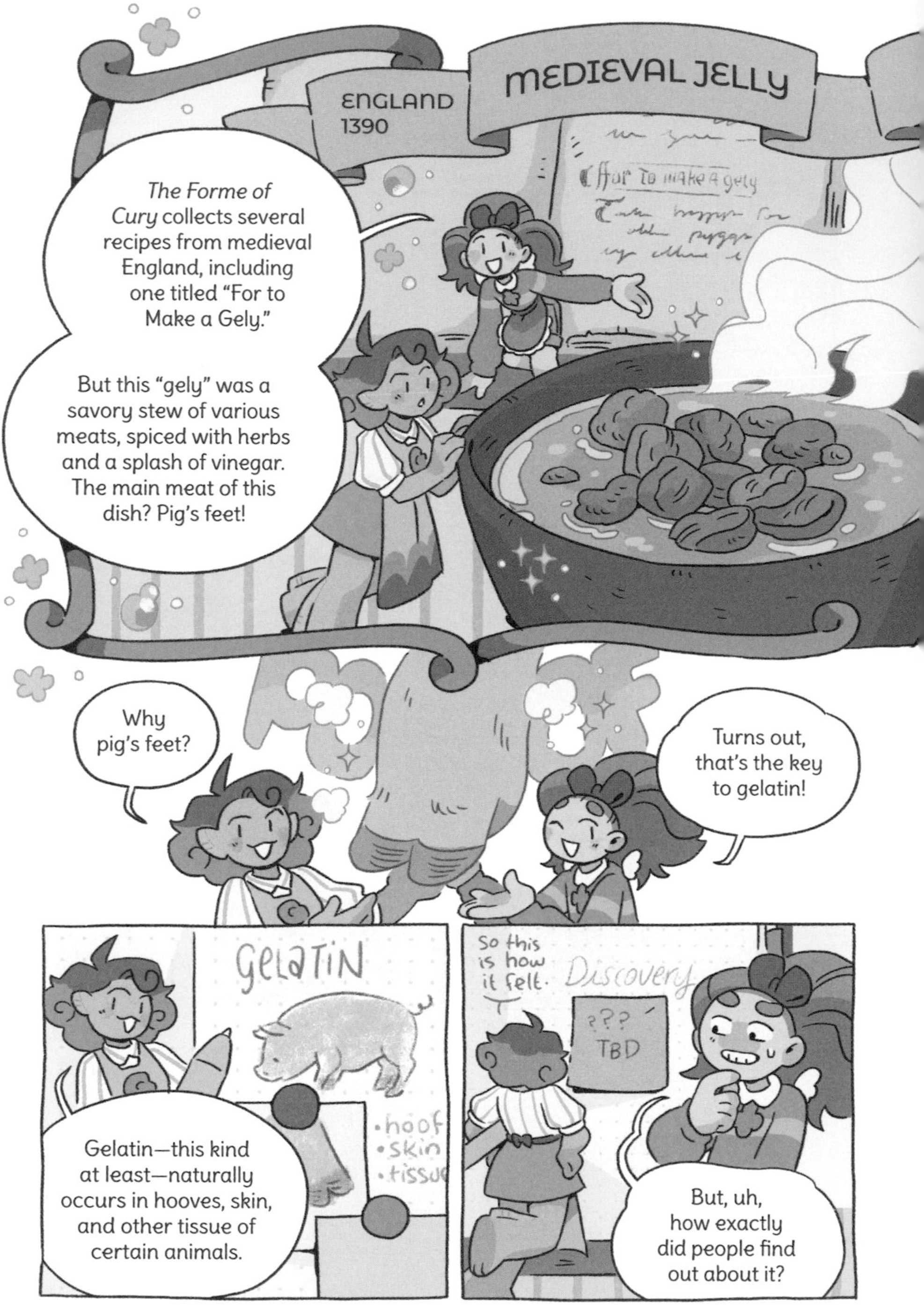

ENGLAND 1390
MEDIEVAL JELLY
For to make a gely
*The Forme of Cury* collects several recipes from medieval England, including one titled "For to Make a Gely."
But this "gely" was a savory stew of various meats, spiced with herbs and a splash of vinegar. The main meat of this dish? Pig's feet!
Why pig's feet?
Turns out, that's the key to gelatin!
GELATIN
• hoof
• skin
• tissue
Gelatin—this kind at least—naturally occurs in hooves, skin, and other tissue of certain animals.
So this is how it felt.
Discovery
??? TBD
But, uh, how exactly did people find out about it?

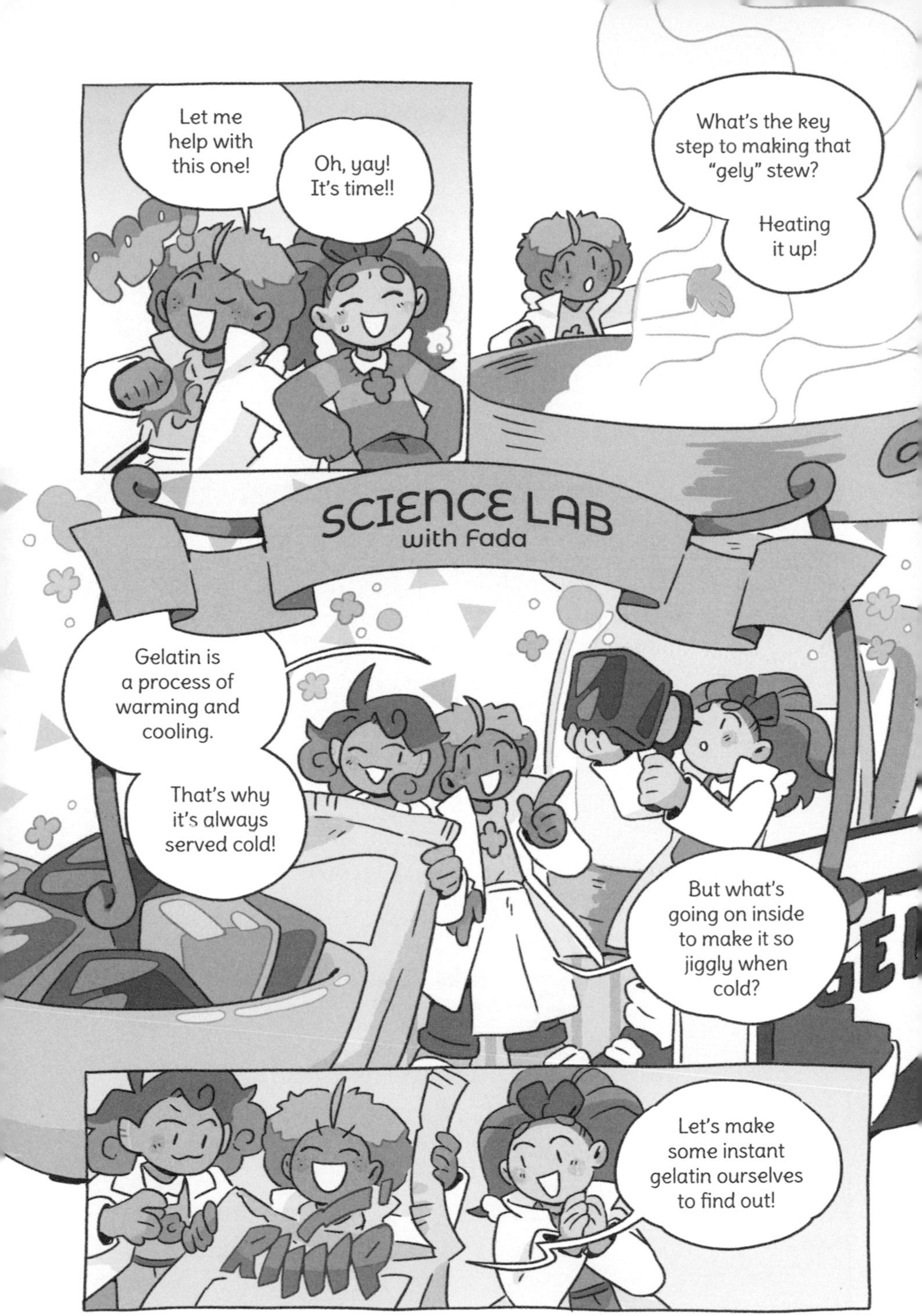
Let me help with this one!
Oh, yay! It's time!!
What's the key step to making that "gely" stew?
Heating it up!
SCIENCE LAB
with Fada
Gelatin is a process of warming and cooling.
That's why it's always served cold!
But what's going on inside to make it so jiggly when cold?
Let's make some instant gelatin ourselves to find out!

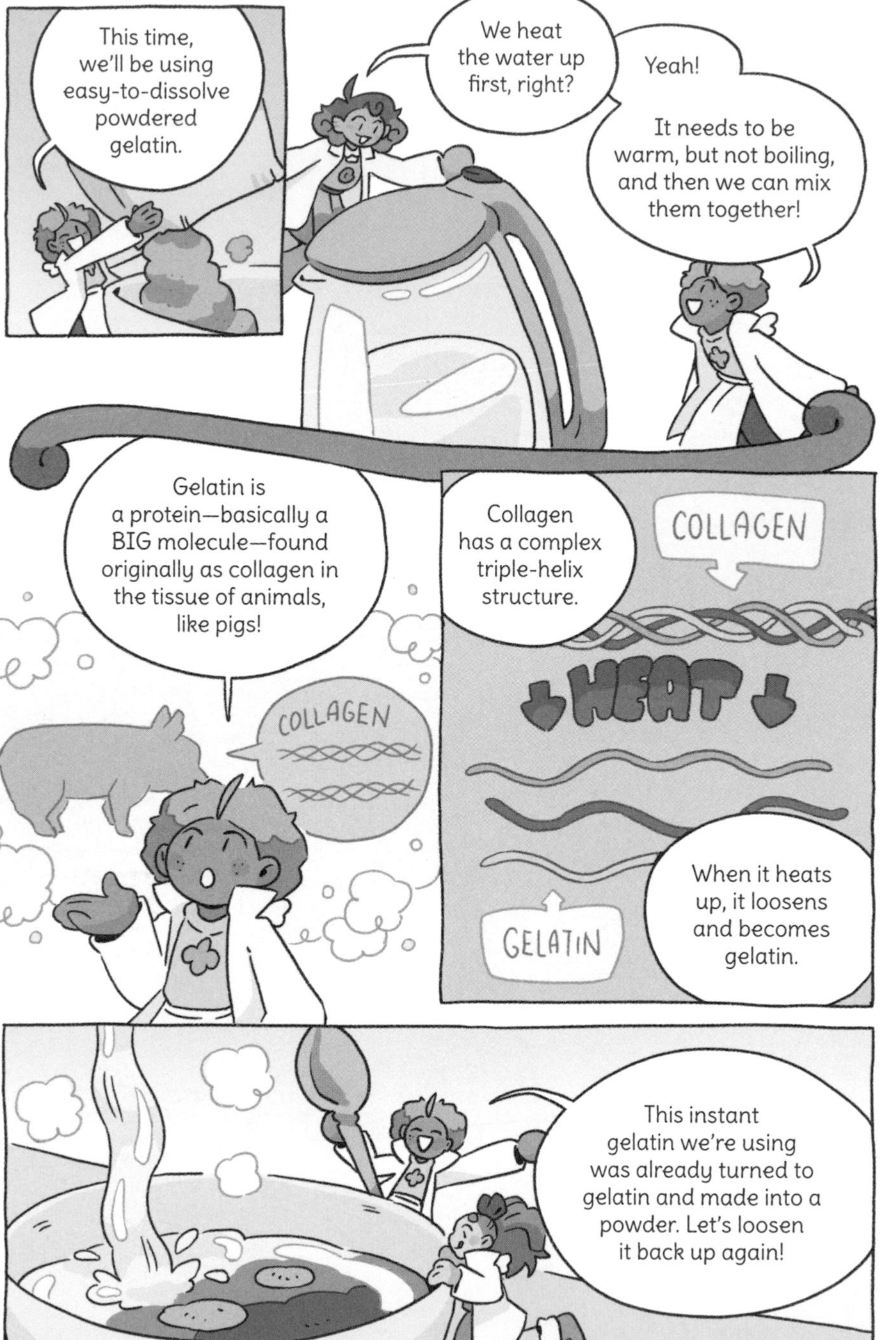
This time, we'll be using easy-to-dissolve powdered gelatin.
We heat the water up first, right?
Yeah!
It needs to be warm, but not boiling, and then we can mix them together!
Gelatin is a protein—basically a BIG molecule—found originally as collagen in the tissue of animals, like pigs!
COLLAGEN
Collagen has a complex triple-helix structure.
COLLAGEN
HEAT
GELATIN
When it heats up, it loosens and becomes gelatin.
This instant gelatin we're using was already turned to gelatin and made into a powder. Let's loosen it back up again!

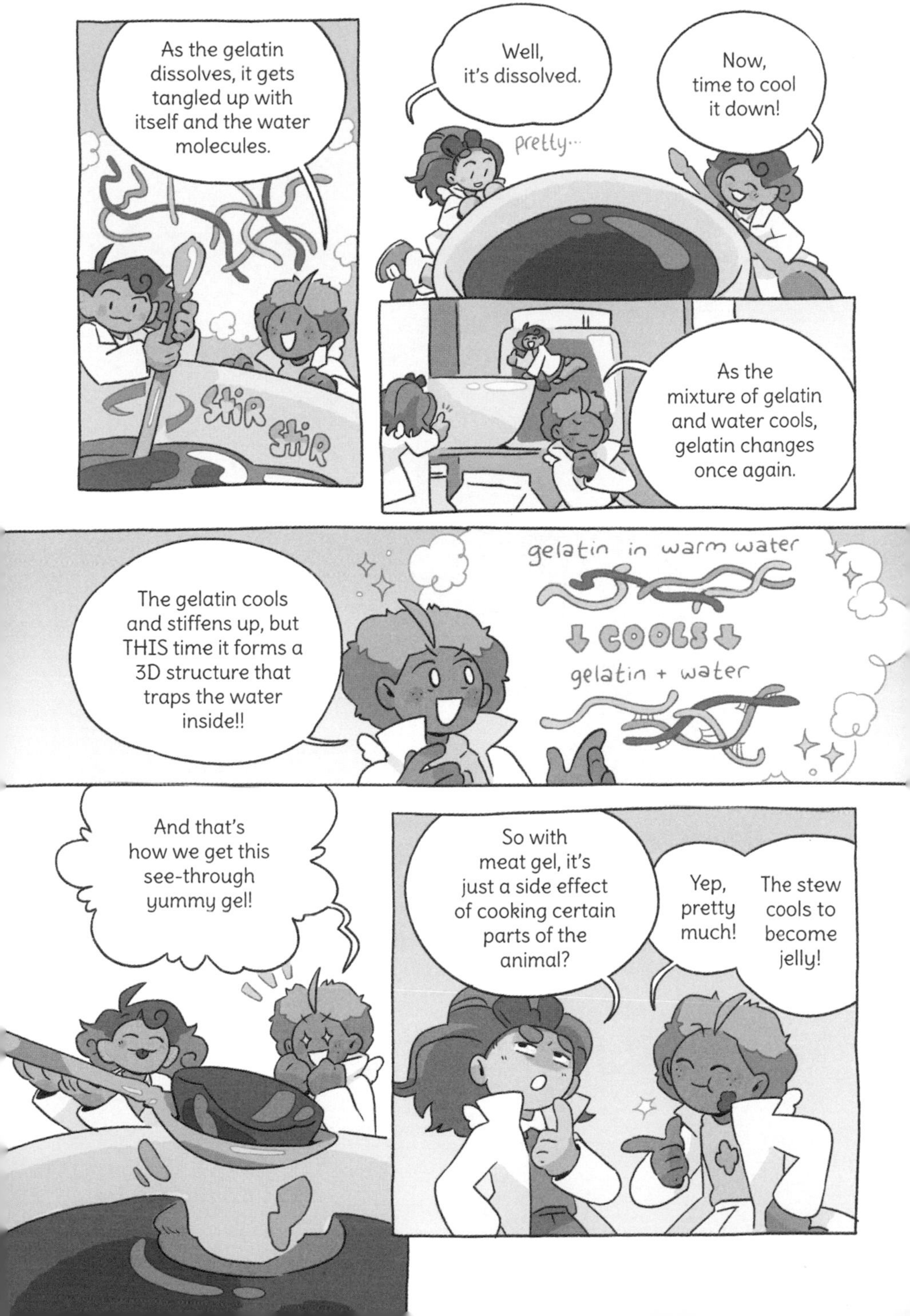
As the gelatin dissolves, it gets tangled up with itself and the water molecules.
STIR STIR
Well, it's dissolved.
pretty...
Now, time to cool it down!
As the mixture of gelatin and water cools, gelatin changes once again.
The gelatin cools and stiffens up, but THIS time it forms a 3D structure that traps the water inside!!
gelatin in warm water
COOLS
gelatin + water
And that's how we get this see-through yummy gel!
So with meat gel, it's just a side effect of cooking certain parts of the animal?
Yep, pretty much!
The stew cools to become jelly!

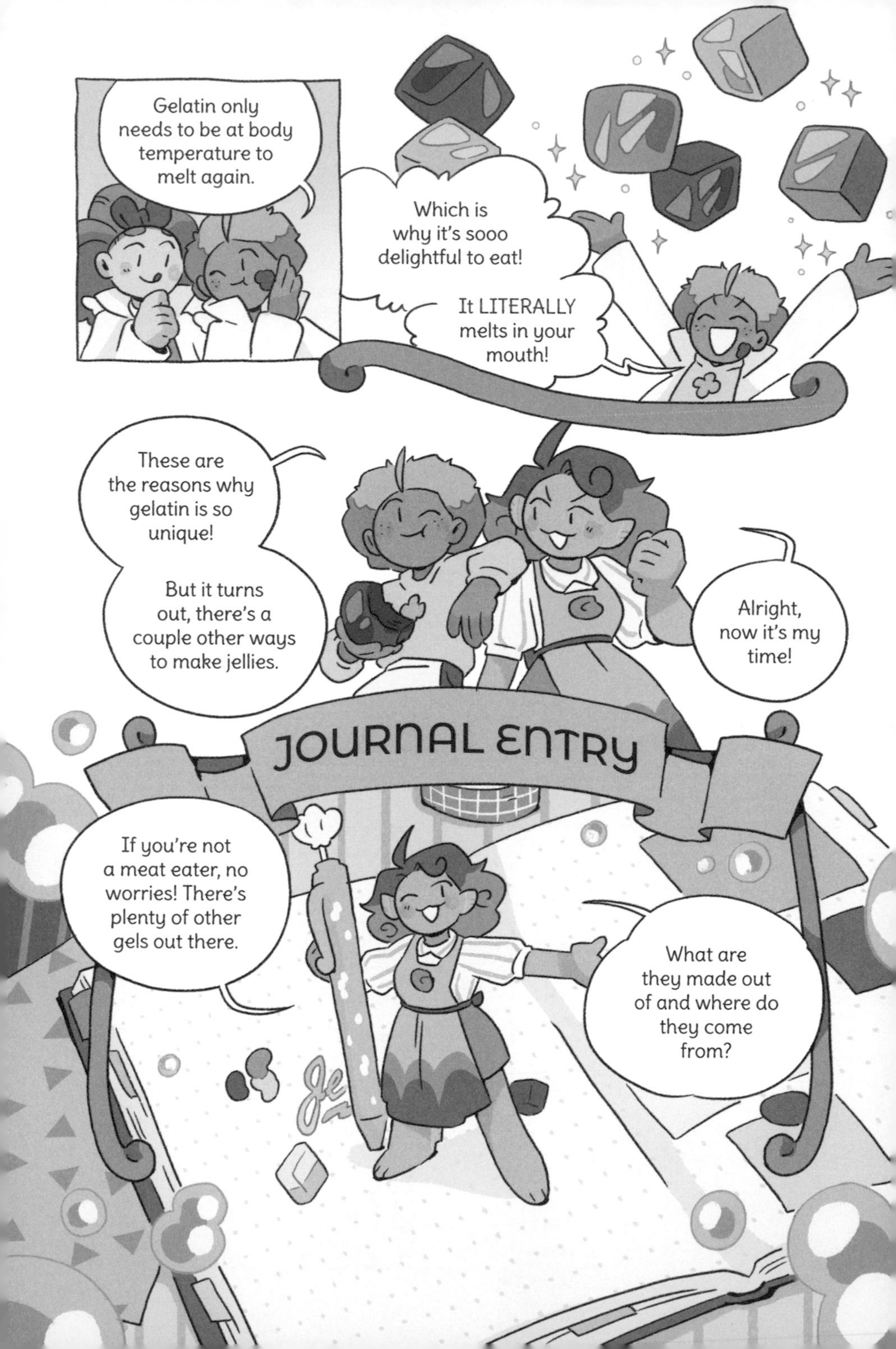
Gelatin only needs to be at body temperature to melt again.
Which is why it's sooo delightful to eat!
It LITERALLY melts in your mouth!
These are the reasons why gelatin is so unique!
But it turns out, there's a couple other ways to make jellies.
Alright, now it's my time!
JOURNAL ENTRY
If you're not a meat eater, no worries! There's plenty of other gels out there.
What are they made out of and where do they come from?

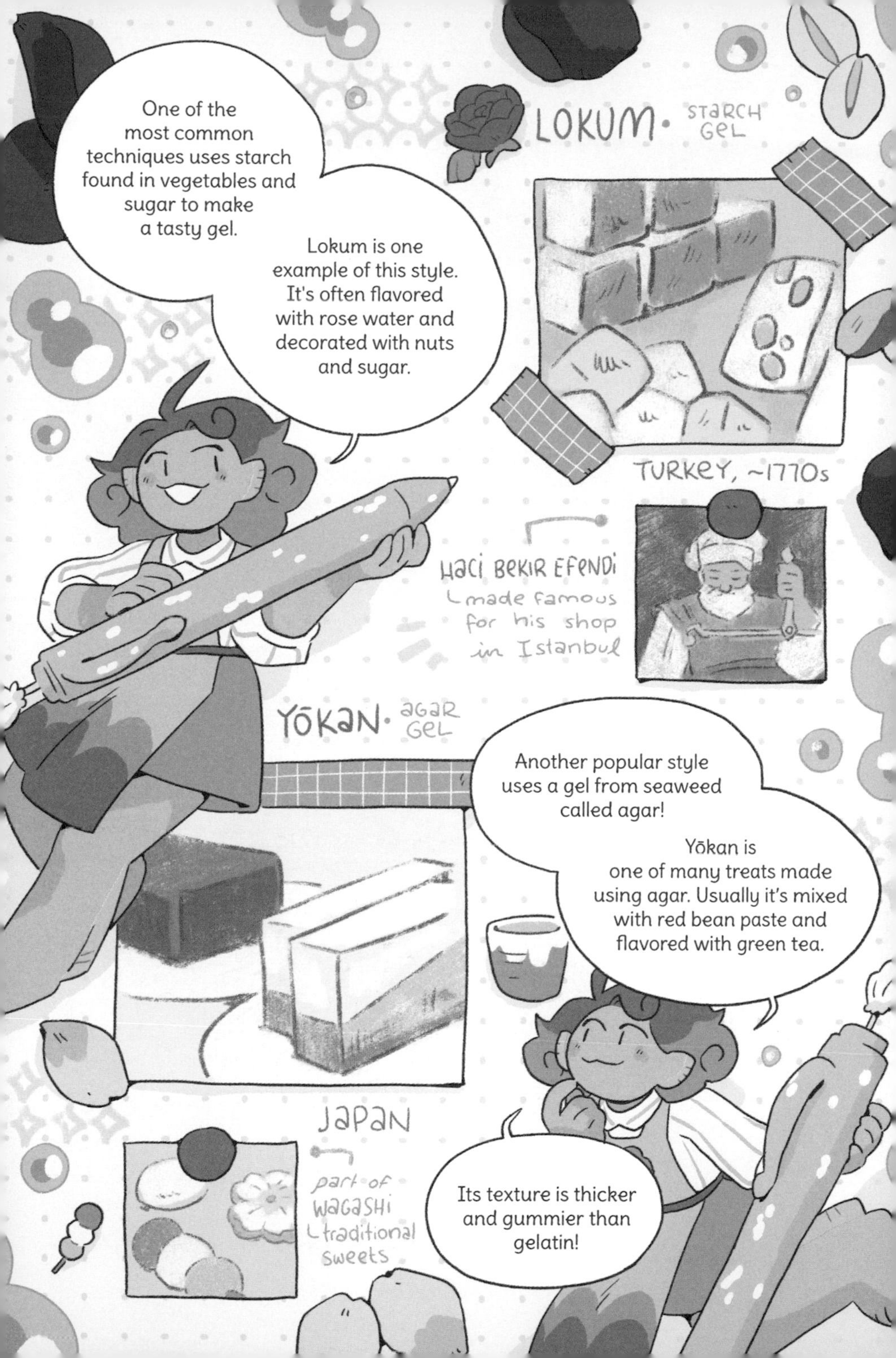

One of the most common techniques uses starch found in vegetables and sugar to make a tasty gel.
Lokum is one example of this style. It's often flavored with rose water and decorated with nuts and sugar.
LOKUM · STARCH GEL
TURKEY, ~1770s
HACI BEKIR EFENDI
made famous for his shop in Istanbul
YŌKAN · AGAR GEL
Another popular style uses a gel from seaweed called agar!
Yōkan is one of many treats made using agar. Usually it's mixed with red bean paste and flavored with green tea.
JAPAN
part of WAGASHI
traditional sweets
Its texture is thicker and gummier than gelatin!

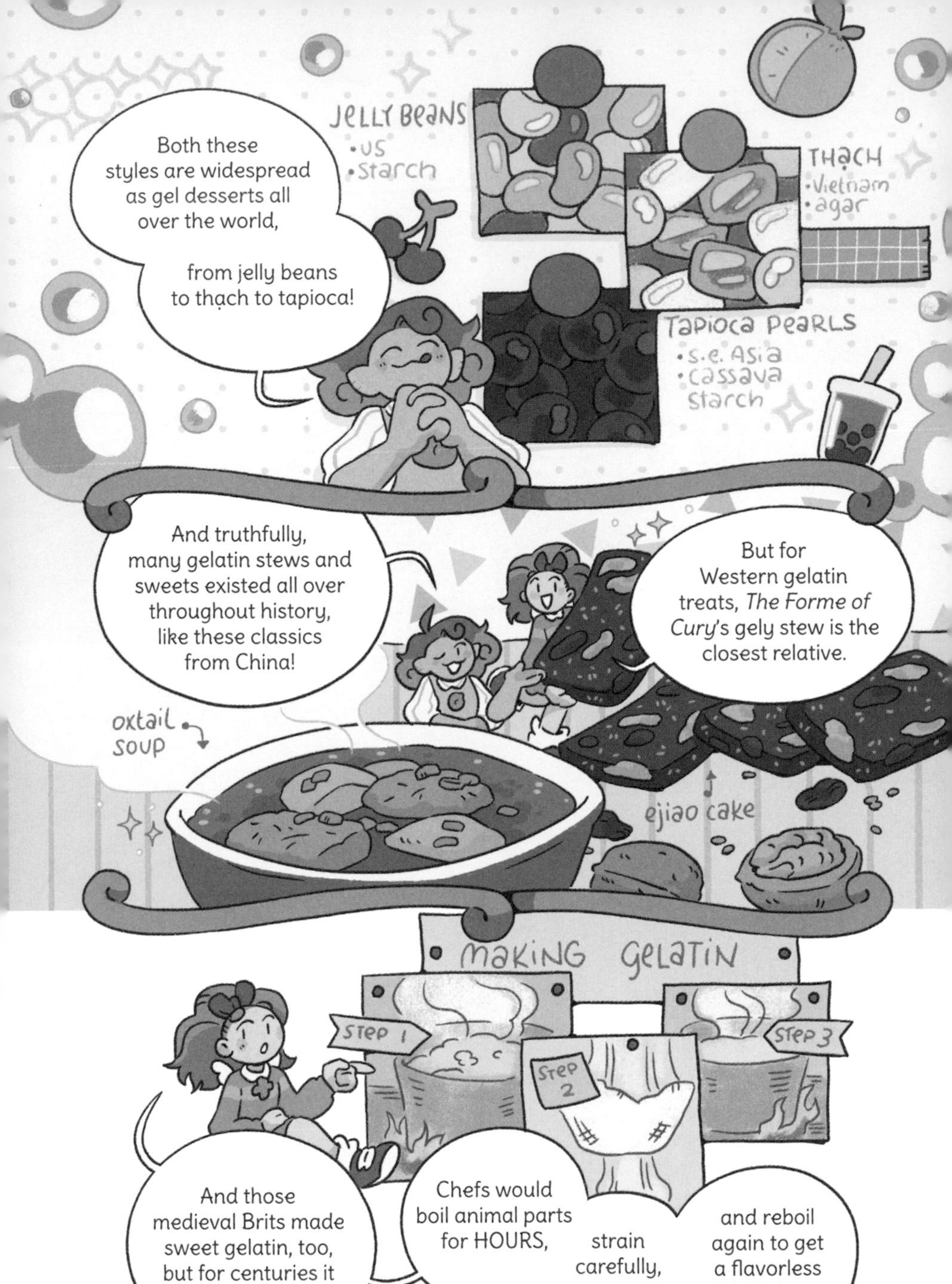

Both these styles are widespread as gel desserts all over the world,
from jelly beans to thạch to tapioca!
JELLY BEANS
•US
•Starch
THẠCH
•Vietnam
•agar
TAPIOCA PEARLS
•S.E. Asia
•Cassava starch
And truthfully, many gelatin stews and sweets existed all over throughout history, like these classics from China!
But for Western gelatin treats, *The Forme of Cury*'s gely stew is the closest relative.
oxtail soup
ejiao cake
MAKING GELATIN
STEP 1
STEP 2
STEP 3
And those medieval Brits made sweet gelatin, too, but for centuries it was a lot of work!
Chefs would boil animal parts for HOURS,
strain carefully,
and reboil again to get a flavorless gelatin base.

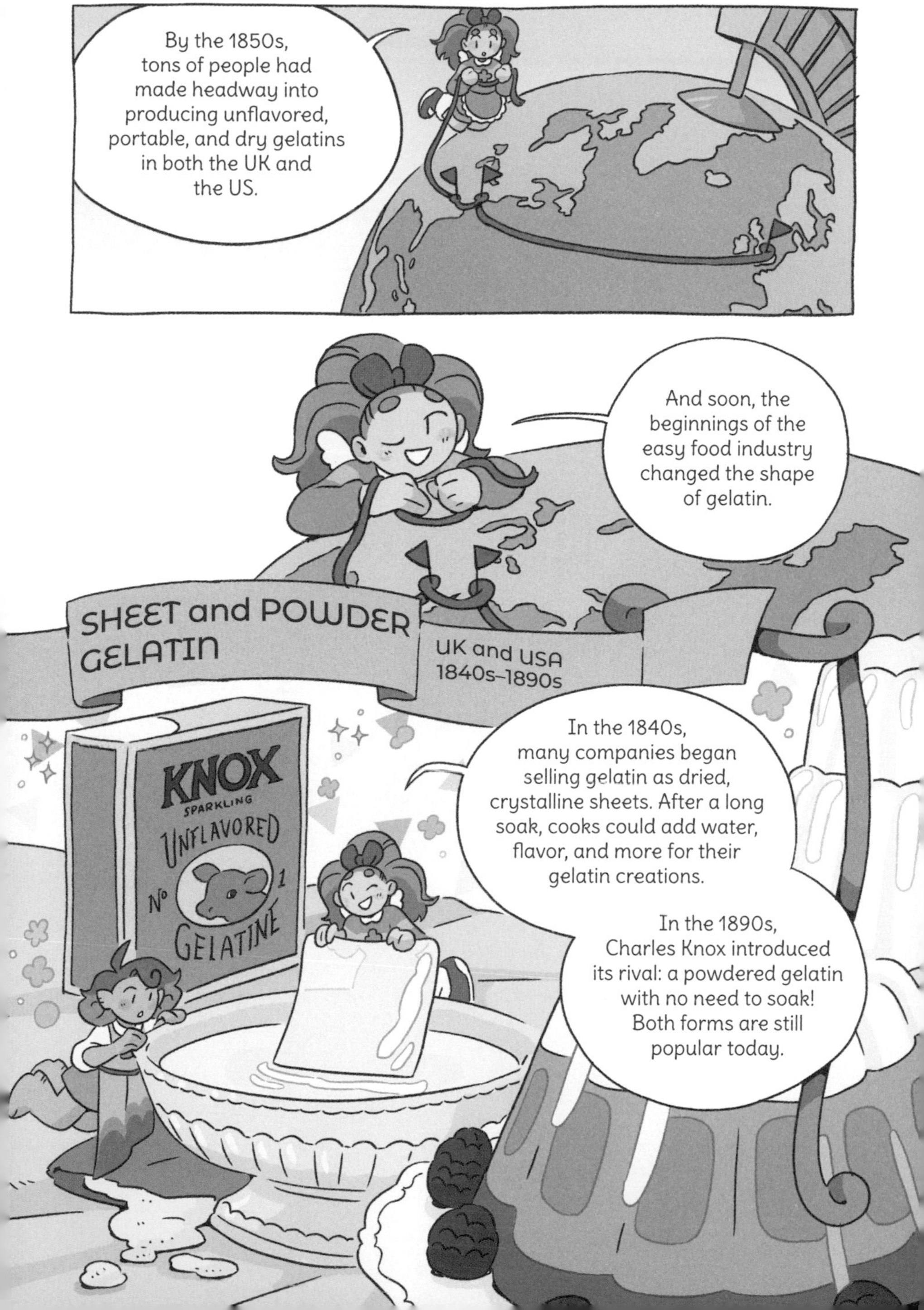

By the 1850s, tons of people had made headway into producing unflavored, portable, and dry gelatins in both the UK and the US.
And soon, the beginnings of the easy food industry changed the shape of gelatin.
SHEET and POWDER GELATIN
UK and USA 1840s–1890s
KNOX SPARKLING UNFLAVORED Nº 1 GELATINE
In the 1840s, many companies began selling gelatin as dried, crystalline sheets. After a long soak, cooks could add water, flavor, and more for their gelatin creations.
In the 1890s, Charles Knox introduced its rival: a powdered gelatin with no need to soak! Both forms are still popular today.

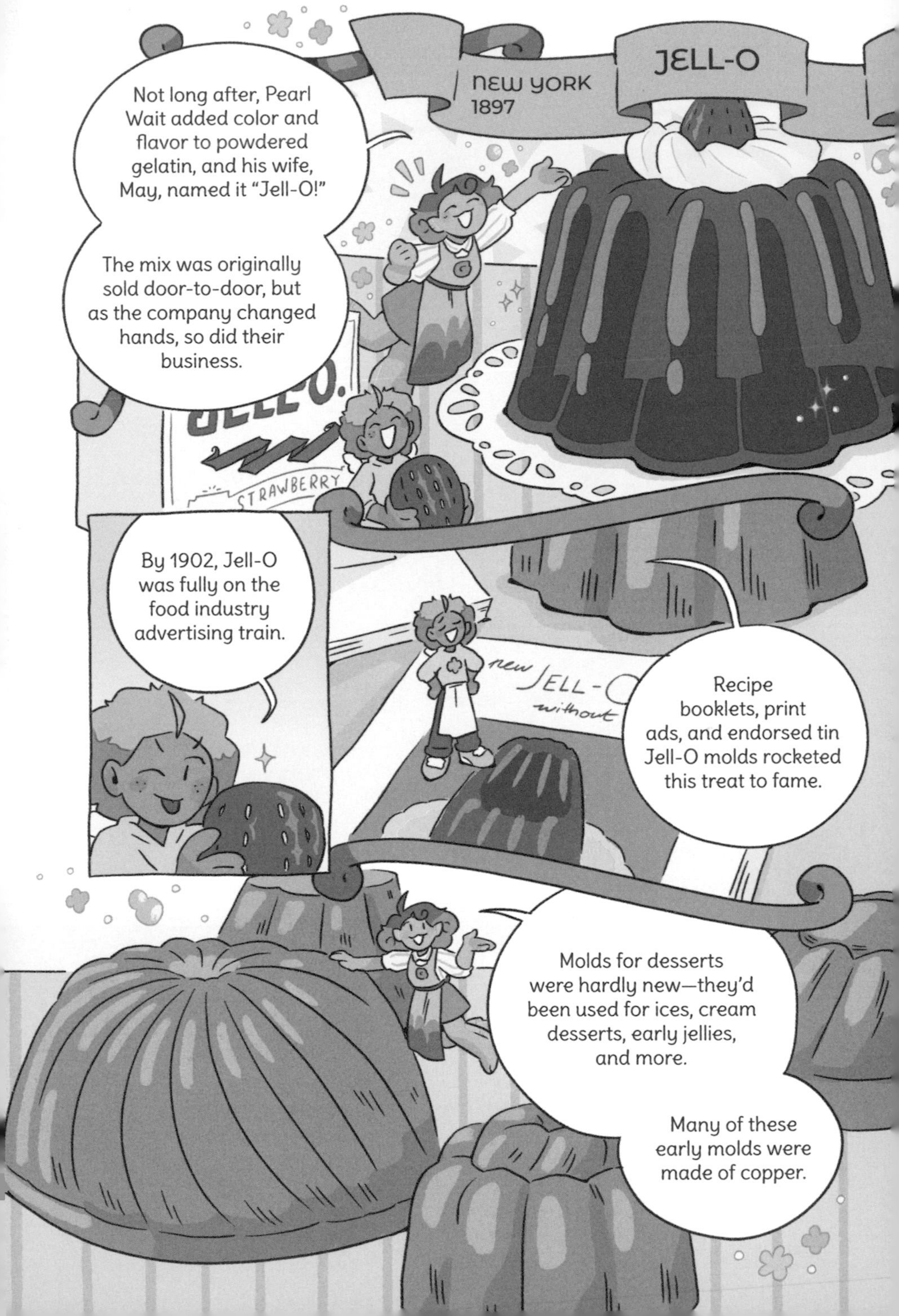
NEW YORK 1897
JELL-O
Not long after, Pearl Wait added color and flavor to powdered gelatin, and his wife, May, named it "Jell-O!"
The mix was originally sold door-to-door, but as the company changed hands, so did their business.
STRAWBERRY
By 1902, Jell-O was fully on the food industry advertising train.
new JELL-O
without
Recipe booklets, print ads, and endorsed tin Jell-O molds rocketed this treat to fame.
Molds for desserts were hardly new—they'd been used for ices, cream desserts, early jellies, and more.
Many of these early molds were made of copper.

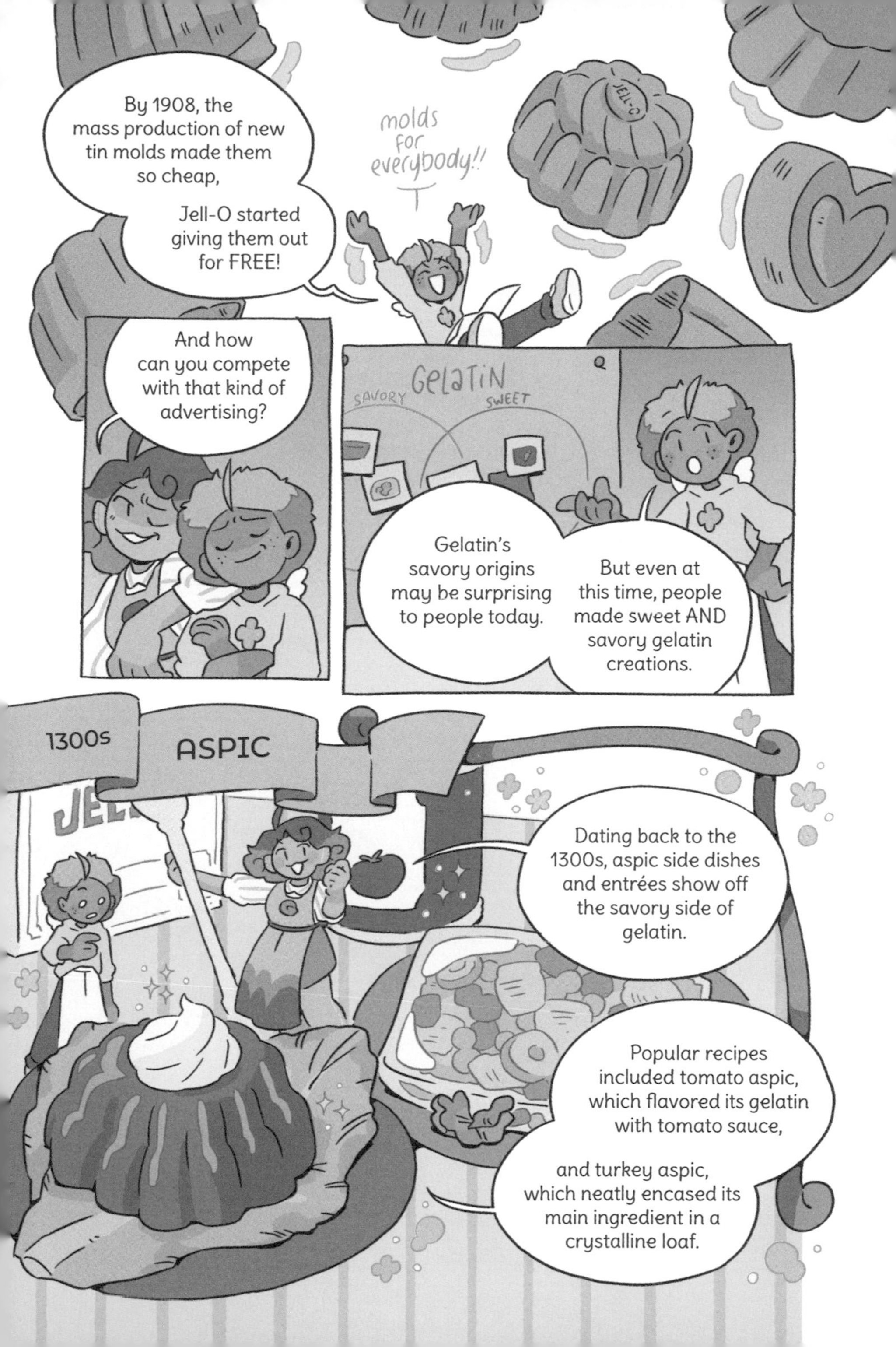
By 1908, the mass production of new tin molds made them so cheap,
Jell-O started giving them out for FREE!
molds for everybody!!
JELL-O
And how can you compete with that kind of advertising?
GELATIN
SAVORY
SWEET
Gelatin's savory origins may be surprising to people today.
But even at this time, people made sweet AND savory gelatin creations.
1300s
ASPIC
Dating back to the 1300s, aspic side dishes and entrées show off the savory side of gelatin.
Popular recipes included tomato aspic, which flavored its gelatin with tomato sauce,
and turkey aspic, which neatly encased its main ingredient in a crystalline loaf.

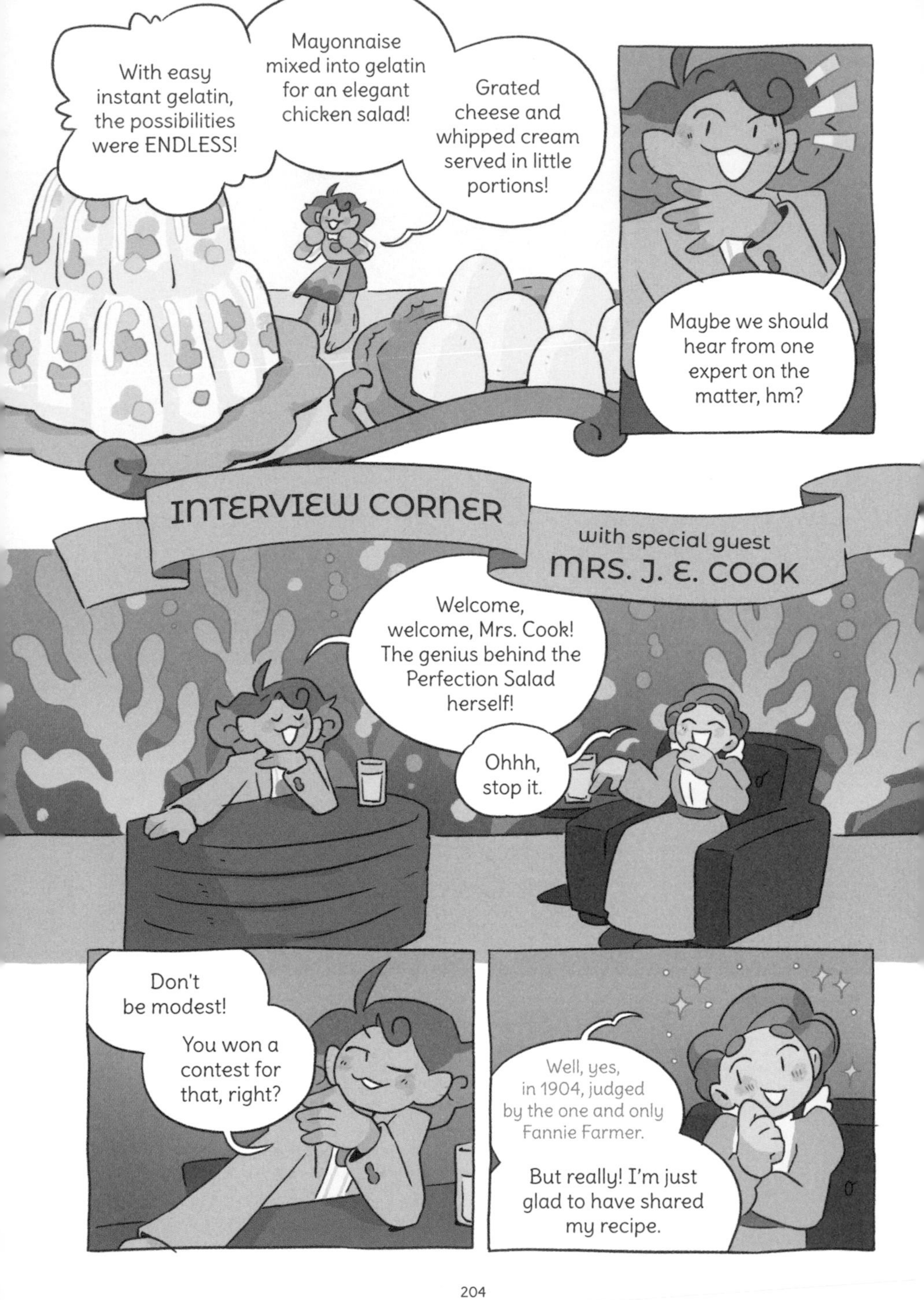
With easy instant gelatin, the possibilities were ENDLESS!
Mayonnaise mixed into gelatin for an elegant chicken salad!
Grated cheese and whipped cream served in little portions!
Maybe we should hear from one expert on the matter, hm?
INTERVIEW CORNER
with special guest MRS. J. E. COOK
Welcome, welcome, Mrs. Cook! The genius behind the Perfection Salad herself!
Ohhh, stop it.
Don't be modest!
You won a contest for that, right?
Well, yes, in 1904, judged by the one and only Fannie Farmer.
But really! I'm just glad to have shared my recipe.

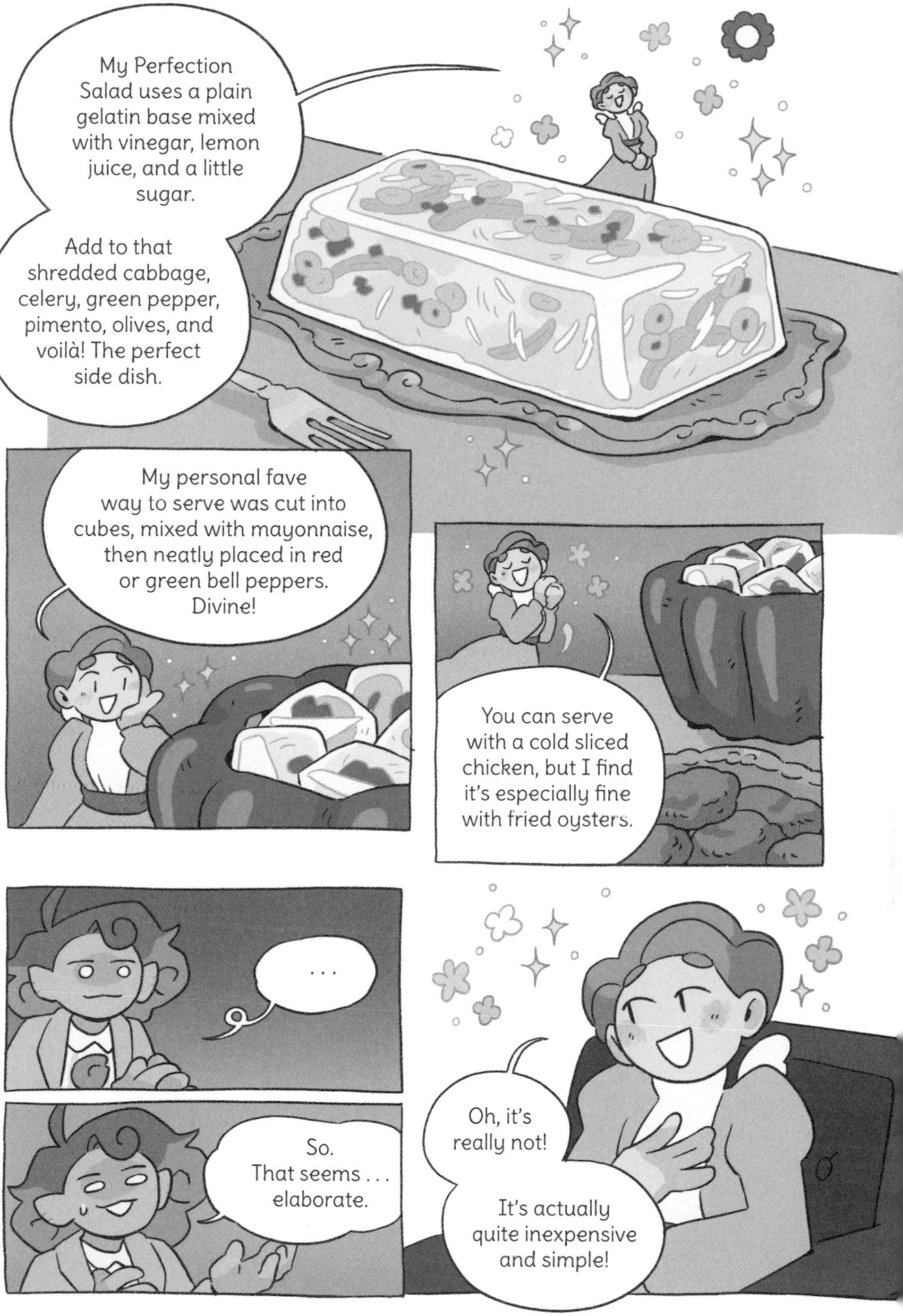
My Perfection Salad uses a plain gelatin base mixed with vinegar, lemon juice, and a little sugar.
Add to that shredded cabbage, celery, green pepper, pimento, olives, and voilà! The perfect side dish.
My personal fave way to serve was cut into cubes, mixed with mayonnaise, then neatly placed in red or green bell peppers. Divine!
You can serve with a cold sliced chicken, but I find it's especially fine with fried oysters.
. . .
So. That seems . . . elaborate.
Oh, it's really not!
It's actually quite inexpensive and simple!

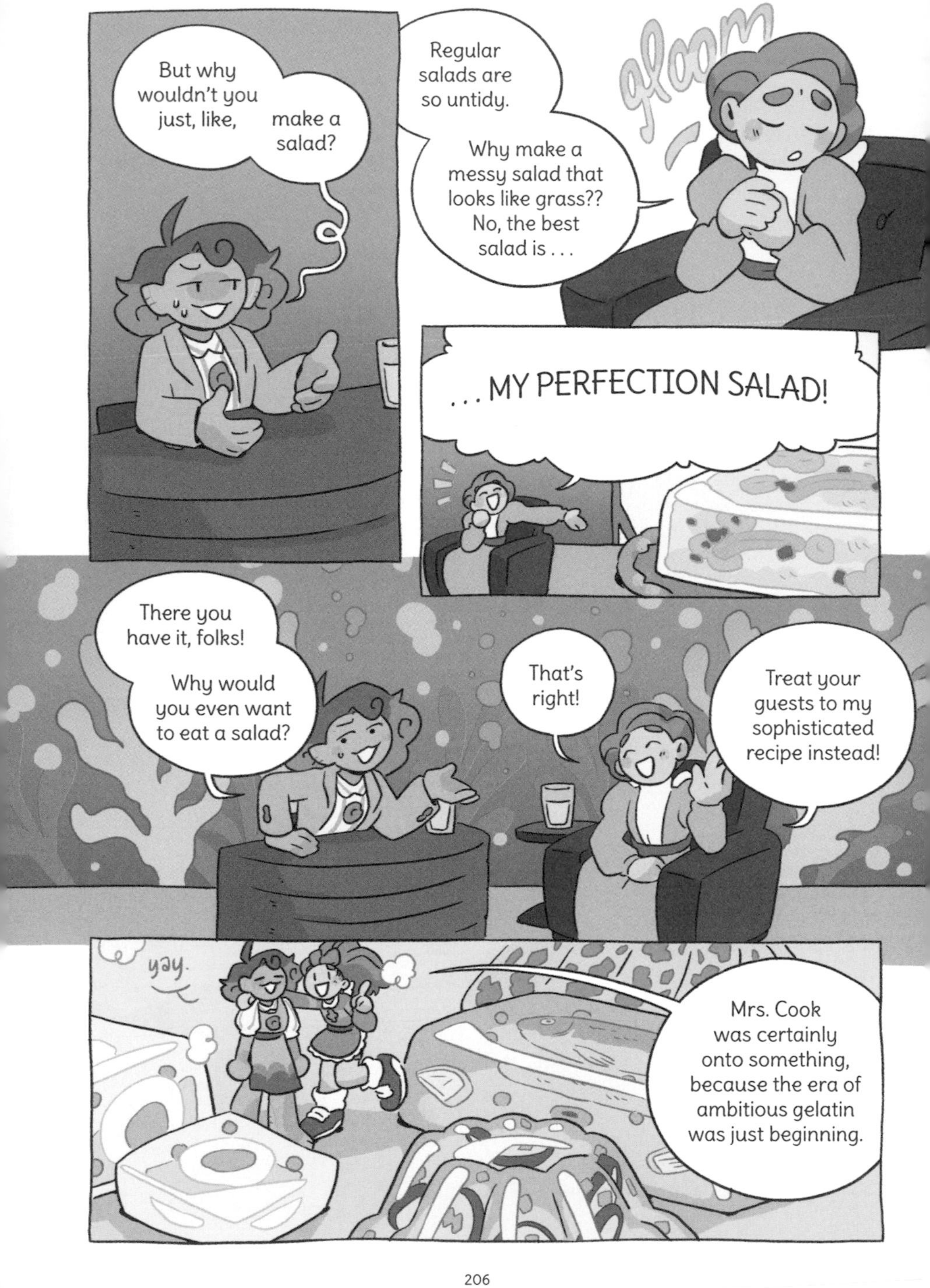
But why wouldn't you just, like, make a salad?
Regular salads are so untidy.
Why make a messy salad that looks like grass?? No, the best salad is . . .
gloom
. . . MY PERFECTION SALAD!
There you have it, folks!
Why would you even want to eat a salad?
That's right!
Treat your guests to my sophisticated recipe instead!
yay.
Mrs. Cook was certainly onto something, because the era of ambitious gelatin was just beginning.

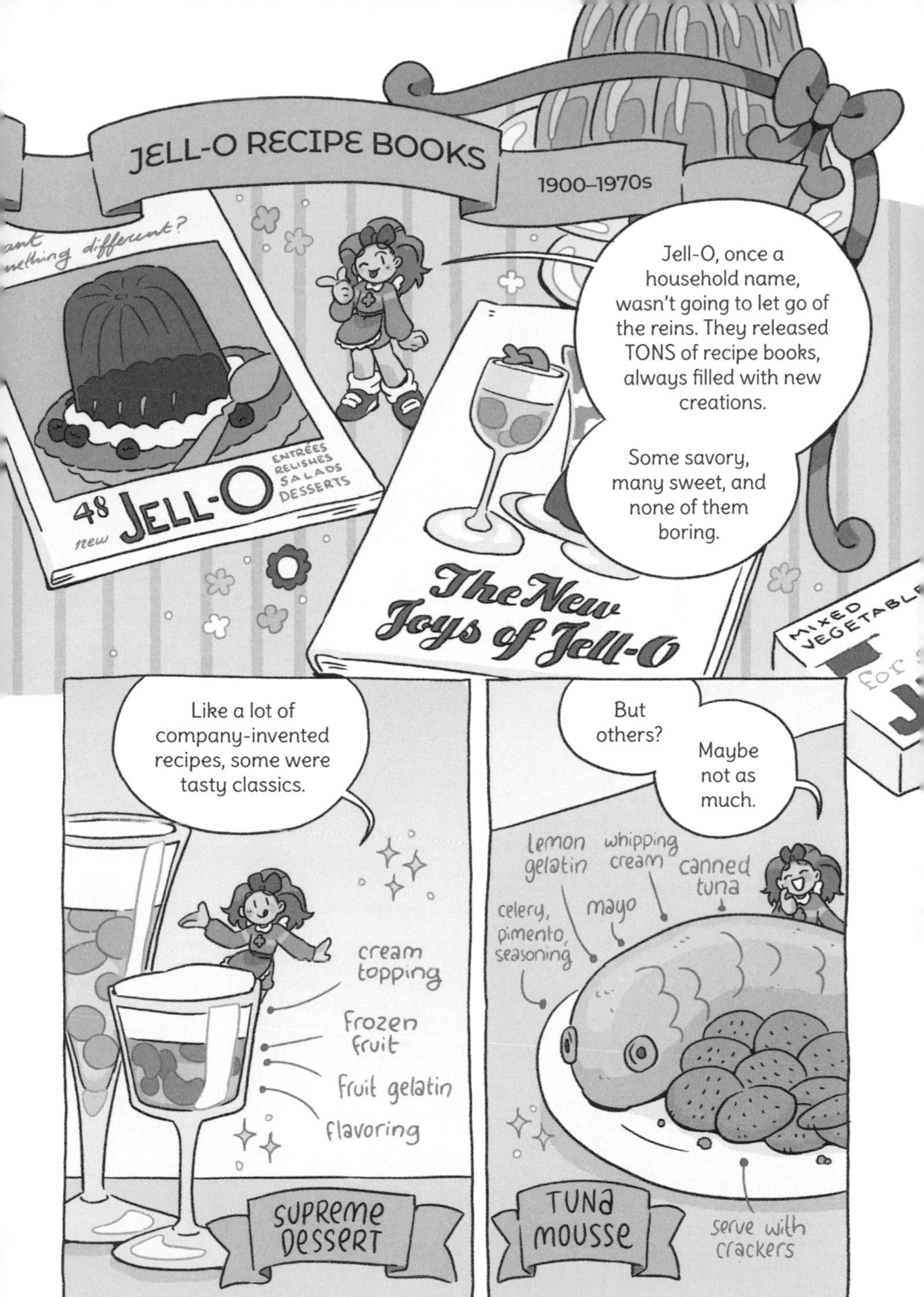
JELL-O RECIPE BOOKS
1900–1970s
Jell-O, once a household name, wasn't going to let go of the reins. They released TONS of recipe books, always filled with new creations.
Some savory, many sweet, and none of them boring.
48 new JELL-O
ENTRÉES RELISHES SALADS DESSERTS
The New Joys of Jell-O
MIXED VEGETABLE
Like a lot of company-invented recipes, some were tasty classics.
cream topping
Frozen fruit
fruit gelatin
flavoring
Supreme Dessert
But others?
Maybe not as much.
lemon gelatin
whipping cream
canned tuna
celery, pimento, seasoning
mayo
serve with crackers
TUNA MOUSSE

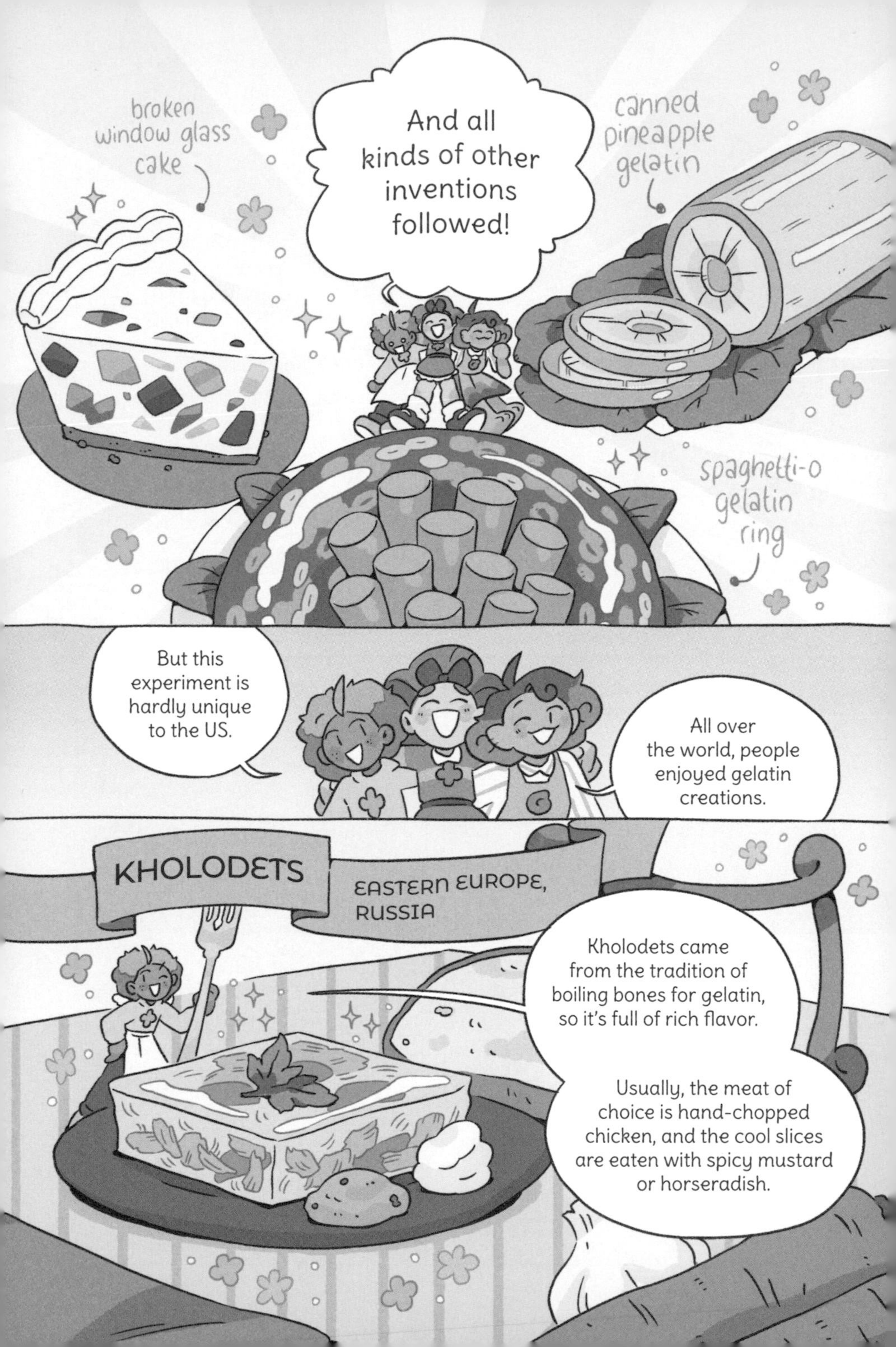
broken window glass cake
And all kinds of other inventions followed!
canned pineapple gelatin
spaghetti-o gelatin ring
But this experiment is hardly unique to the US.
All over the world, people enjoyed gelatin creations.
KHOLODETS
EASTERN EUROPE, RUSSIA
Kholodets came from the tradition of boiling bones for gelatin, so it's full of rich flavor.
Usually, the meat of choice is hand-chopped chicken, and the cool slices are eaten with spicy mustard or horseradish.

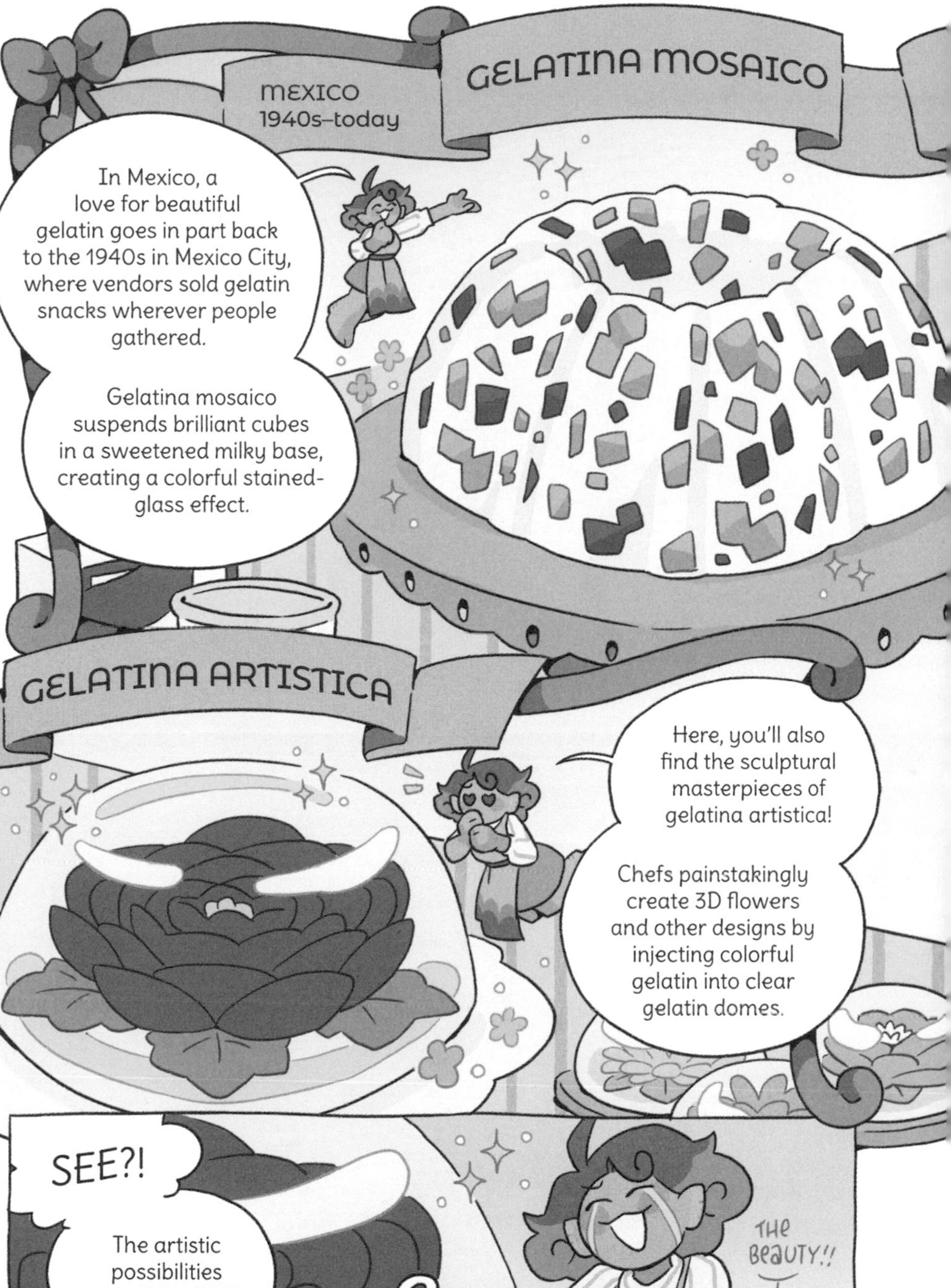
GELATINA MOSAICO
MEXICO
1940s–today
In Mexico, a love for beautiful gelatin goes in part back to the 1940s in Mexico City, where vendors sold gelatin snacks wherever people gathered.
Gelatina mosaico suspends brilliant cubes in a sweetened milky base, creating a colorful stained-glass effect.
GELATINA ARTISTICA
Here, you'll also find the sculptural masterpieces of gelatina artistica!
Chefs painstakingly create 3D flowers and other designs by injecting colorful gelatin into clear gelatin domes.
SEE?!
The artistic possibilities are ENDLESS!
THE BEAUTY!!

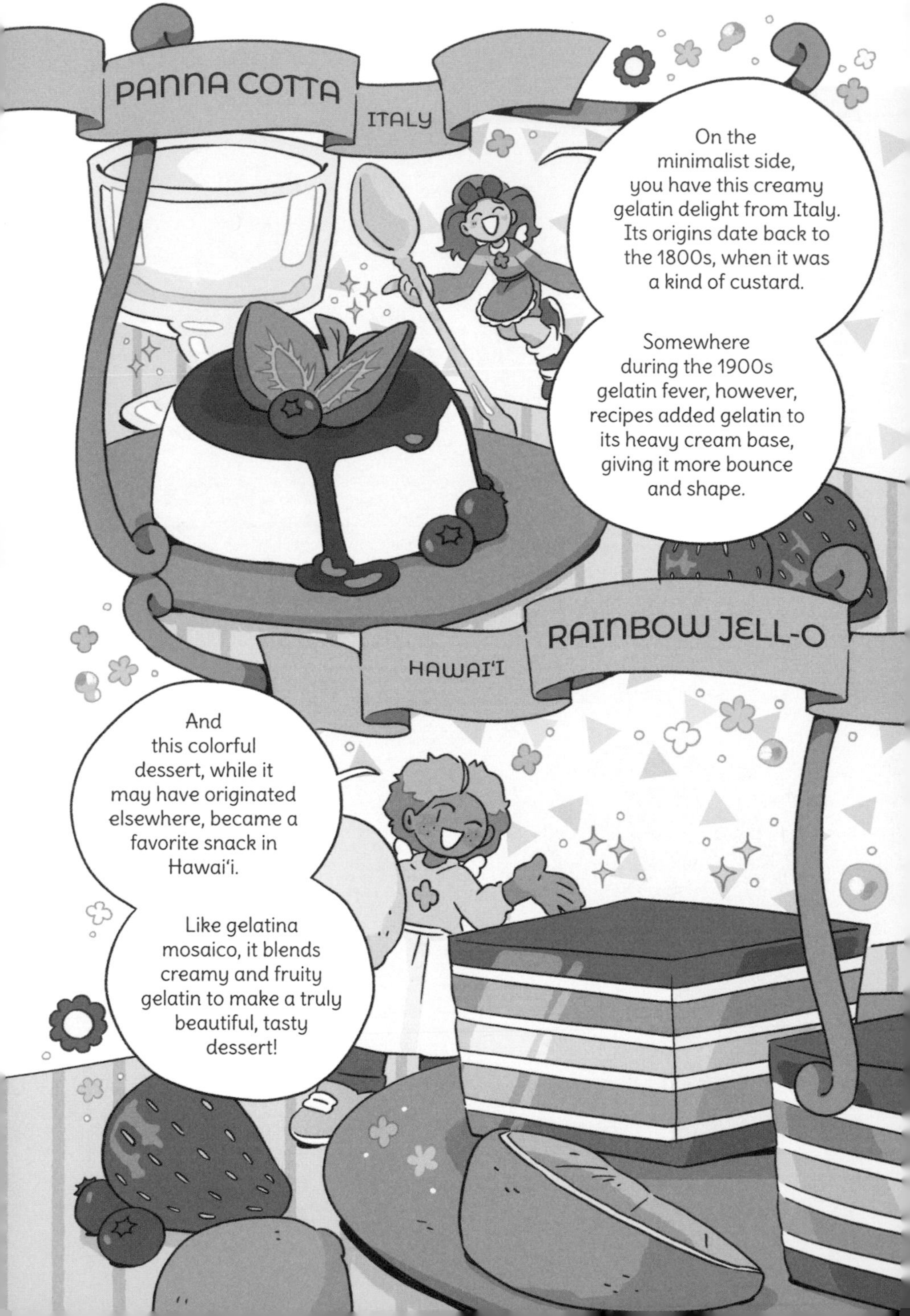
PANNA COTTA
ITALY
On the minimalist side, you have this creamy gelatin delight from Italy. Its origins date back to the 1800s, when it was a kind of custard.
Somewhere during the 1900s gelatin fever, however, recipes added gelatin to its heavy cream base, giving it more bounce and shape.
RAINBOW JELL-O
HAWAI'I
And this colorful dessert, while it may have originated elsewhere, became a favorite snack in Hawai'i.
Like gelatina mosaico, it blends creamy and fruity gelatin to make a truly beautiful, tasty dessert!

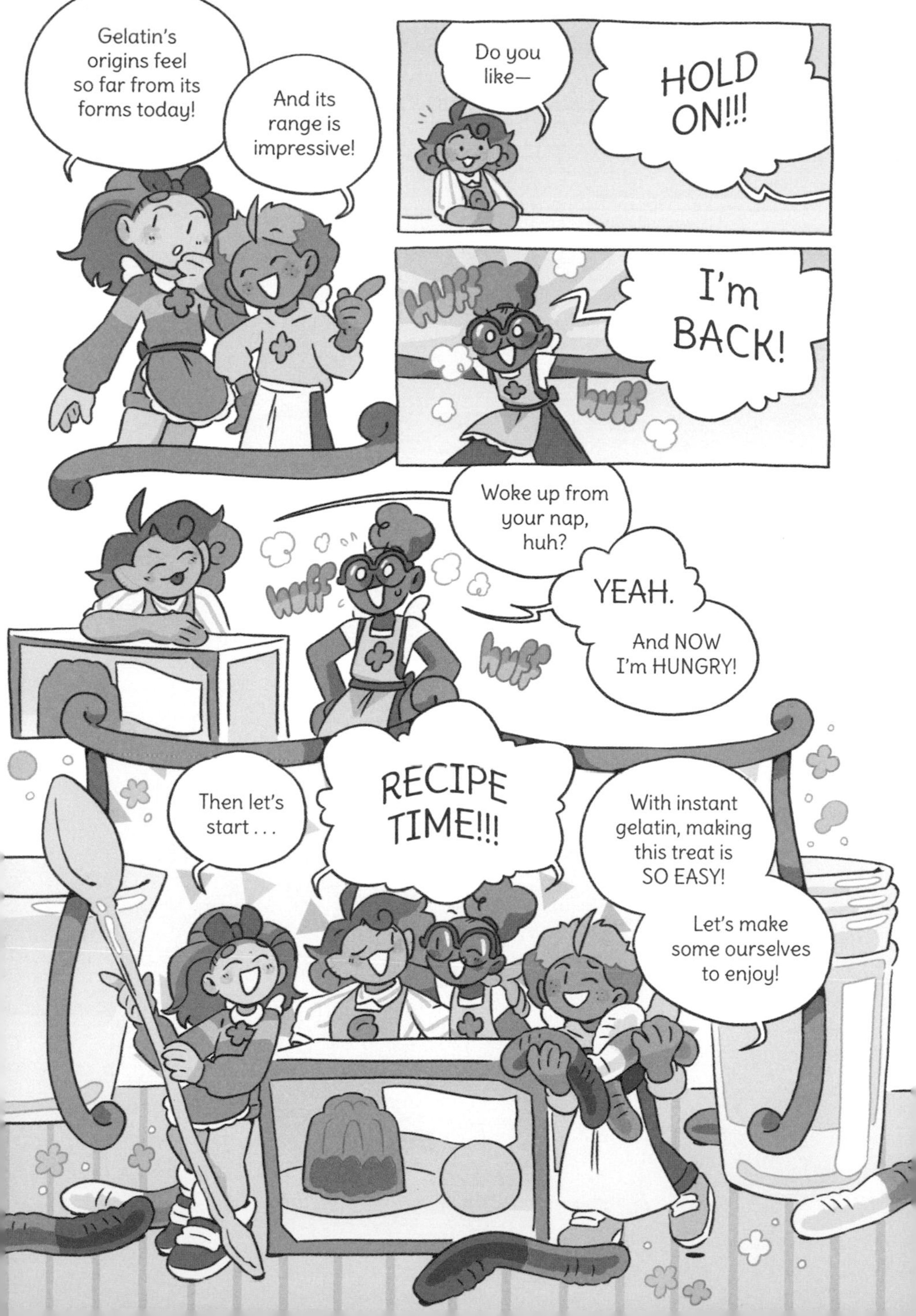

Gelatin's origins feel so far from its forms today!
And its range is impressive!
Do you like—
HOLD ON!!!
HUFF
I'm BACK!
huff
Woke up from your nap, huh?
HUFF
YEAH.
huff
And NOW I'm HUNGRY!
Then let's start . . .
RECIPE TIME!!!
With instant gelatin, making this treat is SO EASY!
Let's make some ourselves to enjoy!

# GUMMY GELATIN CUPS

## YOU WILL NEED:

1 box of your favorite instant gelatin flavor

1 cup warm water

1 ¼ cups cold water

1 bag of your favorite gummies

If you prefer fruit, use berries instead of gummies!

mixing bowl

spoon

4 clear cups

## OPTIONAL TOPPINGS:

whipped cream

sprinkles

sweetened condensed milk

Whatever you want!!

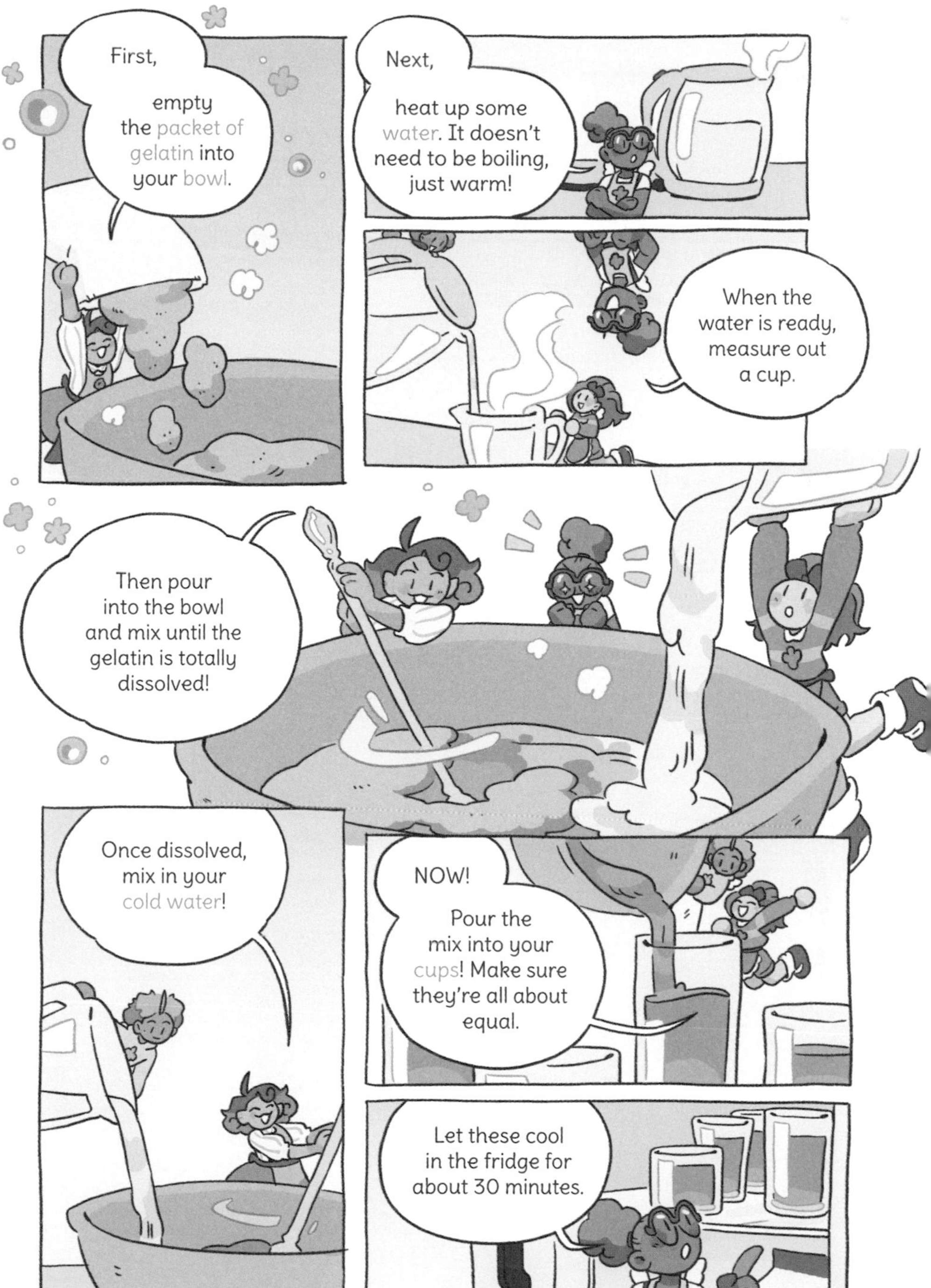
First, empty the packet of gelatin into your bowl.
Next, heat up some water. It doesn't need to be boiling, just warm!
When the water is ready, measure out a cup.
Then pour into the bowl and mix until the gelatin is totally dissolved!
Once dissolved, mix in your cold water!
NOW! Pour the mix into your cups! Make sure they're all about equal.
Let these cool in the fridge for about 30 minutes.

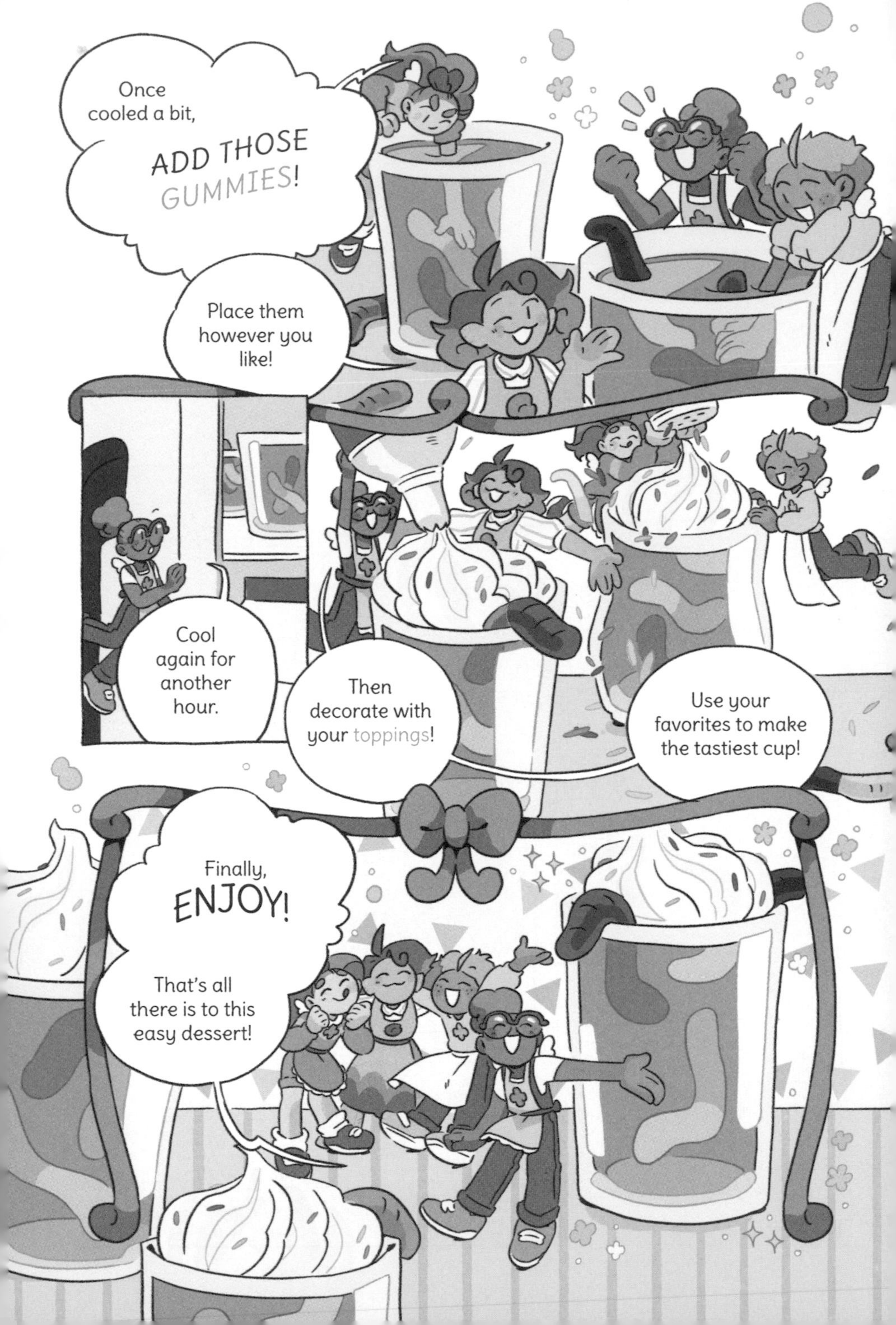
Once cooled a bit, ADD THOSE GUMMIES!
Place them however you like!
Cool again for another hour.
Then decorate with your toppings!
Use your favorites to make the tastiest cup!
Finally, ENJOY!
That's all there is to this easy dessert!

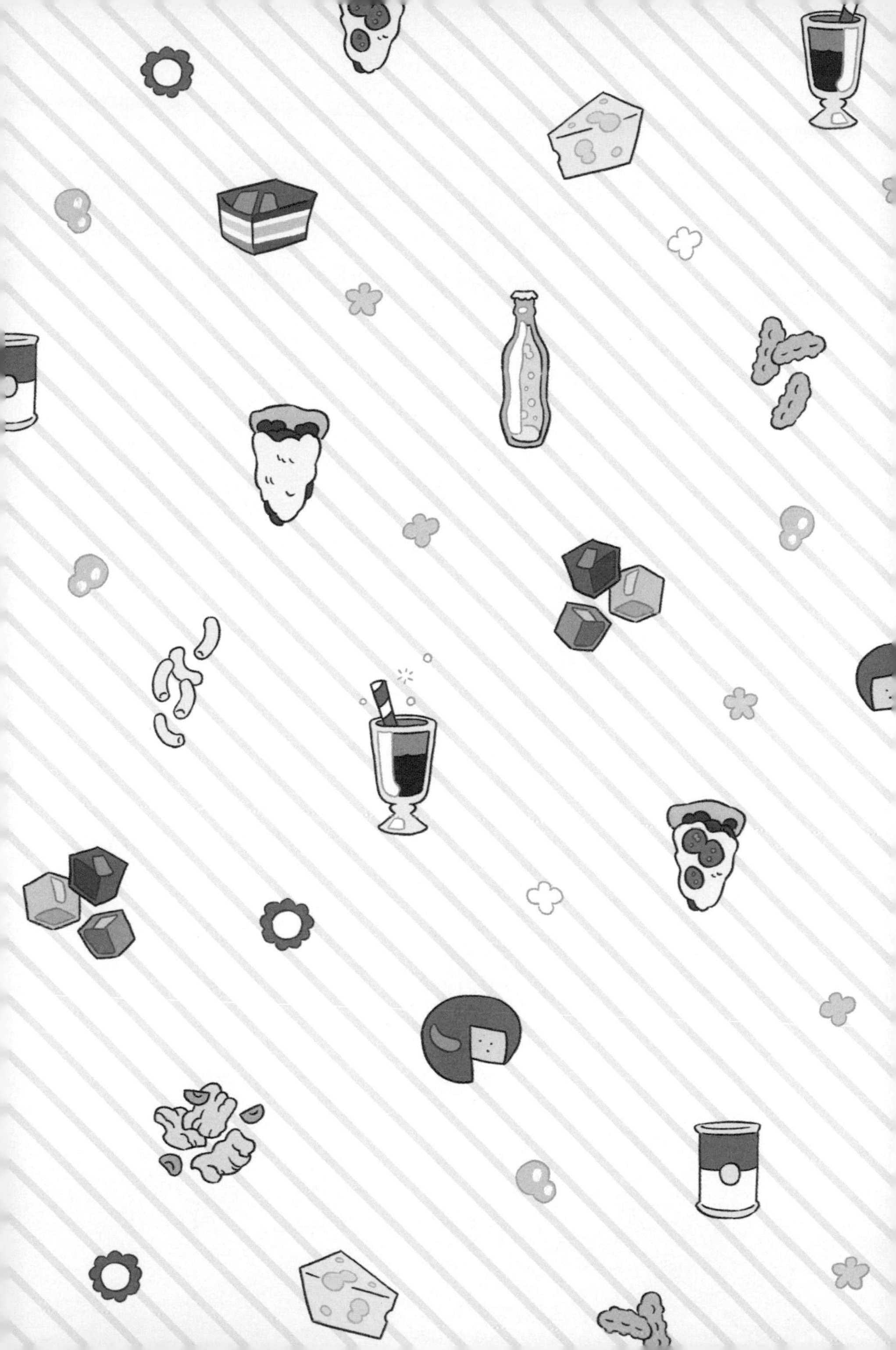

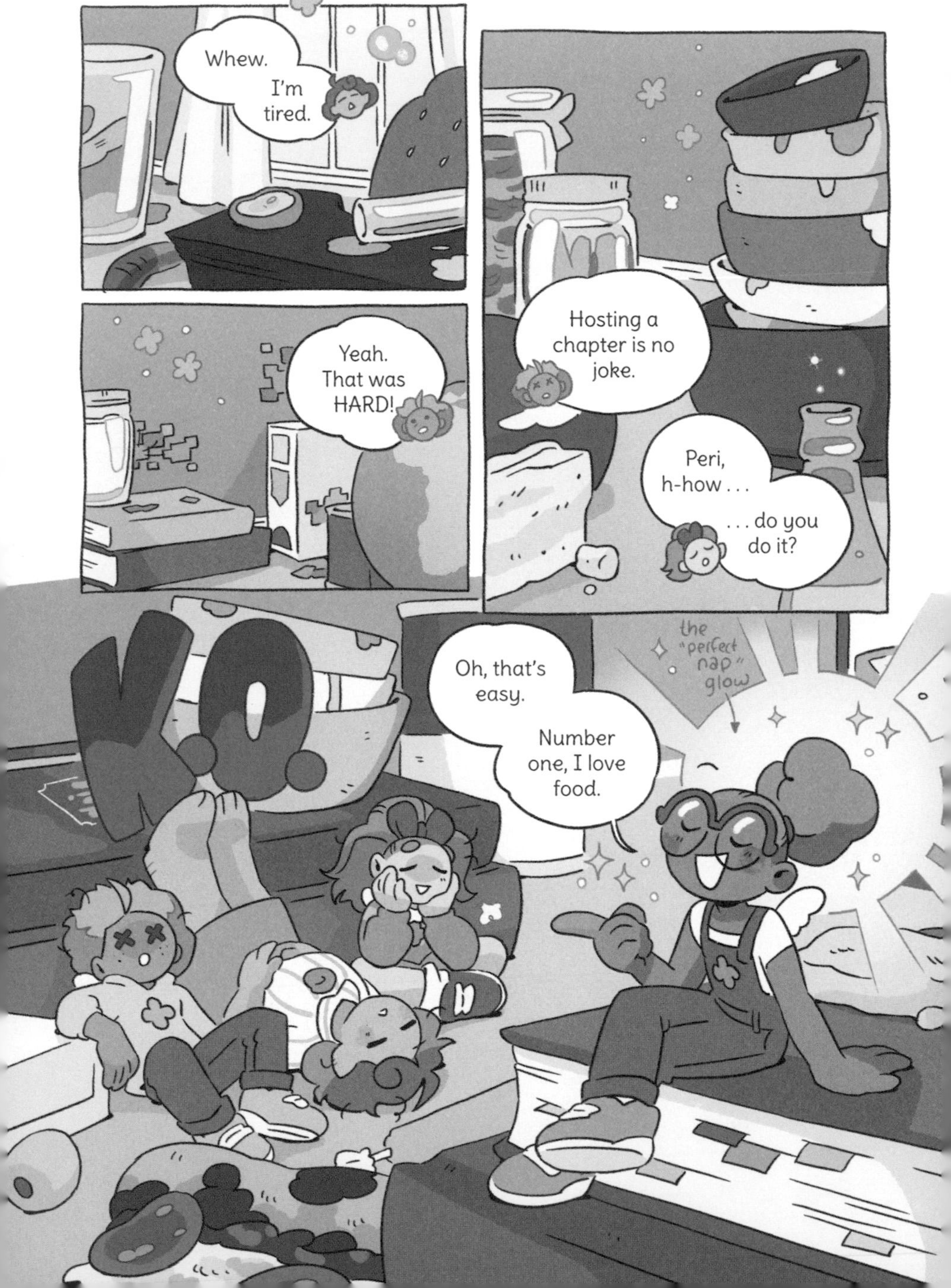
Whew.
I'm tired.
Yeah. That was HARD!
Hosting a chapter is no joke.
Peri, h-how . . .
. . . do you do it?
K.O.
Oh, that's easy.
Number one, I love food.
the "perfect nap" glow

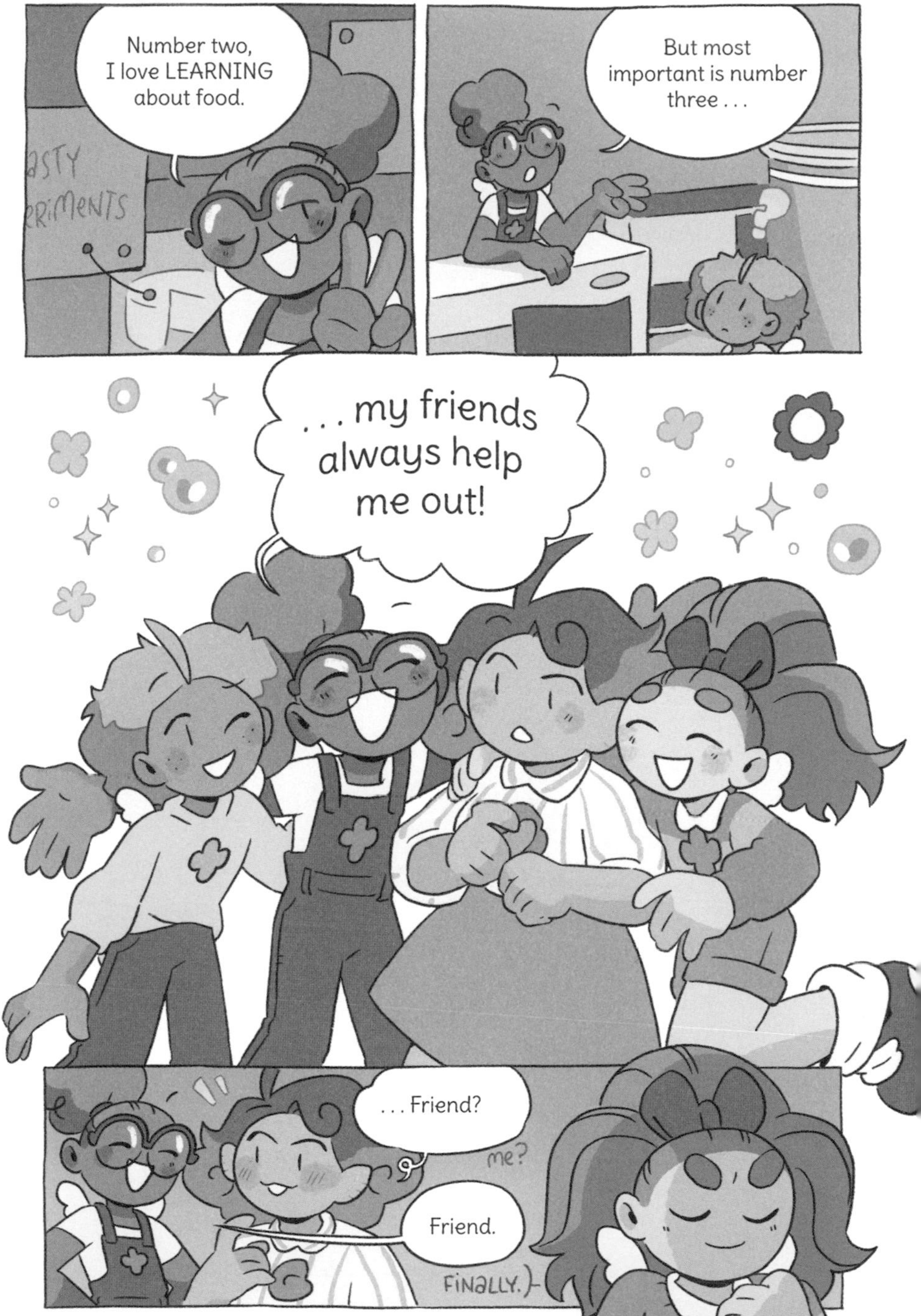
Number two,
I love LEARNING
about food.
But most
important is number
three . . .
. . . my friends
always help
me out!
. . . Friend?
me?
Friend.
FINALLY.

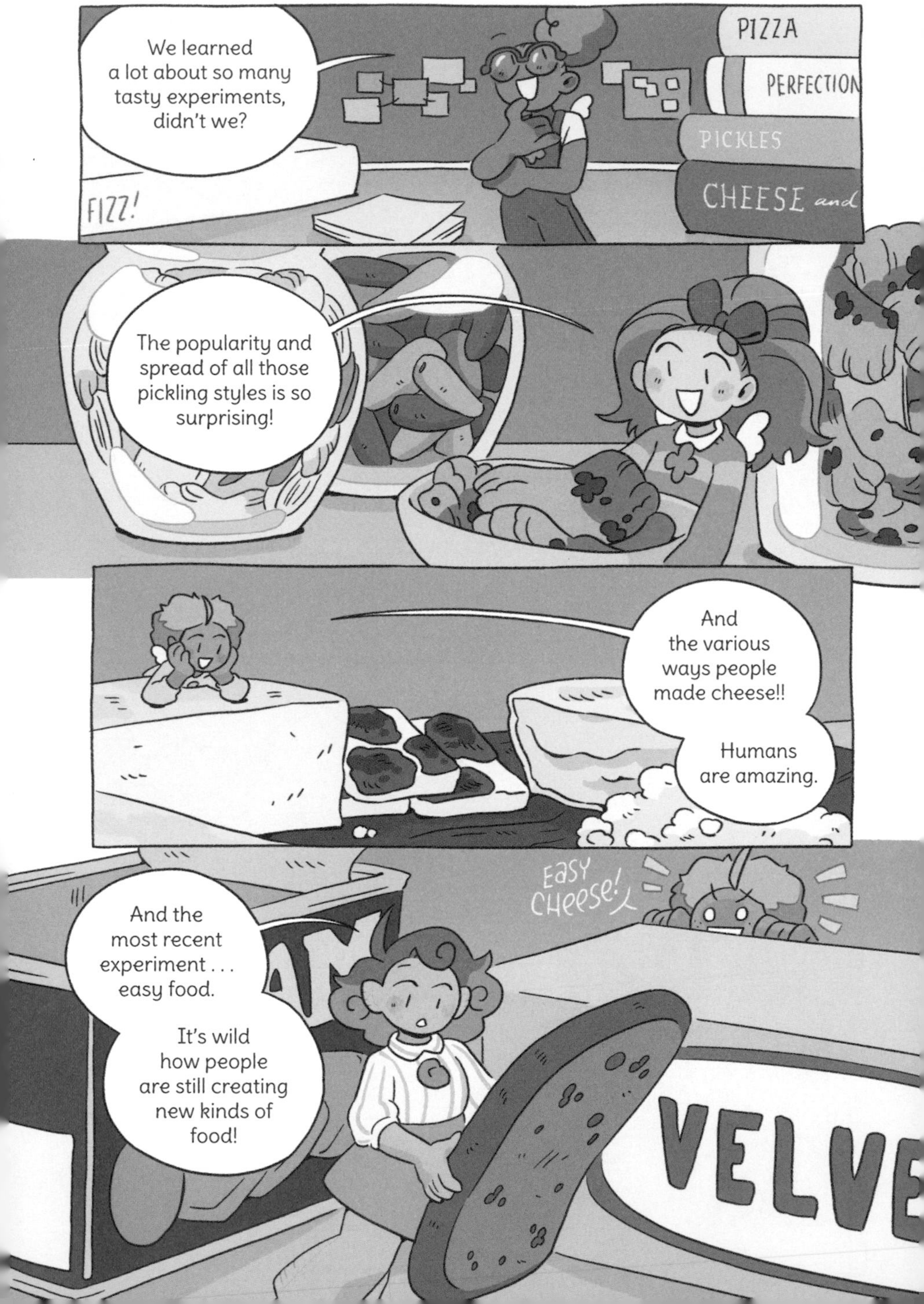

We learned a lot about so many tasty experiments, didn't we?
PIZZA
PERFECTION
PICKLES
CHEESE and
FIZZ!
The popularity and spread of all those pickling styles is so surprising!
And the various ways people made cheese!!
Humans are amazing.
EASY CHEESE!
And the most recent experiment . . . easy food.
It's wild how people are still creating new kinds of food!
VELVE

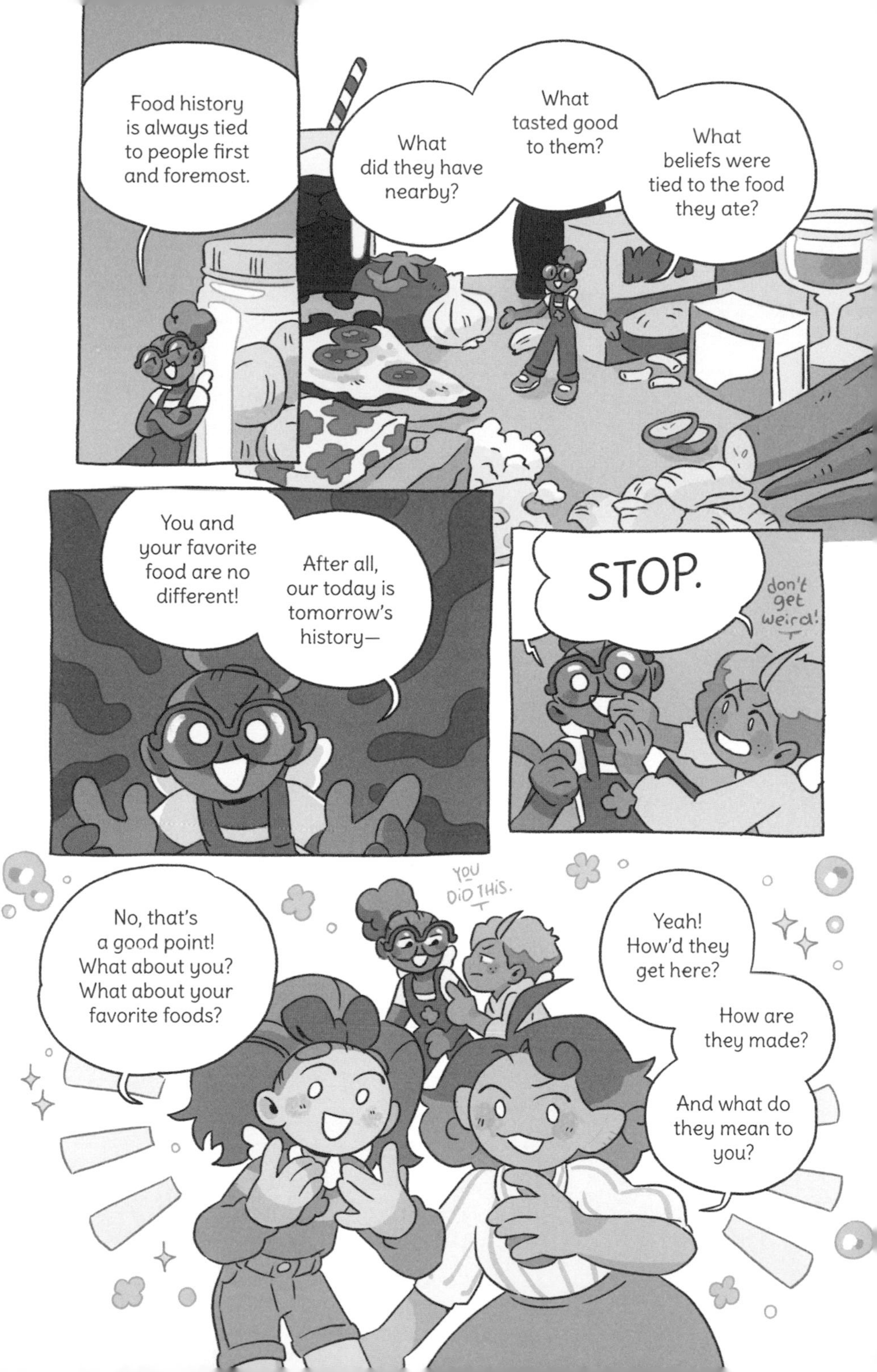
Food history is always tied to people first and foremost.
What did they have nearby?
What tasted good to them?
What beliefs were tied to the food they ate?
You and your favorite food are no different!
After all, our today is tomorrow's history—
STOP.
don't get weird!
No, that's a good point! What about you? What about your favorite foods?
YOU DID THIS.
Yeah! How'd they get here?
How are they made?
And what do they mean to you?

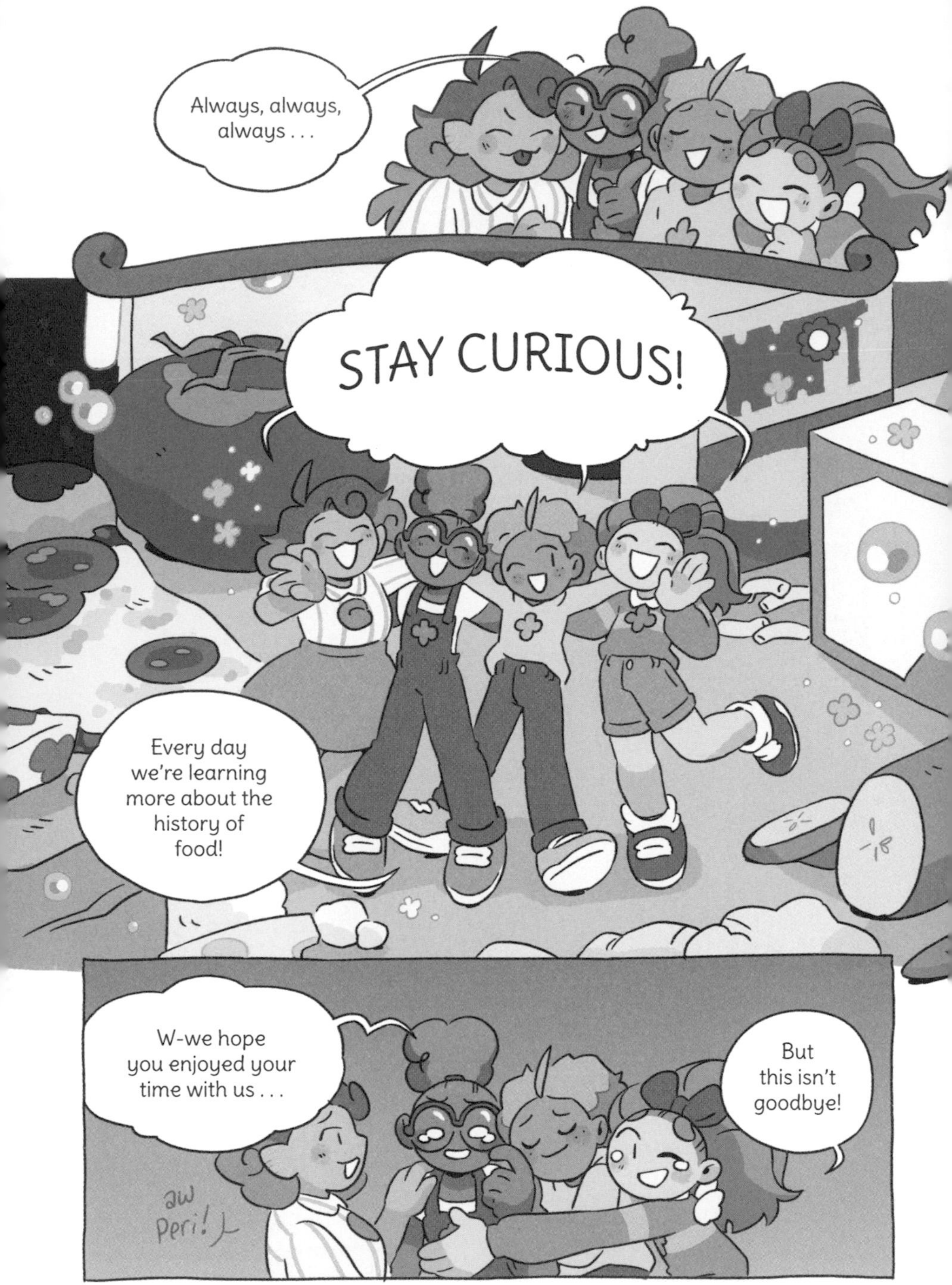
Always, always, always . . .
STAY CURIOUS!
Every day we're learning more about the history of food!
W-we hope you enjoyed your time with us . . .
aw Peri!
But this isn't goodbye!

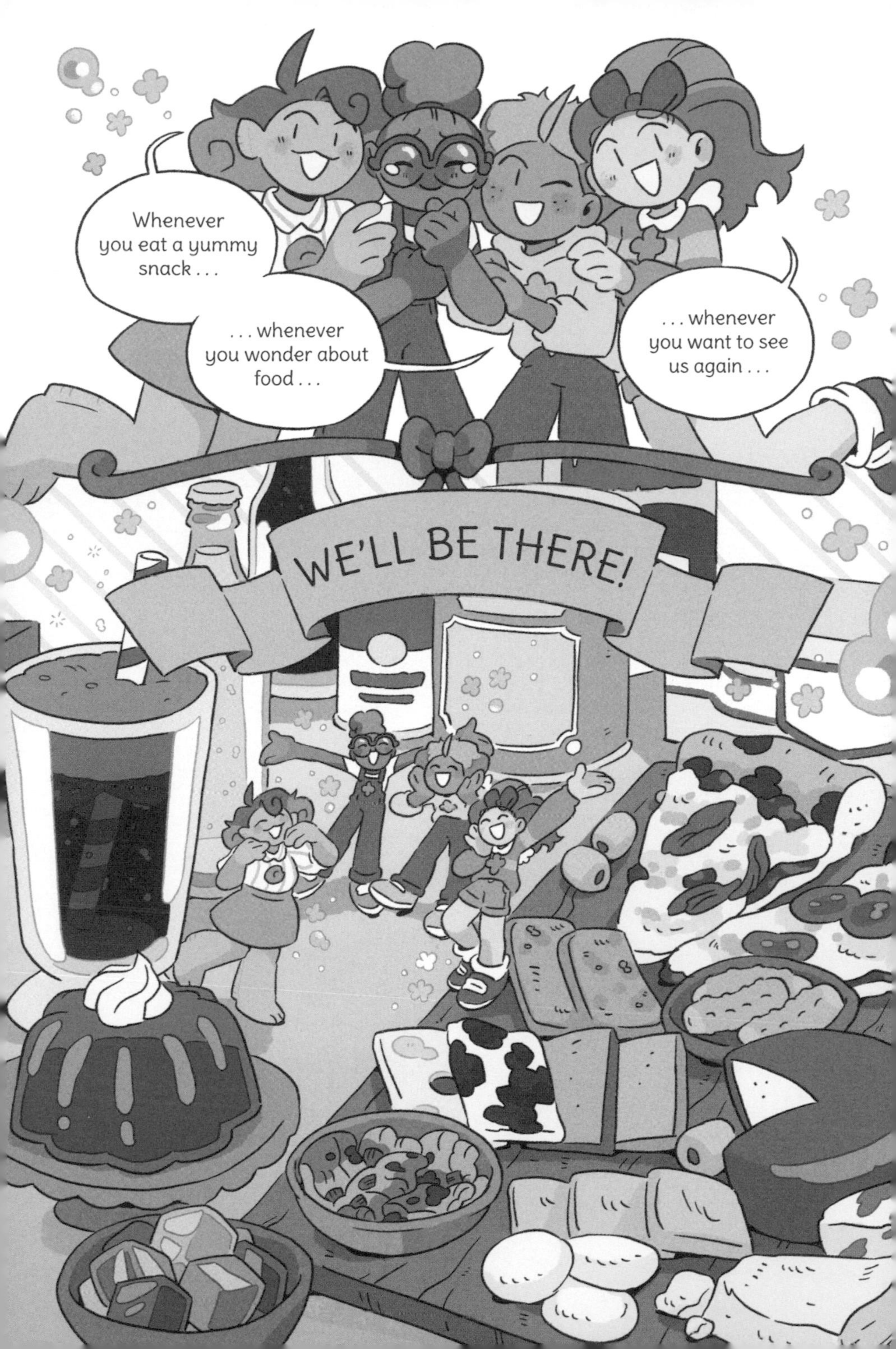
Whenever you eat a yummy snack . . .
. . . whenever you wonder about food . . .
. . . whenever you want to see us again . . .
WE'LL BE THERE!

# Bibliography

Allen, Bryan, and Silvia Allen. "Mozzarella of the East (Cheese-making and Bai culture)." *Ethnorêma* 1 (2005): 19–27. readkong.com/page/mozzarella-of-the-east-cheese-making-and-bai-culture-4265859.

Anter, Tarig. "Who Are the Fulani People & Their Origins?" Modern Ghana. modernghana.com/news/349849/who-are-the-fulani-people-their-origins.html.

Barrett, Liz. *Pizza: A Slice of American History.* Minneapolis, MN: Voyageur Press, 2014.

Barrow, William. "The Late Freda DeKnight: Tribute to a Lady Titan." *Negro Digest,* August 1963.

Berzok, Linda Murray. "Gelatin." *Encyclopedia of Food & Culture.* Encyclopedia.com. encyclopedia.com/science-and-technology/biochemistry/biochemistry/gelatin.

Boston Cooking School, The. *The Boston Cooking School Magazine of Culinary Science and Domestic Economics,* 1896–1914. Accessed via Hathi Trust Digital Library. catalog.hathitrust.org/Record/000521406.

British Museum, The. britishmuseum.org/.

Cam, Lisa. "What's the story behind instant ramen noodles—and how did post-war America influence their invention?" *South China Morning Post,* April 1, 2020. scmp.com/magazines/style/news-trends/article/3077785/whats-story-behind-instant-ramen-noodles-and-how-did.

Chanin, Natalie. "The History of Ambrosia." Alabama Chanin Journal, December 4, 2013. journal.alabamachanin.com/2013/12/the-history-of-ambrosia.

Cho, Grace M. "Eating Military Base Stew." *Contexts* 13, no. 3 (2014): 38–43. jstor.org/stable/24710550.

Corning Museum of Glass. cmog.org/.

Davidson, Alan. *The Oxford Companion to Food.* New York: Oxford University Press, 2014.

Davison, Jan. *Pickles: A Global History.* London: Reaktion Books Ltd., 2018.

DeKnight, Freda. *A Date with a Dish.* New York: Hermitage Press, 1948.

Donnelly, Catherine. *The Oxford Companion to Cheese.* New York: Oxford University Press, 2016.

Donovan, Tristan. *Fizz: How Soda Shook Up the World.* Chicago: Chicago Review Press, 2013.

Fujimoto, Dennis. "Barbara Funamura, creator of Spam musubi, dies at 78." Nichi Bei, June 9, 2016.
nichibei.org/2016/06/barbara-funamura-creator-of-spam-musubi-dies-at-78/.

Goldstein, Darra. *The Oxford Companion to Sugar and Sweets.* New York: Oxford University Press, 2015.

"Gooey Butter Cake History and Recipe." What's Cooking America.
whatscookingamerica.net/History/Cakes/GooeyButterCake.htm.

Harper, Donald. "The Cookbook in Ancient and Medieval China." Paper presented at the Discourses and Practices of Everyday Life in Imperial China Conference, Columbia University, New York, NY, October 2002.
studylib.net/doc/7720058/the-cookbook-in-ancient-and-medieval-china-donald
-harper.

Harris, Jessica B. *High on the Hog: A Culinary Journey from Africa to America.* New York: Bloomsbury USA, 2011.

Helstosky, Carol. *Pizza: A Global History.* London: Reaktion Books Ltd., 2008.

Hyams, Gina. "The Joy of Mexican Gelatina." Eat Mexico, January 6, 2019.
eatmexico.com/the-joy-of-mexican-gelatina/.

Jie Li (producer), and Hu Zhitang (director). "Salted Flour." *Flavorful Origins,* Yunnan Cuisine. Netflix, 2019. Video, 12:00.
netflix.com/title/80991060.

Katz, Brigit. "The Woman Who Invented the Green Bean Casserole." *Smithsonian Magazine,* October 26, 2018; updated November 19, 2018.
smithsonianmag.com/smart-news/remembering-dorcas-reilly-inventor-green-bean
-casserole-180970635/.

Kim, Evelyn. "The Amazing Multimillion-Year History of Processed Food." *Scientific American,* September 2013.

Kindstedt, Paul S. *Cheese and Culture: A History of Cheese and Its Place in Western Civilization.* White River Junction, VT: Chelsea Green Publishing, 2012.

Li, Ang. "Asian American Chefs Are Embracing Spam. But How Did the Canned Meat Make Its Way Into Their Cultures?" *Time,* May 28, 2019.
time.com/5593886/asian-american-spam-cuisine/.

Met, The. metmuseum.org/.

Miyares, Ines M. "Expressing 'Local Culture' in Hawai'i." *Geographical Review* 98, no. 4 (Oct 2008): 513–531.

Morrison, Allan. "Hold Last Rites for Fashion, Food Expert Freda DeKnight." *Jet,* February 14, 1962.

Moss, Robert. "How Ambrosia Became a Southern Christmas Tradition." Serious Eats, August 10, 2018. seriouseats.com/ambrosia-southern-christmas-tradition.

Moula, Fauzia. "WAGASHI, HOW TO MAKE WAGASHI AT HOME/GHANA AND AFRICAN LOCAL CHEESE." YouTube, May 28, 2020. Video, 7:19. youtube.com/watch?v=2gzsc0IN7HQ.

Muckenhoupt, Meg. *Cabbage: A Global History.* London: Reaktion Books Ltd., 2018.

Neil, Marion Harris. *The Story of CRISCO.* Cincinnati, OH: The Proctor & Gamble Co., 1913. Accessed via Project Gutenberg. gutenberg.org/files/13286/13286-h/13286-h.htm.

*New Royal Cook Book.* New York: Royal Baking Powder Co., 1920. Accessed via Project Gutenberg. gutenberg.org/files/38193/38193-h/38193-h.htm.

"Our Founder." Nissin Foods. nissin.com/en_jp/about/founder.

Pegge, Samuel. *The Forme of Cury: A Roll of Ancient English Cookery Compiled.* England, c. 1390. Accessed via Project Gutenberg. gutenberg.org/cache/epub/8102/pg8102.html.

Pierce, Donna Battle. "Freda DeKnight: A 'Hidden Figure' and Titan of African-American Cuisine." NPR, February 16, 2017. npr.org/sections/thesalt/2017/02/16/514360992/meet-freda-deknight-a-hidden -figure-and-titan-of-african-american-food.

"Rennet in cheese – the science: how does rennet work?" The Courtyard Dairy. thecourtyarddairy.co.uk/blog/cheese-musings-and-tips/rennet-in-cheese-the -science-how-rennet-works.

Shapiro, Laura. *Perfection Salad: Women and Cooking at the Turn of the Century.* New York: Farrar, Straus and Giroux, 1986.

Shapiro, Laura. *Something from the Oven: Reinventing Dinner in 1950s America.* London: Penguin Books, 2005.

Smith, Andrew F. *The Oxford Encyclopedia of Food and Drink in America.* 2nd ed. New York: Oxford University Press, 2012.

Soda & Beer Bottles of North America. sodasandbeers.com/.

"The 'Zha' with Chilies Contributes a Lot to Various Delicacies." iChongqing. ichongqing.info/culture/chongqing-local-food/the-zha-with-chilies-contributes-a-lot-to-various-delicacies.

"What Is Pickling?" Exploratorium. exploratorium.edu/cooking/pickles/pickling.html.

Williams, Roger Ross, and Jonathan Clasberry. "Our Founding Chefs." *High on the Hog: How African American Cuisine Transformed America.* Netflix, 2021. Video, 52:00. netflix.com/title/81034518.

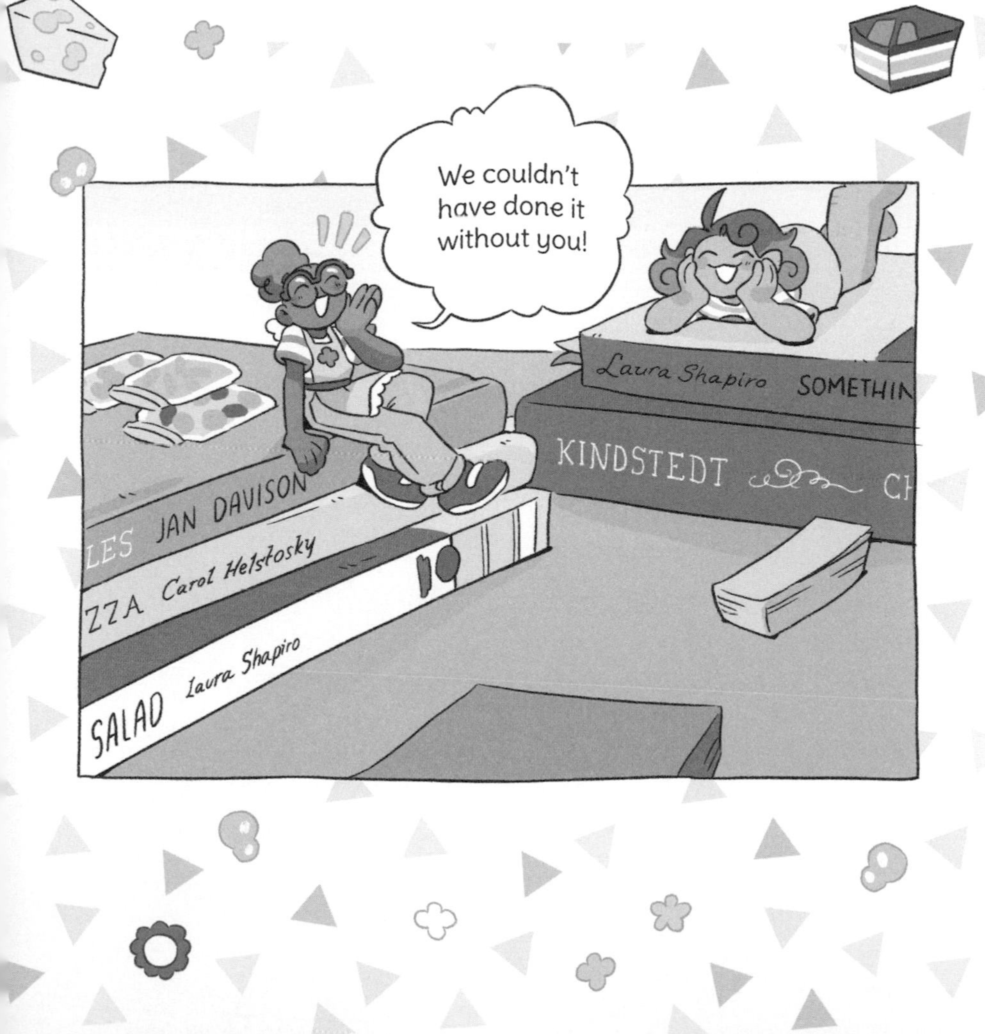
We couldn't have done it without you!
Laura Shapiro SOMETHIN
KINDSTEDT CH
LES JAN DAVISON
ZZA Carol Helstosky
SALAD Laura Shapiro

# HOW TO DRAW PERI

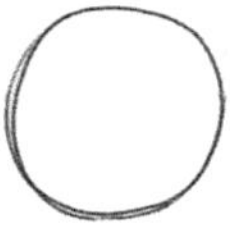

1. Draw a circle.

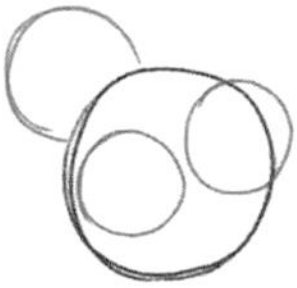

2. Draw three more.

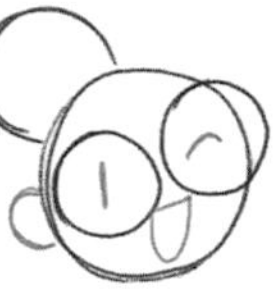

3. Add lines for eyes, one ear, and mouth. Make her wink or smile if you like!

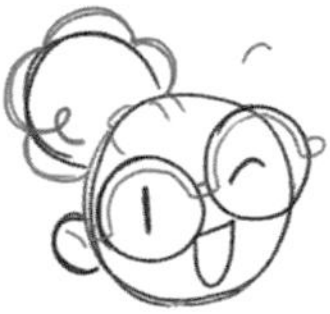

4. Add curves for hair and an eyebrow over her head, and some hair lines. Add the extra lines to her glasses.

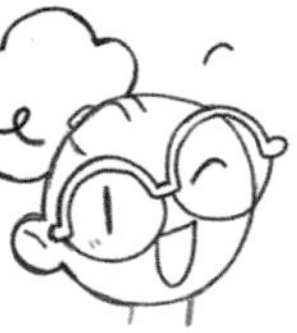

5. Clean up the lines you don't need! Add two lines for her neck and two tiny lines for her cheek.

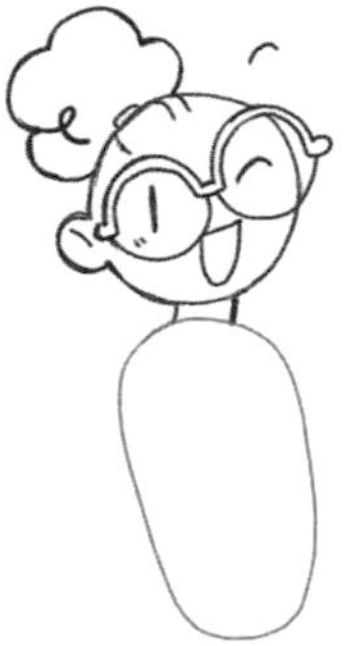

6. Add a big oval for her body shape.

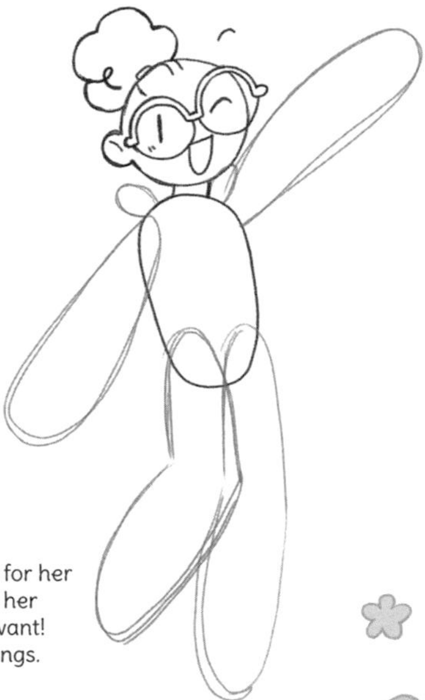

7. Then add two looong ovals for her arms and two more ovals for her legs. Pose her however you want! Add two little ovals for her wings.

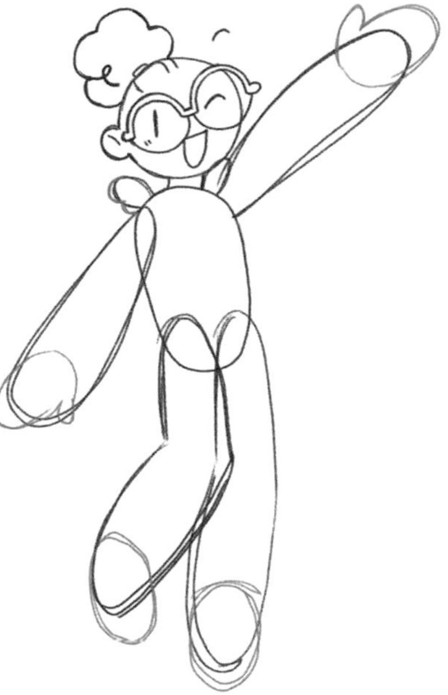

8. Draw little mittens for her hands and little potatoes for her feet. Add curves to the bottom of her wings.

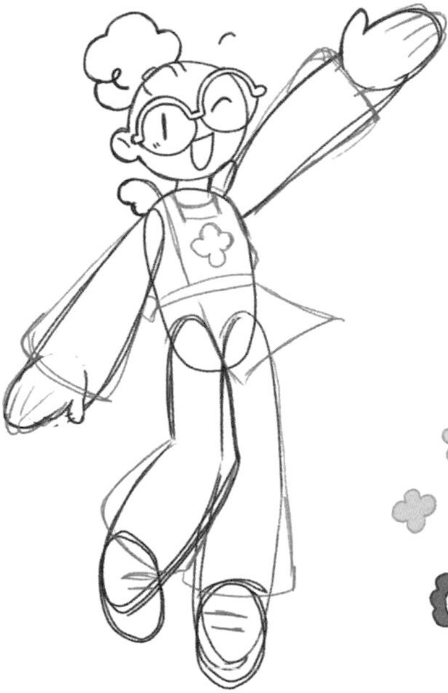

9. Here's where you can have fun dressing Peri! Her basic apron is two rectangles with a strip around her waist and a clover on the chest. Add lines for her fingers.

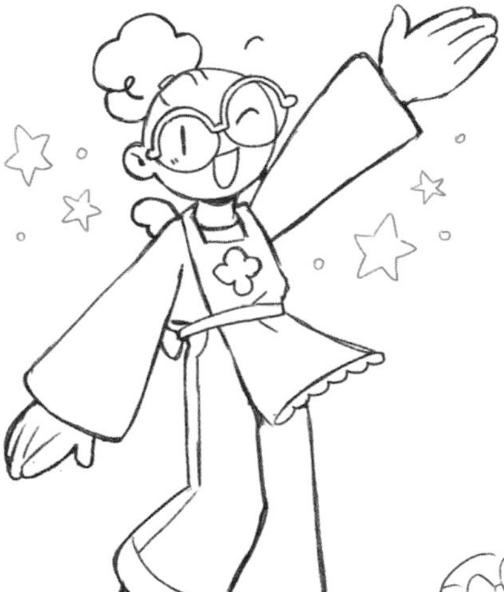

10. Clean everything up and add whatever extra details you want!

Do you want to make your own sprite? Every sprite has their own unique traits!

Fee has bigger eyebrows, Fada has freckles, and Naia has fins on her ears and feet. What would your sprite look like?

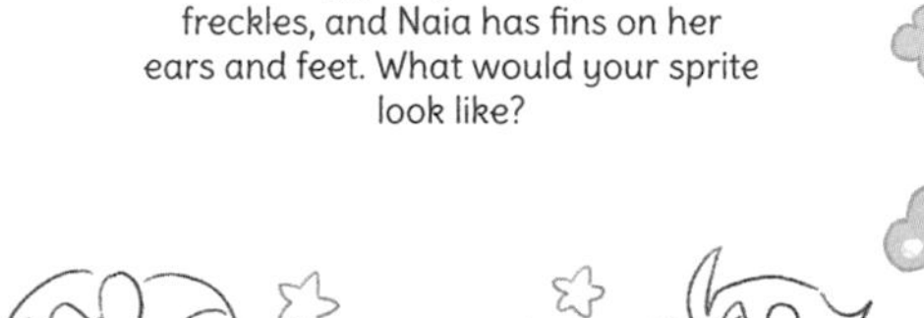

## PERI

**FAVE CHEESE:**
wagashi

**FAVE PICKLE:**
THE SAUCE!!

**FAVE EASY FOOD:**
gooey butter cake

## FEE

**FAVE CHEESE:**
Roquefort and Brie!!

**FAVE PICKLE:**
cucumber

**FAVE EASY FOOD:**
fruity gelatin

## FADA

**FAVE CHEESE:**
EASY CHEESE!!

**FAVE PICKLE:**
cabbage

**FAVE EASY FOOD:**
mac and cheese!

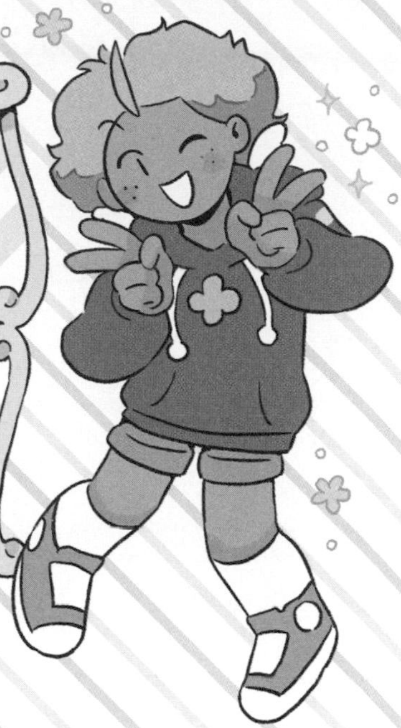

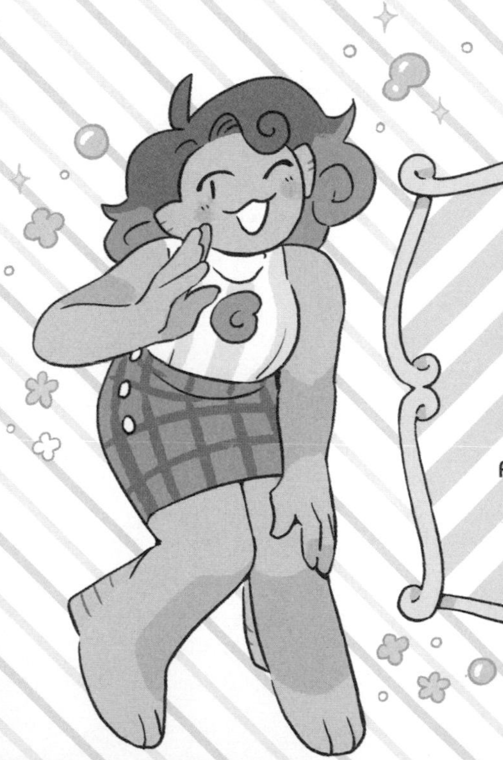

## NAIA

**FAVE CHEESE:**
rubing

**FAVE PICKLE:**
salsa and ceviche!

**FAVE EASY FOOD:**
the WEIRD ones!!

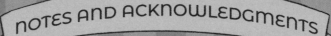

# NOTES AND ACKNOWLEDGMENTS

I want to acknowledge the political nature of food, as I did in *Yummy*, and how so much of it is informed by war, colonization, imperialism, and slavery. This book especially touches on topics of war, racism, and imperialism, none of which justify the creation or spread of any of these foods. As always, we must acknowledge these histories to pay our necessary respects. Food history is, quite deeply, human history.

I'd also like to acknowledge that this book was written and drawn in Austin, Texas, on the traditional land of the Jumanos, Tonkawa, Nʉmʉnʉʉ, and Sana people, the rightful stewards of this beautiful land, where I am grateful to live.

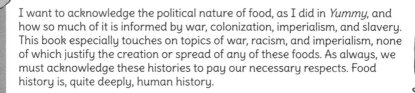

Thank you, dear reader, for picking up this book! If you happen to like dessert history, you should read *Yummy: A History of Desserts*! If you've already read *Yummy,* I hope you enjoyed *Tasty*, too!

While I researched to the best of my ability, *Tasty* is an introductory look at the foods mentioned in this book. With many old, old foods like pickles and cheese, there's so much we still don't know and so much we're still finding out! Our understanding of history is always growing and changing in fun and surprising ways, so I hope you'll keep an open mind as you learn more about history and your favorite foods!

I'd like to thank the incredible team at RH Graphic—Whitney Leopard, Danny Diaz, and Patrick Crotty—and Steven Salpeter for making this book a reality. I'm so pleased to have more food history to share, and without their hard work, it simply couldn't have happened.

I'd love to thank my beloved partner, Sergio, for always giving me wonderful feedback and suggestions and learning about food history with me.

I made this book entirely during the coronavirus pandemic, so I didn't get to share nearly as much food with my friends and loved ones as I have in years past. I'm thankful to those who found ways to spend time together despite that, and somehow found a way to share food, too, even if we couldn't enjoy it in person.

## ABOUT the AUTHOR

I'm Victoria Grace Elliott, a comic artist living in Austin, Texas. I love food (cooking, eating food, collecting tiny toy food, and learning more about different kinds of food), watching soap operas, and singing karaoke. My books include *Yummy: A History of Desserts*, *Please Be My Star*, and this book you're reading now!

Hungry for more?

Satisfy your sweet
tooth with *Yummy:
A History of Desserts*

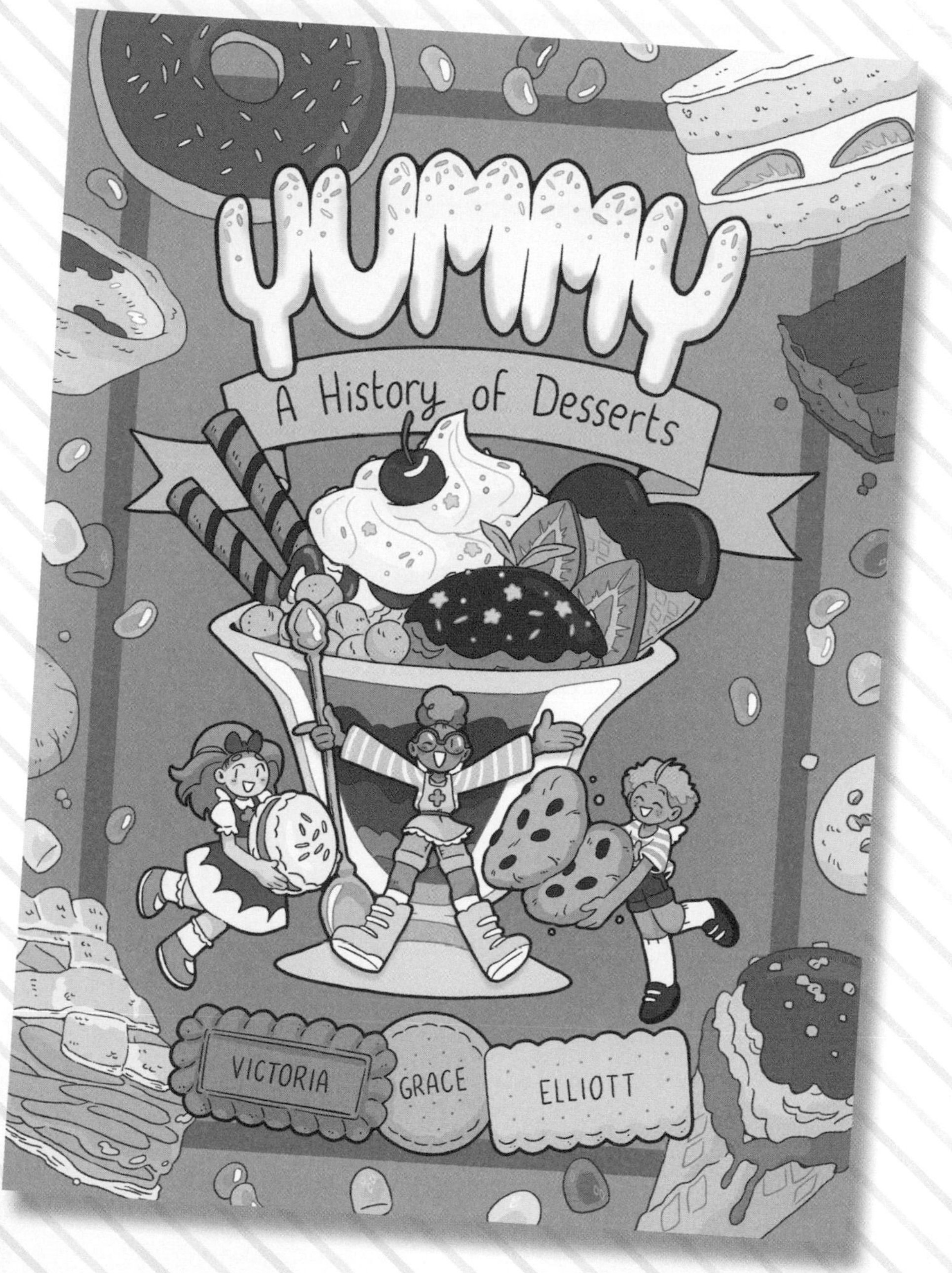
YUMMY
A History of Desserts
VICTORIA
GRACE
ELLIOTT

# JUMP INTO
# AN EXCITING NEW
# GRAPHIC NOVEL!

# RH ▢ GRAPHIC

A graphic novel on every bookshelf

Learn more at RHCBooks.com

RHCB